Lawyers' Ethics and the Pursuit of Social Justice

CRITICAL AMERICA
General Editors: Richard Delgado and Jean Stefancic

Lawyers' Ethics and the Pursuit of Social Justice

A Critical Reader

EDITED BY

Susan D. Carle

FOREWORD BY

Robert W. Gordon

New York University Press

NEW YORK AND LONDON

NEW YORK UNIVERSITY PRESS
New York and London
www.nyupress.org

Library of Congress Cataloging-in-Publication Data
Lawyers' ethics and the pursuit of social justice : a critical reader /
edited by Susan D. Carle.
p. cm. — (Critical America)
Includes bibliographical references and index.
ISBN-10: 0-8147-1639-3 (cloth : alk. paper)
ISBN-13: 978-0-8147-1639-7 (cloth : alk. paper)
ISBN-10: 0-8147-1640-7 (pbk. : alk. paper)
ISBN-13: 978-0-8147-1640-3 (pbk. : alk. paper)
1. Legal ethics—United States. 2. Social justice—United States.
I. Carle, Susan D. II. Series.
KF306.A5L378 2005
174'.3'0973—dc22   2005006775

New York University Press books are printed on acid-free paper,
and their binding materials are chosen for strength and durability.

Manufactured in the United States of America
c 10 9 8 7 6 5 4 3 2 1
p 10 9 8 7 6 5 4 3 2 1

Contents

Foreword

Robert W. Gordon

Publication of this thoughtfully assembled reader on lawyers' ethics is a significant event. Susan Carle has a discriminating eye. She gathers here the harvest of some of the best and freshest research and debate on lawyers' ethics and the role of lawyers in society. The collection makes available to law teachers and their students and to practicing lawyers and their apprentices a sophisticated guide to ethical reflection and decision-making. These essays don't pretend to give clear answers to the hardest questions lawyers face in practice. Indeed, because they disagree on so many issues, they make clear that there are no clear answers. But they sharpen and illuminate those questions, especially by pointing to alternative ways of thinking about how to answer them.

This book would be useful to any lawyer, or for that matter, anyone interested in justice, the legal system, and the professions. Probably the immediate and obvious audience for this book is legal academics who have signed up—or, as often happens, have been conscripted—to teach a course in professional responsibility. Law schools have until very recently not had much success teaching professional responsibility. Many of them would still probably not offer any course in the subject at all were it not that the American Bar Association has, since the Watergate scandals, required some instruction on legal ethics and that state bar associations require aspirants to entry to pass an exam on the ethics rules. Law faculties, mostly refugees from practice, tend to avert their eyes from the careers and practice settings in which their graduates will spend most of their lives. Law teachers probably do a pretty good job of preparing students to be (or to argue before) appellate judges, legislators, and philosopher-kings. Outside law school clinical programs, we don't teach students a lot about being lawyers, with the exception of teaching them to write research memos and argue cases. We assume they will learn all the rest later on, in practice.

Students, for their part, are skeptical about ethical training. They assume ethics is a matter of ordinary morality, learned in early childhood if ever, which at this point in their lives they either have or haven't acquired. Or else, since most law schools have taught professional responsibility as a course in the disciplinary rules, and since the bar exam tests knowledge of those rules, students assume learning ethics is an exercise in memorizing rules. If they are cynics, they assume the whole enterprise is just a lot of abstract and hollow preaching that has no relevance to the real world or to careers in practice.

Of course all these beliefs are mistaken. Being a good person isn't sufficient to make one a good lawyer. (In fact, some think it gets in the way.) People of exemplary honesty, fairness, and generosity in personal dealings can be real stinkers in professional settings—especially if prodded by a set of ethical precepts and institutional incentives that seem to license—and sometimes even actively to encourage—antisocial behavior. Memorizing the rules isn't much help either. The rules at best set a minimum standard of ethical conduct—how to stay out of jail and to avoid being disbarred. The rules in any case turn out to be least helpful where guidance is most urgently needed, as when the lawyer's obligations to clients are in greatest tension with obligations to the legal system. The rules conflict with one another and there are no rules to resolve the conflicts.

Fortunately, law schools have slowly, gradually, begun to do better. Law school clinics, for one thing, make it possible to begin socializing students early into ethics of care, loyalty, and confidentiality. Actually having to take on responsibility for someone in trouble—more responsibility than a firm would give an associate for many years—is a breathtakingly educational experience. Clinical work presents live everyday ethical dilemmas—the conflict between what a client says he wants and what he actually seems to need; the temptations to stretch fact and law to the limits or beyond to fit the client's situation into something qualifying for a legal solution; the problem of the lying client or witness; the problem of indifferent, unresponsive, or actually hostile legal agencies. In the clinical setting, the day's ethical problems generated by the caseload can become the objects of shared reflection and analysis.

Law teachers also now have access to a much richer body of scholarship about the profession. Twenty-five years ago the study of the legal profession and legal ethics was a nearly dead field, avoided by the intellectually ambitious. Only a handful of brave pioneers did work of lasting value on the subject. As this collection reveals, all that has changed. The study of the legal profession and the exposition and critique of its ethical rules and precepts is now a booming field. Law schools are now able, if they want to take up the challenge, to play a distinctive and valuable role in the training of lawyers, because they are in a position to examine the profession with more detachment than those who have to make a living in it. One thing in particular that law schools can probably do better than practice settings is education in the structural determinants—the economics and sociology —of lawyers' situations and lawyers' practices. Ethical orientations, after all, are only partly a matter of internal disposition. They are as much or more importantly a function of structures and incentives embedded in markets, institutions, and cultural systems. In corporate law, of course, both "lawyers" and "clients" are organizations, not individuals; or rather, they are individuals embedded in organizations, and making decisions and looking for cues to organizational leadership and incentives. Almost everyone recognizes that pressures on lawyers to engage in dubious behavior—overbilling clients, dumping lower-fee in favor of higher-fee clients in cases of conflicts, taking "aggressive" positions with regulating and taxing authorities, allowing corporate clients to skate near to or over the borders of legal conduct, skimping on work for lower-paying clients—come from competition among firms for clients and within firms for profit shares and chances at partnership.

But while a course in economics and sociology of professional and client organizations and markets may be crucial, it is not enough either. Law schools must be the place, one hopes only the first of many places, in which to subject the ethical principles themselves to critical scrutiny— preferably in dialogue with, and with the active engagement of, practitioners. Some ethics teachers have been very successful in examining how the lawyer's differentiated role-morality can be reconciled (if at all) with principles of ordinary (Kantian, Aristotelian, utilitarian, or any other) morality. Also, any legal ethics course has to be partly a course in jurisprudence. As lawyers we are supposed to pursue our clients' interests "within the bounds of the law." But what is the "law" whose bounds set the limits of our clients', or our own, self-interested action? How is it constructed, and what is the appropriate part the lawyers contribute to constructing it?

And, ultimately, what are the legitimate social purposes of lawyering, besides allowing lawyers to make a living, and a comfortable living if they can? The profession's standard answer is that lawyers perform a valuable social service by helping clients use the tools of law, or to maneuver through or around the maze of law, to accomplish their freely chosen ends. But that answer is facile and insufficient. Just helping people to do things more effectively does not necessarily lead to a more just or decent or prosperous society, especially if the things some people want to do are exceptionally destructive or selfish or antisocial. The standard answer doesn't tell you much of anything about how to choose clients, or to allocate scarce resources among clients, or to trade off benefits to clients against harms to society and the legal system. Do poverty and public-interest lawyers tend to unduly dominate their clients? Are corporate lawyers unduly dominated by theirs? Is it legitimate for cause lawyers to privilege the cause they are working for over the immediate interests of clienteles? To help lawyers make the crucial decisions they will have to make, and to design the principles that should guide their decisions, there must be some reflection on how the lawyer's role may be supposed to lead, directly or indirectly, to socially valuable ends.

One of the best features of the essays in this collection is that they are "critical." They show how the most basic questions concerning lawyers' ethics and social responsibilities are contested, how they are subject to debate and vigorously debated, within the profession itself. There simply is no standard conventional wisdom or consensus, and certainly no source of unambiguous directive rules, that novice lawyers can simply sign on to and complacently accept—at least, none that provides any real guidance to resolving the hard dilemmas of professional practice life. Like anything else really important, the practice of law is a messy, dispute-riddled, contentious, politicized field of ideas and action, calling for sustained reflection and complex discretionary judgment.

And perhaps best of all, from a law teacher's point of view, this book helps to show what an incredibly exciting field legal ethics has become. Once one is freed from routinized rule-bound responses to ethical questions, one can appreciate the richness of alternative modes of thinking about practical ethics. It seems to me that these are chief among the many benefits this valuable book has to offer: a good deal of sharp questioning of standard and formulaic wisdom in thinking about how what lawyers do serves or disserves the cause of justice, and serious thought about alternatives.

Introduction

In philosopher and legal ethicist David Luban's 1983 reader, *The Good Lawyer* (unfortunately now out of print), one contributor noted that the study of ethics is, most basically, the study of how to be a "*good X.*"[1] Thus, the study of legal ethics is nothing more or less than the study of how to be a *good lawyer*. Yet this phrase can have many connotations. Many law students believe that being a *good* lawyer involves having excellent skills and preparation and bringing these to bear aggressively on behalf of clients. Note, however, that this conception contains not merely a view about how to be a technically proficient lawyer—i.e., one who has excellent skills and preparation—but also a vision of a lawyer's goodness in the sense in which we usually use the word *ethics*. A good lawyer, from these students' perspective, is a lawyer who aggressively exerts unmitigated zeal, within the bounds of the law, on behalf of her clients. Indeed, it is safe to say that this formulation characterizes the dominant conception of lawyers' primary ethical duty—cabined somewhat by other duties to the court system and to third party others, of course, but primary nonetheless: the lawyer owes her primary duty to the zealous representation of her clients.

What many legal ethics students do not know is that this dominant idea of a lawyer's duty of zealous advocacy on behalf of any taker as client is not the only ethical conception of the good lawyer present in contemporary thought on legal ethics. Nor was it the only conception present in the historical traditions underlying American legal ethics doctrines. Throughout that history and to this day, legal ethics thinkers have aired competing views about lawyers' primary ethical duties. Some of those ideas to be explored in this book include: that lawyers should concern themselves with assuming leadership roles in their communities as citizen statespersons; that lawyers should give higher priority to seeking justice than to advancing their clients' interests; that lawyers should give of their talents and skills to solve the public problems of their day; that lawyers should maintain a high degree of professional independence from their clients; that lawyers should provide legal services for all members of the community, including those who cannot pay; that lawyers should devote their energies to fighting on behalf of downtrodden, underrepresented, and/or unpopular clients; and that lawyers should be engineers for social justice.

Indeed, the opportunity to pursue social justice goals is one of the primary motivations for many prospective law students in deciding to endure the three years of legal training required to begin a career in law. Too often, however, students who start law school with an interest in social justice issues end up abandoning this career path, possibly as the result of professional socialization during law school and/or the crushing burden of law school loans.

This reader was compiled in the belief that students need not abandon their vision of the *good lawyer* as one committed to furthering social justice through law practice. Training in the norms of conduct that govern the legal profession can and should include exposure to the alternative strains of legal ethics thought that focus on social justice concerns. To be sure, the questions that arise from this perspective are no less contested, conflicted, or complex than the questions posed in studying legal ethics from the dominant, more technocratic approach. Indeed, certain perennial problems or *trouble spots* for which we do not have easy answers are central to the writing of almost all legal ethicists who espouse alternative visions of law practice as a means of advancing social justice.

This reader emphasizes several of these themes. One such theme involves the question of how to conceive of *power* in legal ethics analysis. This concept is important both to the analysis of power within and among sectors of the profession and to the analysis of power between lawyers and others. It includes the key issue of the distribution of power between lawyers and clients, as well as questions about how power operates in relations among different sectors of the profession, and between the legal profession and other sectors of society. The questions the concept of power introduces are innumerable: To what extent can or should ethical precepts control the exercise of lawyers' power over relatively powerless clients? To what extent can or should ethics rules constrain lawyers' response to the influence of powerful clients, including large corporations? How should we understand power in the first place—in Foucauldian terms as something that circulates in the micro dynamics of everyday practice? in macro terms from the view of broad institutions and systems? All of these and other questions are matters to which we return throughout this reader.

Another important theme involves the historical and social construction of legal ethics doctrine. As Robert Gordon points out in his Forward, legal education presents an excellent forum—and for many lawyers, probably the last opportunity—for sustained interrogation of the historical traditions on which the values of the contemporary profession rest. Yet a legal pedagogy that focuses predominantly on teaching doctrine neglects this opportunity to give law students the knowledge and critical tools required to understand their future work historically and reflectively. This is a particularly important supplement in the teaching of legal ethics, which involves, after all, the direct study of lawyers' values and why they have come to have them.

Along with an emphasis on history comes an interrogation of the connections between legal ethics doctrine and jurisprudence. As many of the reader's contributors observe, ethics rules do not exist in a vacuum. They instead emerge as one aspect of a generalized jurisprudence, so that, along with shifts in jurisprudential trends, come changes in legal ethics perspectives. This reader compiles scholarly works that trace and analyze the significance of these connections between jurisprudence and legal ethics, as well as the connections between and contests among jurisprudential principles and ethics approaches. It aims, in short, to guide students to understand legal ethics doctrine as the product of particular histories, to see neglected possibilities embedded in those histories, and to see the connections between history, jurisprudence, and the contested terrain of legal ethics doctrine.

A third important theme that flows through this reader is an emphasis on the connections between ethics and experience. This theme especially ties together works based in social identity movements such as feminist legal theory and critical race praxis. It is also an emphasis in the literature from the rebellious lawyering and clinical practice movements. If experience shapes knowledge, then differently situated experiences may tend to produce different ethics ideas. From this perspective, we are led to ask: What would a feminist legal ethics look like? A legal ethics of critical race praxis? What results might we reach if we examined social class and privilege as mechanisms that affect the construction and operation of ethics rules? This reader seeks to challenge students to think about these and similar questions as a means of teaching a critical reflective ethics through practice.

In addition to serving as an educational resource for law students in ABA-mandated legal ethics courses, this reader has a second purpose. It aims to display the breadth and depth of the exciting work currently underway in what I term the *critical* strains of legal ethics inquiry. Recent decades have seen a growth in many different kinds of critical theory in American jurisprudence. There are or have been movements in critical legal studies, critical race theory, feminist theory, sociolegal studies, and many other forms of so-called critical analysis. Thus far, however, too little attention has been paid to another emerging field of critical studies—namely, the study of legal ethics. In legal ethics inquiry, critical approaches have led to many new insights about the American bar's professional regulation projects, and to many alternative visions about the ethical ideals that should govern law practice. This reader aims to provide an introduction to this emerging field.

As used here, *critical* means "critical of the status quo."[2] Critical theory asks why the world cannot be different from what it is. It seeks to turn conventional assumptions on their heads—to see what insights can be gained from scrutinizing the contradictions and gaps in our received beliefs. At their best, critical approaches reflect a joy in debate and dialogue, ample skepticism, and an openness to challenge and disagreement. Indeed, I have often selected pieces precisely for the contrasts they offer when placed together. In doing so, I do not mean to imply that one author must be wrong and the other right. Instead, I hope to show the flourishing diversity of approaches and arguments as a way of encouraging students to enjoy disagreement and contestation as aspects of intellectual play (rather than as deathly serious matters, involving displays of overabundant self-importance and a lack of capacity for humor). I hope that readers will approach this text in the spirit of mutual respect and experimentation in which I intend it.

The book is organized into two parts. Part A focuses on the theory and history underlying critical approaches to legal ethics issues. Chapter 1 introduces four contrasting theoretical approaches to legal ethics analysis, each of which evokes themes that reemerge in later chapters. Chapter 2 looks at selected themes in the literature examining the historical development of contemporary legal ethics doctrines. It aims both to familiarize the student with this history and with leading examples of this literature, and also to raise some of the provocative questions that arise out of a consideration of that history, including the key question of what parts of this history are worth resurrecting and what parts should be discarded because of their connection to the more unsavory aspects of the legal profession's past.

Chapter 3 looks at two case studies of the development of legal ethics precepts in the context of public interest law. The first, examining the history of the NAACP's public impact litigation campaigns, arises out of my research on this topic. The second, considering the poverty law movement of the 1960s and 1970s, sets us up for a better understanding of the development of contemporary approaches that trace their histories directly back to this movement.

Part B moves on to the study of the panoply of contemporary critical approaches to legal ethics inquiry. Chapter 4 looks at clinical law professors' flourishing scholarly literature, which experiments both with new ethical visions of law practice and with new forms of legal analysis to develop those visions through narrative and storytelling. After reading some selections from the client-centered or collaborative lawyering skeins of this literature, we turn to the rebellious or community lawyering literature. Colleagues closer to these movements than I tell me that collaborative and community lawyering have largely become indistinguishably intertwined today, but I separate them for conceptual purposes so that we can compare and contrast their emphases.

Chapter 5 looks at a few selected examples of legal ethics inquiries undertaken by scholars writing from the perspectives of critical legal studies, critical race theory, and feminist legal theory. Chapters 6 and 7 look at other flourishing areas of alternative legal ethics inquiry—namely, law and popular culture and legal ethics and religion, respectively. Finally, Chapter 8 considers the pressing issue of lawyers' ethical duties in the face of corporate power, a perennial question most recently brought to a head by lawyers' involvement in massive financial scandals such as the collapse of the energy giant Enron, Inc.

I hope this book will appeal to a variety of audiences, including, first and foremost, law students, who sometimes suffer (needlessly, in my view) through their mandatory legal ethics courses. For these students, investigating the history and theory underlying the normative commitments of the professional community they are about to join could be one of the most fascinating topics they will encounter in law school. This reader also offers a useful introduction to the legal profession for undergraduate or graduate students in an introduction to law course. It may also provide a lively introduction to the field of legal ethics to interested members of the lay public—of which there appear to be many, given the great popularity of television shows and movies focusing on lawyers' ethical dilemmas, including *The Practice, Law and Order, The Firm,* and *The Pelican Brief.*

Indeed, the study of the intersection between lawyers' ethics and popular representations in film and literature constitutes one of the subject areas of this reader—it provides the focus for Chapter 6 and is evident in other work included in this reader as well.

This reader is designed as a relatively short and inexpensive supplement to more traditional course materials. In order to keep the price of the book as low as possible, I have, with great reluctance, drastically pared down from their original versions almost all of the excerpts included. They now appear as short, accessible passages, suitable for class assignment as supplemental reading to law students rushing through busy semesters. The cuts required to achieve this format have made it necessary to sacrifice much of the richness and complexity of the ideas of the authors who agreed to allow me to include their writing here, and I highly recommend that interested readers consult the full works, as cited in the first endnote to each entry, to further explore ideas they find interesting. The second endnote lists the current institutional affiliations of the authors (which may, of course, differ from the authors' affiliations at the time their articles were written).

In order to preserve reading ease, the cuts taken in each author's work have been made without any indication of their locations. Although many interesting ideas in each piece have been eliminated, I have tried throughout the editing process to avoid distorting the authors' meaning or intent. All footnotes, except direct source attributions, have been cut in the interests of space, and virtually all charts and other graphs have been omitted. Because of these dramatic cuts, readers are urged, in critiquing these pieces, to read charitably, with the awareness that much of the supporting documentation and rebuttal arguments for the authors' positions have been stripped away.

This reader has been structured to mesh with the traditional topics of a legal ethics course. Chapters 1 and 2 make useful companions to the usual history and background introductory chapters in traditional legal ethics textbooks. Chapter 3, containing the case studies of legal ethics dilemmas facing lawyers in the civil rights and poverty law movements, would be helpful to a professor who wishes to provide historical perspective on the development of ethical models for public interest law practice, and could also be assigned as optional reading for students interested in these topics.

Chapters 4 through 7 provide introductions to many exciting avenues of contemporary critical legal ethics scholarship. One way of using these chapters would be to invite students to read whichever chapter(s) are of most interest to them, and then hold a report-back session in which student groups would summarize, for the benefit of other students, what they found most interesting in their reading. This suggestion offers the advantage of covering a great deal of material with less assigned reading, and encourages students to pursue their own areas of interest as well. Students could also be asked to write short "compare and contrast" essays on one or more of these chapters, an assignment I have found useful as a way of enriching the curriculum and allowing students to gain credit for reflective analysis and writing in what can often be a large class with too few opportunities for personalized attention. This technique also allows the professor to learn more about what students find most interesting. Chapter 8, on legal ethics in counseling corporations, provides a useful supplement to the chapters on this subject found in most legal ethics case books.

At the opening of each chapter, I offer an introduction that briefly reviews the background to the readings and highlights the common themes that weave together the selections. I also offer a list of suggested questions for discussion and reflection, which may help the student focus her assessment of the materials. An Appendix offers suggestions for further reading and some additional, more detailed commentary for each chapter.

The hardest part of editing this book has been deciding what to leave out. Not only many impressive works of leading scholarship, but also entire topics, have had to be pared from the final product. Perhaps the most significant omission is the lack of any international focus in the face of an ever-expanding globalized world of law practice. Law students today will face a practice world in which they will not be able to avoid grappling with cross-cultural differences in practice rules and norms. My ultimate decision not to cover this fertile area of legal ethics inquiry stemmed from the fact that several excellent collections already exist that focus on lawyering in international or comparative contexts. Chief among these is an excellent series titled *Cause Lawyering*, edited by Austin Sarat and Stuart Scheingold.[3] Another excellent collection is Richard Abel's magnificent comparative work on the legal professions in civil and common law countries,[4] also available in a short compendium form suitable for classroom use.[5] Rather than do a mediocre job trying to capture the richness of this vast field of scholarship, I decided to refer the serious student of comparative legal ethics in the new millennium to these excellent sources as a starting point.

Two other glaring areas of omission are civil government lawyering and the ethical challenges posed to lawyers in the post-9/11 era. Both of these areas of legal ethics inquiry merit a great deal more attention, but I was not able to find materials on these subjects that fit the scope of this reader. A few suggested leads are noted in the Appendix.

In the final stages of editing this work to fit with the publisher's space restrictions, I found myself compelled to cut out two entire sections from my original plan—one titled "Legal Ethics in Practice Contexts," and the other "Contemporary Policy Debates." These chapters would have taken our critical inquiry further in exploring the legal ethics issues that arise from context-specific examinations of the worlds of public interest practice, criminal defense, prosecution, small-firm and solo practice, and alternative dispute resolution. We would also have read leading works on pressing policy issues, including the meaning of legal ethics prohibitions against engaging in various forms of invidious discrimination; the debate about mandatory pro bono requirements; and critical perspectives on unauthorized practice restrictions, a field pioneered by Deborah Rhode. I owe both thanks and an apology to the many authors who agreed to have their work appear in these excised Chapters; my editors promise to bring out a second edition that includes these works if the market displays sufficient interest.

Acknowledgments

Working on this book has been a labor of love, and I have a great many people to thank for its completion. First, my thanks go to Richard Delgado, Jean Stefancic, and Deborah Gershenowitz, my editor at NYU Press, for having faith in this project and helping with its formulation. I also owe a great debt of gratitude to the reviewers who commented on the book proposal and manuscript at various stages. Their suggestions greatly improved the final product.

Second, my most special thanks go to each of the contributors, who graciously allowed me to reprint their work and suffered the trauma of having their work drastically pared during the excerpting process. There was nothing more rewarding than watching the pages of brilliant ideas grow as I compiled these excerpts, knowing that it was not *I* who had endured the great mental labor of producing such excellent scholarship.

Third, I owe great thanks to many professional colleagues within my home institution and elsewhere who generously gave of their time to share with me their expertise on the various topics covered in this book, including Richard Abel, Susan Bennett, Mary Clark, Angela Davis, Bob Diner-stein, Binny Miller, Elliott Milstein, Russell Pearce, Penny Pether, Brenda Smith, and Rick Wilson. Most importantly, Dean Claudio Grossman gave generous funding and many other kinds of material as well as more intangible institutional supports that allowed this project to be conceived and completed.

I also owe special thanks to Frankie Winchester (Ph.D. A.B.D., History, American University) for careful and precise work on the manuscript, for good cheer, and for tips on doing historical research. And I owe great gratitude to my spouse and co-parent, Henry S. Friedman, for "walking the walk" rather than just "talking the talk" in shifting roles with me to assume primary child care duties at certain points toward the end of my sabbatical so that I could finish this manuscript.

This project was inspired by my students at American University Washington College of Law; their energy and idealism refreshes me daily. Most important were my research assistants, including Jen Birlem, Heather Collier, Elizabeth Elia, Farrah Fontaine, Lei Hart, Benjamin Holt, David Lee, and Yamini Menon, who tested potential contributions for their law student "interest quotient" and helped greatly with research, editing, and proofreading. I owe Minyoung Ohm (J.D., 2004) special credit for a seminar paper that deepened my appreciation of the distinctive features of the rebellious/community law movement.

Finally, this book is dedicated to my parents, Gloria L. and Jack M. Carle, for bringing me to adulthood and for their continuing support.

Theory and History

Chapter 1

Theories of Professional Regulation

This chapter considers several different theoretical perspectives on the legal profession's efforts to establish ethical rules for law practice. Observers of these ethics regulation projects often use theory to organize and prioritize the information they collect. Even when writers do not make their theoretical commitments explicit, the lenses they look through in describing the world of legal ethics regulation are often profoundly shaped by theory. Interdisciplinary cross-fertilization has led legal scholars to borrow from many fields, including political science, economics, anthropology, and social theory. The student perusing these selections will thus observe writers on the legal profession referring often to the work of many prominent social theorists, including Max Weber, Talcott Parsons, Clifford Geertz, and Michel Foucault.

The choice of such sources of theory in turn has normative implications, since descriptions of what exists often suggest what *should* exist as well. Thus, for example, Richard Abel argues that the legal profession's efforts to develop ethics rules are primarily aimed at preserving lawyers' economic monopoly over law-related services. On this theory we should give little value to the bar's ethics regulation projects, since monopolies generally cause economic harm. On the other hand, Terence Halliday suggests that bar organizations perpetuate a public service ethic among lawyers and provide important services to the state. If Halliday's perspective is correct, efforts at professional self-regulation should be applauded because they advance important public-spirited aims. In short, theory is important because it provides the lenses through which we make judgments, including ethical judgments about what is *good* in lawyers' conduct and approaches to practicing law.

To illustrate the wide array of theoretical perspectives that influence current critical work in the legal ethics field, this chapter highlights four contrasting approaches. First, Abel summarizes the sequence of professional regulation projects the American Bar Association (ABA) engaged in over the course of the twentieth century and analyzes how these projects fit within his theory of professional monopolization. (Note that the version of the ABA Model Rules ["Model Rules"] Abel discusses is the 1983 Model Rules of Professional Responsibility, then in draft form, which is now being superseded as the states deliberate on a new version the ABA adopted in 2002, based on the work of the ABA Ethics 2000 Commission.)

Abel provocatively argues that a major purpose of legal ethics regulation is to restrain competition in order to perpetuate lawyers' economic control over the market for legal services. In support of his argument, Abel points to rules such as those prohibiting persons who do not hold a bar license from engaging in the practice of law. He further argues that even rules that do not have a direct monopoly-enforcing effect serve a related purpose—namely, that of legitimation, or "offering a normative justification" for what lawyers would do anyway. The rules are, in Abel's words, "an attempt by elite lawyers to convince themselves that they have resolved their ethical dilemmas." We will return to some of the implications of the fact that elite sectors of the bar typically draft and enforce legal ethics rules in later chapters, including chapters 2 and 3.

Abel's approach is often criticized for being unduly cynical. What is the point of studying legal ethics if lawyers' self-interest and the propagation of justificatory myths are all that is involved? Abel does not always adopt this view: he was a legal services lawyer early in his own career, and he is deeply committed to producing alternative ethical norms that will motivate new generations of law students to engage in public interest practice, as noted in the Appendix. But Abel's approach throws down the gauntlet: if ethics regulation is not primarily for the purposes Abel claims, then what justifications can be offered for legal ethics doctrines? The other writers featured in this chapter explore this question from a variety of perspectives.

The second theorist we read, Terence Halliday, takes a sociological perspective just as Abel does, but poses a challenge to Abel's theory. Halliday begins by laying out two views of professional regulation. The first is the neo-Weberian approach, which views professional regulation as a means of economic monopolization, as Abel does. The second, which Halliday labels the neo-Marxist approach, focuses on ethics rules as reproducing ideology, much like Abel's legitimation claim. Halliday argues that neither of these approaches adequately explains legal ethics regulation, and he offers a third theory of his own. Halliday's theory is that the legal profession's collective organization allows it to bring its special expertise to the service of *state power*. The organized bar contributes important resources to the state, such as legal referral and public education services, expert bodies to carry out law reform projects, and volunteers to design and staff lawyer disciplinary tribunals. In portions of his book not included in the brief excerpt that appears here, Halliday develops this argument through a case study of the Chicago Bar Association.

Both Abel and Halliday focus on the American tradition under which lawyers design and enforce their own ethics rules, a system often referred to as *professional self-regulation.* As this term suggests, the legal profession historically has handled ethics regulation by itself, through the ABA at the national level, and, at the level of state jurisdictions, through state bar committees. Some such committees propose legal ethics rules to their state supreme courts; other committees, composed primarily of practicing lawyers, hear cases and recommend professional disciplinary measures.

In the third excerpt, David Wilkins develops a ground-breaking argument based on the observation that self-regulation is not the only form of regulation that is imposed on, or could be imposed on, lawyers' conduct. Instead, Wilkins notes, there are a variety of regulatory systems that bear on lawyers' activities. These include not only the state bar ethics committees that propose ethics rules, the state judicial systems that adopt them, and the disciplinary boards that enforce them, but also state and federal legislatures that may enact laws that affect lawyers' conduct, individual judges who have the power to sanction lawyers who appear before them, and the legal malpractice system. To evaluate which of these systems make the most sense for regulating lawyers' conduct, Wilkins applies the methodology of *new institutionalism,* which seeks to compare the benefits and drawbacks of various regulatory choices.

In his talk of cost and benefits, efficiencies and externalities, Wilkins sometimes sounds like a law and economics scholar, but the conclusions he reaches are far from the justifications for the status quo for which some versions of law and economics analysis are known. Wilkins wrote his article in the wake of the savings and loan crises of the mid-1980s, in which a number of poorly managed and insured savings and loan institutions collapsed, leaving many large and small investors in financial ruin. Well-respected lawyers who represented these failing savings and loans had sometimes successfully stalled federal agencies' attempts to investigate their clients' financial stability, thus increasing the economic losses incurred. Wilkins seeks to identify what went wrong in a legal ethics system that allows lawyers to act in such a way as to exacerbate these great harms. Today, a similar scandal in the wake of the collapse of the energy giant

Enron has led to similar reevaluations of the legal ethics rules that should guide corporate lawyers, as we see in chapter 8.

After examining the benefits and drawbacks of different systems of lawyer regulation, Wilkins concludes that the best combinations of regulatory methods vary with *practice context.* Lawyers representing less powerful individuals face ethical dangers very different from those faced by lawyers representing sophisticated and powerful clients, such as large corporations; therefore they require rules tailored to their practice contexts that take these dangers into account. Wilkins's arguments that lawyers should abandon attempts to devise universal rule systems to regulate lawyer conduct, and should instead focus on context-specific regulation, were an important step forward in freeing legal ethics inquiry to take a variety of critical directions. Wilkins starkly posed a question underlying many commentators' discomfort with the current system of legal ethics rules: should clients' relative *power* make a difference in the permissible conduct of lawyers representing them?

In the final selection included in this chapter, Lucie White focuses on ethics issues related to lawyers' relationships with their clients, and specifically, to clients with very little power. White applies poststructuralist conceptions of *power* to analyze lawyering roles. Unlike Abel, Halliday, and Wilkins, she scrutinizes lawyers' values and ethical norms on the *micro level* of daily practice rather than on the *macro level* of formal institutions and systems. She urges lawyers to examine on a micro level "how and when we deploy power within the routines of lawyering," with a view to developing "different habits—different ways of talking and paying attention—that may make our deployments of power less disruptive of our clients." Following others, White calls this project the development of a "theoretics of practice." Chapter 4 includes further study of the *theoretics of practice* movement, along with one of White's self-studies of the power dynamics between herself and one of her clients.

As you read these excerpts, here are some questions you may wish to keep in mind to help you synthesize and evaluate the material:

Questions for Reflection and Discussion

1. Do you agree with Abel's argument that a significant motive for lawyers' self-regulation is to protect their monopoly on legal practice? Which Model Rules seem to have this motivation? Which do not fit this theory?

2. Do you agree with Abel's claim that legal ethics rules serve legitimation purposes? What evidence do you see for and against such arguments?

3. What evidence do you see in the Model Rules or elsewhere to support Halliday's claim that an important dimension of lawyers' ethics is the creation of a culture of civic responsibility that encourages lawyers to lend their skills and services to aid the functioning of the state? Is this the best way to understand the admonishment contained in many states' ethics rules that lawyers donate a certain portion of their professional services to pro bono work?

4. What does Wilkins see as the advantages and disadvantages of professional self-regulation? Do you agree with his analysis? Do you anticipate being more comfortable with professional regulation undertaken by your peers in the bar or with that imposed from outside by legislatures or administrative agencies? Why? How much of your perspective is influenced by your perceptions of your own self-interest? (For more on recent moves to impose federal regulation on lawyers' conduct in representing publicly traded corporations, see chapter 8, discussing reevaluations of corporate lawyers' ethical responsibilities following the lawyer-aided collapse of Enron.)

5. Do you think clients' relative power should make a difference in the permissible conduct of lawyers who represent them? Why or why not?

6. Can you think of examples of telling micro-level experiences that you have had as a student lawyer in a clinic or in another legal setting, such as a summer job or legal internship? What insights would be revealed by a "thick description" of what you observed in such a setting?

Why Does the ABA Promulgate Ethical Rules?[1]

Richard L. Abel[2]

Before attempting to answer this question, let me explain why I believe it is a meaningful one. If all occupations promulgated rules of conduct and were constantly engaged in revising them, then there would be no problem. Such rules would be a given; they would be part of the definition of an occupation. But that is obviously not the case. Many occupational groups presently do not have such rules—for instance, retail clerks, or bus drivers or school teachers. Occupations that have such rules in the United States may not have them in other countries. And occupations in the United States that now have such rules may not have had them in the past. Indeed, the ABA first promulgated rules for lawyers only in 1908. Thus, there is variation in the behavior of occupational rulemaking and, therefore, in the possibility of social analysis.

But would the analysis be worthwhile? Is the activity of formulating rules of conduct for lawyers significant? It certainly consumes a considerable amount of energy. Following the drafting of the original thirty-two Canons, not only did periodic amendments increase the number of canons by nearly half, but four committees attempted complete revisions, in 1928, 1933, 1937, and 1954. In 1964 a fifth, the Wright Committee, was created; it spent nearly five years reevaluating the rules and finally proposed a Code of Professional Responsibility that the ABA adopted in 1969.[3] Yet the pace of change is still accelerating: less than ten years later the ABA established still another body, the Kutak Commission, which produced the Model Rules of Professional Conduct.[4] Throughout this period the ABA Committee on Professional Ethics and the committees of state, local, and specialty bar associations issued hundreds of opinions construing the prevailing rules each year, and these opinions were periodically collected, organized, and cross-referenced in codifications. These legislative and judicial materials, in turn, have elicited a mass of scholarly commentary. The whole has been synthesized into numerous casebooks and other teaching materials used in the courses on the legal profession that are required of the more than 120,000 students enrolled in the more than 170 law schools accredited by the ABA (and probably required of most graduates of unaccredited law schools as well). All of these activities, of course, find parallels in the fifty states, which have actual control over the conduct of lawyers. Each state promulgates, revises, and interprets its own rules, inspires local scholarly commentary, requires law schools to instruct students in the rules, tests student knowledge in its bar examination, and may require further education and testing as a condition of readmission for those suspended or disbarred. Enough is going on, it seems, to justify an effort at understanding.

The Rules Do Not Promote Ethical Behavior

Neither the ABA nor the Kutak Commission dwells on why the profession has rules or why they are in need of revision. The reason must have seemed too obvious: "clarification of the ethical judgments lawyers must daily make in the practice of law."[5] Implicit in that goal are the following premises: lawyers constantly encounter ethical dilemmas; the law and morality that guide the rest of society are inappropriate to resolve those dilemmas; the profession has unique competence to discern and respond to those problems; by declaring norms, the profession can guide the conduct of its members, who wish to behave ethically and look to the profession to define ethical conduct; to the extent that guidance, exhortation, and informal pressures are insufficient, conformity can be secured by the professional disciplinary apparatus. This, of course, is simply the instrumental justification commonly offered for law, here applied to rules of professional conduct: they function to shape behavior through instruction and sanction.

The trouble with obvious reasons is that they are often wrong. I think that the instrumental view of law is usually a legitimation rather than a description. It is clearly inadequate as an explanation for most rules of professional conduct. In order for rules to mold behavior they must set forth the boundaries of that behavior with clarity; the vaguer they are, the less effect they can have (or at least the less predictable that effect will be). Yet the Model Rules are drafted with an amorphousness and ambiguity that render them virtually meaningless.

Rules of professional conduct are likely to make a significant contribution to directing behavior only if they differ from prevailing law and morality. Furthermore, an essential claim of professions—and a basis of their relative immunity from state regulation—is that they hold their members to a standard of conduct higher than that of the lay public. Yet many of the Model Rules simply restate the most commonplace morality: do your work promptly,[6] stay in communication with your client,[7] do not represent adverse interests,[8] hold client property in trust.[9] Indeed, lawyers reject the rigors of a higher morality: they resent ethical restrictions on dealings with legislative and administrative bodies for "fear that [they] will thus be put at a competitive disadvantage with nonlawyers."[10] It is hard to imagine that lawyers would act differently if these precepts were not restated by the Rules. If they would act differently, it says little for the ethical standards or respect for law of those who become lawyers. Some of the Rules actually excuse lawyers from ethical obligations that most lay people accept as binding. Lawyers, for instance, are held to higher standards of truthfulness when they apply to the bar (that is, when they are seeking to enter the profession) and when they advertise (that is, whey they are acting in a commercial rather than a professional capacity) than when they function as advocates in litigation or negotiation.[11]

To summarize the last two paragraphs, the Rules are both underinclusive (in the double sense of overlooking salient behavior and being unduly lax) and overinclusive (in restating ordinary law and morality) when viewed as an instrument of social control.

Study after study has shown that the current rules of professional conduct are not enforced. Misconduct is rarely perceived. If perceived, it is not reported. If reported, it is not investigated. If investigated, violations are not found. If found, they are excused. If they are not excused, penalties are light. And if significant penalties are imposed, the lawyer soon returns to practice, in that state or another. Lawyers constantly condemn the failure of the criminal justice system to deter crime for precisely these reasons— because of its alleged indifference, procedural niceties, or excessive lenience. Indeed, we know that the efficacy of social control varies even more strongly with the likelihood of punishment than it does with the severity of the sanction. Yet on both counts, especially the former, the professional disciplinary system falls far below the wholly inadequate standards of the criminal law. Lawyers can hardly present their travesty of a penal system as an effective deterrent.

The Rules Contribute to Market Control

To return to the original question posed by my title, the obvious answers —the answers the Kutak Commission gives or implies—are incomplete or incorrect. The Rules cannot adequately be understood as an effort to induce the behavior they prescribe, nor are they a spontaneous reform expressing the commitment of the ABA to fundamental change. Why, then, did the ABA engage in a revision of the rules of professional conduct, and why has it done so now? We can identify some of the reasons by analyzing the process through which occupations strive to become professions.

All occupations in a capitalist system seek to control the markets in which they sell their labor. Some occupations organize unions. Others form associations that attempt to secure state support for their control over entry to the market. In other words, they aspire to control the supply of services by controlling the production *of* and *by* producers of those services. The justification for control, typically, is that the services require a high level of technical skill and that only those who already possess such skill can determine whether others have acquired it. An occupation is a profession to the extent that it exercises such a mode of supply control. To summarize a long and far more complicated history, American lawyers lost much of their control over supply in the Jacksonian period, when many states eliminated all restrictions on the practice of law. The last two decades of the nineteenth century saw the beginning of a movement to reassert control, which largely succeeded in the decades following the Second World War, when most states required four years of college, three years of study at a law school accredited by the ABA, and passage of a bar examination and a character test.

Because I am going to argue that ethical rules contribute to market control, let me try to forestall at the outset some obvious objections to this interpretation. First, to say that the struggle for market control throws some light on the activity of professional rulemaking is not to deny that many of the Model Rules have little or no direct bearing on the struggle, or that much of the struggle is waged outside the framework of the Rules —over ABA accreditation of law schools, for example. Second, to maintain that the struggle is *waged* through rules is not to insist that it is *won*;

indeed, as I argue below, supply control has recently been diluted. The logic of capitalism dictates that all occupations engage in the struggle, but the outcome is contingent on the particular historical constellation of social, political, and economic forces. Third, the contention that ethical rules contribute to market control is not inconsistent with my earlier claim that many of the Model Rules do not achieve their declared purposes. For one thing, I am talking here about different rules: those that seek to regulate competition are enforced because their implementation is in the interest of lawyers. For another, market control is not, and could not be, a declared purpose of the Rules; it is a latent, not a manifest, function. Finally, I am not advancing a conspiracy theory: I am not concerned with the motives of the rulemakers but with the consequences of their rules for the structure of the market for legal services. From a structural perspective, a profession *must* seek to control its market or else commit collective suicide.

The Rules Are a Means of Legitimation

The profession's response to its economic and social problems offers only a partial explanation for the content of the Model Rules. Even if, in practice, lawyers are primarily concerned with market control through restraints on competition, many of the Rules have at most only a tenuous relationship to that issue. We can approach a satisfactory explanation of professional rulemaking only by abandoning the insistence on seeing all laws as instrumental. Instead, we must turn to their symbolic functions. And the principal symbolic function of rules of professional conduct, clearly, is legitimation. Although social analysis has both overused and abused this concept, I believe it can be given a clear definition. Legitimation is the attempt by those engaged in some realm of social activity to offer a normative justification for their actions. The attempt may be addressed to an external audience, as in public relations, but it may also be a dialogue among the participants themselves.

Viewed from this perspective, rules of legal ethics are an attempt by elite lawyers to convince themselves that they have resolved their ethical dilemmas. I have deliberately been very cautious in advancing this claim because there is little evidence that anyone pays attention to ethical rules beyond the small proportion of lawyers who draft, discuss, and enact them, or those who request ethical opinions. Certainly most lay people know little more than that such rules exist, and those who are aware of the rules are probably skeptical about their contents.

This perspective immediately makes sense of those data that seemed most inconsistent with the instrumental interpretation of the Model Rules. It is precisely so that they can be advanced as a solution to insoluble ethical dilemmas that rules of legal ethics, including the Model Rules, are vague, unrealistic, riddled with gaps, duplicative of ordinary law and morality, unknown to most practitioners, and systematically unenforced. The purpose of such rules is not to describe reality or even to prescribe right behavior, but rather to create a myth about what lawyers might be in order to disguise what they are. Ethical precepts thus necessarily perform two simultaneous functions: they formulate ideals for human behavior and they suggest that behavior can attain these ideals. If the latter function is generally implicit, it is no less important. The less it is possible to realize the ideals, the more their reiteration contributes to the construction of a myth. And if those who proclaim the ideals know, or should know, that they set impossible goals, the myth is not noble but hypocritical.

The promulgation of ethical rules carries two important implicit messages: first, that the rules themselves can resolve the ethical dilemmas of lawyers, with no need for structural changes; second, that the rules offer an exhaustive statement of the ethical dilemmas of lawyers, or at least address the most important ones. The latter message distracts attention from problems not discussed. We can finally understand why it is important for the profession to declare that the Model Rules are both new and the product of the profession's own initiative. They must be new so that they can be seen as untainted by past failures. And they must be self-directed so that the profession can show itself capable of putting, and keeping, its own house in order.

Conclusion

The Rules of Professional Conduct purport to resolve the ethical dilemmas of lawyers. They do so in order that those who draft, discuss, and consult them may be reassured that their conduct is morally correct. But the Rules do not resolve those dilemmas; they merely restate them in mystifying language that obscures the issues through ambiguity, vagueness, qualification, and hypocrisy. The capacity of these precepts to legitimate is constantly being eroded as internal inconsistencies, the meaninglessness of the language, and the empirical falsity and impossibility of their claims and prescriptions become apparent or are exposed by criticism. Hence, the Rules must constantly be rewritten in a vain effort to renew their legitimating force.

The Rules cannot resolve the ethical dilemmas of lawyers because those dilemmas are inherent in the structure of the lawyer's role. First, legal representation, like all other goods and services under capitalism, has become a commodity. This means that clients can buy loyalty, which should be given freely out of a sense of social and political commitment. It means that clients *must* buy justice, which should be theirs by right, and will obtain only as much justice as they can afford. And it means that lawyers *must* seek to maximize their profits (especially as competition within the market for legal services intensifies), with the result that they must sell their services to the highest bidder and withhold them from those who cannot pay the price. In a capitalist society, the highest bidders will necessarily be those who own large amounts of capital and, within that group, those who wield monopoly power. Lawyers are, therefore, partisans in the class conflict that capitalism generates and cannot resolve, and virtually all lawyers are enlisted on the side of capital and against the numerous groups it oppresses, disenfranchises, and exploits—workers, the nonworking poor, women, minorities, citizens of the Third World, and all those who must live in a polluted environment and suffer the depletion of its resources.

Beyond Monopoly: Lawyers, State Crises, and Professional Empowerment[1]

Terence C. Halliday[2]

An essential problem for the neophyte profession is the establishment of control over a sphere of work. It is this, and the cluster of concepts surrounding monopoly, that has become the conceptual pivot around which have revolved many recent treatments of professions and professionalism. The discourse has been cast in two molds, the one neo-Weberian and the other neo-Marxist. The neo-Weberian treatments have focused on the process of economic monopolization; the neo-Marxist discussions have gone on from monopolies of competence to their consequences for the reproduction of bourgeois ideology. Both, however, have been prone to a form of theoretical imperialism that has lost sight of most images but monopoly.

Monopolistic interpretations of the rise of professions too readily become wrongheaded and unbalanced. In part the fallacy of universal monopoly results from a methodological lapse. Ex post facto reinterpretation of a sequence of historical developments allows an observer to assume that monopoly is the overriding motive of most professional actions when it may well be an unintended consequence of some other motivation. In this mode of analysis, where professional actions can be attributed to more benign or malevolent motivations, the latter seem always to be preferred. Higher educational standards may have had a salutary effect on quality of care and on research and the advancement of professional knowledge; professional ethics may have produced higher levels of professional responsibility; and licensure may have protected the gullible from exploitation and personal tragedy. That some of those aspects of professionalism have also had monopolistic effects seems to have largely eclipsed any beneficial consequences. Even if actions are not explicitly monopolistic, that can be reinterpreted as strategic retreat or cunning strategy. Demonopolization becomes indirect monopolization. Moreover, advocates of the monopoly thesis are inclined, at critical points in their arguments, to fall back on an assumption of internal professional cohesion that, in other sections of their discussions, they have been at pains to deny. Consequently, little attention is given to those monopolistic actions by one section of a profession that partially dismantle the monopoly of another section. For example, more prestigious and more powerful specialties within professions may be more readily inclined to adopt measures, such as no-fault laws, that effectively demonopolize areas of less prestigious professional specialties. In sum, then, the defect of an unchecked theory of professional monopolies is that all motivations and most consequences other than those that are explicitly or intentionally monopolistic become debased by that label.

Consequently, the chief lapse of market interpretations of professional activity is not that they draw attention to professional self-interest or to economic motivations or to the consequences of professionalism. To a point, they can be validated empirically. The impediment of vulgar monopolistic theories is that *one* consequence or even intent of professionalism becomes the raison d'être of the entire professionalization enterprise. The part is taken for the whole. Latent consequences become explicit intents; accompanying motives become sole bases of action. Results of professionalization are assumed to be the outcome of a professional "project." In a word, the entire interpretative model is overdetermined.

In the legal profession, whose "modern" bid for professionalization emerged principally from the last quarter of the nineteenth century, there has been a perceptible shift away from the primacy or centrality of market and professional control. A preoccupation with market dominance marked only one, and a developmental, stage in the emergence of the profession and the expansion of its associations. Once that stage was reached, and its "developmental tasks" accomplished, the importance of monopoly in collective professional action and to professional identity began to fade.

The shifts away from the formative stage in the legal profession have been reflected in numerous indicators. Evidence from bar associations demonstrates that there has been a steady relative decline in the size and number of committees on professional fees, professional education, and professional discipline.

The concept of *established professionalism* can be defined both nega-tively and positively. Defined positively, the established phase of profes-sionalism is that point—or, more accurately, that succession of points—at which growth of resources allows a profession to take on a broader range of functions and action than market control. As a result, organizational size, stature, and tradition allow an established profession some putative independence from the statutory or judicial powers on which rests its legitimate domination of service domains. The profession can be more detached and more autonomous from the fiat of the original grantors of monopolistic authority. Privileges become rights. A complete reversal of institutionalized monopoly appears inconceivable. Thus the profession can largely take for granted what previously it had constantly to negotiate. With the energies and resources released from securing and maintaining monopolies, professions attain new capacities for the exercise of influence through assertive collective action.

The expanded capacities and functions of the established profession are reflected both internally and externally. Internally, associations have en-gaged in a wider spectrum of services to members: continuing education; licensing of specialists; channeling of work to practitioners through refer-ral programs; advice on the economics and management of professional offices; and the like. The more fundamental mark of professional matu-rity, however, can be found externally, particularly in changes in relations between professions and the state. The dependency relations with the state in the formative period can be transformed into contributory relations in the established phase. Whereas in the former a vulnerable occupation is at the behest of an empowering state, in the latter a vulnerable state can rely on the expertise of empowered professions. The dependency relation casts professions on the state for the critical structural elements of professional-ism itself; the contributory relation provides the profession with increased leverage on strains in the primary responsibilities of government itself.

Civic Professionalism: Some Normative Considerations

By casting the relations between professions and the state in these terms, the ideal of professional service—a powerful value in many theories of professions—can be reconstructed. In American writings of the postwar period, the concept has been treated individualistically. In the microsoci-ology of professional role performance, relations of lawyer and client or doctor and patient were construed not only as economic, but, more vigorously, as service relations. The argument here does not rest on this assumption but expresses a macrosociology more consistent with the concept of collective service enunciated by Carr-Saunders and Wilson and intimated by Durkheim. The established profession can mobilize its concentration of expertise and bring its associational influence not at the individual but at the *collective* level to the service of state power. To make this claim is not to displace an old heresy of unbridled monopolism with a new orthodoxy of collective civic professionalism. To do so would merely reflect in mirror image the tendentiousness of theories wed entirely to material interests. It is rather to hold monopoly considerations in tension with considerations of collective professional civility. Professions have monopolies of competence; they command specialized skills and advanced knowledge. Very often, as conditions of these, they have developed organizational infrastructures for mobilization as circumstances demand. But it is naive to suppose that professions will commit their distinctive resources to the state irrespective of the interests of the profession—as it were, to write a blank check for the state to cash in on professional expertise when the state finds it expedient without any expectation of a quid pro quo. The state must recognize that a profession bringing its competencies to the needs of institutional and societal adaptation is not without its interests.

Above both sectional and communal interests rise interests beyond the profession—an orientation to a civic professionalism. Transcending the particularism of specialties, the pecuniary interests of employment, and even the community commitment to proceduralism, some segments of bar elites—practitioners, judges, or legal academics—pursue courses of action animated by a civic consciousness. One element of that consciousness may arise from a sense of individual responsibility as a citizen; another element arises from some sense of collective obligation. If an organization can be a fictive corporate individual, then an association of lawyers can be a collective citizen. As the individual has responsibilities as well as rights, the organization has duties as well as perquisites.

It is imperative to insist immediately that interests are frequently incompatible, and that, indeed, just as often as not, sectional claims prevail over communal values and personal advantages are espoused at the cost of civic responsibility. Instances of rapaciousness by individual lawyers can be matched by repeated examples of self-interested and even cynical mobilization by specialties. Recent drafts of professional codes of ethics have been at one moment construed as championing narrow professional interests and at another moment as aspiring to some ideal of public service, even at the expense of those interests. If an enduring struggle between self-interest and altruism underlies individual motivation, a never stable tension between civic and monopolistic values permeates the collective professionalism of lawyers.

In the nature of things, therefore, it is unlikely that professions will serve the state without any consideration of cost to themselves. But it is equally implausible to believe that the only driving motivation of professions is an unbridled bid for collective gain. Consequently, for the state to profit from professional resources it must sometimes recognize, sometimes guard against, and sometimes appropriate the interests of professions—indeed, press them beyond monopoly. The consequence may be, and in some cases already has been, an implicit concordat between states and established professions: in exchange for the state's implicit guarantee that the traditional monopoly of the profession will be largely preserved, notwithstanding occasional adjustments in response to public pressure or professional lapses, the profession will commit its monopoly of competence and its organizational resources to state service, so long as the substance of its service does not directly erode the general control of the market the profession has attained, although it may be prepared to roll back monopoly in certain areas. Indeed the actual service function of the profession provides one of the best forms of insurance that the state will not dismantle the traditional perquisites of the profession. In effect, aspects of such a contract already exist.

Such an implicit concordat has substantial consequences for the legitimacy of the state. The contributions of professions to social institutions or society at large offer more than the ideological gloss or a veneer of legitimation. It is true that professions generate and maintain an ideology or system of beliefs about the system that they serve; but it is a mistake to conclude that their principal function is little more than to polish and patch an ideology that bears little relation to empirical situations. If legitimacy for the state is to be broadened in advanced capitalist societies with the assistance of professions, it will be founded on structural and institutional changes that professions themselves have precipitated or supported. It will not occur only through the elaboration of a distracting ideology that bears only a tangential relation to class relations or social formations. Neither will it be sustained by skirting over the strains in society or the periodic crises faced by the state.

Greater legitimation for social institutions and the state in advanced capitalist societies will occur when professions take some responsibility for the relief of crises through the adaptation of those institutions in which they have authority and whose legitimacy is most at threat. Accordingly, legitimacy derives not merely from a more skillful and refined elaboration of a bourgeois ideology but from the practical utilization of professional competencies and the expertise from which their monopolies are derived. By not ignoring or dismantling professional monopolies but by critically appraising, periodically revising, and systematically appropriating them for its own purposes, the state gains an additional means of upgrading its capacity to meet new demands.

By harnessing the resources of established professions to its more pressing needs, not only does the state obtain an advantage from vestiges of the monopoly with which it originally invested professions, but, in preserving a core if not the totality of that monopoly, it can also better induce the profession to take on itself a more constructive relation that incorporates not only monopoly but much beyond. The evidence suggests that the movement to this new symbiosis between professions and the state may already have begun for the legal profession at the subnational level in the United States.

Who Should Regulate Lawyers?[1]

David B. Wilkins[2]

"Where were [the attorneys]" and "[w]hy didn't any of them speak up or disassociate themselves from the[se] transactions?" These questions, posed by Judge Stanley Sporkin as he reviewed the events leading up to the multi-billion-dollar collapse of Lincoln Savings and Loan, capture the sentiments of many Americans when they discover the extent to which some of this country's leading law firms may be implicated in the tawdry events surrounding the savings and loan crisis. In the eyes of many, these revelations are part of a larger pattern of lawyer misconduct that has contributed to a diverse array of modern woes, including the litigation crisis, the spiraling cost of medical care, the insider trading scandals on Wall Street, and the proliferation of fraudulent tax practices. Indeed, in a recent speech to the American Bar Association (ABA), the Vice President of the United States strongly suggested that lawyers who "overuse and abuse the legal system" are partially to blame for America's failure to compete effectively in the global economy.[3] Although ABA President John Curtin disagreed with this assertion,[4] even the ABA concedes that "the public continues to be critical of lawyer regulation."[5]

This consensus disappears, however, when the discussion focuses on controlling lawyer misconduct. Predictably, the ABA clings to the traditional view that disciplinary agencies operating under the supervision of state supreme courts should retain primary responsibility for ensuring that lawyers live up to their professional obligations. This position has become more difficult to maintain in light of the burgeoning number of alternative systems for controlling lawyer misconduct. For example, judges now routinely use Rule 11 to sanction lawyers for filing frivolous claims or defenses or otherwise needlessly increasing the costs of litigation. Federal regulators bring enforcement actions, both administratively and in the courts, against lawyers who aid and abet their clients' violations of applicable regulatory statutes. State legislatures and Congress continue to expand the range of liability actions that can be filed against lawyers, while judges dismantle many of the restrictions against suits by third parties under existing statutory and common law theories. Even traditional malpractice liability has been transformed as courts have removed many of the evidentiary and procedural impediments that have traditionally made it difficult for clients to sue their lawyers successfully. More changes could soon be on the way, as policymakers contemplate new enforcement schemes ranging from the Competitiveness Council's recommendation for a "loser pays" rule in diversity cases and a moratorium on one-way fee shifting to a variety of state initiatives that would place some or all of the disciplinary process under the control of the legislature.

The presence of these alternative enforcement models has sparked a heated debate over who should have responsibility for regulating lawyers and how that authority should be exercised. The debate proceeds on several levels. On the policy level, lawyers, judges, and legal academics argue whether the benefits of particular control systems outweigh their costs. This debate, however, is often merely a surrogate for a deeper theoretical and methodological disagreement about the criteria for conducting a cost-benefit analysis in this context. On this theoretical level, partisans of particular enforcement strategies argue about the proper goals of professional regulation and the assumptions and processes that should guide any attempt to determine whether these goals are likely to be met.

This article attempts to provide a framework for resolving these disputes. First, I separate the most commonly discussed enforcement systems into four paradigmatic models: disciplinary controls, liability controls, institutional controls, and legislative controls. Second, I divide the claims made on behalf of these models into "compliance arguments," which are efficiency claims about the costs and benefits of a particular enforcement strategy, and "independence arguments," which are claims about whether a given form of regulation promotes or undermines lawyer independence. Third, I assert that reaching an accurate judgment in either of these categories of argument requires paying careful attention to differences in enforcement contexts. I conclude that no single enforcement system is likely to address all categories of lawyer misconduct efficiently. Each system nevertheless has certain comparative advantages in particular contexts. As a result, placing independence claims to one side, an optimal enforcement strategy would utilize some combination of all four regulatory approaches.

The Enforcement Systems

Enforcement proposals can be grouped into four models: disciplinary controls, liability controls, institutional controls, and legislative controls. Although these four models share many features, each system accomplishes its objectives through a different mix of structures and practices. These distinctive characteristics have important implications for the costs and benefits of utilizing these control strategies.

1. *Disciplinary Controls.* The reference point for this model is the current disciplinary system, in which independent agencies acting under the supervision of state supreme courts investigate and prosecute violations of the rules of professional conduct. The basic structure resembles a criminal prosecution. To avoid the appearance of favoritism or bias, disciplinary enforcement is consciously set apart from the day-to-day performance of legal work. The process is conducted almost exclusively ex post by independent officials who have no prior association with the case. These officials are instructed to reach their judgments solely on the basis of the evidence presented at a formal hearing in which the accused lawyer is accorded a full panoply of due process protections. In keeping with the criminal justice analogy, disciplinary agencies primarily focus on punishment and deterrence. Compensation, although allowed under limited circumstances, remains a secondary goal.

2. *Liability Controls.* Injured clients, and to a limited extent third parties, have traditionally had the right to sue lawyers under a variety of statutory and common law theories. Although bar leaders and others have tried to separate "malpractice" from "discipline," these efforts have been largely unsuccessful. Recent developments are likely to blur the distinction even further. For example, the Resolution Trust Company has filed a number of lawsuits alleging that several prominent law firms committed malpractice when, in conjunction with the managers of various savings and loans, they prevented regulators from discovering massive financial improprieties at these federally insured institutions. Similarly, as courts and legislatures relax the traditional restrictions against suits by nonclients, a growing

number of third parties are suing lawyers for breaching ethical duties. As a result, litigation is now a viable alternative to professional discipline.

Like the disciplinary model, liability controls operate on the basis of ex post complaints by injured parties. A victorious claimant, however, is entitled to full compensatory and even punitive damages. Restrictions on the lawyer's right to practice law, on the other hand, are generally not available. Finally, claims are subject to the normal rules of practice and procedure that govern litigation in state and federal courts, including, when appropriate, trial by jury.

3. *Institutional Controls.* Lawyers work either directly in, or in the shadow of, state institutions. With increasing frequency, these institutions are expressly taking responsibility for uncovering and sanctioning lawyer misconduct. For example, Rule 11 now authorizes judges to impose sanctions for certain kinds of litigation-related misconduct. Similarly, several federal administrative agencies, including the Securities and Exchange Commission (SEC), the Office of Thrift Services (OTS), and the Internal Revenue Service (IRS) are now seeking to sanction lawyers who do not properly advise their clients about their duties under these regulatory regimes.

These and similar efforts share a common goal: to locate enforcement authority inside the institutions in which lawyers work. As a result, the structure and operation of any particular system will be primarily a function of the institution within which it is situated. Nevertheless, a few generalizations are useful. First, enforcement authorities are in a position to observe lawyer misconduct directly. A judge, for example, will know if a lawyer has failed to file a pleading. Second, because the enforcement official and the lawyer to be disciplined are involved in a continuing relationship, sanctions can be imposed either immediately or after a separate hearing. Finally, the substantive jurisdiction of these institutional enforcement officials is likely to be confined to the area in which the institution operates. For example, SEC officials cannot discipline lawyers outside of the securities area.

4. *Legislative Controls.* Certain public officials and other commentators have proposed a new administrative agency that would have sole responsibility for investigating and prosecuting lawyer misconduct. Although such an agency might be patterned after the agencies that currently regulate doctors in many states, nothing requires this particular form. Instead, an agency might adopt procedures utilized by other regulatory agencies, such

as the Occupational Safety and Health Administration (OSHA) or the SEC. All that is required of this form of control is that its authority and operation ultimately rest in the hands of the executive or the legislative branch rather than the courts.

Supporters and opponents of these four regulatory developments deploy a wide range of arguments to justify their positions. For expository purposes, these arguments can be classified as "content arguments," "compliance arguments," and "independence arguments" according to whether they focus on the substantive content of the rules to be enforced, the ability of an enforcement system to produce substantial compliance at acceptable costs, or the relationship between a particular sanctioning system and the status of lawyers as independent professionals.

The Role of Context

Participants in the various enforcement debates often speak as though their compliance and independence arguments capture universal truths about lawyers, clients, and the state. For example, the ABA's claim that judicially supervised disciplinary agencies should exercise "exclusive" control over the enforcement process implicitly asserts that this form of regulation is the best system for controlling all lawyer misconduct in all contexts. Similarly, when lawyers oppose "external" regulation on the ground that it would undermine "professional autonomy," they usually couch their assertions about the proper relationship between the lawyer and the state in universal terms. These universalist claims ignore relevant distinctions in both the content of professional norms and the market for legal services.

Acknowledging Conflict within the Lawyer's Role

It is axiomatic that lawyers are expected to be both zealous advocates for the interests of their clients and officers of the court. Each of these roles generates distinct professional duties. As an advocate, a lawyer is expected to keep the client informed, safeguard the client's secrets, provide competent and diligent services at a reasonable fee, and abide by the client's wishes concerning the purposes of the attorney-client relationship. As an officer of the court, however, a lawyer should not counsel or assist the client in fraudulent conduct, file frivolous claims or defenses, unreasonably delay litigation, intentionally fail to follow the rules of the tribunal, or unnecessarily embarrass or burden third parties. These disparate professional duties complicate the comparative analysis of various enforcement alternatives.

Understanding the Role of the Market

Discussions on this topic often assume a uniform lawyer-client relationship in which the client is incapable of understanding and evaluating lawyer conduct. This assumption fails to capture the complexity of contemporary legal practice. Clients vary widely in their experience and sophistication concerning legal practice. Some clients will hire a lawyer only once in their lifetime. For others, interacting with lawyers is a way of life. Corporations are likely to dominate this latter category. As "repeat players," these sophisticated consumers usually have a considerable baseline of experience from which to formulate the goals of the representation and to evaluate lawyer performance. In addition, corporations have comparatively more resources to devote to the task of understanding and evaluating lawyer conduct. Given these differences, we would expect that the average corporate client will have much greater access to information about lawyer conduct than the average individual.

This gap between corporate and individual clients is amplified by stratification and specialization within the bar. The formal and informal relationships lawyers form with colleagues, adversaries, and state officials produce unique and effective norms, procedures, and sanctions. These embedded control systems are likely to be different for corporate and individual lawyers. Corporate lawyers tend to work in larger firms, make more money, and have greater professional status and occupational mobility than lawyers who primarily represent individuals. Similarly, corporate and individual lawyers tend to concentrate in different fields of law and interact with different state officials. These and other differences have led many to conclude that lawyers who represent corporations occupy a separate hemisphere from those who primarily represent individuals. A lawyer's hemisphere of practice plausibly will affect the operation of whatever enforcement system coexists with these embedded controls.

A Contextual Model

Contextual differences relating to the lawyer's role and the identity of the client suggest a matrix of possible lawyer-client interactions. Figure 1 illus-

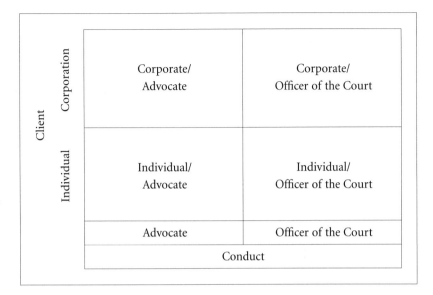

Figure 1

trates this matrix. The vertical axis charts the identity of the client, from "individuals" to "corporations," as a surrogate for the range of embedded controls likely to influence the conduct of a particular lawyer. The horizontal axis delineates lawyer conduct as it relates to the two faces of the lawyer's role: "advocacy duties" represent obligations to clients and "officer of the court duties" symbolize responsibilities to the legal framework, identifiable third parties, and the public at large.

Deciding where any given case falls within this matrix will always be a matter of judgment, particularly at the margins. Certain individual clients undoubtedly will have more in common with the average corporation than with other individuals. For example, the relationship between de-throned investment banking czar Michael Milken and his principal lawyer, Arthur Liman, a partner in one of New York's most prestigious law firms, probably more closely resembles interactions between Drexel Burnham and its lawyers than the experience of most individual criminal defendants. Similarly, many professional duties can fairly be characterized as being owed both to clients and to the legal framework. A lawyer who knowingly files a frivolous lawsuit without informing the client of the weakness of the claim may be simultaneously violating both her duty to assist in the efficient administration of justice and her obligation to serve her client's interests competently. Nevertheless, each end of the two axes—individual/corporate and advocate/officer of the court—captures something important about the context in which any enforcement system must operate. These categories therefore serve as useful reference points for the multiplicity of contextual factors that will affect the operation of any regulatory regime.

Matching Solutions to Problems

Each of the four sanctioning systems generates unique compliance and independence effects. Targeting the systems at specific quadrants of the matrix should increase the benefits of certain forms of control and avoid some of the drawbacks that would result from applying a single sanctioning system in all contexts.

For example, individual clients complaining about inattention, low-level negligence, overpayment, or conversion of trust funds will often be better served by the kind of flexible, informal, and relatively inexpensive procedures found in many disciplinary agencies than they would be by malpractice suits. Although the responsibility for enforcing these violations might be transferred to a new, legislatively created OSHA- or SEC-inspired regulatory agency, the case has yet to be made that this agency would be any more aggressive in ferreting out complaints or developing innovative solutions than the kind of independent disciplinary agency that now exists in most states. Moreover, because individual clients are also the group most vulnerable to the chilling effect of state controls, the wholesale transfer of regulatory jurisdiction to state authorities should await more persuasive evidence of the effectiveness of legislative controls than the record of most consumer protection agencies currently provides.

Recognizing that disciplinary agencies should focus primarily on individual agency problems also suggests the need for further reforms. Because of the difficulty that most individual clients have in recognizing agency problems, disciplinary authorities must concentrate more of their limited resources on investigation and prevention. Although there are structural limits on how zealous agencies can be in this regard, much more could be done. Building on the model of random audits of client trust accounts endorsed by the ABA, disciplinary counsel could conduct random "quality audits" to determine whether a lawyer provided competent, professional services in a particular case. Moreover, these organizations could do much more to standardize the expectations of both clients and lawyers about the quality, timing, and cost of legal services.

Institutional controls, on the other hand, will be specialized simply as a result of where they are located and the stratification within the bar. Thus, SEC or OTS enforcement systems will by definition apply only to corporate lawyers. Moreover, because of the growing specialization within the bar, lawyers who do securities or banking work are likely to spend a majority of their time in these areas. Therefore, specialized rules and enforcement practices can be tailored to the unique requirements of these regulatory contexts without undue confusion or contradiction. For present purposes, this specialization means that agencies can develop a wide spectrum of sanctioning procedures designed to control corporate externality problems without chilling zealous advocacy. Such efforts will be particularly effective when applied to the advising phase of these corporate relationships.

For example, consider OTS's efforts to discipline lawyers who fail to advise their federally insured clients to comply with the legal obligation to operate in a safe and sound manner. Although critics of OTS's proposal do not dispute that lawyers should counsel their clients to obey the law, the critics vehemently object to giving the agency the authority to punish lawyers for giving other advice. But these arguments ignore the substantial incentives that these lawyers have to be overzealous in their construction of applicable limitations and the fact that a lawyer's failure to carry out his admitted obligation is likely to go unnoticed in the absence of agency monitoring and investigation.

A quite different situation is presented in areas in which achieving greater compliance through institutional controls poses a credible threat to professional independence. For example, the IRS has recently brought a wave of enforcement proceedings against criminal defense lawyers who refuse to disclose the identity of clients from whom they have received more than $10,000 in cash. The express purpose of these actions is to force lawyers to comply with the terms of a recent federal statute that makes it a crime for anyone to fail to report such a transaction. Not surprisingly, many criminal defense lawyers claim that these enforcement efforts "undermine the attorney-client privilege, threaten the integrity of the criminal justice system and gut important constitutional rights, including the right to counsel."

These claims deserve serious consideration. Although the terms of the disclosure statute are relatively clear, there is a dispute over whether its command is consistent with a lawyer's duty of confidentiality. Because the clients in question, most notably those allegedly involved in narcotics trafficking or organized crime, are among the most unpopular in contemporary society, the claim that their lawyers should not be subjected to government pressures that might cause them automatically to resolve this ambiguity in favor of disclosure is quite strong. This concern may not be sufficient to stop these enforcement actions altogether, but it does underscore the importance of providing defense lawyers with a neutral forum for challenging the government's actions.

Finally, in areas such as protection proceedings for abused children or commitment hearings for the mentally ill, institutional controls aimed at preventing externality problems might not be appropriate at all. Because of the potential for agency problems in these settings, the risk of further disadvantaging already underserved client populations outweighs any likely enforcement gains. Government authorities should instead institute proceedings designed to deter client-centered misconduct.

Conclusion

This article does not provide definitive answers to many of the difficult questions that policymakers must confront when they choose a particular sanctioning system. There may be, for example, good reasons unrelated to either compliance or independence for preferring one enforcement system over another in particular cases. The analysis presented here does, however, underscore the fact that many of those seeking to make or influence these decisions are asking the wrong questions.

Implicit in the many claims about how lawyers should be regulated is the assumption that a single enforcement structure will be appropriate for all lawyers in all contexts. This unitary vision, however, fails to account for the diversity in both the structure of the legal marketplace and society's expectations of the profession. Corporate clients are substantially different from individual consumers of legal services. Duties to the legal framework require different kinds of maintenance than obligations owed to clients. As a result, the question to be asked is not who should regulate lawyers, but rather how should policymakers coordinate the various resources at their disposal to increase the likelihood that all segments of society can benefit from a competent and independent legal profession.

Seeking the Faces of Otherness[1]

Lucie E. White[2]

When I went to college, our intellectual gurus—in addition to Timothy
Leary and John Lennon—were people like Noam Chomsky and Claude
Lévi-Strauss. Their theories talked about boxes, bipolar oppositions, ex-
changes (usually of women, it seemed), and law-ruled transformations.
Their intellectual maps were geometric and symmetrical, and covered the
entire social world, as we then imagined it. Although there was a lot of
movement within their paradigms, that movement resembled a military
drill more than a dance. Those days, the late 1960s, were the salad days of
what we now disparagingly call "structuralism."

I remember reading during those years an essay by a young anthropologist named Clifford Geertz. This essay used the technocratic talk of the
times, but its message was out of synch with the positivism that such talk
often assumed. The essay made reference to a new "meta-concept" that
Geertz called "terminal screens."[3] This term is a wonderful reminder of
how the words we use are inevitably colored by the historical moment in
which we write. Clifford Geertz does not talk about "terminal screens" any
more. Instead, he writes about "thick descriptions,"[4] and works and lives.[5]

By "terminal screens," Geertz meant something similar to what one
might describe, in the lingo of the 1990s, by reference to the array of
designer "shades" that one can buy in places like Los Angeles, to color the
world different tints for one's varying moods. Geertz used "terminal
screens" to point out that one can view the same social "reality" through
a range of different conceptual or theoretical screens or filters. Depending on the screen one looks through—the matrix of terms or concepts
through which one filters what one sees—the same event can take on
many different appearances.

In the days when structuralism was still in vogue, this was a marginal, though by no means novel, idea. Since then, it has entered the intellectual mainstream. Many people now talk of the partiality—or inevitably interpretive nature—of all of the "discourses," "paradigms," or "lenses" through which we make sense of our human world, and in turn constitute ourselves. Many scholars now teach us how our understandings of the world both reflect and define the positions from which we view it.

At the same time that Clifford Geertz's star was rising in the world of social theory, Noam Chomsky's was falling: structuralism was overtaken by new "post-structuralist" ways of thinking. The intellectual leader of this movement was Michel Foucault. Foucault, with a little posthumous coaching from Nietzsche, was indisputably a genius, a paradigm smasher. He, more than any other single figure, moved us beyond the "conventional," structural understanding of power. In this conventional view, power is a thing that people have and wield over others, usually on the basis of their roles in stable institutional hierarchies. Foucault gave us a new meta-theory of power—one that was so intriguing, so fitting for the uncertain times of the 1970s, that many other theorists—sociologists, linguists, and historians—took up the joint project of filling in its details, and of using it, lens-like, to sharpen their view of social life.

According to this new meta-theory, power is not a tool. Rather, like an evanescent fluid, it takes unpredictable shapes as it flows into the most subtle spaces in our interpersonal world. In this picture, we no longer see distinct "persons" controlling power's flow. Indeed, we cannot really separate the agents of the movement from the movement itself. Sometimes we may think we see more or less familiar human actors, who seem to guide the fluid, like children might make giant soap bubbles in a park. Yet at other moments, these familiar "persons" disappear, and we see only the patterns that linger as the bubbles dance.

This theory of power offers a very interesting lens through which to view social interactions, including interactions between lawyers and their clients. It is especially important to progressive law teachers, scholars, and advocates for at least two reasons. First, this lens is bringing forth a new body of situated microdescriptions of lawyering practice. For the first time, these descriptions give us a substantial base of data that we may use to reflect on our work. This new data enables us to see exactly how and when we deploy power within the routines of our own lawyering. With this new insight into what we do, we can begin to ask why we do it and how we might change. We can begin to envision different habits—different ways of talking and paying attention—that may make our deployments of power less disruptive of our clients' efforts to empower themselves. This kind of reflective reconstruction of our day-to-day lawyering routines can make our practice, as progressive lawyers, more consistent with our aspirations of greater social justice. Thus, the descriptive project makes possible a new field of critical reflection on advocacy and pedagogy —a "theoretics" of practice—the potential of which we are just beginning to explore.

The second reason that Foucault's picture of power is so important to progressive advocates is that it has opened up new possibilities in the political practice of relatively disempowered groups. The conventional theory of power reveals a dichotomized world of domination and subordination; through such a lens, the hegemony of the dominant class is virtually absolute. Not only does that class confine the actions of the subordinated, but it also dictates their language, preferences, thoughts, dreams, and indeed their most deeply held moral and political intuitions. In American legal scholarship, Catharine MacKinnon has used this dichotomized picture of power with great skill to challenge claims that women can experience authentic subjectivity in contemporary society.[6]

MacKinnon posed this challenge in an encounter with Carol Gilligan at Buffalo Law School in 1984.[7] In that exchange, MacKinnon argued that values of "caring" and "connection" that Gilligan and other feminists sought to reclaim and celebrate are symptoms of women's subordinate position in a closed system of power.[8] According to MacKinnon, even women's feelings of sexual pleasure are suspect; these feelings, like every other feature of Woman, define a colonized subject, a being whose essence has been shaped by and for men.

Thus, as Angela Harris has demonstrated in her critique of Catharine MacKinnon's work,[9] a conventional understanding of power locks women, and indeed every subordinated group, in a discursive "prisonhouse" from which there is no escape. Just as the dominators can do nothing except wield their power, the subordinated can speak nothing except their masters' will. No change is possible in this universe; indeed, even the most creative tactics of resistance or gestures of solidarity reinforce the bonds of domination. This understanding of domination, designed to reveal injustice, leads to two perverse results. First, it excuses those in the dominant class from attempting to reflect on or change their own conduct, or to ally themselves with subordinate groups. Second, it reinforces in relatively disempowered groups the very doubts about their feelings, capacities, and indeed human worth that subordination itself engenders.

Foucault's picture of power disrupts this closed circle of domination. By showing that the dominators do not "possess" power, his picture makes possible a politics of resistance. It opens up space for a self-directed, democratic politics among subordinated groups, a politics that is neither vanguard-driven nor co-opted, as the politics of the colonized subject inevitably is. At the same time, and of more immediate relevance to lawyers, this new picture of power makes possible a self-reflective politics of alliance and collaboration between professionals and subordinated groups. Given the new theaters of political action that Foucault's theory of power has opened up, it is not surprising that it has stolen the stage in historical, cultural, and finally legal studies from those who speak of power in more conventional terms. The Foucaultian picture of power makes insurgent politics interesting again; it brings possibility back into focus, even in apparently quiescent times when resistance is visible only in the microdynamics of everyday life.

Yet with the power of this new lens comes a risk. With such an instrument in our hands, it is easy to forget the lesson that Professor Geertz taught. Any "terminal screen" gives us only a partial view of the world: it enhances some features of reality—probably those that its inventors most wanted to see—while erasing or obscuring others. The risk for those who use Foucault's lens is that they will forget this lesson, and begin to think of their own meta-theory as the last word on how power "really" works—the terminal screen. Foucault's lens reveals such a longed-for landscape of possibility that it has begun to entrap our imagination, deluding us into thinking that with this lens we have finally seized the power to comprehend the world.

One consequence inevitably follows when we forget that our latest theories are not absolute. This is the risk that, in our own certainty, we will lose patience with those who do not share our faith. As Professor Delgado points out, such intolerance often reveals itself only after time renders our certainties obsolete, and thereby ridiculous.[10] At least two further risks are specific to Foucault's lens.

The first risk has been identified by feminist scholars such as Nancy Fraser and Robin West.[11] While the Foucaultian lens reveals the fluidity of power, it does not show how power can become congealed in social institutions in ways that sustain domination. It may be true that everyday interactions create and maintain social institutions, but this insight does not enable us to map those interactions against the institutional matrices they create. Nor does this insight show us how institutions constrain the circulation of power, channeling it to flow toward some social groups and away from others. In short, the Foucaultian lens does not move us toward a theoretics and a reconstructive politics of institutional design.

Without richer meta-theories—stronger lenses—that focus on institutional as well as interpersonal realities, we will remain bewildered by exactly how our actions reiterate what has been called "structural" or "institutional" subordination. We will remain unable to critique and repattern our actions, so that we enact more democratic institutions as we seek to live more ethical lives. These other lenses need not replace Foucault's; rather, they can provide a second filter on the same landscape, enabling us to study the geology of the ocean floor as well as the action of the waves. Without these other lenses, the dynamics of systemic injustice—dynamics that stunt the life-chances of some social groups with more than random frequency—will remain invisible and therefore go unchallenged.

Getting stuck inside the Foucaultian worldview carries a second risk as well. In addition to stunting our ability to rethink institutions in emancipatory ways, this lens obscures our human capacity—or, more accurately, our longing—to realize ourselves in the world by feeling with other people, as well as by winning against them. Foucault's lens defines and thereby reveals human interactions as strategic contests. Our personhood takes form in those moments when the contest shifts power our way. This lens does not pick up those moments when we feel the force of another's emotions or the resolve behind her commitments. If such moments appear at all, they look like surges of the other's power rather than images of the other's face.

We must not discount the risks imposed by theories that make human connection seem too easy to attain. Such theories have typically sanctioned domination of the most insidious kind, by encouraging the privileged to name the feelings of less powerful others, without cautioning that to name another's feelings is also to silence her voice. We cannot give up Foucault's contest-focused theory to return to a simplistic, imperialist version of humanism. At the same time, however, we must recognize that Foucault's theory is ultimately—and indeed, inevitably—incomplete. For although Foucaultian power is always in motion, it hovers outside of the other, circling in what is ultimately a closed field. Foucault's theory does not make sense of our yearning for, or our occasional movement toward, a more fully and freely interconnected human world.

Chapter 2

Historical Perspectives

This chapter looks at the historical development of lawyers' ethical rules and values, an area in which a great deal of exciting new scholarship is underway. We return, this time from a historical perspective, to some of the questions explored in chapter 1, where we examined contrasting theoretical approaches to the study of lawyers' professional regulation. These questions include: Are the lawyers who promulgate legal ethics rules motivated by other-regarding motives, such as protecting clients and the proper working of the legal system, or by self-regarding motives, such as protecting a professional monopoly? How should we understand the role of elites within the profession in shaping legal ethics norms? Conversely, what should we make of the legal profession's exclusion, up to the end of the nineteenth century, of women, racial minorities, and persons outside the upper socioeconomic strata of society? Is there a connection between the homogeneity of the bar during this period and its greater moral certainty about lawyers' proper ethics? What parts of the historical traditions underlying the development of legal ethics rules should we retain or revive, and what parts should we discard? Finally, is it possible to construct better visions of ethical lawyering based on the lessons of history?

This chapter begins to examine these and other questions by focusing on writing about lawyers' ethics in four historical periods: (a) the antebellum period (before the Civil War); (b) the so-called Progressive Era, defined as the decades surrounding the turn from the nineteenth to the twentieth century; (c) the early twentieth century, in which our focus is on the entry into the profession of traditional *outsiders*, defined on lines of race, class, and gender; and (d) the later twentieth century, characterized by still greater diversification of the profession, and, as is explored further in chapters 4 and 5, decreasing consensus about lawyers' ethical norms.

Section A, "Antebellum Ethics," begins with Russell Pearce's examination of a legal ethics treatise drafted in the 1850s by George Sharswood, a

Pennsylvania lawyer, judge, and law professor. After summarizing the historical progression of nineteenth-century legal ethics regulation, Pearce turns to a textual analysis of Sharswood's legal ethics treatises. Pearce sees in that writing the strong influence of civic republicanism, a tradition that emphasized citizens' duties to advance the common good of the community rather than individual self-interest. Applied to the legal profession, the civic republican model saw lawyers' primary duty as being to serve as community leaders, safeguarding the public interest and advancing justice, rather than advocating single-mindedly for their clients.

Pearce contrasts civic republican ideas about lawyers' role as caretakers of the common good with the countervailing view that lawyers' overriding duty should be to serve as zealous advocates for their clients. Under this second model, the outcome of an adversarial process determines the "justice" of a case, and the lawyer's role is simply to serve as the best advocate possible within this system. Pearce acknowledges that Sharswood understood that lawyers had to play an adversarial role in some situations. He argues, however, that the balance Sharswood struck between adversarialism and civic republicanism was very different from the balance struck in the dominant contemporary legal ethics conception. According to Pearce, the contemporary conception tilts too far in the direction of lawyer adversarialism and gives too little weight to civic republican concerns about the common good.

Norman Spaulding challenges Pearce's claim that civic republicanism predominated over adversarial ethics in early nineteenth-century America. Relying on Sharswood and earlier legal ethics writing, Spaulding argues that the picture is more complex than Pearce and other contemporary critics of lawyer adversarialism admit. Spaulding points to a decline in civic republican certainties about lawyers' roles through the course of the nineteenth century. He argues that this decline followed from the erosion of the easy moral certainties that were possible when legal ethics deliberation took place in relatively homogenous, stable social settings. In today's world, many competing visions of lawyers' ethics, arising from diverse viewpoints, experiences, and concerns, must collide and mutually inspire and challenge one another. We begin to explore this cacophony of diverse voices later in this reader.

Section B, "Elite Lawyers in the Progressive Era," examines lawyers' ethics at the turn from the nineteenth to the twentieth century. Robert Gordon surveys the nineteenth century for historical ideas about how to preserve—or, more accurately, resurrect—lawyers' commitment to an ethics that called for the maintenance of independence from clients. Gordon finds examples in great lawyer-statesmen figures such as Louis Brandeis, who, before he became a U.S. Supreme Court justice in 1916, was both a highly successful corporate lawyer and a leading public interest advocate. Brandeis did significant pro bono service, including acting as a champion for utility rate regulation, protective labor legislation, and many other progressive civic reform causes.

Brandeis coined the term "lawyer for the situation" to describe a lawyering model under which an attorney seeks to find a just or fair solution to a dispute rather than to advocate solely for his own clients' interests. To give one frequently mentioned example, Brandeis once represented a shoe manufacturer, William McElwain, who faced a labor dispute after he cut wages during an economic downturn. Brandeis listened to the workers' grievances, and then counseled his client to make the improvements in working conditions—including regularizing workers' terms of employment—that Brandeis considered a fair and appropriate resolution of the dispute. The client accepted Brandeis's recommendations and the workers halted their protest.[1]

Brandeis remains an important model for scholars seeking alternative legal ethics visions. Clyde Spillenger, however, examines the flip side of Brandeis's desire to maintain independence from clients. Spillenger argues that too much distance from one's clients fails to achieve the ethical ideals of active engagement and dialogue with those one has agreed to represent. Spillenger also makes telling connections between Brandeis's independent lawyering style and a model for elite public interest representation that continues to hold sway today. Under that model, lawyers in well-compensated corporate practices devote a (usually relatively small) portion of their time to uncompensated work for worthy causes, nonprofit organizations, and/or indigent clients, while remaining very much apart from these clients in most aspects of their professional (and personal) lives. Spillenger measures this model against ethical standards that value dialogue and engagement. In a prescient conclusion written almost a decade ago, Spillenger compares Brandeis's refusal to be influenced by others' perspectives with the mindset of contemporary public-interest-lawyer-turned-politician Ralph Nader, whose stubborn independence of mind threatens at the time of this writing to swing the 2004 presidential election.

In the final excerpt in Section B, historian Jerold Auerbach energetically argues that the legal ethics and civic reform projects of late nineteenth-century corporate lawyers were based not in any high-minded civic motives, but in more base desires to limit outsiders' entry into a cozy professional monopoly. (Note that Auerbach, drawing on Sharswood's writings just as Pearce and Spaulding did, finds in them evidence to support his thesis concerning the exclusionary motives for legal ethics regulation.) Auerbach also describes one of the most sordid chapters in the ABA's history, its 1914 decision to exclude African Americans from membership—a policy it maintained until the 1940s.[2]

Section C, "Insiders/Outsiders: Lawyers' Lives/Lawyers' Agency," begins to explore the work and perspectives of early lawyers who belonged to social categories that were historically excluded from law practice on grounds of race and/or gender. It is easy for current law students to overlook the legal profession's not-so-distant history of exclusion and discrimination on both sex and race grounds, but that history deserves attention as we reflect on the development of lawyers' ethical norms. To briefly summarize some of that history here: until the turn of the twentieth century, the majority of lawyers gained admission to the bar after apprenticing in a lawyer's office.[3] Only the most elite lawyers went to law schools, and those schools were much like country clubs, dominated by the sons of the country's leading families. By the end of the 1800s, however, this situation had started to change. Proprietary law schools that offered night classes to students who lacked the resources for full-time studies began to open up in many cities, allowing new immigrants and others lacking family wealth to study law and sit for the bar exam. In the late 1800s, land grant colleges began to offer legal education to African-American students, and some elite schools began to let in very small numbers of African-American students as well. Law schools such as Howard University and the Washington College of Law began to allow women to obtain law degrees, and State courts began to repeal their rules prohibiting African Americans and women from obtaining bar licenses. But bar associations, including the American Bar Association as already noted, were much slower about dismantling their discriminatory membership policies. The ABA admitted its first woman member in 1918 and did not repeal its rule barring the admission of African Americans until 1943.[4]

Even with the removal of such explicit prohibitions excluding women and attorneys of color from practicing law, traditional outsiders faced many discriminatory barriers to professional achievement. Legal employers blatantly discriminated on race, class, ethnicity, and gender lines; many judges remained hostile to nontraditional practitioners; and outsiders often had a harder time obtaining clients and desirable legal work.

Students who wish to explore this history further may refer to the excellent and growing literature summarized in the Appendix.

Section C provides two samples of the growing literature exploring the experiences of traditional outsiders in fighting for opportunities and recognition within the legal profession. I include these excerpts to allow us to begin thinking about whether and how this history has influenced and potentially can affect the development of legal ethics conceptions of what it means to be a *good* lawyer. We explore the contemporary literature examining the intersection of legal ethics and various forms of what I call *outsider jurisprudence,* such as critical race theory and feminist legal theory, in Part B. In order to appreciate that literature in terms of its historical development, it is helpful to examine the experiences of traditional outsiders who first penetrated the exclusionary barriers to law practice.

Virginia Drachman, as part of a much larger project examining women lawyers' experiences in various periods through the late nineteenth and twentieth centuries, writes about the challenges faced by women lawyers in the 1920s and 1930s, as it became clear that discriminatory barriers in the legal profession were not going to fall easily. Kenneth Mack examines the life of one early African-American woman lawyer, Sadie T. M. Alexander, who began law practice in 1928. Mack argues that legal historians should focus more on the experiences of such lawyers, rather than confining their analyses to legal elites. He finds that, despite the dual forms of race and sex discrimination she faced, Alexander exhibited remarkable agency in shaping her professional life. Mack notes, however, that Alexander's agency must be understood as partial or constrained; traditional understandings of women's role in the domestic sphere continued to influence her life choices.

Drachman likewise emphasizes the important relationship between domestic ideologies and women's ability to achieve professional equality. Although Mack and Drachman both focus on women lawyers, they also discuss the effects of race discrimination on African-American male lawyers, a subject to which we turn in more detail in chapter 3.

In section D, "The Later Twentieth Century and a Changing Profession," Carrie Menkel-Meadow explores the later-twentieth-century implications of continuing diversification of the legal profession. Menkel-Meadow notes the increasing competitiveness of the profession, which corresponds with insiders' loss of their monopolistic hold on law practice. These changing conditions have increased the business pressures lawyers face, and have led to greater work-hour demands, less job security, and a lower quality of life for many attorneys. Menkel-Meadow hopes, however, that the accelerated pace of change in the profession may also create spaces for new structures and approaches to law practice.

Note that, with respect to the increasing feminization of the legal profession, the trends identified in Menkel-Meadow's 1990s statistics have continued; today a majority of law students are female, and demographers predict that this preponderance of female students in law school will increase still further in the near future.[5] The likely future with respect to increasing diversification of the legal profession on lines of class, race, and ethnicity unfortunately is not as bright, as literature summarized in the Appendix discusses.

Questions for Reflection and Discussion

1. What support do you see, in the current Model Rules or in other less formally codified aspects of lawyers' ethics, for Pearce's civic republicanism? Do you support the civic republican conception of lawyers serving as community leaders with responsibility to tend to the public good? Does this model give too little emphasis to lawyers' duties to serve as zealous advocates for their clients?

2. What are Gordon's main suggestions for how to mine history for ideas to promote contemporary lawyers' ethical aspirations to civic-mindedness and independence from client pressures? Which of his suggestions are the most persuasive in your view?

3. Are you persuaded by Spillenger's arguments questioning the benefits of lawyers retaining too much independence from their clients? In what respects is Spillenger most persuasive? least persuasive?

4. As noted, Auerbach, Pearce, and Spaulding draw on some of the same historical texts for evidence in support of their very different theses. How can this be? Do you find any one of these theses more persuasive than the others based on the evidence presented? How could you independently evaluate the three authors' claims about what these texts reveal?

5. Are you convinced by Auerbach's argument that the ABA's 1908 legal ethics canons were largely a product of class and ethnic hostility?

6. Whereas Gordon urges lawyers to return to the more active involvement in civic work that elite corporate lawyers displayed at the end of the nineteenth century, Auerbach argues that these involvements were merely a shield to deflect growing public criticism of lawyers' ethical failings. Do you see similarities between Auerbach's thesis and Abel's monopoly theory, which we examined in Chapter 1? Between Gordon's and Halliday's arguments that elite lawyers' civic involvements can promote the public good in ways the state could not otherwise accomplish? Where along the spectrum stretching between Auerbach's and Abel's view, on one side, and Gordon's and Halliday's, on the other, do your own views lie as to lawyers' motives for engaging in civic and professional service projects? Is the picture a complex and contradictory one? Would it be better on the whole to have more or less of this kind of civic involvement by lawyers today? What are your own plans for becoming involved in civic and professional service work in your legal career?

7. What significance does the legal profession's history of discrimination and exclusion on the basis of race and sex have today? Have you observed or experienced discrimination in your life in the law? Do you think that this history has any connection, positive or negative, to the values and ethical conceptions of the profession today? Would ethical rules written by traditional outsiders to the profession be likely to look different from the rules we have inherited? If so, in what respects?

8. Do you agree with Menkel-Meadow's arguments that the increasing diversification of the legal profession presents opportunities for transforming the values and structures of law practice? What evidence do you see supporting or contradicting her hopes?

Rediscovering the Republican Origins of the Legal Ethics Codes[1]

Russell G. Pearce[2]

The consensus among leading commentators on legal ethics issues is that the legal ethics codes embody an adversarial ethic. An examination of the historical roots of the legal ethics codes in the work of George Sharswood, a nineteenth-century jurist and scholar, provides an alternative interpretation.[3] Although largely ignored by commentators today, Sharswood's essay on ethics was the original source of most of the modern legal ethics codes. Sharswood believed that a lawyer's principal obligation was the republican pursuit of the community's common good even where it conflicts with either her client's or her own interests. Sharswood defined the common good as the protection of order, liberty, and property in order to provide individuals with the opportunity to perfect themselves.

Although Sharswood's essay does not govern interpretation of the modern codes, it has had significant influence on their content and language. The drafters of the first national code, the American Bar Association (ABA) *Canons of Ethics*,[4] expressly acknowledged that they were borrowing language and ideas from Sharswood's treatises. The ABA's subsequent codification of the *Model Code of Professional Responsibility* in 1970[5] and the *Model Rules of Professional Conduct* in 1983[6] have retained much of the subject matter the *Canons* adopted from Sharswood, departing from the *Canons* only in the mechanisms for enforcing ethical standards. Therefore, the *Model Code* and the *Model Rules,* like the *Canons* before them, preserve lawyers' opportunities to act primarily as public officers with broad discretion and authority to substitute their moral judgments for those of their clients. The profession's purported adherence to the adversarial ethic demonstrates that modern commentators have not fully appreciated the implications of these concepts retained from Sharswood's treatise.

When the ABA adopted the first national legal ethics code in 1908, Sharswood's text was well known and its formative contribution acknowledged. The *Canons* setting forth the lawyer's major duties to the courts, the bar, and the client, and all but seven of the original thirty-two *Canons,* are drawn in whole or in part from Sharswood. The current ethical guidelines, the *Model Code* and the *Model Rules,* have retained the substantive content of the *Canons* and have changed only the mechanisms for enforcement of the ethical standards.

Despite Sharswood's significant contribution to the development of the modern legal ethics codes, commentators have failed to appreciate the importance of Sharswood's essay when interpreting the *Model Code* and the *Model Rules.* Most modern commentators acknowledge that Sharswood's essay was the source of the *Canons.* However, they generally treat Sharswood's contribution in a cursory manner. Commentators generally assert that legal ethics originated in Henry Brougham's famous "credo" that "'[a]n advocate, in the discharge of duty, knows but one person in all the world, and that person is his client.'" Indeed, one leading commentator has described Brougham's statement as "[t]he legal profession's basic narrative . . . sustained over two centuries notwithstanding pervasive changes in American society and in the profession itself."[7]

An examination of Sharswood's essay raises questions about the wisdom of this description. Sharswood's work, which was the basis for the *Canons* and later evolved into the *Model Code* and the *Model Rules,* expressly rejects Brougham's credo as the basis for legal ethics standards. Sharswood propos[ed] a system of legal ethics that embraced a republican vision of the lawyer's role. This vision conceived a lawyer's first obligation to be the common good: the rule of law and the protection of property rights. Once that duty was satisfied, lawyers owed a duty of loyal and zealous representation to their clients. Sharswood addressed much of his study of legal ethics to the task of balancing these sometimes competing adversarial and republican obligations.

The Republican Role of Lawyers

Historians have traced the roots of republicanism to ancient Rome,[8] to Renaissance Italy,[9] and to English opposition thought.[10] Professor William

Treanor has noted that "[a]t the center of republican thought lay a belief in a common good and a conception of society as an organic whole. The state's proper role consisted in large part of fostering virtue, of making the individual unselfishly devote himself to the common good."[11] According to what most historians consider the dominant ideological force behind the American Revolution, individuals had little to fear from republican government which emphasized the right of the people to participate in the political system.[12] The legislature, "[a]s the voice of the people, . . . could be trusted to perceive the common good and to define the limits of individual rights."[13]

Traditional republican thought saw in commerce and the attendant pursuit of self-interest a threat to proper governance and to virtue. Persons "involved in the marketplace were usually overwhelmed by their [self-]interests and were incapable of [the] disinterestedness" necessary to virtue and realization of the common good.[14] Moreover, "[w]ealth encouraged greed in its possessors and enabled them to wield undue power."[15]

In the wake of the American Revolution, influential republican thinkers came to reconsider this view, accepting and in some cases even welcoming the role of wealth and commerce in society. Professor Gordon Wood has observed that many republicans conceded "that private interest ruled most social relationships . . . [and that] to expect most people to sacrifice their private interests for the sake of the public good was utopian."[16] In the economic sphere, some republicans adopted theories that recognized both the inevitability and the legitimacy of self-interest. For example, a leading historian has brought forth James Madison's argument that "republican governments must protect the rights of property, as well as of persons," in part to encourage industry with the incentive of potential wealth.[17]

Despite this shift, thinkers like Madison remained distinctly republican because they did not give up hope for "virtuous politics" predicated on the existence of a common good.

Having lost faith in the people's capacity for virtue, these modified republicans viewed the duty of governance as the role of a virtuous elite. Two groups would provide much of this leadership. The first was "disinterested gentry who were supported by proprietary wealth and not involved in the interest-mongering of the market place."[18] The second was "lawyers and other professionals [who] are somehow free of the marketplace, are less selfish and interested and therefore better equipped for political leadership and disinterested decision-making than merchants and businessmen."[19] Accompanying this shift to faith in elites and away from majoritarian processes was a break with traditional republican stress on the centrality of deliberation.

In the structure of government, the ultimate protection against majority interference with the rights necessary to achieve virtue would be the judiciary and the legal system. Professor Gordon Wood has noted that one major way of protecting liberty was to remove issues "such as property and contract rights . . . from popular tampering [by defining them as] 'fixed principles of law to be determined by judges.'"[20]

In the context of this modified republicanism, Professor Robert Gordon has described what he calls the "traditional 'republican ideal'" of the lawyers' role.[21] In this ideal, lawyers possess the independence from faction necessary for virtue in addition to a counter-majoritarian obligation to protect property and other rights. Last, they have a responsibility "to serve as a policy intelligentsia . . . and to use the authority and influence deriving from their public prominence and professional skill to create and disseminate, both within and without the context of advising clients, a culture of respect for and compliance with the purposes of the laws."[22]

Professor Gordon's description of the republican lawyer's role accords with Alexis de Tocqueville's famous observations. Although not a republican, Tocqueville in *Democracy in America* described lawyers as the leaders of American government.[23] Lawyers protected the seemingly contradictory interests of democratic institutions and property interests. While lawyers' work drew them toward the interests of property and order, Tocqueville wrote, "their disproportionate influence results from the existence of democratic, rather than aristocratic or oligarchic, governance."[24] Similar to Professor Gordon's description of the republican tradition of lawyering, Tocqueville observed that lawyers used democratic institutions, especially the jury system, to promote public acceptance of counter-majoritarian values.

The role that Gordon and Tocqueville describe encompasses Sharswood's vision of the role of the lawyer. More broadly, Sharswood's vision is consistent with the modified republicanism that historians have found to be influential in the post-revolutionary era. In Sharswood's vision of the lawyer's role, much as Professor Gordon describes the republican model of lawyering, lawyers provided the enlightened political leadership that protected "life, liberty, and property." Sharswood observed that "more frequently than from any other profession, [lawyers] fill the highest public stations," including dominance of the legislative process, and exclusive administration of the judicial system as advocates and judges. Lawyers were experts schooled in the science of law and capable of impartial or, in classic republican terms, "virtuous" legislation and jurisprudence.

Sharswood provided illustrations of the lawyer's duty to society. Lawyers were to secure "[t]he obligation of contracts" and restrict "the right of eminent domain . . . by the provision for compensation."[25] Protection of contract and property rights also required clear, predictable rules, the achievement of which required vigilant defense of *stare decisis* and prohibition of retroactive legislation. Judicial respect for precedent and legislative avoidance of class legislation were necessary to impartial governance. To limit interference with liberty, the taking of property through taxation should be limited to the extent necessary to protect life, liberty, and property.

Protecting property by influencing judicial and legislative processes was only part of the obligation of Sharswood's ethical lawyer. Similar to the observations of Professor Gordon and of Tocqueville, Sharswood suggested that lawyers had a duty to secure popular acceptance of the lawyers' counter-majoritarian values. In this effort, Sharswood's own language illustrated how the language of democracy and equality could be used to defend counter-majoritarian values. Sharswood argued that a legal system that respected order and property would provide equal justice under law, and would protect the widow and orphan as well as the business person. The legal profession, in its republican role, "counsel[ed] the ignorant, defend[ed] the weak and oppressed, and . . . [stood] forth on all occasions as the bulwark of private rights against the assaults of power."[26]

Employing this democratic language, the legal profession sought to gain the confidence of and "to diffuse sound principles among the people."[27] The profession did so in providing counsel to clients, making arguments in court to judge and jury, and through publications. Lawyers succeeded in this effort because of their pervasive role in government which "comes home so nearly to every man's fireside."

The Lawyers' Adversarial Role

After describing lawyers as republican public servants, Sharswood's essay then explained their adversarial role. Sharswood discussed why an adversarial system was necessary and whether this type of system would result in lawyers aiding injustice by arguing for the "wrong side."[28] Sharswood defended the adversarial system as the best, though imperfect, method of deciding disputes. In this type of system, a neutral judge and jury decided issues of law and fact after full presentation of evidence and arguments by adversary parties. For this system to work, the advocate who presented each party's case must present it as well as possible and was "not morally responsible" for the party. If lawyers as advocates had full moral responsibility for their clients, "they would usurp the functions of both judge and jury."

Sharswood also explained why professional advocates were necessary. A complex system of law required expertise, as did presentation of a case in court, and parties were not likely to possess this expertise. Moreover, the same complexity that made the profession of law a practical necessity also required the profession as a guarantor of relative equality between the parties. Without counsel, "there would be a very great inequality between [parties], according to their intelligence, education and experience, respectively."

Balancing the Republican and Adversarial Roles

Sharswood reconciled the lawyer's republican and adversarial roles by creating an ethical system which valued both. His attempt to resolve "the limits of [the lawyer's] duty when the legal demands or interests of [the] client conflict with his own sense of what is just and right"[29] focused on the tension between these roles. Sharswood acknowledged that no conflict existed for proponents of the adversarial view that "all causes are to be taken by [a lawyer] indiscriminately, and conducted with a view to one single end, *success*," which he described as the "prevailing tone of professional ethics."[30] Indeed he noted that this ethic had been eloquently described by Lord Brougham "in his justly celebrated defence of the Queen," when he asserted that "'[a]n advocate . . . in the discharge of his duty knows but one person in all the world, and that person is his client."[31] Lord Brougham proposed that the lawyer's first and only duty was "[t]o save that client by all means and expedients, and at all hazards and costs to other persons, and among them to himself." The lawyer should not consider the implications of actions for third parties, even if it causes "alarm . . . torments, [and] destruction." Lord Brougham noted that the lawyer must even "[s]eparat[e] the duty of a patriot from that of an advocate," and represent the client zealously even if it would put the "country in confusion."

While a strong defender of the adversarial system in principle, Sharswood rejected Brougham's approach. Sharswood acknowledged that the successful functioning of an adversarial system required the legal profession to provide access to the courts for all. However, in light of the lawyer's republican role, such an adversarial system could not require each individual lawyer to represent any client and to seek the greatest success for every client represented. Accordingly, Sharswood endorsed Pennsylvania Chief Justice Gibson's repudiation of the "'popular but gross mistake . . . to suppose that a lawyer owes no fidelity to anyone except his client. . . .'"[32] Justice Gibson urged the contrary view that the lawyer was a public officer with duties to the public and the court as well as the client. He observed that "'[t]he high and honorable office of a counsel would be degraded to that of a mercenary were [the lawyer] compelled to do the biddings of his client against the dictates of his conscience.'"

Conclusion

An examination of the origin of the legal ethics codes in Judge George Sharswood's essays supports a new reading of the legal ethics codes. Sharswood's ethical standards were derived from the lawyer's republican role as a public officer exercising independent moral discretion. He concluded that when republican duties conflicted with adversary duties to the client, the adversary duties must yield. Sharswood's essay was the basis for the *Canons* and its concepts and language survived in the *Code* and the *Rules*. Accordingly, although current commentators describe the codes as embodying the adversarial ethic, the codes in fact continue Sharswood's approach to the extent that they permit the lawyer discretion to reject or ignore client instructions.

This rediscovery of Sharswood and his contribution has implications for the recent debate regarding the lawyer's role. While providing critics of the adversarial ethic with historical grounding, it challenges them to clarify their strategies for achieving their goals, including explaining how to achieve consensus on normative objectives and elevate lawyer's moral standards. For proponents of the adversarial ethic, on the other hand, the challenge is to modify the codes to require lawyers to serve their clients.

Sharswood leaves us with one final challenge. By his republican approach to lawyer's ethics, he asserts in effect that legal ethics standards in large part define the nature of our society. This claim is stunning, especially at a time when the reputation of lawyers is so low. If, upon assessing Sharswood's assertion, we find that it has any merit, we will have to remake the field of legal ethics.

The Myth of Civic Republicanism: Interrogating the Ideology of Antebellum Legal Ethics[1]

Norman W. Spaulding[2]

The argument of this article is that the morally activist concept of lawyering so often said to prevail among nineteenth-century civic republican legal elites is more mythical than real. Contemporary scholars attracted to this morally robust idea of law practice (scholars I have elsewhere called "role critics"[3]) have made "concessions to the technique of legend"[4] in reporting the history and ideology of antebellum law practice. These concessions have suppressed a rich and exceedingly complex antebellum debate on the definition and justifiability of the lawyer's role. Not only has this debate been suppressed, but the context that gave rise to the debate and the array of motives that made the debate so lively have been pushed off the horizon of analysis. Role critics rely almost exclusively on the work of David Hoffman of Baltimore, and George Sharswood of Philadelphia, to show the prevalence of a morally activist republican ethic in early and mid-nineteenth-century thought. Both men merit closer examination.

Hoffman published his fifty Resolutions in Regard to Professional Deportment as part of a two-volume Course of Legal Study. First published in 1817, the book sets out an extended, heavily annotated syllabus of readings to prepare the young lawyer for law practice.[5] The republican thematics of the book are unmistakable. First, Hoffman embraces the concept of the lawyer as a virtuous citizen entrusted with the highest tasks of governance. Working from the premise that "law as a moral science is without doubt based . . . on the soundest systems of moral philosophy, and of metaphysics," the book begins not with common law or an introduction to legislation, but rather with an ambitious set of readings in moral and political philosophy.[6] "To be great in the law," he contends, "it is essential that we should be great in every virtue,"[7] and so the Course of Study is structured not simply to train competent lawyers, but to form good men.

Like other republican legal elites, Hoffman also believed that law should be conceived and taught as a science and that only such an approach would ensure the production of lawyers qualified to play their special role in society. As an anonymous reviewer emphasizes in an 1830 article for the *North American Review* on Hoffman's book, when the question is about forming able advocates, wise judges, and perspicacious lawgivers, it is plain that this ordinary education will do no longer. Hoffman was so enthralled with the promise of law, scientifically conceived, that he argues students will be drawn to a higher standard of conduct by the sheer force of their studies.

Finally, Hoffman appears to embrace the republican conviction that law practice should be dominated by an exclusive elite—that sound practice of the science demands a class worthy of the power it confers and the labor it exacts. As G. Edward White has argued, Hoffman's *Course of Study* fits squarely within the discourse of "a new class of lawyers—elite commentators—who defined their role as educating the profession and the public in the 'science' of law."[8]

Even if it is beyond peradventure that Hoffman's *Course of Study* reflects the values of republican ideology, it is far from clear that his *Resolutions on Professional Deportment* (his effort to translate those values into a code of ethics) are representative either of practice at the time or of the consensus of republican legal elites on the specific legal duties entailed by their self-appointed role as the "governing class." Role critics have treated Hoffman as though he stood at the center of a republican ideal of morally activist lawyering, but on this very question he may properly belong at the margin—as the exponent of a rather extreme version of that ideal.

Indeed, far from expressing then-prevailing professional norms, Maxwell Bloomfield contends that the *Resolutions* were a reaction against them —a post hoc "protest against the debasement of professional mores that he perceived in the Jacksonian era."[9]

Other legal instructors, even those who endorsed a scientific approach to law, generally omitted Hoffman's expansive moral and humanistic curriculum, focusing instead on more narrow legal principles. Bloomfield reports, for instance, that Joseph Story (to whom the *Course of Study* is dedicated) sheared off nearly everything from Hoffman's course except the readings in common law and the Constitution soon after he adapted the curriculum for his lectures at the nascent Harvard Law School.[10]

As a personal protest against the perceived evils of Jacksonian democracy, however, Hoffman's *Resolutions* become more understandable. Bloomfield observes that Hoffman was a devout, highly educated son of a prosperous Baltimore mercantile family, and a proud member of the Baltimore bar. Hoffman was thus situated in rarified professional air. And for just this reason, his sharp response to the "leveling process" that threw into doubt the "traditional society of the late eighteenth century [and] its cohesive elite leadership"[11] gives the *Resolutions* an idiosyncratic, reactive, even wistful tone.

Role critics have also ignored the extent to which "Hoffman's approach to legal ethics, like his jurisprudence generally, was steeped in religious conviction."[12] Strong religious faith not only renders law and morality inseparable for Hoffman, it seems to have given him a profound confidence in the capacity of properly trained lawyers to make correct moral judgments about the justice or injustice of the law and of their clients' legal objectives. In the preface to the Resolutions he says he believes that "in most cases one of the disputants is knowingly in the wrong."[13] Thus while a lawyer may be tempted by the interests and passions that animate those who wish to bring unjust suits, Hoffman was confident that religion, morals, and the "elevated honour" which scientific law study provokes will normally forestall the lawyer's corruption.[14]

On each of these grounds—his reactive motivation for drafting the Resolutions, the singularity of his heavily moral and interdisciplinary approach to scientific law teaching, his membership in an insular, hyper-elite bar, and his religiously based objectivism on legal ethics—we have occasion to question whether Hoffman's thoroughgoing commitment to moral activism in lawyering in fact speaks for the "governing class" of lawyers in the early nineteenth century.

The view of the role expressed in Sharswood's *Essay on Professional Ethics* is more complex than David Hoffman's in a number of respects, and this complexity has produced interpretive dissonance among role critics and other scholars. At least one commentator has argued that the essay endorses a client-centered theory of the role; others counter that it fits squarely within the republican justice-centered tradition; and a few, moved by the internal tensions of the essay, claim that it presents a middle position between the extreme moral activism of Hoffman and the radically client-centered maxim offered by Lord Henry Brougham in a speech before the House of Lords in 1820. The interpretive dissonance alone is reason enough to question the dominance of civic republican moral activism among antebellum lawyers. But by and large, role critics have ignored this dissonance, lumping Sharswood together with Hoffman and "depict[ing] a smooth process in the transmission of legal ethics doctrines" through the nineteenth century.[15]

Interpretive dissonance exists for good reason. The *Essay* both reflects and resists the republican premises that animate Hoffman's *Resolutions*. On the one hand, Sharswood embraces both the scientific theory of law and the idea that lawyers bear special obligations to governance as professional elites. On the other hand, he carefully distinguishes law from moral obligation, and assiduously avoids any pretension to the kind of moral objectivism that enables Hoffman to assume lawyers and clients will, in most cases, know who stands in the right. On the latter point, Sharswood repeatedly admonishes readers that questions regarding fidelity to client are "the most difficult questions in the consideration of the duty of a lawyer,"[16] and that even a lawyer's considered judgment on the justice of his client's case may turn out to be incorrect.

This epistemological skepticism not only makes Hoffman's confident moralism seem brazen by contrast, it directly affects Sharswood's view of the lawyer's role. Sharswood bifurcates the right to refuse representation by distinguishing between suing and defending: on the one hand, a lawyer (whether civil or criminal) should never prosecute a case he believes to be unjust (since the office of lawyering would then be "'degraded to that of a mercenary'"[17]), a lawyer for the defendant, on the other hand, may use all his abilities to hold the plaintiff to the facts and the law, even if he believes his client is culpable. And in cases where the defense lawyer believes justice is on the side of his client, Sharswood endorses unchecked zeal—the lawyer may not only use all his "ingenuity and eloquence" to ensure success, but may "fall back upon the instructions of his client, and refuse to yield any legal vantage-ground, which may have been gained through the ignorance or inadvertence of his opponent."[18]

Pearce has argued, and others have assumed, that on balance morally activist republican principles prevail over client-centered values in this bifurcated scheme.[19] Be that as it may, three things are equally clear. First, Sharswood's endorsement of moral activism is far more circumspect than Hoffman's, suggesting that a range of views on the ethics of lawyering may have been thought consistent with republican values. Second, his endorsement of moral activism is (as we saw with Hoffman) more a reaction against than a reflection of prevailing professional norms. Third, Sharswood's bifurcated scheme is internally inconsistent. At least in civil cases, holding plaintiffs' lawyers morally accountable for the causes they represent while exempting defense lawyers is difficult to square with Sharswood's skepticism about lawyers' ability to accurately prejudge the merits of cases, his concerns about allowing lawyers to usurp the role of judge and jury, and his emphasis on the importance of equal representation by competent experts to the proper functioning of the adversary process. All of these points have been lost in role critics' haste to present Hoffman and Sharswood as archetypical exponents of a coherent republican theory of morally activist lawyering.

At least one reason to embrace both the division and the rich debates it has provoked is that greater dangers lie in their suppression or superficial resolution. Both client-centered and morally activist conceptions of the role are pernicious in their extreme forms since both can lead to injustice and, ultimately, to lawlessness—a tyranny of omnipotent clients or a tyranny of omnipotent lawyers. If nothing else, then, openly acknowledging, carefully studying, and even coming to enjoy the contest between the two ideals may operate to preserve an essential "habit of reluctance" in their proponents.[20]

The Independence of Lawyers[1]

Robert W. Gordon[2]

I know perfectly well that when lawyers start talking about their public duties, being officers of the court and so on, most of us understand that we have left ordinary life far behind for the hazy aspirational world of the Law Day sermon and Bar Association after-dinner speech—inspirational, boozily solemn, anything but real. But try for a moment to suspend disbelief. The vision of lawyering as a public profession has real historical content, even if the "republican" tradition that gave it content happens for the moment to be in recession. It even has a real current content, meaning that in some forms it is (and, as I'll argue, must be) actually though differentially instantiated in the conventional practices of lawyers. Finally the vision has tremendous–though mostly as yet unrealized—potential to transform lawyers' practical conceptions of their work in constructive ways.

In America the earliest and most powerful articulations of the ideal came from leading (usually) Federalist lawyers, nourished on Montesquieu. These lawyers, in turn, influenced Tocqueville's view of American lawyers as a substitute for the Montesquieuvian aristocracy, forming a separate estate in society, committed by professional instincts and habits to functioning as a balance wheel in political life.[3] This view ascribes to lawyers both negative and positive roles. The negative role is that of resolutely obstructing, out of their instinctive conservatism, any attempted domination of the legal apparatus by executive tyrants, populist mobs, or powerful private factions. Lawyers were to be the guardians, in the face of threats posed by transitory political and economic powers, of the long-term values of legalism.[4] Performing their positive functions entails the assumption of a special responsibility beyond that of ordinary citizens. They are to repair defects in the framework of legality, to serve as a policy intelligentsia, recommending improvements in the law to adapt it to changing conditions, and to use the authority and influence deriving from their public prominence and professional skill to create and disseminate, both within and without the context of advising clients, a culture of respect for and compliance with the purposes of the laws.

In the republican vocabulary, independence from the dominant factions of civil society was the essential precondition to the "civic virtue" or "patriot capacity" that lawyers needed to perform these functions.

The lawyer dependent upon the continuous patronage of a faction would no longer be able even to perceive, much less act upon, a view of the general interest. The need for people capable of maintaining such a general perspective was considered particularly important in a commercial republic like the United States. The pursuit of self-interest through commerce might well be the road to general prosperity, but it also had potential to deflect attention from social issues, to devalue public service and to corrupt politics by turning the public sphere into a trough of private favor-seeking. Some group had to be habitually oriented towards a longer-run, less particularistic perspective on state and society.

Lawyers and others believed that in America, lawyers were peculiarly qualified to be that group. They furnished a disproportionate share of Revolutionary statesmen, dominated high offices in the new governments and the organs of elite literary culture, had more occasions even than ministers for public oratory, and were the most facile and authoritative interpreters of laws and constitutions, rapidly becoming the primary medium of America's public discourse and indeed its "civic religion."[5] Also —this has been since so completely eclipsed that it now seems almost a joke, though it wasn't one at all in the early nineteenth century—they seemed to have exceptional opportunities to lead exemplary lives, to illustrate by their example the calling of the independent citizen, the uncorrupted just man of learning combined with practical wisdom. Lives of eminent lawyers were written up and circulated for schoolchildren and popular readers. As an inspiration to the younger bar, lawyers endlessly eulogized their dead brethren's disinterestedness and devotion to professional craft and public service, often at considerable sacrifice to income.

The "republican" vocabulary of civic "virtue," once employed to explain why lawyers should be at least somewhat independent of the major powers and factions of civil society, is now rather out of fashion. But in fact we cannot do without some such concept. Even someone committed to the most thoroughly reductionist versions of modern liberal theory—that there is no public interest, save that in fair rules for the free competition of private interests in the market, the provision of public goods, and the correction of market failures—must still imagine some mechanism for maintaining the basic framework of legal rules that constitute and support the market. To provide such a mechanism, it turns out that it is very difficult to manage without some notion that lawyers must be committed to helping to maintain the legal framework. The system of adversary representation can only work, can only be justified, if it's carried on within a framework of law and regulation that assures approximately just outcomes, at least in the aggregate. At a minimum, lawyers must be independent enough from their clients to support the rules and institutions of the framework, even when doing so hurts their clients.

In the early years of the republic the upper bar was dominated by gentlemen who thought of law not only as a living, but as a branch of statesmanship and high culture. The revival of professionalism in the late nineteenth century was largely accomplished by an aspirant WASP middle class, mobilized to preserve for itself sources of status and social influence distinct from business success, and career paths outside and not subordinate to the new giant corporate hierarchies.[6] In this century, both patricians (for example, Henry Stimson, Grenville Clark, Francis Biddle, Dean Acheson) and middle-class WASPs (for example, Elihu Root, John J. McCloy, David Lilienthal Jr., A. A. Berle Jr., W. O. Douglas) have embraced the ideal of independent lawyering. The ideal also has found some of its greatest exponents among Jewish lawyers (for example, Louis Brandeis, Louis Marshall, Felix Frankfurter, Jerome Frank), who, excluded from the inner circles of the WASP elite, had the vantage point of marginality to scold that elite for selling out its public service traditions to big business clients.

But leanings toward public service and noncommercial values, even when combined with alienation from business culture, can never constitute sufficient conditions for mobilizing lawyers to assert their political independence. After all, there are many other ways to deal with dissonance between one's practical situation and professional ideals. Lawyers can adjust their ideals to the situation, or leave corporate practice for teaching or government service or a judgeship, or leave law entirely, or (among corporate lawyers a very common strategy) narrow their conception of professionalism to technical skill, or simply cultivate an alienated ironic distance from their work and seek satisfaction in personal life. Unless lawyers possess exceptional force of individual character, mere motivation, though indispensable, is not enough. Neither is exhortation enough. To have any real force, the norms of independent practice need to be authoritatively declared and promoted, acted upon by powerful lawyers, and institutionalized in elite legal practice. Thus we need to examine the institutional conditions necessary to foster an ideal of independence that lawyers not only pay homage to, but also rely on for practical guidance in concrete situations.

The first requisite of independence is that the lawyer have some source of norms, rules, or conventions to refer to in resisting client pressures. These include both norms governing the clients, such as the ordinary rules of substantive law as applied by regulatory agencies or courts, and those governing the lawyers, such as rules of practice before agencies or courts, liability rules for neglect or malfeasance, professional ethical codes, and standards of practice drawn up by bar committees. Strong professional norms of autonomy may also come from ideologies of legalism, both "traditional" and "technocratic."

The second requisite of independence, which historically has been a lot harder to achieve, is to create norms powerful enough to constrain the lawyer's conscience and calculations, especially outside practice settings such as the courtroom where unprofessional conduct is easily detected. Informal norms and conventions are sometimes more powerful than formal ones. Lawyers riding and dining on circuit together in the last century, for example, were able to enforce upon each other conventions restricting advantage-taking through procedural or pleading maneuvers.[7] Lawyers in the upper echelons of their markets can set the standards distinguishing proper from sleazy practice for the rest of the profession.

It should help the cause of independence to have a client base that is as diverse as possible in its interests and ideologies. With such a base, lawyers will not risk losing all their clients if they argue for a position that one of the clients dislikes. A lawyer is less likely to become an ideological captive of a heterogeneous clientele. The English bar since the early nineteenth century, for example, has manifested its reliance on this principle by trying to enforce client diversity through the principle that the barrister must take any case that is offered.[8]

Brandeis used to stress the importance of thorough knowledge of the client's business operations as the precondition to influential counseling.[9] According to Brandeis, only such knowledge could place the lawyer in a position to devise creative alternatives to the client's plans which would harmonize the clients' interests with long-run social purposes expressed in law.[10] Brandeis's theory remains persuasive today.

Historically it has been of considerable importance that leading corporate lawyers were also famous citizens, men who at some time had held high public office, had directed armies or foreign relations or the national treasury. Such grandees were not likely to be overawed by business and financial tycoons, however rich and powerful, but rather able to invest their counseling with special authority.

One of the reasons that lawyers have been able to serve as a leadership elite in politics and community affairs is that unlike many other business people, they are in a position to control their time. Early nineteenth-century law practice, for instance, was structured so as to leave lots of leisure time for other pursuits—politics, writing, cultural affairs—that were conventionally integrated into a lawyer's life. A typical law office consisted of three men: the senior partner who handled the office's big clients and trials and argued appeals of public moment, the junior partner who took care of the bread-and-butter work of the firm, and the law student or clerk who did the copying.[11] As one's career progressed more time was expected to open up for projects outside practice. In current large-firm practice, of course, the amount of one's own or one's associates' time that can be released from hours billed to clients is no longer a purely individual but rather a collective decision, a function of the internal culture and politics of the firm.

Like any type of law practice, public interest work requires money. How may lawyers fund their public-interest practices today? A short list: (a) they may be the kind of people that Federalists like Hamilton thought would staff political leadership elites, people of independent wealth; (b) more likely they may be individuals at a stage in their careers where they have either already made enough money to satisfy their needs for private consumption, or simply are willing to forgo a lot of private consumption for the satisfactions of working for public causes; (c) even if not well-off themselves, they may belong to a collective, such as a law firm with a strong public interest orientation or a two-career marriage, which is well-off, and whose members are happy to trade off some joint income for the chance for some of them to engage in public service—in effect the members rely on their profitable pursuits to subsidize their unprofitable work; (d) they may take on public interest lawsuits which, if successful, will yield lawyers' fees; (e) they may donate money to other organizations such as public interest firms; (f) they may donate their own or their associates' services to public interest or legal services groups largely funded by other sources, such as foundations or direct-mail solicitations; (g) they may use their influence in bar groups to lobby for fee award or legal services legislation, to encourage the use of bar funds (such as interest on lawyers' trust accounts) to subsidize public interest or legal services organizations, or to defend such organizations against attempts to defund them; (h) they may use their contacts to raise private or foundation funds for public interest groups.

Face it: the key ingredient on this list is willingness to forgo individual or individual-share-of-group income. I know that to many it will seem incredible that lawyers in a position to make a lot of money would sacrifice it to other goods. "If that's what it takes," they will say, "forget it." All I can do is point out that historically lawyers have sacrificed income repeatedly. I will give only a few examples among many. In the midst of his extremely lucrative practice, Hamilton took time off to hold public office, even though he had no other source of income and died without enough to pay his debts.[12] Brandeis articulated an explicit theory that the purpose of private practice income was to permit the independent lawyers to engage in public causes; he followed his own preaching, living ascetically and taking on his major public causes without fee. Antebellum lawyers expected to spend a large part of their working lives in politics and public office.[13]

To a large extent, public activity was instrumental to their private ambitions, for politics brought them public exposure and contacts with important potential clients (just as today young lawyers often do a stint at the SEC or the Antitrust Division of the Justice Department as preparation for private practice). But clearly to some extent it wasn't, because lawyers would return to the public realm after their careers were made, at considerable sacrifice to their fortunes. My own research on the New York City corporate bar of 1870–1910 shows that at least 67 of the most successful members of that elite were heavily involved in legal, social, and political reform movements while in practice.[14] Today, lawyers still trade law-firm partnerships for judgeships or administrative posts paying a quarter to a tenth as much.

Clearly we need to develop a much richer sociology of professional aspirations than is provided by the banal observation that people pursue their self-interest. Granted that is so, what is it that lawyers perceive to be in their self-interest: do they want to maximize only wealth, or some other goods such as power, status, honor, fame, exciting work, and the sense that their lives are meaningful and worthwhile? If at any particular time and place some segments of the bar turn out to be interested in making money to the exclusion of other interests, that in itself is a striking cultural phenomenon that requires explanation. To find such an explanation, we need to turn once more to an examination of professional culture.

Elusive Advocate: Reconsidering Brandeis as People's Lawyer[1]

Clyde Spillenger[2]

No one holds a surer place in American legal iconography than Louis D. Brandeis. And, unlike most celebrated jurists, Brandeis is almost as revered for his exploits as a lawyer as for his judicial works. Brandeis's biographers regularly call attention to the public spirit and daring he displayed as "the people's attorney."[3] Scholarly critics of mainstream legal professionalism likewise point approvingly to Brandeis's approach to the practice of law, sometimes citing it as an alternative to the crabbed and uninspiring ethic that is said to dominate American legal practice.[4] Since academic writing on lawyering has a characteristic concern with praxis, emphasizing norms of lawyer behavior (unlike, say, scholarship on constitutional law, whose content is mostly propositional), these paeans to Brandeis have the instructional tone of "edifying" literature. They invariably leave the reader with the message that, if she is a lawyer, she would do well to emulate Brandeis.

The reasons for Brandeis's heroic stature, the building blocks of his reputation as "the people's lawyer," are familiar. As an attorney who was both fabulously successful and deeply committed to the public interest, he is a consoling reminder that one can "do good while doing well."[5] He made a policy of refusing compensation for legal work that he thought raised "public" issues, a practice that speaks to our own sanctification of pro bono services. He is supposed to have scrutinized potential clients with a careful eye, refusing to handle cases in whose justness he did not believe and sternly commanding clients to refrain from taking manifestly anti-social positions in their legal disputes. During the Senate hearings on his nomination to the U.S. Supreme Court in 1916, he faced fierce accusations that he had violated legal-ethical norms in his law practice, which is generally taken to mean that his ethical standards were superior, or at least visionary. He was the original "counsel for the situation," an appealing phrase whose provenance I will explore in some detail. His 1905 address "The Opportunity in the Law"—urging lawyers to stand "between the wealthy and the people, prepared to curb the excesses of either"[6]—is cited or excerpted in virtually every introductory casebook on professional responsibility. And, most significantly, a good deal of detail adorns the account of Brandeis's heroics. In general, we have little information about the dilemmas lawyers face in their day-to-day encounters with clients and others, and the way in which they navigate those dilemmas. But, largely because the 1916 hearings aired many episodes from Brandeis's lawyering career, we may learn about his lawyering methods from fact rather than myth.

In this article, I take a different view of Brandeis as lawyer. Most writers treating the subject have celebrated Brandeis's fierce independence from the constraining hand of powerful clients and his humanity in encouraging clients to understand their own interests as well as those of their adversaries and of society at large. But I see the same phenomena in a more ambiguous light. There was a downside to Brandeis's independent and directive approach to lawyering—an unwillingness to submit to the discipline of engagement with others (in particular, clients) that the act of representation necessarily imposes. This unwillingness was especially salient where matters of "public" import were concerned, for Brandeis's overriding priority seems to have been the integrity of his self-presentation in the public sphere. As Robert A. Burt has suggested, autonomy was not simply a lawyering ethic but was native to Brandeis's character; in his related pursuits of public interest law and political reform, Brandeis adopted a rhetorical and behavioral strategy distinguished by resistance to close identification with any group, political party, cause, or client.[7] His approach brings to mind words like "freedom," "independence," "autonomy"; it suggests his profound antipathy to acting as a mere "representative" of an anterior "interest." As a lawyer, Brandeis had numerous virtues, and he did not literally abandon or coerce clients. But his independence at times diminished client voice in a way that I would hesitate to erect uncritically as a lawyering ideal.

The aspiration to autonomy can be highly principled, and in Brandeis it accompanied an unfailing wisdom and commitment that make criticism seem almost uncivil. At first blush it may appear that Brandeisian independence is precisely what we need in a political and legal world with a diminished sense of ethical agency and autonomy. But the question of how, indeed if, one is to act in concert with others in such a world complicates the choice of Brandeis as a model for lawyering. In any relational context—and the realms of politics and lawyer-client interaction obviously qualify as such—one person's "freedom" or "autonomy" can come at a sacrifice of the power that others are able to assert. Of course, there is no easy answer to the choice between aloneness and solidarity, a choice that lies at the heart of all questions of social relations. The demands of personal and political loyalty, on the one hand, and the aspiration to self-construction, on the other, can make it difficult to know where to draw the line between autonomy and engagement. But Brandeis drew it consistently and severely at the point where engagement threatened political self-definition, and this is a crucial part of his legacy as lawyer and reformer. In the end, I am more critical than previous scholars have been of the autonomy exemplified by the most celebrated episodes in Brandeis's lawyering career; I find its impulse to be too escapist, too hostile to the spirit of engagement that ought to inform one's actions within the lawyer-client relationship and in the public sphere more generally.

Besides the light it sheds on Brandeis himself, my discussion of Brandeis's approach to lawyering in the public interest takes up more generally the ideals of lawyering and its paradigmatic function, representation. Valorization by other scholars of Brandeis's lawyerly "independence" or, in some cases, his "situational" approach to client representation has tended to assume that those ideals are themselves unproblematic. But Brandeis's manner of lawyering in the public interest suggests that neither engagement nor autonomy can serve as a comfortable resting place in our conception of the lawyer-client relationship, indeed of any relationship.

Since Brandeis's public representations were often undertaken without fee, they also seem relevant to current efforts to expand lawyers' pro bono activities. And, like many foundational images, Brandeis's public interest persona has its own canonical text—his oft-quoted speech "The Opportunity in the Law," in which he called for lawyers to abandon their vassalage to corporate interests.[8]

A second image that pervades the treatments of Brandeis-as-lawyer is that of the mediator, the harmonizer of conflicting social interests. The central exhibit in this rendition of Brandeis's lawyerly virtues is his role in mediating [a] New York garment workers' strike. But one can find this image of Brandeis as harmonizer in other parables as well—for example, in the episode involving Brandeis's use of the phrase "counsel for the situation." A celebrated example is Brandeis's counseling of his friend and client, the shoe manufacturer William McElwain, who found himself in a labor dispute arising out of his effort to cut wages during an economic downturn. After visiting McElwain's plant and consulting labor leader John Tobin, who was representing the workers, Brandeis counseled (commanded, really) McElwain to devote greater efforts to regularizing employment, and he told Tobin, in McElwain's presence, that the workers were "right." Brandeis, in the eyes of some writers, thus demonstrated that he privileged human relationships or "situations" over the mere individualized interests of clients. Not surprisingly, this part of Brandeis's image has seemed to support modern-day efforts to enlist lawyers in roles that transcend the narrow and conventional confines of adversarial justice.

The third image, closely linked with the previous two, is that of Brandeis's steely independence. A favorite illustration of this independence is Brandeis's storied policy of refusing to take cases in whose justness he did not believe, which serves as a stern reproach to the "hired gun" reputation that has long plagued the American legal profession. Brandeis doubtless departed from this policy from time to time—it is hard to believe that so successful a counselor and advocate could have been quite so fastidious —but there certainly are particular instances to support its attribution to him.

In offering a less celebratory account of Brandeis's political and lawyerly persona, I have tried to suggest, not that Brandeis misbehaved, but that his style in politics and lawyering had as much to do with a chosen mode of self-presentation as with larger ideals of the good lawyer or the public-spirited citizen. That choice necessarily came at the expense of competing values, those of dialogue and engagement with others. In interpreting his actions as I have, I am not so much devaluing Brandeis's choice as I am underscoring the dilemma that awaits anyone faced with the alternatives of aloneness and solidarity.

Reconsideration of Brandeis's approach to lawyering begets other questions. The first entails a more general examination of our lawyering ideals. If one is to assess his approach critically, one must at least outline a more general theory of legal representation that mediates between the ideals of autonomy and engagement.

The concepts of both independence and engagement that I have distilled from consideration of specific episodes involving Brandeis are themselves too abstract to support a universal lawyering ethic or a critique of such an ethic. There would be something faintly irrelevant in advising associate corporate counsel for RJR Nabisco to develop an attitude of greater empathy toward her client, and something downright bizarre in commending an attitude of steely independence to the legal services lawyer representing a member of a traditionally subordinated group, such as Mrs. G. in Lucie White's illuminating article.[9] Any hope of drawing either positive or negative general lessons for lawyering from consideration of Brandeis's approach must be chastened by the knowledge that one can scarcely imagine Brandeis as either associate corporate counsel for RJR Nabisco or attorney for Mrs. G.—a fact that those who celebrate Brandeis's lawyerly virtues sometimes overlook.

Stated with the requisite generality, or embedded in a sufficiently poignant scenario, the lawyering traits attributed to Brandeis have unquestionable appeal. For example, when Robert W. Gordon advocates lawyerly independence and points to Brandeis as an inspiring example thereof, concededly he is not calling for lawyers to adopt an attitude of contempt or neglect toward their clients. What he has in mind is Brandeis's willingness to guide his business clients, forcefully if necessary, toward morally acceptable behavior and to engage in public interest work of his own, regardless of what they might think.[10] Luban's conception of "moral activism"[11] and Simon's phrase "ethical autonomy"[12] speak to the same point. Likewise, a subtly different ethic associated with Brandeis—that of "counsel for the situation"—has clear and fruitful application to the more nuanced portrait of lawyers as counselors, negotiators, and intermediaries that has partially supplanted the image of lawyers as adversarial litigators that structured the set of legal-ethical norms prevalent in Brandeis's day. Thomas Shaffer's argument concerning the responsibilities of lawyers to represent relationships and not merely individuals is only one example of the invocation of Brandeisian imagery to support the notion of the lawyer-as-intermediary.[13]

These visions of lawyering differ in some respects, but they share one important feature: they ascribe to the lawyer a responsibility for articulating larger values (whether those of the "public interest" or of the "situation" or "relationship") that must structure or qualify the ends desired by an individual client. In this sense, Brandeis is indeed an apt source of inspiration for modern critiques of the ideology of lawyering. No lawyer ever assumed this responsibility with fewer qualms. But this seemingly salutary principle is itself the source of my ambivalence concerning Brandeis and his meaning for the ethos of lawyering.

It is one thing to speak of the lawyer's "ethical autonomy" or her "moral activism" as a basis for declining, in specific instances, to assist in the furtherance of the client's goals.

Therefore, while critiques of the nonaccountability principle and the concomitant exaltation of moral activism are inspiring in the abstract, the more complex kind of autonomy exhibited by Brandeis seems more troubling.

Dialogue usually involves two people talking and two people listening. The fixation among legal ethicists upon the figure of the immoral client and the amoral lawyer has almost concealed the possibility that moral dialogue might be edifying for the lawyer as well as the client. Brandeis's very lack of interest in this enterprise of dialogue takes us beyond the question of whether the lawyer should be a frictionless conduit for the client's views and ends, a question to which few would now give an unqualifiedly affirmative answer. It raises the question as well of whether the client should constitute the pedestal from which the lawyer attains political standing.

Brandeis's distinctive commitment to political self-definition is meaningful precisely because his consuming interest was the public weal; that commitment comes into view when we see his activities in lawyering and reform encounter "public" issues. Because of Brandeis's commendable devotion to the public good, it will seem to some that my resistance to his approach is simply the post-Progressive's corrosive skepticism concerning what is and who is entitled to define and speak for the public interest, and that it implicitly derogates the "cause lawyering" that has done so much to promote political and social change. One cannot scrutinize Brandeis's activities without coming to grips with impact litigation (especially class actions), legislative advocacy on behalf of the public, and the other forms taken by public interest law. Political opponents of these developments in the practice of law invariably have crafted their arguments in terms of their supposed violation of traditional conceptions of representation and the duties implied by it.

But I do not challenge the legitimacy of the public interest law movement, whose source Luban finds in Brandeis's "moral activism."[14] The question raised by Brandeis in his roles as lawyer and reformer is, rather, how political meaning—the identification of ends and means, in the smallest dispute as well as the largest conflict—is created. I am less troubled by the "arrogation of power" of which some accuse the activist lawyer than by the implications of an ideal of withdrawal, the aspiration to an Emersonian autonomy, embodied in Brandeis's quest to have his political voice wholly self-defined. Anyone for whom the application of critical intelligence to the larger world partakes of a creative individual act understands, at least dimly, the allure if not the compulsion of that aspiration: to say only what one thinks, to advocate only the precise thing that one believes to be just and true. That ideal is an indispensable part of the tradition of conscience and dissent suggested by the figure of Emerson himself (who maintained a famous remoteness from the political controversies of his time).

But in nurturing "devotion to a thought," one eventually encounters a world of others, some bearing claims that conflict with such a devotion. To join with others in political action, or to stand up for a client in court or elsewhere, may entail some surrender of individual prerogative if those others are not to be made simply role players in one's own script. For those of us tempted to look back wistfully on him, fixation upon the larger public good that is transcendently embodied by a figure like Brandeis is poignant, not because no one has the right to define the public good, but because that fixation can hide from us the virtues of dialogue, negotiation, and accommodation as politics. It is no coincidence that the person most often revered as a modern-day Brandeis, Ralph Nader, seems as little committed to a communal or "dialogic" approach to the substance and process of politics as Brandeis was. It may be that Brandeis and Nader represent an essential type in the realm of rebellious or dissenting politics—charismatic figures who bear an inspiring and egalitarian message, but whose effectiveness is due in part to the very aloofness that makes them uninterested in accommodating dialogue even with followers. Whether this is an equally essential type in the realm of client representation is another question.

A Stratified Profession[1]

Jerold S. Auerbach[2]

Early in the twentieth century lawyers began to contemplate the impact of social change upon their profession. "Commercialization" was the protean term of invective that most vividly expressed their unease. At one extreme, it expressed anxiety about concentrated economic power and hostility toward corporation lawyers, whose rapid professional ascendance and apparent subservience to businessmen were deeply unsettling. At the other, as an indication of concern with immigrant ghettos and urban poverty, it demonstrated antagonism toward lawyers from ethnic minority groups —the profession's new and growing underclass. Both the Wall Street lawyer and the ambulance chaser threatened models of professional independence and esteem associated with a homogeneous society and an Arcadian past.

Lawyers who clung to older values launched a crusade for professional purification. The immediate impetus was provided by President Theodore Roosevelt, who, in his Harvard address in the spring of 1905, sharply rebuked corporate lawyers for aiding their clients in evading regulatory legislation. Stung by the president's speech, Henry St. George Tucker, president of the American Bar Association and scion of a venerable Virginia family of lawyers, urged his associates to inquire whether "the ethics of our profession rise to the high standards which its position of influence in the country demands." The association authorized a committee to consider the wisdom of a code of professional ethics. It reported back a year later with a vigorous affirmative recommendation. In soaring rhetoric it implored the bar to return to its golden age of virtue. "Our profession is necessarily the keystone of the republican arch of government," it declared. "Weaken this keystone by allowing it to be increasingly subject to the corroding and demoralizing influence of those who are controlled by graft, greed and gain, or other unworthy motive, and sooner or later the arch must fall." An influx of new lawyers who pursued an "eager quest for lucre" had diverted the bar from its traditional standards and from its "pristine glory." A code of ethics, drawing upon the wisdom of the past, "should provide a beacon light on the mountain of high resolve to lead the young practitioner safely through the snares and pitfalls of his early practice up to and along the straight and narrow path of high and honorable professional achievement." Although Roosevelt had denounced those who counseled the malefactors of wealth, and the cry of "commercialization" bracketed lawyers in the highest and lowest professional strata, the committee report was more selective. Indeed, once bar associations exerted control over the campaign for canons of ethics, corporate lawyers, who were disproportionately represented in their councils, shifted the onus to "ambulance chasers" and "shysters," who were disproportionately excluded.

The new canons drew heavily upon George Sharswood's *Essay on Professional Ethics,* published in 1854. Sharswood's *Essay* was at best antiquated, and at worst irrelevant. He had addressed it to a generation accustomed to moral exhortation and confident that its own definitions of character, honor, and duty were eternal verities. Warning even in the 1850s of "a horde of pettifogging, barratrous, money-making lawyers," Sharswood had urged "high moral principle" as the bedrock of professional dignity. Passivity and patience were his cardinal virtues. Like young maidens awaiting suitors, aspiring lawyers must await clients. "Let business seek the young attorney," Sharswood insisted. It might come too slowly for profit or fame (or never come at all), but if the lawyer cultivated "habits of neatness, accuracy, punctuality, and despatch, candor toward his client, and strict honor toward his adversary, it may be safely prophesied that his business will grow as fast as it is good for him that it should grow." Sharswood's safe prophecy may have comforted a young nineteenth-century attorney in a homogeneous small town, apprenticed to an established practitioner, known in his community, and without many competitors. It could hardly reassure his twentieth-century counterpart, the new-immigrant neophyte in a large city where restricted firms monopolized the most lucrative business and thousands of attorneys scrambled for a share of the remainder. He could draw scant comfort from Sharswood's confident assertion that some preordained rule determined that his practice grew no faster than was good for him. He either hustled or starved.

Yet the new ABA Canons, which were quickly adopted at the state level, measured the social texture of twentieth-century urban practice against antebellum memories. Emphasis on reputation as the key to professional dignity and success—understandable in the tight and comfortable social structure of Sharswood's Philadelphia—presupposed the vanished homogeneous community whose lawyers were known, visible, and accessible and whose citizens recognized their own legal problems and knew where to turn for assistance. In twentieth-century cities, ironically, these conditions flourished only in the subculture inhabited by corporate law firms and their business clients. Here, too, was a small homogeneous community whose members enjoyed shared values, ease of communication, and a network of mutually reinforcing educational, religious, and social ties. The Canons, reflecting values appropriate to a small town, were easily adaptable to an equally homogeneous upper-class metropolitan constituency, where they served as a club against lawyers whose clients were excluded from that culture: especially the urban poor, new immigrants, and blue-collar workers. These lawyers confronted problems of client procurement that were never encountered by an established corporate practitioner.

A cluster of canons pertaining to acquiring an interest in litigation, stirring litigation, and division of fees almost exclusively affected the activities of struggling metropolitan solo lawyers. They did not apply to the conduct of the firm members or securely established practitioners who formulated them. The canon that uniformly prohibited lawyers from indicating publicly that they engaged in a specialty practice equated the firm known to serve a roster of corporate clients with the solitary lawyer, especially the newcomer, who specialized in negligence work and depended upon a constant client turnover for economic survival.

The prohibition against advertising instructed lawyers that success flowed from their "character and conduct," not from aggressive solicitation. It thereby rewarded the lawyer whose law-firm partners and social contacts made advertising unnecessary at the same time that it attributed inferior character and unethical behavior to attorneys who could not afford to sit passively in their offices awaiting clients; it thus penalized both them and their potential clients, who might not know whether they had a valid legal claim or where, if they did, to obtain legal assistance. The canon prohibiting solicitation discriminated against those in personal injury practice, who bore the pejorative label "ambulance chasers." And although the fee-fixing canon reminded lawyers that their profession was "a branch of the administration of justice and not a mere money-getting trade," only the contingent fee (the hallmark of negligence lawyers) was explicitly subjected to judicial scrutiny. That distinction suggested that the decisive question was who earned the fee, not the size of the fee earned.

In tandem, these canons condemned the acquisitive urge (especially among lawyers who earned least), consigned the lawyer to his office to await a client who wandered by with a case that assured fame and fortune, and attributed success (hardly unrelated in American society to monetary accumulation) to good character. The lower the fee a lawyer earned, and the less discreet he was in pursuit of it, the more likely it was that his "money-getting" activities would be scrutinized and criticized. The Canons especially impeded those lawyers who worked in a highly competitive urban market with a transient clientele. Little wonder that they made more sense to an attorney in Sullivan & Cromwell or in Fairfax County, Virginia, than to a personal injury lawyer on the lower east side of Manhattan.

The ethical crusade that produced the Canons concealed class and ethnic hostility. Jewish and Catholic new-immigrant lawyers of lower-class origin were concentrated among the urban solo practitioners whose behavior was unethical because established Protestant lawyers said it was. There were serious "social, economic and occupational differences between the rulemakers and others subject to the rules. . . ." Elite practitioners insulated themselves from "ethically contaminating influences" while they compelled lawyers whose low status was attributable to their ethnic and class origins to bear the brunt of such pressures. Rules of ethical deviance were neither universal nor timeless. They were applied by particular lawyers to enhance their own status and prestige. Deviance was less an attribute of an act than a judgment by one group of lawyers about the inferiority of another.

The Canons were justified in quite different terms. Their purpose, declared one member of the American Bar Association, was "to elevate the standing of the profession. . . . The public and the press expect that we shall formally promulgate some decalogue. The time is opportune, if we wish to maintain the traditional honor and dignity of our profession."

The Canons reflected and reinforced an increasingly stratified profession. Particularly in larger cities, declared *Bench and Bar,* "where the practice of law has become more nearly than ever a mere commercial pursuit, in which the wiles and deceits of the horse-trader are deemed good form by many, it is necessary to set up, so that all may see, some of the more elementary ethical precepts of our professional forebears of the 'old school.'"[3] (Professional forebears, of course, had registered the same complaint: back in 1879 the president of the New York State Bar Association complained that "men are seen in almost all our courts slovenly in dress, uncouth in manners and habits, ignorant even of the English language, jostling, crowding, vulgarizing the profession.")[4] The Canons embodied these "old-school" precepts. Ironically, however, it was the low-status lawyer, the target of the Canons, whose generalized practice and range of human contacts most closely approximated the traditional professional ideal of the accessible generalist. He had become the Abraham Lincoln "gone urban," whose ethnic origins and urban habitat destroyed any resemblance to his idealized rural ancestors and made him professionally vulnerable.

More important in the years to come, as the children of new immigrants entered the legal profession in unprecedented numbers, the Canons separated the bar's best men, Protestants of English and northern European origins, from the "unfit"—Jews and Catholics from eastern and southern European backgrounds. In the end, ethnic bonds mitigated fears that corporation lawyers had wrought destructive dislocations upon the profession. Old-style practitioners could cooperate with them in a united front to preserve the legal profession—or, at least, its elite stratum—as an Anglo-Saxon Protestant enclave.

In the years before World War I the structural transformation of the legal profession neared completion. White Anglo-Saxon corporation lawyers were concentrated at the professional apex, and new-immigrant metropolitan solo practitioners were restricted to the professional base. Ethical norms were promulgated; whether enforced or not they distributed status and morality according to social origin and type of professional practice. Legal services were available according to economic resources, not need. Yet professional stability was only tentative, never final. Recurrent threats required attention, and bar associations began to serve as caretakers of elite interests.

Bar associations did venture timidly into the shallower waters of law reform, but they usually skirted the dangerous shoals of substantive change. In 1912 ABA president Stephen Gregory declared that professional associations were "the chief instrumentality of constructive legal reform." Rarely, however, did their concern extend to such problems as the provision of legal services. At best, they preoccupied themselves with the most technical, professional aspects of legal issues—for example, the ethical proprieties of contingent fees rather than the social and individual costs of lives broken in industrial accidents. The result was that law reform served as "a banner of rectitude waved in the public eye," a shield to deflect public criticism. The law reform movement, sponsored by bar associations after the turn of the century, became the plaything of the legal specialist, whose job "was not to turn society on its head, but to refine and embroider his own special product. . . . Law was supposed to be socially relevant; but the areas chosen for reform were not the areas of law most socially relevant."[5]

During the second decade of the twentieth century the American Bar Association began to assert itself aggressively as a professional protective organization. In 1912 the executive committee of the American Bar Association unknowingly admitted three black lawyers to membership. Informed of its carelessness, it quickly passed a resolution rescinding the admission and—"since the settled practice of the Association has been to elect only white men as members"—referring the matter for determination by the entire association. Moorfield Storey, a past president of the bar association and the first president of the National Association for the Advancement of Colored People, was incensed. "It is a monstrous thing," he complained, "that we should undertake to draw a color line in the Bar Association." The association was in a quandary. Claiming to be a national organization, it functioned as a restricted social club. The admission of blacks, in the words of its membership chairman, posed "a question of keeping pure the Anglo-Saxon race." Prodded by Storey, members permitted the three duly elected black lawyers to remain but provided that all future applicants must identify themselves by race. The association thereby committed itself to lily-white membership for the next half-century.

The New Woman Lawyer and the Challenge of Gender Equality in Early Twentieth-Century America[1]

Virginia G. Drachman[2]

In 1917, Denver lawyer Mary Lathrop became the first woman admitted into the American Bar Association; in 1930, she confessed that she was tired of the equality she had achieved in the legal profession. Moreover, she yearned for the feminine privileges women lawyers had received in the past. "Women have gained rights but they have lost privileges. They receive no more courtesy and chivalry. Personally, I'm rather tired of rights. I'd love to have a few privileges. . . . I advise any girl who contemplates entering laws to stay away from marriage and concentrate on the legal business."[3] In one brief moment, Lathrop unveiled the sacrifices inherent to women lawyers' quest for professional equality with men. Moreover, she revealed that they had not even achieved their goal of gender equality. As far as Lathrop was concerned, women lawyers still could not balance the dual responsibilities of marriage and career with the same ease as men. Rather, the only way for women to succeed in law in 1930 was to accept the same separation of marriage and career as nineteenth-century women lawyers had endured.

It had not always seemed so discouraging. Rather, the generation of the new woman lawyer began the twentieth century with great hope and optimism about the promise of gender equality for women in the legal profession. And they had good reason. The new woman lawyer was part of a generation of women who did not have to face the rigid legal and institutional barriers that had obstructed women's entry into the legal profession in the nineteenth century. By 1920, every state bar was open to women, all but twenty-seven of 129 law schools admitted women, and the suffrage amendment made women full and equal citizens. As the gender barriers crumbled, the number of women lawyers soared. Whereas there were only 200 women lawyers in 1880, by 1920 there were 1,738. Moreover, another 1,171 women were enrolled in law schools and would join the ranks of the 3,385 women who were lawyers by 1930.

Having been spared the struggles of nineteenth-century women lawyers to gain admittance to bar associations and law schools, women lawyers in the early twentieth century faced their future with optimism and self-confidence, believing in their ability to succeed in the legal profession. Embracing the new ideal of gender equality, they relished competition with men and anticipated success on male terms in all areas of their professional lives. For one, they cast their sights beyond the office, the appropriate arena for the nineteenth-century woman lawyer, and claimed the courtroom as their rightful domain. In doing so, they signaled an end to the gendered division of labor in legal practice. In addition, whereas nineteenth-century women lawyers had made a special claim to protect the legal rights of women and children, the generation of new women lawyers claimed the once male-identified areas of legal practice such as litigation, bankruptcy, and criminal law as well.

The new women lawyers also brought gender equality into their private lives. Rejecting the notion of a woman's so-called natural domesticity, they redefined marriage and motherhood as lifestyle options rather than womanly obligations. They insisted that the new woman lawyer who chose this route could confidently expect to balance the needs of her family with the obligations of her professional life. In both their private and professional lives, new women lawyers sought to throw out the rules of the past and expected to play the game like men.

In the minds of these new women lawyers, their claim to gender equality signaled the end of the deep conflict between femininity and professional identity. This conflict had plagued women lawyers in the nineteenth century, demanding that they be at once sentimental and objective, domestic and career-oriented. Instead, the new women lawyers of the 1910s and 1920s proudly proclaimed that the era of gender equality had arrived, permitting them to shed the burden of their feminine identity. One woman lawyer expressed the faith of her generation in the new gender equality, explaining that "the day has arrived when there are only lawyers, and not men and women lawyers."[4] Another woman echoed this view. "For my part, I want merely to be known as a 'lawyer' and not as a 'woman lawyer'...."[5]

While the generation of new women lawyers began the century believing in the promise of gender equality for women in the legal profession, by the end of the 1920s they understood that their optimism had been misplaced. Despite the remarkable success of some individual women lawyers, most women lawyers never came close to achieving the professional prestige, autonomy, fulfillment, or financial security of women like Lathrop.

Despite the many claims about an era of great opportunity and professional progress for women in the law, women lawyers discovered that profound gender discrimination still impeded their professional success. As early as 1912, Boston attorney Alice Parker Lesser exposed the hard reality behind the claims of progress. "I realize that for years I and other women lawyers have lied when we said that we were on an equal basis with men in our professions. It is not so, and I am going to tell the real truth about the situation now. The field of law is no better today for girls than it was 20 years ago when they entered it." Women had more opportunities than ever before to study law, she explained, but they still lacked the opportunity to practice it. "Of course, she has all the book learning any lawyer can have. . . . But practice of law tells another tale."[6]

In 1920, in the midst of the heady days of the suffrage success and the claims of feminist victory, many women lawyers acknowledged that they were losing the battle to make it in the law. In 1920, New York lawyer Anna Parrons complained to the BVI that women had no opportunities for lucrative corporate work. "The big corporations will never give their work to women, and unless one can get big business the chances of financial success are small."[7] But while some women lawyers deplored the dearth of opportunities for women in the elite corporate law firms, others lamented an even more serious problem—the near impossibility of finding even a modest clerkship or office position. One woman lawyer claimed that male lawyers in New York City only hired women "if they haven't the money to pay a man."[8]

This was precisely the experience of Anna Moscowitz Kross, a Jewish immigrant from Russia and a graduate of New York University Law School. Law firms continually rejected her with the brazen claim, "We want a man." She finally found work in the office of a friend where she gained experience but earned no money. Gertrude Smith, another graduate of New York University Law School, encountered the same hostility in her search for a clerkship. In a letter to lawyer Inez Milholland, Smith explained that she had answered every ad for a legal position and was willing to accept a small weekly salary of only five dollars to cover the costs of cab fare and lunch. But despite her law degree from New York University and her desperate willingness to accept any position, she was always turned down. "They inform me very politely that I must not forget I am a woman and therefore would not be of any service to them." With little money to spare and no prospect of work in sight, she asked: "My dear Miss Milholland, are there no men in this city who have enough to give a woman lawyer a chance to show her worth . . . ?" Nearly broken by the relentless discrimination she encountered from male lawyers in New York, Smith confessed to Milholland: "I have lost all my ambition and courage."[9]

The gender discrimination Smith encountered was not unique to New York City. In Chicago, Irene Hanks reported that she had "been denied openings on the sole objection of sex."[10] Alice Greenacre explained that not only had she failed to find a clerkship in Chicago, but other women lawyers had informed her that "no woman had ever had a law clerkship in a law office in Chicago."[11] In addition to facing discrimination in the search for employment in Chicago, one woman lawyer reported that the Chicago Bar Association was "not cordial in its treatment of its women members."[12]

Women lawyers in the South encountered particularly strong resistance. Tiera Farrow could not find one male attorney in Kansas City, Missouri to hire her. As a result, she and another woman lawyer had to open an office together at a greater financial expense than either could afford. Their office was a very modest venture; they shared one room with two desks, four chairs, a bookcase of law books, and a typewriter. Despite their efforts to economize, business was so meager that survival forced both women to find other jobs. They were insulted or ignored by male lawyers and judges, and after two years of working together, they had made no money. Farrow's partner became so discouraged that she quit the law and went to New York to become a secretary. On her own, Farrow moved to an even smaller office, tried to live even more modestly, and settled into a solo practice which barely allowed her to make ends meet.

In Baltimore, the city bar association refused to admit women as late as 1931. This policy effectively locked the women lawyers of Baltimore out of both the Maryland state bar and the American Bar Association because both associations required its members to belong to their local bar association.

The situation for women lawyers in Georgia was even worse because the Georgia bar did not open to women until 1916 and then only after a bitter struggle. The debate began in 1911 when Minnie Anderson Hale, a graduate of the Atlanta Law School, applied for, but was denied, admission to the bar. Several weeks later, the Georgia legislature defeated a bill which would have made women eligible for the bar; but it could not escape the issue. The following year, Georgia McIntire-Weaver, a onetime dressmaker, stenographer, and finally honors graduate of Atlanta Law School, forced the Georgia legislature to reconsider reforming the law, which prohibited women's admission to the bar. Despite the support of eminent male attorneys and judges, the legislature again refused to pass the reform. However, even the Georgia legislature could not stop Georgia McIntire-Weaver. She relocated to West Virginia, which had admitted women lawyers since 1896, passed the bar, and set up practice. Having passed the bar in another state, McIntire-Weaver was finally eligible to return to Georgia to practice.

The situation in Georgia was closely monitored by the press, including professional journals such as *Law Notes* and *Women Lawyers' Journal* as well as the popular women's magazine, *Good Housekeeping*. In its article, "Your Daughter's Career," *Good Housekeeping* used the example of Weaver-McIntire in Georgia to warn its female readership of the obstacles awaiting the aspiring woman lawyer.[13] In 1916, the Supreme Court of Georgia once again denied women admission to the bar; but this was the last time. Within months, the Georgia legislature passed an act to permit women to practice law; and on August 19, 1916, Georgia joined the ranks of the other forty-five states or territories that had already admitted women to the bar on equal terms with men.

Two women lawyers, Mary Johnson and Betty Reynolds Cobb, immediately gained admission to the Georgia bar in 1916. Nevertheless, women lawyers in Georgia still faced an uphill fight. There were only twenty-five of them in the entire state by 1920. Compared to states such as Massachusetts with over 100 women lawyers and California with almost 350, the women lawyers of Georgia were a very small and insignificant group. Representing barely 1 percent of the practicing attorneys in the state, they made their careers alone under conditions strikingly similar to the pioneer generation of women lawyers a half century before. Cobb admitted that, even though she had what she described as a "pleasant and reasonably remunerative" office practice, Georgia was still reticent to welcome women lawyers.[14] "I do not think our section of the country is ready, quite yet, to make 'easy sailing' for a woman lawyer."[15] Moreover, Cobb linked what she perceived to be the deep hostility against women lawyers in Georgia to the women's suffrage movement and the advancement of women in general. In a blunt warning to women not to try to establish a legal career in the South, she explained: "To put it in a nutshell, I would not advise any young woman to study law with a view to practicing it below the 'Mason and Dixon Line' for the next generation at least. We haven't the vote yet; and if we ever get it, it will be when it is forced upon our law makers by a Federal Amendment and will not come as a State Law. Can I say anything more illuminating on the attitude of our men toward women?"[16]

While the situation for women lawyers may have been unusually harsh in Georgia, it was not unique. The difficulties encountered by women lawyers in New York, Chicago, Baltimore, Nebraska, and Washington indicate the existence of a national pattern of discrimination against women in the legal profession. Frances R. Calloway, Office Manager and Registrar at DePaul University Law School in Chicago, attested to the pervasiveness of this gender discrimination. "Out of hundreds of requests for law clerks ... I have never received one request for a young woman, nor have I been able to place one unless through influence, as the daughter of a lawyer."[17]

African-American women suffered even deeper discrimination as race combined with sex to yield tougher obstacles to overcome. While a few were able to overcome the hardships of economic struggle and racism to make it in the legal profession, for the most part, black women who became lawyers were part of the privileged elite in the African-American community. Jane Bolin grew up in the middle-class town of Poughkeepsie, New York, went to Wellesley College and then to Yale Law School, and married a lawyer. Sadie Mossell Alexander's father was the first African American to graduate from the University of Pennsylvania Law School, and her husband was a graduate of Harvard Law School. Inez Fields of Hampton, Virginia was the daughter of a lawyer and the wife of a professor of industrial education. Sallie White of Kentucky was the wife of the dean of faculty at the Central Law School, the so-called "colored" state university in Kentucky.

The economic comfort, social status, and professional advantages they derived from the men in their lives, either their fathers or husbands, linked these women. For women such as Alexander, White, and Bolin, marriage to a lawyer eased their way into the legal profession and moderated the dual handicaps of their sex and race. Yet, even these most privileged of African-American women faced obstacles white women lawyers never knew. Racial discrimination was a harsh reality that left women like Sadie Alexander with little patience for the problems of white women lawyers.

"When I hear white women lawyers complaining about their lot it amuses me. It is the same problem I have been facing all my life."[18]

In the end, no degree of social privilege could fully shelter an African-American woman lawyer from the dual prejudices of racism and sexism. The paltry number of African-American women lawyers testifies to that fact. While three black women lawyers practiced law in Virginia in the 1920s, they remained the only African-American women to practice law there until after World War II. Black women lawyers fared even worse in other southern states. None practiced law in Mississippi, Louisiana, Kentucky, or Arkansas before 1945. Nor did they do much better in other regions of the country. There were only four African-American women lawyers in the District of Columbia, three in New York, and none in Massachusetts in 1930. By 1940, there were only thirty-nine African-American women lawyers scattered throughout the country. These thirty-nine black women lawyers stood in stark contrast to the 4,146 white women lawyers in the country in 1940. And these white women lawyers were still but a small group when compared with the 172,329 white male lawyers in 1940.

A Social History of Everyday Practice: Sadie T. M. Alexander and the Incorporation of Black Women into the American Legal Profession, 1925–1960[1]

Kenneth W. Mack[2]

In April of 1939, Sadie Tanner Mossell Alexander, Pennsylvania's first and only black woman lawyer, began corresponding with several dozen African American women attorneys practicing law in the United States. After slightly more than a decade of practice in Philadelphia, Alexander was on her way to a career that would place her among the most noteworthy women lawyers of her era. Having obtained her B.S. (1918), M.S. (1919), Ph.D. (economics, 1921), and J.D. (1927) from the University of Pennsylvania, she could already count herself as one of the most highly educated women of her time, and one of the relatively few to establish herself successfully in the private practice of law. After law school, she joined the prestigious African American law firm founded in 1923 by her husband, Raymond Pace Alexander, where she became a well-respected practitioner of probate and domestic relations law. Sadie Alexander practiced there until the firm's demise in 1959, after which she created her own firm. During that time the Alexander firm was Philadelphia's leading civil rights law firm—litigating desegregation cases, defending racially biased criminal prosecutions, mobilizing community support for integration, and lobbying legislators and public officials for changes in civil rights laws and policies.

Sadie Alexander served for twenty-five years as the secretary of the National Urban League, and was elected to the national board of the ACLU. In 1946, President Harry Truman appointed her to his President's Committee on Civil Rights. The Committee's report, "To Secure These Rights,"[3] was one of the most important documents of the post–World War II civil rights movement. In 1952, she was appointed to the Philadelphia Commission on Human Relations, the city's watchdog agency on civil rights issues. After becoming its chair in 1962, she remained involved in the local and national civil rights movements, campaigning against housing discrimination and police brutality in the city and joining Martin Luther King, Jr. in the historic 1965 Selma-to-Montgomery march. Alexander rounded out her career at the age of eighty-one, when President Jimmy Carter appointed her to chair the White House Conference on Aging in 1978. When she passed away in 1989 at the age of ninety-one, news of her death was carried nationally.

In 1939, however, this was all still ahead of her, and Sadie Alexander's correspondence with her black women lawyer peers focused on more mundane issues. Alexander initiated the correspondence by sending out form letters, asking for information on black women's law practices, and initiating a fledgling professional network among women who previously knew little about each other. She discovered fifty-seven African American women admitted to practice by the time she published the results of her research in 1941.[4] Alexander wrote with evident pride about the accomplishments of women who were becoming respected practitioners, such as Jane Bolin, Yale Law School's first black woman graduate, who had established herself in private practice in Poughkeepsie and New York City before securing a position as trial counsel in the New York City Corporation Counsel's office. While in private practice, Bolin succeeded where even Alexander failed, affiliating herself with a firm where her name appeared on the firm's letterhead—Mizelle and Bolin. Eunice Hunton Carter also corresponded with Alexander about her pursuit of a career that was unusual for a woman in the 1930s: first, as a low-level criminal prosecutor in New York City, and later as a trial attorney in New York prosecutor Thomas Dewey's anti-racketeering office. Alexander herself was a well-known attorney in her native Philadelphia. Before the 1920s, when Sadie Alexander's generation of black women lawyers began practicing, few, if any, black women practiced law full time. However, two decades later, dozens were in full-time practice, and many were building careers that would earn them the envy, and sometimes hostility, of their male colleagues.

This article contends that a careful and nuanced analysis of the professional lives of this small group of black women lawyers challenges the prevailing interpretation of the history and sociology of the early twentieth-century American legal profession. The leading interpreters of this period share many of the assumptions of *Unequal Justice,* Jerold Auerbach's influential history of the twentieth-century American bar.[5] Auerbach argued that unprecedented demographic changes in the turn-of-the-century American bar—the entry of ethnic and religious minorities into the profession in large numbers—provoked a hostile response from the profession's elite. Native-born lawyers' concerns about the profession's ethnic composition led to new standards for law school accreditation, prelegal and legal education, and bar admission that helped exclude immigrants from the profession. The mainstream bar's hostile response to the growth of personal injury litigation in the early twentieth century was partly a reaction to the new modes of practice through which many immigrant lawyers made their living. Another defining moment occurred in 1912, when the admission of just three black lawyers to the American Bar Association caused the organization to adopt a resolution that effectively barred African Americans from its membership for the next several decades. Similarly, studies of women's entry into the profession have found that the bar's structure and ideology steered women toward unprofitable and low-prestige areas of practice, and that women lawyers were particularly unwelcome in the courtroom.[6] With regard to these women's experiences in the profession, a number of scholars, influenced by the work of the eminent women's historian, Nancy Cott, have argued that the male-dominated bar was particularly cruel, promising equality in its professional dogmas but delivering careers that led to frustration and marginalization.[7]

The interpretive stance of this article does not quarrel with most of these factual descriptions, but rather differs with the methodology that lies behind them. Most analyses of the bar in this period focus on the ideologies of elite lawyers and the structure of the profession as their preferred sites of historical and social inquiry. The unstated assumption of much of this literature is that the professional identities of lawyers are formed largely by these ideologies and professional structures. Thus, the professional worlds of early twentieth-century immigrant lawyers were largely defined by their exclusion from high-prestige practice, and those of women lawyers were mainly defined by the gender segmentation that prevailed within the profession. As women who were doubly marginalized by the intersection of race and gender prejudices, the professional lives of Sadie Alexander and her black women lawyer peers should encapsulate this story of exclusion and frustration. Professional advancement, which was precarious enough for white women, would seem all but impossible with the added impediment of race. The analysis presented here, however, reaches the opposite conclusion. Peering behind the veil of gender- and race-based discrimination, it finds a rich and complex professional world where black women lawyers' identities were constituted as much by everyday interactions with professional colleagues, judges, clients, and opponents as by the structural features of an exclusionary bar. Explicating this quotidian world of gender role contestation, lawyer-client conflict, professional relationships, and other features of black professional life, this article argues that Alexander and her peers were able to obtain a surprising, and often ironic, degree of power and prestige in the profession—surprising, at least, from the perspective of the dominant interpretive paradigm for the bar in this period.

The dominant paradigm's privileging of bar associations and elite lawyers is rooted in the prevailing methodological approach to the history and sociology of the legal profession. Recent scholarship in this area has applied a critical lens to the analysis of the profession, in large part superseding an earlier body of work that focused on the functions that the bar provided in a modernizing society. This newer, critical work has provided tantalizing insights into the structure of the American bar, the comparative analysis of national legal professions, and the ideological conflicts of elite lawyers in the United States and elsewhere. At the same time, many legal historians have begun calling for, and practicing, legal history "from below," arguing that social history (often encompassed in the voices of outsiders in the law) performs a critical function by complicating and informing the dominant narratives of legal history. These social historians of American law argue that analyses of the everyday experiences of outsiders—workers, women, ethnic and racial minorities—critically contribute to a full and nuanced picture of the history of American law and sociolegal change. With few exceptions, the methodologies of the social historians have yet to be applied to the history of the legal profession.

As the dominant paradigm would predict, Sadie Alexander and her peers at the black woman's bar often began their careers in segregated spaces—accepting stereotypical positions that kept them out of the courtroom and confined them to office practice. By her second decade of practice, however, Alexander was actively recreating her role as a lawyer. She did not lack for templates on which to model her social and professional interactions. As J. Clay Smith has argued, black women lawyers of her era were successors to a late-nineteenth-century "feminist intelligentsia,"[8] composed of middle-class black women such as Gertrude Mossell, Anna Julia Cooper, and Ida B. Wells, who began to carve out a place for educated black women in a society that often did not recognize them. As a strategy for acceptance in a world where black respectability was supposed to be an oxymoron, many in this group internalized the late-Victorian manners and mores of the respectable whites of their era.

Alexander drew on this reservoir of respectability to become an effective negotiator, such that by the 1940s her negotiating skills were attracting institutional clients to the firm. By her third decade of practice, she had even turned her negotiating skills on her husband, successfully beating back his efforts to unilaterally merge the firm with another without her consent. By that time, her skills had made her a more well-known figure in civil rights circles than her husband.

Even as Alexander was pushing the boundaries of women's practice, she penned a seemingly incongruous note to a young woman interested in studying law, telling her "your only hope [to succeed at practice] is to be associated with a man." At about the same time, when Jane Cleo Marshall Lucas sought out Alexander's advice shortly before her graduation from law school, Alexander told her to "marry a black lawyer." Fifty years later, Lucas recalled: "I thought that was hilarious!" Her advice to Lucas is perhaps less surprising in the context of a letter written several years earlier to an acquaintance, in which Alexander observed, somewhat flippantly, that "anybody can stay in school long enough to get degrees, but everybody cannot get a husband. Therefore, I am much prouder of my title, Mrs. Alexander, than of any degree or professional distinction." Sadie Alexander thought that the surest route to professional success came about through the intervention of men, both in private and professional life, precisely because that described her own career trajectory.

When asked about tensions between her marriage and her professional duties, Alexander remarked, "We didn't have any at all." Marriage and practice with her husband were reinforcing relationships. Just as she accepted reciprocal, but differing, obligations in marriage, she accepted them in the office. The firm remained the Raymond Pace Alexander law firm until it closed.

Sadie Tanner Mossell Alexander was a fierce critic of gender discrimination and believed that women and men should have equal opportunities at the bar, but her definition of equality was mediated by the late-Victorian ethos of her generation. That definition might seem strange to us today, but for her it was natural. Liberal, equal-rights feminism would have to wait for another day. Although Alexander shared many of the movement's objectives, she took another route in her quest for equality within the profession. Gender separation at home was the rubric through which Alexander interpreted her professional world and she, along with many African American women lawyers of her generation, was willing to accept a degree of separation and subordination within the profession at the beginning of her career. For Alexander and her generation, stereotypical women's lawyering roles were not solely the imposition of a male-dominated bar; adoption of such roles carried certain advantages for women who still assumed that they were responsible for household and childrearing duties. It made sense, both in practical and cultural terms, for home and work roles to reinforce one another. Moreover, while the legal profession defined success in masculine terms, as these women knew, success within the profession did not always mean the same thing. As time went on, the skills that they developed in subordinate roles provided entry points to more prestigious positions, as demonstrated by their own careers. In fact, the negotiation and advising skills that they learned in office practice were more in line with the profession's long-term trends than the jury trial work on which many of their black male colleagues thrived. The relationship between gender, power, and domination could change with time, making what was subordinating at one moment liberating at another.

In many ways, the professional lives of Sadie Alexander and her black women lawyer peers were a response to the question posed perhaps most provocatively by Audre Lorde: "Can the master's tools dismantle the master's house?"[9] Can socially subordinated groups contest their subordination using the same social structures and ideologies that define those groups as inferior? With regard to women in the early twentieth-century American legal profession, the conventional answer to this question has been "no." According to the traditional interpretation, the early twentieth-century mainstream bar began to articulate norms of professional advancement that were based on meritocracy rather than status, and a number of women lawyers took the profession at its word. These women lawyers began to define home and work roles for themselves that were identical to those of men. The "new woman" lawyer was optimistic about her chances of succeeding in the profession on the same terms as her male colleagues. Much of this optimism, however, dissipated in the late 1920s and 1930s, as women lawyers began to run up against roadblocks to their personal and professional aspirations—the prejudices and discrimination of male lawyers that would relegate them to careers at the bottom of the professional hierarchy. According to this interpretation, professionalism was a trap for these women, and women lawyers' experiences at the early twentieth-century bar would be defined largely by discrimination and exclusion. The struggle for gender equality would have to be taken up by succeeding generations of women lawyers.

One of the theses of this article is that, for the first generation of practicing black women lawyers, Audre Lorde's question should be answered with a qualified "yes." The early twentieth-century American bar, like other professions, exerted a strong disciplinary force on its entrants. Most lawyers, even those who were members of groups against which the profession defined itself, were forced to conduct their professional lives on terms largely dictated by the mainstream bar. Sadie Alexander and her correspondents were no exception. Doubly disabled, they felt the press of discrimination and exclusion even more harshly than their black male or white women peers. Yet, there were gaps within the bar's discriminatory structure, spaces where outsiders could find some room for play, maneuver, and sometimes an ironic power. Discriminatory professional practices may have been pervasive, but such practices did not define everything about the day-to-day life of a lawyer. Alexander and her generation of black women lawyers found places of opportunity in their everyday practice, and used them to step into positions of power within the profession. While they could never escape the race- and gender-based ideologies that helped define their place at home and at work, many of them managed to carve out careers that must have surprised their male colleagues, although certainly not themselves.

Culture Clash in the Quality of Life in the Law: Changes in the Economics, Diversification, and Organization of Lawyering[1]

Carrie Menkel-Meadow[2]

There is no question that law practice has changed in recent decades. More lawyers work in larger units or newer forms of practice. Increasing numbers of lawyers come from previously excluded groups, including both women and minority demographic groups. After a period of economic boom there is general economic anxiety about the continued health and growth of the law "industry." This occurs as there is a general "speed up" in American work, the forms of law practice organization and billing for legal work are being renegotiated, and rates of dissatisfaction with the practice of law increase, especially among younger and newer lawyers. These are just some of the changes, broadly labeled, by this writer and others, as "transformations" in the legal profession, that have undoubtedly inspired the current effort to understand what the legal profession of the twenty-first century will look like. These changes in the structure and organization of lawyering will have a profound effect on the way in which people labor as lawyers.

As one who is generally skeptical about the predictions of "futurists," because I do not think we can accurately predict how various "trends" will interact with each other, I find my task, to suggest proposals or resolutions to deal with the "economics and work environment" of legal practice, particularly difficult. Change in the legal profession is clearly afoot—but how the various changes outlined above will interact with each other is difficult to assess.

My themes and biases here should be stated at the outset. In my view, the quality of life in the legal profession needs improvement, if lawyers are to lead socially useful and productive lives, for their clients, for their colleagues, for their families, and for themselves, as well as for the future of our legal system. There is room for hope in achieving positive changes for the profession with the entrance and contribution of more diverse members of the profession. However, it is also clear that a variety of other factors, such as the economics of law practice, resistant occupational structures, and persistent, but outmoded, ideologies may have countervailing influences on the innovations most likely to improve the quality of life and work environments of lawyers. My theme here is that change in the legal profession will come from a clash of cultures—demands for more humane and horizontally satisfying work on the one hand and the requirements and exigencies of the economic (and vertical) bottom line on the other. Thus, ultimately, the story of change in the legal profession is a story of how culture and social structural change are negotiated. Like the current effort, official conferences with specific resolutions are one way of trying to put things on the social change agenda. Ultimately, however, the resolutions of social, political, and economic negotiations in the legal profession are much more likely to occur in more subtle ways, behind the closed doors of law firms, government agencies, and bar associations. Whether particular changes in the professional culture will ultimately be considered to be progressive innovations or deformations and regressions will depend primarily on who makes up the profession and how much clients and the lay public will be involved in the cultural and economic negotiations.

The story of the development of the legal profession in the United States in the nineteenth century is the oft-told tale of limited competition and increased barriers to entrance to the profession, characterized by the movement from apprenticeships to proprietary schools and increasingly to formal requirements for university and law school formal education, state examinations, and licensing and certifications. Whether seen as an economic project to limit competition or a social project to keep out immigrant and non-"nativist" men, the tale of the nineteenth century is an exclusionary one. Historians and sociologists of the profession have documented how attempts to "reform" the profession, by adding educational requirements or demanding adherence to ethical standards, all coincided with increasing enrollments of law students and attempts at greater diversification of the profession—first by class, then by ethnic origin, race, and gender. Fluctuations in the size and development of the legal profession vary both with these efforts to control the supply of lawyers and with the political and economic variations of war and recession. The practicing profession nearly doubled between 1890 and 1930, but dropped during the Depression and the Second World War, with similar cycles in the years of the Korean and Vietnam wars. As Richard Abel points out, the lawyer-to-population ratio was about the same in 1950 as it had been in 1900 and the same in 1960 as in 1885.[3] Between 1960 and 1980, the legal profession experienced growth; law school enrollment increased three times, bar admissions four times, and the lawyer-to-population ratio halved. The last ten years have seen some leveling off of this expansive growth period. At least one scholar of the legal profession attributes most, if not all, of this recent growth to the entrance of women into the profession.[4]

Entry barriers to immigrants, blacks, and women were both "official" and more subtle. Blacks and women were formally excluded from legal education and from licensure, while some immigrant groups persevered through night schools and the development of their own law firms to service their own constituencies. Particularly successful were Catholics and Jews, who began with separatism in their own law firms, but eventually gave way to an assimilationist strategy.

By the late 1960s, women began entering the profession in greater numbers. They currently represent about 40 percent of the student body and just under 20 percent of the profession. On the other hand, entrance into the profession has been less successful for minorities—putting Blacks, Hispanic Americans, Asian-Pacific Islanders, and American Indians together, all minorities constitute just about 10 percent of the total enrollment in law schools and much less than 10 percent of total bar membership. A recent article in the American Bar Association Journal points out that only 3 percent of all partners in our largest firms are minorities[5] (compared to about 8–9 percent for women).

After the expansion of the 1980s, we are currently in a period of "downsizing" and doom-and-gloom forecasts for the large firms. Profits are down and many firms have chosen to retain partner profits by reducing associate "overhead," just as higher and higher rates of job dissatisfaction are reported by younger lawyers. What began as a "women's issue"—how inhospitable the large law firm was—has grown into an issue that affects all who work in law firms—associates, partners, women, men, minorities and whites, as well as the clients served. Several structural aspects of the large firm deserve mention here. Although there is a continued increase in the number of large law firms, it is also true that greater numbers of law firms have dissolved in recent years, beginning with the national "scandal" of Finley, Kumble. Large numbers of lawyers and interstate and multi-state clients increase the number of possible conflicts of interests. As firms specialize, different firms may do some of the work for the same clients (common are splits between securities work and litigation or bankruptcy and labor). Most firms report fierce competition in the acquisition and retention of clients. What solo attorneys have previously been disciplined for in client solicitation, large firms now do through "client workshops and seminars." Law firms now compete with their own clients as in-house counsel begin to "retake" the litigation work that was previously farmed out. The need for constant new and old business has, by all internal and external reports, led to changing measures of partner profit and associate evaluation. The measures of "eat what you kill" and overvaluation of "finders" as compared to "minders and grinders" have placed economic contribution to the firm at the center of attorney compensation and valu-ation. Many commentators decry this "commercialization" of the practice, claiming that the practice of a profession has become a "business."

With an increased emphasis on "billable hours" as the measure of suc-cess within a law firm, there have been several important developments for lawyers on both economic and quality-of-life grounds. To the extent that the bottom line or billable hours control evaluation (in more polite law firm lingo this is called "productivity"), more quantitative than qualitative decisions are made about partnerships. This increases predictability for associates but often creates some instability for the law firm, by reducing "bonding" by senior partners with particular associates, and creates what some critics have labeled a "time famine." Billable hours continue to rise to such levels that at least one study documents that over 50 percent of asso-ciates bill more than 2,400 hours a year and take less than two weeks of vacation a year. Associates claim that law firms require total commitment such that their family and other aspects of their outside lives are almost nonexistent, as their every minute is clocked and monitored in the law firm. The emphasis on individual billable hours has also had the effect of decreasing some forms of collective action in the law firm, including both sociability and collegiality, as well as more altruistic, pro bono, and public interest activities.

While most of the attention on the economics of law practice has fo-cused on the large law firm, a few scholars have focused their attention on what may be the source of real innovation in the profession—the new

forms of entrepreneurial lawyers consisting of solos, small firm practices, or prepaid legal plans or clinics that attempt to deliver volume legal
services. Following the decision of *Bates v. State Bar*,[6] lawyers began advertising to attract directly volumes of middle- and lower-income clients
who had previously been thought to have inadequate access to the expensive, bar-fixed rates of private lawyers. This "revolution" in client-getting
techniques, accompanied by the Supreme Court's approval of a variety of
group and prepaid legal plans,[7] has resulted in a number of economic and
technological innovations in how law is practiced that affect other dimensions of the quality of life choices for lawyers.

These new forms of practice are also distinguished by their demographic profile—a larger proportion of these lawyers are women, and in
urban areas greater numbers of minority lawyers will be found in this
form of practice. For many women and minorities disenchanted with the
ways of the large firm, these new forms of practice provide an alternative
that allows them to use their "personal qualities" to deal directly with
clients, master a new form of professional knowledge (the technology of
computer delivery of services), and maintain a less totalized personal existence. Yet undoubtedly these lawyers will suffer from a larger economic
recession as well.

The 1970s saw the development of "alternative law collectives" of political and ideological commitments in which work was shared, salaries were
divided evenly among professional and nonprofessional staff, and cases
were taken purely for their law reform potential, rather than for their
economic value. While few of these offices survived the era of greed in
the 1980s, they continue to provide evocative visions of how law practice
could be alternatively arranged.

In the public sector, different organizational models of less hierarchy
and more consensual decision-making, often attributed to women or
other "outsider" lawyers, may temporarily alter both the organization and
culture of a law practice unit.

In a sense, then, the census and other data we have on the forms and
organization of law practice do not fully reflect the variations on law practice structures that do and could exist. More importantly, despite the attempts to use economic theories (particularly of the firm) to explain the
structures of law firm practice, there are no easy predictive models for
understanding the relationship of particular economic arrangements to
particular forms of law firm organization.

Chapter 3

Historical Case Studies

This chapter presents two historical case studies to further explore how American lawyers' ethical self-conceptions came to encompass particular understandings of law practice as an important avenue for fighting social injustice. The first case study involves the history of the NAACP. The second looks at the strategic and ethical challenges of the poverty law movement of the 1960s and 1970s. This movement is interesting in its own right, and also deserves examination because it was the direct precursor to the clinical legal education movement. As we shall see in chapter 4, that movement has spawned some of the most creative new critical writing on the intersections among law practice, law teaching, and legal ethics issues.

In section A, "Legal Ethics and the NAACP," J. Clay Smith documents the professional accomplishments of the first African-American lawyers, including their work filing some of the first civil rights cases in the country. As Smith describes, the nation's second African-American lawyer, Robert Morris Sr., filed what was probably the first school desegregation lawsuit, in Boston in 1848. Although Morris was unsuccessful in this suit, it led the way for the successes of the civil rights movement a century later. In the 1890s, Louis André Martinet engineered a test case strategy leading to *Plessy v. Ferguson*,[1] a case that challenged the "separate but equal" doctrine that segregated African-American rail passengers into separate cars. That case was also unsuccessful, but it set off a chain of events and doctrinal developments leading eventually to the abolition of the separate but equal doctrine in education in *Brown v. Board of Education*.[2] Test case litigation strategies were further refined by African-American civil rights organizations such as W.E.B. DuBois's Niagara Movement and then the NAACP.

In an excerpt from my work on the early history of the NAACP, I explore the development of these test case litigation strategies and the tensions they posed in relation to traditional legal ethics principles. This tension came to a head in the southern assaults against the NAACP on legal ethics and other grounds following the organization's victory in *Brown*. As first documented by Mark Tushnet in books cited in the Appendix, and as I have further explored in other articles (see Appendix), NAACP lawyers Charles Hamilton Houston and Thurgood Marshall were well aware of the organization's vulnerability to legal ethics charges and struggled mightily, but eventually unsuccessfully, to avoid them.

An excerpt by Charles Hamilton Houston's biographer, Genna Rae McNeil, captures Houston's great significance in the development of new ethical conceptions of lawyers' role as public interest lawyers. As McNeil shows, Houston stands as a figure bridging many divides. He enjoyed access to the developing *sociological jurisprudence* being taught at elite law schools, as a result of his admission as one of a very small number of African-American students at Harvard Law School. But he also remained an outsider to this elite world by virtue of his race, class origins, and first-hand experiences with racial injustice. Inhabiting this space of creative tension, Houston transformed the ideas of sociological jurisprudence to develop his concept of lawyers as "social engineers," who could apply their legal skills to advocate through the courts for civil rights—-and, in a fight Houston would turn to later in his life, against economic injustice as well. Houston envisioned Howard Law School, where he served as a professor and dean, as a training ground for such new lawyers, and in his life example combined the ethical ideals of public interest practice, scholarly reflection on new directions implicit in received jurisprudential traditions, and the transference of such ideals to new generations of students through mentoring and teaching.

The ethics assaults against the NAACP culminated in *NAACP v. Button*.[3] In that case, the U.S. Supreme Court finally resolved the half-century-old tension between test case litigation and traditional legal ethics doctrines by ruling that nonprofit public interest organizations are constitutionally protected from some kinds of legal ethics discipline.

Although *Button* was an important victory in many respects, Derrick Bell explores the unintended legal ethics consequences of that holding. Bell, who had then only recently resigned from a position as a civil rights lawyer for the NAACP, examines the NAACP's public-interest litigation model in the period following *Brown*. He points out that, in this nation-wide remedial phase of the *Brown* litigation, the desegregation strategy the NAACP's lawyers adopted sometimes contravened the desires of the parents of affected African-American schoolchildren. Many of these parents would have preferred to focus on improving educational quality rather than insisting on busing and other methods of achieving desegregation that placed great burdens on their children without necessarily leading to better educations for them. Bell asks whether the public interest lawyers who singlemindedly pursued the NAACP's post-*Brown* remedial strategy achieved the proper balance between their own views of the public interest and their duty to advocate for their clients' desires. Bell thus brings us full circle back to the tension between lawyers' conceptions of the public good and their duties as zealous advocates for their clients—the fundamental problem with which this chapter began in examining legal ethics issues in the early 1800s.

Bell's paradigm-shifting article marked the beginning of an enormous outpouring of literature examining ethical issues in public interest practice. In Section B, "The Poverty Law Movement," we begin our look at some of that literature. Inspired by the successes of civil rights lawyers, lawyers involved in the poverty law movement sought to use public impact litigation strategies to address the problems of poverty and class inequality in the United States. Gary Bellow and Jeanne Charn (then Kettleson) examine some of the special ethics issues these strategies raise. They note that simply adding more legal services lawyers does not necessarily solve the power imbalance problems that lead to poor people's legal interests not being adequately represented in the legal system. As Pearce did from a different perspective in chapter 2, Bellow and Charn criticize the legal system's emphasis on adversarialism. But they critique the proposed alternatives to adversarialism as well, including the hopes some held out for alternative dispute resolution (ADR) procedures as a better means of resolving disputes. (Some of the literature exploring the intersection between ADR and legal ethics is listed in the Appendix.) Bellow and Charn conclude that the legal ethics problems the poverty law movement highlights implicate deep structural issues in the profession. We will return to more of this literature on ethics issues in public interest lawyering later in this reader.

Questions for Reflection and Discussion

1. McNeil documents how Houston struggled with both race discrimination and class issues in his years at Harvard Law School. Do you see remaining vestiges of this legacy in legal education today? If so, what are some examples?

2. Sociological jurisprudence was the intellectual precursor to legal realism and saw law as policy rather than as a science based on logically determined legal rules (as late nineteenth-century legal formalists had). Do you see any connections between Houston's study of sociological jurisprudence and his vision of lawyers as social engineers? If so, what connections do you see?

3. In your own legal education, have you seen connections between ways of thinking about law, on one hand, and conceptions of how lawyers should practice law, on the other? Can you reflect on what these have been? Has any aspect of your legal education deeply influenced or changed your views about law practice? (This topic might be one for a reflection paper or small group discussion.) Are there connections between theories of law and the practice of law that you wish your professors would make more explicit? If so, what are these connections?

4. Bell and Carle both note that the ABA's model ethics codes do not adequately take into account the fact that, in any litigation that has a significant public impact, a lawyer's decision in one case may have profound effects on future litigants who are not before the court. Do you think this problem should be addressed in the Rules? If so, how would you address it?

5. Do you see any ethics issues raised by Bell's decision to critique publicly the practices of the public-interest legal organization that had formerly employed him? If so, what are these issues? Do you think Bell's conduct was proper under the circumstances? Why or why not?

6. Bellow and Charn define public interest law as involving the provision of "subsidized legal services, on a full or almost full-time basis, to those who would otherwise be under- or unrepresented" and as services provided by lawyers "specifically paid to devote most or all of their efforts to the 'legally disadvantaged.'" Is this a different definition of public interest law from that suggested by the historical models Pearce and Gordon discuss? What assumptions about how the legal system works and how the public interest should be determined are built into the Bellow and Charn model? Do these differ from the assumptions underlying the civic republican and Progressive-Era lawyer-statesmen models? If so, what are these differences? As considered in question 3, do you see connections between

theories of how the legal system operates and conceptions of how to be a good lawyer?

7. Do you see solutions to the underlying structural problems of imbalance in client power and resources on which Bellow and Charn focus? If so, what changes do you propose to fix the problems these authors describe? Do any of these involve or include changes in lawyers' ethical orientations?

8. The façade of the United States Supreme Court building in Washington, D.C., is inscribed in large letters with the phrase "Equal Justice for All." Is this true in the American legal system? If not, why are these words inscribed in such a visible location? Is this an example supporting Abel's argument that lawyers' ethical ideals are mere justificatory myths?

Emancipation[1]

J. Clay Smith Jr.[2]

Robert Morris Sr., America's second black lawyer, commenced the study of law in Boston under the tutelage of Ellis Gray Loring, a white man connected with the antislavery movement. Loring, an 1827 Harvard University law graduate, hired Morris as a house servant in 1837, when Morris was fifteen years old. Loring also had a white lad in his employ. Robert Morris Sr. got a chance to study law because the white servant "neglected his duties," which allowed Morris to move up to "help out by doing copying in Loring's law office." Pleased with the intellect of young Morris, Loring encouraged him to study law. On February 2, 1847, Robert Morris Sr. was admitted to the Superior Civil Court of Suffolk County and thereafter began to practice law.

Morris was an aggressive and assertive lawyer whose technical skills were recognized by many in the community and by members of the local bar. In 1847, in what may be the first lawsuit filed by a black lawyer on behalf of a client in the history of the nation, a jury in Boston ruled in favor of Morris's client, though the details of the trial are unknown. Morris, however, recorded his feelings and observations about his first jury trial:

> There was something in the courtroom that made me feel like a giant. The courtroom was filled with colored people, and I could see, expressed on the faces of everyone of them, a wish that I might win the first case that had ever been tried before a jury by a colored attorney in this country. At last my case was called; I went to work and tried it for all it was worth; and until the evidence was all in, the argument on both sides made, the judge's charge concluded, and the case given to the jury, I spared no pains to win. The jury after being out a short time returned, and when the foreman in reply to the

clerk answered that the jury found for the plaintiff, my heart pounded up
and my people in the courtroom acted as if they would shout for joy.

After his victory in this trial, Morris's popularity soared: a black man had
prevailed against a white lawyer. A few months later Robert Morris Sr. was
approached by a group of citizens led by Benjamin F. Roberts and asked
to file a lawsuit to desegregate the Boston public school system. Roberts
complained that his daughter was precluded from attending a neighborhood school because she was black. Morris accepted the case, and in 1848
he filed, and personally tried, the first civil rights case challenging a segregated public school system in Boston. The name of this celebrated case
was *Roberts v. City of Boston.*

The complainants in the lawsuit were Sarah Roberts, a five-year-old
black child, and her father, Benjamin F. Roberts. At the trial Morris attempted to prove (without success) that a resolution passed by the local
school board in Boston requiring "colored children" to attend "colored
schools" was illegal. In this instance, Sarah Roberts was required to travel
a fifth of a mile further from her house than the nearest public primary
school. In fact, the nearest public school was nine hundred feet from
Sarah Roberts's house, and five schools for white children lay between
Sarah's home and her school. But the local court ruled in favor of the local
school board, represented by P. W. Chandler, and Morris was required to
pay court costs of $51.30. Morris immediately appealed the ruling to the
Supreme Judicial Council of Massachusetts, the highest court in the com-
monwealth, and won the support of Charles Sumner, an abolitionist Boston lawyer who in 1851 would be elected to the United States Senate.

Attempting to overturn the lower court's ruling, Robert Morris and
Charles Sumner filed, in 1848, the first civil rights appellate brief ever
co-signed by a black lawyer and a white lawyer in any case in America.
The brief argued that the constitution and laws of Massachusetts made all
persons, without distinction of age, sex, birth, color, origin, or condition,
equal before the law. However, the court refused to overturn the lower
court's decision, holding that it was reasonable and "practical" to require
black children in Boston to travel further distances to attend "colored
schools."

Although Morris and Sumner lost this case, their effort helped set in
motion a jurisprudence of opposition to segregated public education that
would culminate one hundred and five years later in *Brown v. Board of
Education,* which held that state-imposed segregation in public school sys-

tems was unconstitutional. Robert Morris lost his case before the Supreme Council of Massachusetts but won the respect of the black citizens of Boston.

In 1874, Straight University, an institution sponsored by the American Missionary Association, opened its law department. For the next twelve years, the law department graduated several black and white law students, including Louis André Martinet, its "first Negro graduate," in 1876. He paid for his legal education by moonlighting as a part-time French teacher. Martinet was elected to the Louisiana state legislature representing St. Martin Parish, where he served from 1876 to 1878.

As was usual in many states, law students in Louisiana were permitted to take the bar at the end of their first year in law school. Martinet took advantage of this opportunity, passed the examination, and was a member of the Louisiana bar when he graduated from Straight University. Two years after Martinet's graduation, the Hayes-Tilden Compromise was reached, and the federal troops that had protected blacks during the Reconstruction era were withdrawn from the South. This left educated lawyers like Martinet "on the scene at a time when the fortunes of the Negro were fast running out."

Martinet's efforts to obtain employment after leaving law school were hard-fought. On August 6, 1877, he applied for a full-time teaching position at Straight University as a professor of Latin and French. In his letter seeking the professorship, Martinet wrote, "I am also one of the graduates of the law class of 1876, though I was admitted previously to the Bar, after a credible examination, by the Supreme Court." At the time Martinet applied for an appointment, he was also "one of the directors of the public schools for [New Orleans]." By August 20, 1877, having received no response to his earlier letter, Martinet wrote that he had waited long enough for a reply to his petition "asking for a teachership in Straight University. I leave tomorrow for the country."

Martinet did not remain in the country for very long. He soon returned to New Orleans to practice law. On June 2, 1885, Martinet was admitted to practice in the United States District Court for the Eastern District of Louisiana, though rigid segregation laws were meanwhile being enacted throughout the South. In an effort to inform the New Orleans black community about news and current political issues, Martinet began to publish the *Daily Crusader* around 1890, the same year in which the Louisiana state legislature passed a series of Jim Crow laws. The paper was used as a tool to help fight the violence toward and political repression of his people. One target of the paper was the "separate car law" passed by the Louisiana legislature in 1890. The separate car law required that blacks and whites ride in separate coaches in all public transportation in the state. Martinet publicly denounced the separate car law in the *Daily Crusader* and quickly became the leader of the protest movement to have the Jim Crow laws in Louisiana declared unconstitutional.

A strategy for a legal challenge against the legality of the separate car law had to be formulated by the lawyers, and the black community had to be mobilized. Martinet called upon "Eugene Luscy, R[udolph] L[ucien] Desdunes and other graduates of [Straight University's] law school [who] took an active part in organizing the Citizens Committee for the Annulment of Act No. 111, commonly known as the separate car law." In 1890, Martinet became one of the first black lawyers to use the term "test case" in planning a litigation strategy to repeal the Louisiana Jim Crow laws. Financial support to pay Martinet and his colleagues for what was to be a long legal fight was raised by the Citizens Committee.

In the early 1890s, Martinet declared, "We'll make a case, a test case, and bring it before Federal courts on the grounds of the invasion of the right [of] a person to travel through the states unmolested." In the first test case, Daniel L. Desdunes was arrested when he refused to vacate a seat reserved for whites in a public streetcar in New Orleans. Desdunes was brought before a local judge, who dismissed the charges against him. The Desdunes decision gave the black community confidence that their cause was just, and another test case was planned.

Homer Adolph Plessy was next used as the guinea pig to test the separate car law. Plessy was arrested and criminally charged for refusing to vacate a coach on a passenger train reserved for whites. An urgent call went out to Albion Winegar Tourgée, a white lawyer living in New York, and to James C. Walker, another white lawyer, to represent Plessy. Tourgée was a Union Army veteran and former "carpetbag" North Carolina judge during Reconstruction. Despite the fact that there were black lawyers in the South, many of them practiced "almost exclusively in the police courts" and thus were not considered to appeal Plessy's case. In addition, an experienced appellate lawyer was needed to take the case to the United States Supreme Court after the Supreme Court of Louisiana denied Plessy's writ of prohibition in 1892.

As the case worked its way to the United States Supreme Court, the nation waited for what may have been the most important race case to be determined by the Court since the Dred Scott decision of 1857. On May 18,

1896, Justice Henry Billings Brown, writing for the majority of the Court, held that state-imposed separate but equal car statutes on interstate railroad travel did not violate the Thirteenth or Fourteenth Amendments to the United States Constitution.

Albion W. Tourgée's efforts to have the Supreme Court strike down the separate car law in *Plessy* cannot be given enough credit, but the courageous efforts of Louis André Martinet, who laid the groundwork for the test case, deserve as much credit. It was Martinet who mobilized the community effort, shaped the case, selected the lawyers, and edited a key document in the appeal.

Race, Class, and Legal Ethics in the
Early NAACP (1910–1920)[1]

Susan D. Carle[2]

The key to the NAACP's litigation success was its use of "test cases," a term used to refer to a strategy in which an organization seeks to find or, if necessary, to create a legal controversy to establish a point of law as precedent in future cases. Today the term invokes images of the NAACP's 1954 victory in *Brown v. Board of Education*,[3] but in fact the strategy was central to the NAACP's objectives from its founding in 1909. The test case idea in turn had its roots in activism by civil rights campaigners and corporations stretching far back into the nineteenth century.

By the late nineteenth century, African-American lawyers working in local communities had begun to experiment with the use of citizens' organizing committees to challenge racial injustice. The most impressive effort to organize a national civil rights organization to sponsor test cases prior to the founding of the NAACP was the Niagara Movement, an African-American group organized in 1905 at a meeting in Niagara Falls, New York. Its founders included W.E.B. DuBois, the brilliant but temperamental scholar and writer who would later provide intellectual leadership within the NAACP during its first several decades. The founding documents of the Niagara Movement, drafted primarily by DuBois, articulated a plan to "push test cases in the courts" challenging Jim Crow cars and other practices.[4] To this end, the Niagara Movement's founders established a "legal department" to oversee nationally coordinated civil rights work.[5] Active in the department were lawyers such as W. Ashbie Hawkins, who would later play a key role at the local level in early NAACP litigation campaigns. The Niagara Movement successfully challenged unequal accommodations in interstate carriers before the Interstate Commerce

Commission and took part in other civil rights cases, but raising funds to finance these and other initiatives proved difficult. By 1909, the Movement had collapsed. A new interracial group, calling itself the "Committee on the Status of the Negro," emerged with the idea of organizing a new national civil rights organization to fill the hole left by the Niagara Movement's collapse. This group founded the National Association for the Advancement of Colored People in 1909.

As first constituted, the NAACP legal committee was composed of five white men. Four were lawyers; one was a former university professor. In 1913, the national legal committee merged with the legal advisory board of the New York Vigilance Committee, which functioned as the local NAACP branch in New York City. Arthur Spingarn, a wealthy Jewish lawyer, joined the legal committee at this point and became its chair, a position he retained until 1940. Arthur Spingarn had received his A.B., M.A., and LL.B. from Columbia University and belonged to both local bar associations that drafted and enforced legal ethics law. He maintained a successful Wall Street trusts and estates law practice, but his correspondence exhibits none of the worry about losing opportunities for paid legal work that other lawyers who were donating significant time to the NAACP displayed. Spingarn's family wealth allowed him the luxury of being a true "gentleman" lawyer, balancing his legal practice with a variety of artistic and pro bono interests.

The newly constituted legal committee had one African-American member, Deborcey Macon Webster. Webster was unusual among African-American lawyers during the period in that he, like most of his fellow legal committee members who were white, had a Wall Street practice. Webster's name appears as counsel in several divorce and estate cases, and he reputedly counted among his clients Lord and Taylor and Tiffany and Company. Although many of the lawyers who were pioneering creative public impact litigation techniques in civil rights cases at the time were African Americans, as we have seen, none of them was on the NAACP legal committee.

The NAACP was, from its earliest years, pursuing ambitious litigation strategies that differed markedly from traditional notions about how the litigation process should work. Whereas traditional notions assumed that legal disputes arose separate from and prior to the initiation of litigation, the NAACP's test case strategy depended on staging the best possible facts for the purpose of *creating* litigation. Whereas traditional models envisioned lawyers sitting in their offices waiting for clients to bring legal matters to their attention (or, more realistically, bringing in business by networking within circles of acquaintances), the NAACP wanted to widely proselytize new causes of action, in order to reach potential plaintiffs who were strangers to the legal world and would not otherwise have been aware of their rights. Finally, whereas traditional models viewed litigation as resulting in judgments that would primarily affect the rights of parties before the court in the present and short-term future, the NAACP designed its litigation to try to affect the legal rights of all African Americans, far into the future.

Traditional notions of litigation were embedded in the prevailing canons of legal ethics and related law. Some of the assumptions were apparent in the silences in the canons—the topics they did not address. The canons, for example, reflected almost no recognition that a lawyer's handling of a legal matter might have broad effects far into the future on persons or interests other than the immediate parties. The canons also failed to discuss the difficulties of reconciling competing interests among client groups. Other traditional assumptions were embedded in legal ethics prohibitions, including rules that barred lawyers from engaging in practices on which the NAACP's litigation model depended. These rules could have caused enormous difficulties for the NAACP's nontraditional litigation experiments. But its national legal committee did not balk at this problem because, I argue, its members had sufficient power within the local legal ethics enforcement community to adopt their own alternative interpretation of these rules without fear of censure.

The most problematic canon for the NAACP's litigation strategy was Canon 28, entitled "Stirring Up Litigation." Canon 28 defined it as "unprofessional for a lawyer to volunteer advice to bring a lawsuit, except in rare cases where ties of blood, relationship or trust make it his duty to do so." Canon 28 had common law and criminal counterparts. These rules fell generally under the rubric of statutes prohibiting "barratry" and took many forms, all aimed at prohibiting lawyers from "inciting" or encouraging litigation.

Other common law doctrines potentially of trouble to the NAACP included prohibitions against "maintenance" or "champerty," which were conceived of as offenses involving the "intermeddling" by a third party in a lawsuit by supporting or assisting a litigant in pursuing a legal claim. Still other legal ethics norms derived from the common law included prohibitions against intermediaries becoming involved in legal relationships and prohibitions against non-lawyers practicing law. These doctrines were not yet codified in 1908 canons, but were well accepted and cited as grounds for attorney discipline.

Such prohibitions against "stirring up" litigation, volunteering advice to bring a lawsuit, or acting as a third-party intermediary between a client and lawyer could have caused problems for the NAACP's test case litigation techniques. For example, organizing pairs of testers to descend on New York City's theaters to test compliance with antidiscrimination laws certainly gave rise to litigation where none would have existed otherwise. Similarly, the NAACP "created" a case when it sought out plaintiffs, planned a transaction, and then coordinated with the opposing side to orchestrate the facts leading to *Buchanan v. Warley*, as Holmes's unpublished dissent in that case complained. In these and many other instances, the NAACP's legal representatives conceived of and championed a dispute in order to bring about a lawsuit, conduct that at least technically ran afoul of rules prohibiting the encouragement or inciting of litigation. Similarly, the NAACP's national office's direction of lawyers in the field could have been viewed as intermeddling by a third party.

Canon 28 and related doctrines were not the only rules that could have caused problems for the NAACP's litigation experiments. Another was Canon 27, which sharply restricted lawyer advertising by providing that "solicitation of business by circulars or advertisements, or by personal communications, or interview, not warranted by personal relations, is unprofessional." This rule could have posed problems for the NAACP's many activities aimed at soliciting plaintiffs for its cases, including not only Brinsmade's and Nerney's practice of writing to strangers to offer the NAACP's legal services, but also NAACP legal representatives' practice of recruiting plaintiffs for test cases and speaking before groups to urge involvement with pending or anticipated litigation.

Local ethics committees had considered cases arising under Canons 27 and 28 and related rules, and had strictly interpreted these ethical strictures. Such cases ran the gamut from straightforward "ambulance chaser" cases to those presenting scenarios analogous to the activities of the NAACP. One such case involved the successful initiation of disciplinary proceedings against a lawyer who had advertised his services in part as follows:

> Samuel E. Neuman, a white lawyer, who is a colored man's friend . . . accident, criminal, and matrimonial actions a specialty. . . .

A local bar association had Mr. Neuman suspended from practice for this advertisement.[6] On its view, advertising oneself to be a white lawyer who would take on cases for African Americans violated both the Canons of Ethics and New York criminal law provisions barring advertisements to procure divorces.

In a similar case, a bar association disapproved of a lawyer placing such an advertisement in the program book for an event "given by citizens who are members of a single race to honor a distinguished man of their number."[7] The association reached a similar conclusion about lawyers advertising that they were willing to do legal work pro bono, disapproving the practice of a lawyer advertising that he would "handle a few deserving law cases without any fees."[8]

Local and national bar associations had also disapproved of practices in which lawyers served as advisors to groups or organizations established for the purpose of promoting individuals' abilities to pursue potential causes of legal action. In light of these precedents, the NAACP's similar strategies in finding and pursuing plaintiffs' claims in the civil rights arena could have presented substantial legal ethics difficulties.

These considerations, however, did not stop the NAACP national legal committee from pursuing its litigation agenda. This fact gives rise to the question of what legal committee members were thinking about the application of traditional legal ethics strictures to the activities of NAACP.

The further explanation required, I believe, is that the members of the legal committee were comfortable in the face of these canons because the motives they were considering were their own, and they felt assured that these motives were beyond reproach. Equally important, they were confident that their peers in the bar associations charged with interpreting and enforcing legal ethics rules would reach the same conclusions. In these men's views, the NAACP's legal work was exempt from the legal ethics strictures enforced against others because the NAACP was acting solely in the "public interest"—their very presence on its legal committee vouched for this fact.

The tendency to think of one's own actions as virtuous and beyond reproach is a common one, of course, but for the lawyers on the NAACP's first national legal committee this tendency received reinforcement in a Progressive Era mentality that viewed the public good as unitary and consensual. Absent from their world view was our contemporary understanding of pluralistic politics—of "cause" litigation as a form of "representation enforcement." To the optimistic early twentieth-century mind set of the lawyers on the legal committee, legal solutions to social injustice were ascertainable through study and analysis—one's perspective did not vary depending on one's position in society. This universalist understanding of social justice translated into a sense of confidence about the reach of legal ethics rules. The purpose of these rules was to prohibit "bad" conduct, but not to interfere with "good," altruistically motivated endeavors. That there could be anything suspect about the legal committee members being the judge of these questions when their own conduct was at issue simply would not have occurred to them.

The story of the NAACP's encounters with legal ethics dictates continues into later decades, as other scholars have explored. Beginning in the 1920s, a shift in the racial balance of the NAACP's staff and legal committee began to take place. In 1934, Charles Hamilton Houston joined the NAACP national staff as special counsel. In 1938, Thurgood Marshall took over this position. In this period, as Mark Tushnet was first to investigate, Houston and Marshall were deeply concerned about the tensions between the organization's nontraditional litigation strategies and traditional legal ethics rules prohibiting barratry, solicitation, and like offenses. Acutely aware of the NAACP's vulnerability to legal ethics charges, Houston and Marshall strived mightily, though ultimately unsuccessfully, to keep the organization out of legal ethics trouble.

In the 1950s and 1960s, in the aftermath of *Brown*, legal ethics law provided one of the main grounds for southern states' fierce legal assaults against the NAACP. Tushnet has described how, when that litigation reached the U.S. Supreme Court, a majority of justices first voted that the NAACP was liable for criminal penalties for its litigation techniques. A fortuitous interim change in the Court's membership led to reargument in the case, however, and a close majority of the Court finally decided, over a strong dissent by Justice Harlan, that the NAACP could not be prosecuted under states' legal ethics laws for solicitation, barratry, or related offenses, because its test case litigation strategies were a protected form of political activity under the First Amendment.[9] *Button* thus finally resolved, as a matter of federal constitutional law, important legal ethics questions about the NAACP's test case litigation strategies that the NAACP's first national legal committee had handled half a century before as a matter of an implicitly shared, scarcely articulated, informal practice norm.

Groundwork: Charles Hamilton Houston and the Struggle for Civil Rights[1]

Genna Rae McNeil[2]

In a deeply personal sense, Charles [Hamilton Houston] understood racism as an irrational, ubiquitous, external force that violated human beings, disrupted plans, bred bitterness, and destroyed dreams. Yet at his very center he also knew that he could not be defined by that kind of assault on his spirit. Charles had been jolted, but his future had not been wrenched from his control. With a new sense of authority he took his stand. The laws that buttressed stifling, oppressive practices and policies had to be fought immediately, directly, and persistently if the opportunities of America were to become options for black Americans. This he would do after law school.

The evening of 18 September 1919, Charles left home to begin his first year of Harvard Law School. Charles had selected Harvard because of its excellence, and his parents agreed that was where he ought to be. Although Harvard admitted a few academically qualified blacks, this did not mean Harvard was without racism. Harvard, as did Yale, Columbia, Princeton, and other private institutions with reputations for excellence and elitism, "discriminated against applicants on the basis of their nativity and religion.... As for blacks and other racial minorities, a handful were tolerated as long as they remained inconspicuous; too many blacks, it was feared, might change the 'complexion' of the campus." It would be important for Charles to be in a position to study without holding an outside job, the Houstons decided. All three used their resources to make this possible. Charles had some savings and his veterans' benefits. William had discretionary funds because of his successful practice, and Mary had ample earnings to assist her son from time to time because of her established reputation as a hairdresser and the occasional needlework she did for fees.

The sacrifices of his parents did not go unrewarded. Undaunted by the rigor and the pace at which Harvard legal education was conducted, Charles "soon proved himself to be an outstanding student despite the keen competition of a remarkable post-war student body." By the end of his first year, Charles had earned one A in contracts and another in property at a time when "[the] grading system [at Harvard Law School had] long been such that an 'A' [was] a mark attained by only a small percentage of the students." Thereafter he kept in his files a memento of his freshman year, an A examination in liabilities signed by a professor whom he admired greatly, Joseph H. Beale.

More comfortable in the Harvard setting during his second year, Charles moved into an apartment with a black classmate, Jesse Heslip. Often when the two left their 1556 Cambridge Avenue apartment they ran into a tall, lanky, but handsome and outgoing young first-year student on his way to the law school. Raymond Pace Alexander (who one day would become president of the National Bar Association) always had something to say or some idea to share.

It did not take long for Charles and other black students at Harvard to discover that there was a dividing line between whites and blacks and to observe that lines were drawn even with respect to such quasi-academic activities as law clubs. One did not come to Harvard and forget one's racial heritage.

Infrequent socializing, hard work, seriousness, and discipline in relation to his law studies despite obstacles or other obligations earned Charles five As and one B, "something which few students are able to do," Dean Roscoe Pound was eager to point out in a letter of recommendation for Charles. This honor average in his second-year work won Charles election to the editorial board of the *Harvard Law Review*. He became the first of his race to be so honored. Alexander remembered how proud the black students were when this happened, for Charles had not only done his own studying, he had also willingly assisted other students and particularly younger black students who looked to him "as a guide post." In talking with white students, black students found that their friend Charles Houston was considered by students and faculty alike "one of the brightest men on campus." "All of his teachers speak highly of him," Harvard dean and renowned scholar Roscoe Pound reported.

Charles's third year of law school, 1921–22, was incredibly busy. Editing volume thirty-five of the *Harvard Law Review,* one of the most prestigious journals of scholarship on the law, was both an honor and a heavy obligation. It required an extraordinary number of hours a week beyond regular studies. Researching legal questions, analyzing cases, evaluating articles written by law professors throughout the country, editing those accepted for publication, reviewing books, and writing lengthy "notes" on issues of law put Charles under constant pressure. Being the first and only black on the *Law Review* made it even more difficult. After a few months, Charles wrote his parents and was very candid: "The editors on the *Review* didn't want me on this fall; now all is one grand harmony. But I still go on my way alone. They know I am just as independent and a little more so, than they. My stock is pretty high around these parts. God help me against a false move."

Although Charles certainly had more than enough to do, he was persuaded that a law club for students excluded from the established clubs was an important part of the legal education. Black and Jewish students had none of the opportunities for outside legal activities such as investigating cases and researching legal authorities for cases being handled by practicing attorneys. White students were able to do these things because of a number of law clubs open to them and because they had constant support from attorneys in the Boston-Cambridge area. His *Law Review* status notwithstanding, Charles had never been approached about a law club. In fact, there had never been invitations extended to nonwhites or non-Protestants. Raymond Alexander, although he had a job and not as much time for activities beyond assigned studies, was sensitive to the significance of this exclusion. He and Charles spoke with other students and, according to Alexander, owing to Charles's efforts both on and off campus, eleven Harvard blacks succeeded in establishing a Dunbar Law Club (named for a Jewish lawyer in Boston who came in and acted as adviser to fourteen students of African and Jewish heritage).

With his [dean and mentor], Roscoe Pound, praising Charles's "excellent work" and stressing that "I should undoubtedly offer him a scholarship if he wishes to stay for another year," Charles Houston qualified for and won the Langdell scholarship. The financial award enabled Charles to study for his doctorate at Harvard in preparation for both practical and scholarly pursuits in law. Ranking in the top 5 percent of his class, Charles graduated with his LL.B. (Bachelor of Laws) *cum laude* (with honors).

In September 1922 Charles became a candidate for the degree of Doctor of Juridical Science. He again distinguished himself, making a 79 graduate average (75 was equivalent to an A). He took five courses, and professors consistently evaluated his work as excellent or superior. This was no small accomplishment, since these courses included Roman Law and Jurisprudence taught by Roscoe Pound, who had recently published *An Introduction to the Philosophy of Law,* and Administrative Law and Public Utilities under the instruction of Felix Frankfurter. With Frankfurter as an adviser, Charles prepared a doctoral thesis titled "Functional Study of the Requirements of Notice and Hearing in Governmental Action in the United States." Although he was a doctoral candidate from 1922 to 1923, Charles maintained contact with black students in the classes below him because he believed some unity was very necessary. He kept abreast of the underclassmen's progress through Raymond Alexander. When called upon, he met with them to protest racial discrimination in the freshman dormitory. Later he assured the younger students of his support and interest in their welfare by joining the newly created Nile Club (named after the river in Africa) for Harvard students of African descent.

While attending Harvard Law School, Charles Hamilton Houston was challenged to a new appreciation of teaching, particularly law teaching. For some reason (perhaps because of his father's emphasis on practice) it simply had not occurred to Charles before (during the years his father regularly spent evenings at Howard Law School) that the formal teaching of law was so important. But he knew better by 1922. He understood that if it were not for teachers and scholars, the law might never be more than precedent—judgments confirming the correctness of earlier judgments.

So it was that in the midst of his Harvard years Charles had pondered his commitment to the use of the law in the struggle for rights and in its relation to the education of lawyers. So it was that he decided it was important not only to practice but also to teach law, and therefore went on to do graduate work at Harvard and the University of Madrid.

Charles Houston, A.B., LL.B., S.J.D., accepted the dean of Howard University Law School's offer [to join the faculty] in 1924. Houston was extremely serious about his teaching at Howard. He worked the students as if he believed they had no choice about becoming first-rate lawyers. His distant cousin by marriage, William Henry Hastie Jr., who followed in Charles's footsteps, remembered that Charles knew that "in the world nobody's going to make allowances. . . . The world takes no excuses even for understandable shortcomings." Naturally, because of this, there were some students who had difficulty with Dr. Houston and others "who disliked him because of his toughness and unwillingness to accept the mediocre." Yet certainly everyone knew, as A. Mercer Daniel, a Howard Law graduate (1909) who later became a professor and law librarian, recalled,

"It was no easy task to study law when the student had to work eight hours during the day, as most of them did, and go to school from 5 P.M. to 9 P.M. three or more days a week." But Charles Houston asked no more of his students than he expected of himself, and for that reason, while "students were sometimes driven to swearing" at Houston "they also swore by him."

Charles Houston "was a law teacher all of his days. . . . Surrounded by an aura of extreme competence, his very presence in legal dialogue commanded respect. His wise advice, accompanied by explanation of analysis and synthesis . . . was a revelation in itself." He was "in the law school night and day." He devoted many hours, beyond his practice, to preparation for his courses, both when large numbers of LL.B. students were concerned and when a few graduate students were dependent on him for advanced study. He made detailed and extensive notes for jurisprudence lectures, and his examinations were indicative of the kind of critical thinking he expected of his students. In the jurisprudence course, for example, less than two months into the term, Houston presented his students with an examination of four questions about material he had covered. Two were "Compare the doctrine held and set forth by the nineteenth century historical school with those held by the nineteenth century analytical school" and "Sketch the philosophy of Kant." By December of the same year, he called on his students to analyze and discuss their lecture and reading materials in answers to such essay questions as "Which nineteenth century school of jurisprudence emphatically denied the power of conscious effort to change or modify the course of law, and why?" "Contrast the principles common to the various schools of sociological jurisprudence of the twentieth century with the principles common to the various schools of jurisprudence of the nineteenth century," and "Write a short discussion of the sociological aspect of capital punishment as applied under our present form of the administration of justice in criminal cases."

As Charles Houston developed his courses over the years, he increasingly insisted that the students think about the broad spectrum of societies, laws, and classes of people. In the course on administrative law he stressed the elements of expediency, social interest, and spheres of influence to illustrate the growing importance of administrative law to black people. Focusing on a related concern in a jurisprudence final exam for 1926, he asked, "Can you trace in the course any evidence of an extension of the protection of the law to wider and less-favored classes of men from the days of the Greeks to the present?" (He would in later years implement changes at Howard to assure that its program of legal education was consistent with an understanding of the interrelationships of race, class, and law in society. This meant offering standard courses but also providing a different emphasis and through standard courses and new courses focusing on the application of the law to the plight of black people.)

Charles Houston was concerned about both the training of excellent lawyers and their continuing education. This concern manifested itself in activities outside the firm and Howard Law School. When he was admitted to practice in the District of Columbia, there was no local bar association in which Houston or any other black attorney was welcome. The D.C. Bar Association, a private voluntary professional organization, excluded nonwhites. In 1925, Charles Houston, with fellow District lawyers who were black, including George E. C. Hayes, Louis R. Mehlinger, and J. Franklin Wilson, organized and incorporated the Washington Bar Association. The "objects" of the association as stated in the charter included "improvement or enhancement of professional skills as well as professional and citizenship responsibilities of the members . . . advancement of the science of jurisprudence and administration of justice; continued improvement of the standards of legal education; [and] encouragement of legal research." Consistent with these aims, Houston, for the Washington Bar Association, communicated with the D.C. Bar Association and such distinguished attorneys as Felix Frankfurter in an effort to have the D.C. bar library facilities open to black lawyers upon application.

After three years of local practice and teaching, Charles Houston wanted more involvement in the effort to train blacks for law and to encourage their participation in the struggle for liberty and the improvement of the quality of black life in the United States.

A specific conception of the role of the black lawyer provided the basis for Charles Houston's proposals regarding the future of Howard University Law School. He maintained that in addition to taking care of legal matters revolving around the individual client's personal problems with individuals or society,

[the] Negro lawyer must be trained as a social engineer and group interpreter. Due to the Negro's social and political condition . . . the Negro lawyer must be prepared to anticipate, guide and interpret his group advancement. . . . [Moreover, he must act as] business adviser . . . for the protection

of the scattered resources possessed or controlled by the group. . . . He must provide more ways and means for holding within the group the income now flowing through it.

Thus, Charles Houston proposed that the "immediate objective" of the school should be "to make itself a more efficient training school" in order to fulfill the race's need for "capable and socially alert Negro lawyers."

From 1935 to 1940, Charles Houston established himself as the "architect and dominant force of [the] legal program" of the NAACP. He devised the legal strategy, charted the course, began a program of political education for the masses, and handled the civil rights cases. He called on former students to accept the challenge of civil rights law and brought into the campaign eager, alert, and astute lawyers. He advised and directed black lawyers throughout the nation about their local campaigns against discrimination in education, transportation, jury exclusion, and denial of the vote. With his philosophy of social engineering, Houston was confident of his cause, his strategy, and his ability and that of his cohorts to engage in meaningful and successful struggle against segregation and inequality. Given an immoral America, the NAACP campaign required that lawyer-social engineers use the Constitution, statutes, and "whatever science demonstrates or imagination invents" both to foster and to order social change for a more humane society. This "Houstonian jurisprudence" pervaded all Houston did in the NAACP campaign.

The concurrent recognition, by Houston, of the NAACP's limited funds and personnel, the separate (i.e., segregated) schools in a large section of the nation and racial discrimination in educational systems throughout the entire United States, led Houston to make specific choices regarding the objectives and tactics of the NAACP's attack on discrimination in education and transportation. In his opinion there were three possible objectives. First, the direct, immediate result such as a court ordering admission of a student or equalization of salaries in a school system could be the object of litigation. Second, the NAACP could go to court realizing the high probability of losing but making use of the case to achieve beneficial byproducts such as calling attention to the evil, using the court as a forum, building public sentiment around the case, and creating a sufficiently strong threat for some temporary ameliorative action to be taken, for example, suing for admission of a student to a university and losing but having legislation for out-of-state scholarships put on the state's books.

Third, the NAACP could go to court in order to use the court as a laboratory to extract information. For example, explained Houston:

> We have very little money, very few trained investigators. But all we need is about $10.00, then we can file a case in court. Five dollars more, and we can bring the whole state education department into court with all its records, put each official on the stand under oath and wring him dry of information.

The "positionary tactics" devised by Houston—within the context of a basic strategy of judicial precedent—building for the erosion of the "separate but equal" principle and establishment of the unconstitutionality of segregation—constituted the program of the NAACP for the legal struggle against educational discrimination for the period of Houston's Special Counselship and subsequent years.

Serving Two Masters: Integration Ideals and Client Interests in School Desegregation Litigation[1]

Derrick A. Bell Jr.[2]

Largely through the efforts of civil rights lawyers, most courts have come to construe *Brown v. Board of Education* as mandating "equal educational opportunities" through school desegregation plans aimed at achieving racial balance, whether or not those plans will improve the education received by the children affected. To the extent that "instructional profit" accurately defines the school priorities of black parents in Boston and elsewhere, questions of professional responsibility are raised that can no longer be ignored:

How should the term "client" be defined in school desegregation cases that are litigated for decades, determine critically important constitutional rights for thousands of minority children, and usually involve major restructuring of a public school system? How should civil rights attorneys represent the often diverse interests of clients and class in school suits? Do they owe any special obligation to class members who emphasize educational quality and who probably cannot obtain counsel to advocate their divergent views? Do the political, organizational, and even philosophical complexities of school desegregation litigation justify a higher standard of professional responsibility on the part of civil rights lawyers to their clients, or more diligent oversight of the lawyer-client relationship by the bench and bar?

This article will review the development of school desegregation litigation and the unique lawyer-client relationship that has evolved out of it. It will not be the first such inquiry. During the era of "massive resistance," southern states charged that this relationship violated professional canons of conduct. A majority of the Supreme Court rejected those challenges, creating in the process constitutional protection for conduct that, under other circumstances, would contravene basic precepts of professional behavior. The potential for ethical problems in these constitutionally protected lawyer-client relationships was recognized by the American Bar Association Code of Professional Responsibility, but it is difficult to provide standards for the attorney and protection for the client where the source of the conflict is the attorney's ideals. The magnitude of the difficulty is more accurately gauged in a much older code that warns: "No servant can serve two masters: for either he will hate the one, and love the other; or else he will hold to one, and despise the other."

Client-Counsel Merger

The position of the established civil rights groups obviates any need to determine whether a continued policy of maximum racial balance conforms with the wishes of even a minority of the class. This position represents an extraordinary view of the lawyer's role. Not only does it assume a perpetual retainer authorizing a lifelong effort to obtain racially balanced schools; it also fails to reflect any significant change in representational policy from a decade ago, when virtually all blacks assumed that integration was the best means of achieving a quality education for black children, to the present time, when many black parents are disenchanted with the educational results of integration.

This malady may afflict many idealistic lawyers who seek, through the class action device, to bring about judicial intervention affecting large segments of the community. The class action provides the vehicle for bringing about a major advance toward an idealistic goal. At the same time, prosecuting and winning the big case provides strong reinforcement of the attorney's sense of his or her abilities and professionalism. Dr. Andrew Watson has suggested that "[c]lass actions . . . have the capacity to provide large sources of narcissistic gratification and this may be one of the reasons why they are such a popular form of litigation in legal aid and poverty law clinics." The psychological motivations which influence the lawyer in taking on "a fiercer dragon" through the class action may also underlie the tendency to direct the suit toward the goals of the lawyer rather than the client.

The questions of legal ethics raised by the lawyer-client relationship in civil rights litigation are not new. The Supreme Court's 1963 treatment of these questions in *NAACP v. Button*, however, needs to be examined in light of the emergence of lawyer-client conflicts which are far more serious than the premature speculations of a segregationist legislature.

The Court deemed NAACP's litigation activities "a form of political expression" protected by the First Amendment. Justice Brennan conceded that Virginia had a valid interest in regulating the traditionally illegal practices of barratry, maintenance, and champerty, but noted that the malicious intent which constituted the essence of these common law offenses was absent here. He also reasoned that because the NAACP's efforts served the public rather than a private interest, and because no monetary stakes were involved, "there is no danger that the attorney will desert or subvert the paramount interests of his client to enrich himself or an outside sponsor. And the aims and interests of NAACP have not been shown to conflict with those of its members and nonmember Negro litigants."

Joined by Justices Clark and Stewart, Justice Harlan expressed the view that the Virginia statute was valid. In support of his conclusion, Harlan carefully reviewed the record and found that NAACP policy required what he considered serious departures from ethical professional conduct. First, NAACP attorneys were required to follow policy directives promulgated by the National Board of Directors or lose their right to compensation. Second, these directives to staff lawyers covered many subjects relating to the form and substance of litigation. Third, the NAACP not only advocated litigation and waited for prospective litigants to come forward; in several instances and particularly in school cases, "specific directions were given as to the types of prospective plaintiffs to be sought, and staff lawyers brought blank forms to meetings for the purpose of obtaining signatures authorizing the prosecution of litigation in the name of the signer." Fourth, the retainer forms signed by prospective litigants sometimes did not contain the names of the attorneys retained, and often when the forms specified certain attorneys as counsel, additional attorneys were brought into the action without the plaintiff's consent. Justice Harlan observed that several named plaintiffs had testified that they had no personal dealings with the lawyers handling their cases and were not aware until long after the event that suits had been filed in their names. Taken together, Harlan felt these incidents justified the corrective measures taken by the State of Virginia.

Justice Harlan was not impressed by the fact that the suits were not brought for pecuniary gain. The NAACP attorneys did not donate their services, and the litigating activities did not fall into the accepted category of aid to indigents. But he deemed more important than the avoidance of improper pecuniary gain the concern shared by the profession, courts, and legislatures that outside influences not interfere with the uniquely personal relationship between lawyer and client. In Justice Harlan's view, when an attorney is employed by an association or corporation to represent a client, two problems arise:

> The lawyer becomes subject to the control of a body that is not itself a litigant and that, unlike the lawyers it employs, is not subject to strict professional discipline as an officer of the court. In addition, the lawyer necessarily finds himself with a divided allegiance—to his employer and to his client—which may prevent full compliance with his basic professional obligations.

Harlan conceded that "[t]he NAACP may be no more than the sum of the efforts and views infused in it by its members" but added a prophetic warning that "the totality of the separate interests of the members and others whose causes the petitioner champions, even in the field of race relations, may far exceed in scope and variety that body's views of policy, as embodied in litigating strategy and tactics."

Justice Harlan recognized that it might be in the association's interest to maintain an all-out, frontal attack on segregation, even sacrificing small points in some cases for the major points that might win other cases. But he foresaw that

> it is not impossible that after authorizing action in his behalf, a Negro parent, concerned that a continued frontal attack could result in schools closed for years, might prefer to wait with his fellows a longer time for good-faith efforts by the local school board than is permitted by the centrally determined policy of the NAACP. Or he might see a greater prospect of success through discussions with local school authorities than through the litigation deemed necessary by the Association. The parent, of course, is free to withdraw his authorization, but is his lawyer, retained and paid by petitioner and subject to its directions on matters of policy, able to advise the parent with that undivided allegiance that is the hallmark of the attorney-client relation? I am afraid not.

NAACP v. Button *in Retrospect*

The characterizations of the facts in *Button* by both the majority and the dissenters contain much that is accurate. As the majority found, the NAACP did not "solicit" litigants but rather systematically advised black parents of their rights under *Brown* and collected retainer signatures of those willing to join the proposed suits. The litigation was designed to serve the public interest rather than to enrich the litigators. Not all the plaintiffs were indigent, but few could afford to finance litigation intended to change the deep-seated racial policies of public school systems.

On the other hand, Justice Harlan was certainly correct in suggesting that the retainer process was often performed in a perfunctory manner and that plaintiffs had little contact with their attorneys. Plaintiffs frequently learned that suit had been filed and kept abreast of its progress through the public media. Although a plaintiff could withdraw from the suit at any time, he could not influence the primary goals of the litigation. Except in rare instances, policy decisions were made by the attorneys, often in conjunction with the organizational leadership and without consultation with the client.

The *Button* majority obviously felt that the potential for abuse of clients' rights in this procedure was overshadowed by the fact that Virginia enacted the statute to protect the citadel of segregation rather than the sanctity of the lawyer-client relationship. As the majority pointed out, litigation was the only means by which blacks throughout the South could effectuate the school desegregation mandate of *Brown.* The theoretical possibility of abuse of client rights seemed a rather slender risk when compared with the real threat to integration posed by this most dangerous weapon in Virginia's arsenal of "massive resistance." Most legal commentators reacted favorably to the majority's decision for precisely this reason. Justice Harlan was criticized by these writers for refusing to recognize the motivation for Virginia's sudden interest in the procedures by which the NAACP obtained and represented school desegregation plaintiffs.

Nevertheless, a few contemporary commentators found cause for sober reflection in Harlan's dissent. And even those writers who viewed the decision as necessary to protect the NAACP conceded that the majority had paid too little attention to Justice Harlan's conflict-of-interest concerns. As one writer noted, Justice Brennan's response—quoting from Justice Harlan's opinion in *NAACP v. Alabama* ex rel. *Patterson*[3] to the effect that NAACP interests were identical with those of its members—was inadequate. In the Alabama case the NAACP was attempting to protect the secrecy of its membership; the Court ruled that the organization had standing to defend the privacy and freedom of association of its members because they could not come forward without revealing their names and sacrificing the very rights at stake. But in school cases, as Justice Harlan observed in *Button,* an individual plaintiff might prefer a compromise which would frustrate attainment of the goals of the sponsoring groups.

The ABA Response

Button's recognition of First Amendment rights in the conduct of litigation led to subsequent decisions broadening the rights of other lay groups to obtain legal representation for their members. In so doing, these decisions posed new problems for the organized bar.

The American Bar Association, faced with the reality of group practice which it had long resisted, has attempted to adopt guidelines for practitioners; but the applicable provisions of its new *Code of Professional Responsibility* provide only broad and uncertain guidance on the issues of control of litigation and conflict of interest as they affect civil rights lawyers.

The *Code of Professional Responsibility* again and again admonishes the lawyer "to disregard the desires of others that might impair his free judgment." But the suggestions assume the classical commercial conflict or a third-party intermediary clearly hostile to the client. Even when the Code seems to recognize more subtle "economic, political or social pressures," the protection needed by civil rights clients is not provided, and the suggested remedy, withdrawal from representation of the client, is hardly desirable if the client has no available alternatives.

The market system mentality of the drafters of the *Code* surfaces in another provision suggesting that problems of control are less likely to exist where the lawyer "is compensated directly by his client." But solving the problem of control by relying on the elimination of compensation from a source other than the client was rejected in *Button.* All that remains is the warning that a person or group furnishing lawyers "may be far more concerned with establishment or extension of legal principles than in the immediate protection of the rights of the lawyer's individual client." The *Code* approach, urging the lawyer to "constantly guard against erosion of his professional freedom" and requiring that he "decline to accept direction of his professional judgment from any layman," is simply the wrong answer to the right question in civil rights offices where basic organizational policies such as the goals of school desegregation are often designed by lawyers and then adopted by the board or other leadership group. The NAACP's reliance on litigation requires that lawyers play a major role in basic policy decisions. Admonitions that the lawyer make no important decisions without consulting the client and that the client be fully informed of all relevant considerations are, of course, appropriate. But they are difficult to enforce in the context of complex, long-term school desegregation litigation where the original plaintiffs may have left the system and where the members of the class whose interests are at stake are numerous, generally uninformed, and, if aware of the issues, divided in their views.

Current ABA standards thus appear to conform with *Button* and its progeny in permitting the representation typically provided by civil rights groups. They are a serious attempt to come to grips with and provide specific guidance on the issues of outside influence and client primacy that so concerned Justice Harlan. But they provide little help where, as in school desegregation litigation, the influence of attorney and organization are mutually supportive, and both are so committed to what they perceive as the long-range good of their clients that they do not sense the growing conflict between those goals and the client's current interests. Given the cries of protest and the charges of racially motivated persecution that would probably greet any ABA effort to address this problem more specifically, it is not surprising that the conflict—which in any event will neither embarrass the profession ethically nor threaten it economically—has not received a high priority for further attention.

Idealism, though perhaps rarer than greed, is harder to control. Justice Harlan accurately prophesied the excesses of derailed benevolence, but a retreat from the group representational concepts set out in *Button* would be a disaster, not an improvement. State legislatures are less likely than the ABA to draft standards that effectively guide practitioners and protect clients. Even well-intentioned and carefully drawn standards might hinder rather than facilitate the always difficult task of achieving social change through legal action. And too stringent rules could encourage officials in some states to institute groundless disciplinary proceedings against lawyers in school cases, which in many areas are hardly more popular today than they were during the massive resistance era.

Client involvement in school litigation is more likely to increase if civil rights lawyers themselves come to realize that the special status accorded them by the courts and the bar demands in return an extraordinary display of ethical sensitivity and self-restraint. The "divided allegiance" between client and employer which Justice Harlan feared would interfere with the civil rights lawyer's "full compliance with his basic professional obligation" has developed in a far more idealistic and thus a far more dangerous form. For it is more the civil rights lawyers' commitment to an integrated society than any policy directives or pressures from their employers which leads to their assumptions of client acceptance and their condemnations of all dissent.

From Ethics to Politics: Confronting Scarcity and Fairness in Public Interest Practice[1]

Gary Bellow and Jeanne Kettleson[2]

Public Interest Lawyers: Special Features of Their Practice

During the past five years, the practice of public interest law has become a fact of the American legal system. Its emergence reflects and responds to longstanding tensions between a lawyer's obligation to clients and to the public generally. As more groups and interests seek representation within the legal system, lawyers find themselves at the center of conflicts that mirror deep-seated differences within American society. Public interest practice thus poses dilemmas that are embedded in the profession's general efforts to make legal services more widely available to a heterogeneous and often divided population. In the next decade the entire bar, not just one segment of it, will have to confront the issues of professional responsibility that the public interest lawyer has begun to bring into focus.

Our purpose in this article is to explore a number of the most persistent ethical dilemmas in public interest practice and to compare them and the choices public interest lawyers make in response to them with similar problems that confront the entire profession.

To place these ethical concerns in the foreground we have tried to relate them to a number of distinctive characteristics of public interest work. Identified from this vantage point, a public interest lawyer is an attorney who provides subsidized legal services, on a full- or almost full-time basis, to those who would otherwise be under- or unrepresented. That is, public interest law is practiced by a group of lawyers specifically paid to devote most or all of their efforts to the "legally disadvantaged," often in ways that seem to generate particular concerns in the bar and special conflicts in their relations with clients and others.

The Ethical Issues: Special Dilemmas of Public Interest Practice

The most troubling ethical problems for public interest lawyers lie in two general areas. The first relates to the enormous gap between what service is presently available and what would be necessary to provide full representation to those who are presently without it. Public interest lawyers must decide, according to some ethically justifiable criteria, who gets what sort of assistance and what obligations are owed to those who are turned away or not reached.

The second set of problems arises from the aggressive stance that the Code requires of all lawyers delivering legal services. Here the question is whether, in the context of a system in which outcomes too often depend upon the financial resources of the parties, the Code's norms permit a *subsidized* lawyer to adequately protect seriously disadvantaged clients and yet avoid unfairly harming opponents. Although there are other ethical issues, these two sources of conflict seem to highlight the dilemmas that the public interest practitioner both confronts and poses for the rest of the bar.

Viewing these problems as paradigmatic, how do we begin to address the choices they entail? To what extent are the dilemmas posed by scarce resources and differential circumstances resolvable within the profession's longstanding commitment to the adversary system? To what extent is our present conception of the role and functions of law and lawyers as much a problem as a potential solution?

The commentators and lawyers who regard the law and its current system of dispute processing as fundamentally sound, albeit flawed, see a much wider distribution of lawyers and legal services as the solution to the ethical problems we have identified. More lawyers would respond to those interests and groups now excluded from the system, and could have an effect on the very conditions that have prevented their being more fairly treated in the past. From this perspective, it is argued that public interest advocacy is an important force in making the existing legal system both more equitable and more accessible.

Unfortunately, despite our desire to see legal resources for the unrepresented expand, such suggestions do not come to grips with the nature of the ethical dilemmas the public interest lawyer encounters. The legal disadvantages with which public interest lawyers deal are rooted in deeply entrenched patterns of inequality and exclusion. Whether linked to poverty, caste, and race, or to the inability of a diffuse majority to bear the costs of aggregating their interests, they are inherent in existing social, political, and institutional arrangements. Lawyers, even many working together, are unlikely to make large inroads on these conditions. Unfortunately, the problems of scarcity and fairness are likely to be with us for a long time.

Moreover, neither public interest lawyers nor the bar have fully confronted the question whether an adversarial, highly complex, professionalized system of dispute resolution will not, in the long run, intensify the legal disadvantages that public interest law is supposed to ameliorate. Making adversarial legal services available to all in this large, heterogeneous, and very unequal society may exacerbate the very problems of unfairness and inequality that access is ultimately intended to resolve. As Sargent Shriver once remarked, "More lawyers is a long way from more justice."[3]

It seems almost contradictory to suggest that the problem of scarcity cannot be satisfactorily resolved by more lawyers. If everyone in need could obtain the services of a competent attorney, public interest lawyers and the bar generally would no longer be caught in the bind of having to choose between more and better legal services for a few—the apparent preference of the Code—or diminished service for many.

The problem is that such a view does not recognize what is involved in the delivery of legal service. First, a large number of human difficulties can be dealt with, in some way, by law and its institutions. The problems currently handled by lawyers, especially public interest lawyers, are in some sense constructed by them and represent only a small fraction of the universe of possibilities. Similarly, what people perceive as a legal problem is a function of the structure and quantity of services that are available. In other words, definitions of legal need are not static; they are elastic and have a tendency to expand as potential beneficiaries see lawyers as capable of responding to their problems. As has been demonstrated in legal services to the poor, demand for services will increase to the limits of the available supply.

Second, even if demand for legal services remained constant at some identifiable level, it would not be possible or desirable to expand the bar to meet the need. A tenfold increase in the existing public interest bar would just begin to equalize the number of lawyers available to the very poor and the rest of the population. It would require something on the order of a tenfold increase in the size of the *entire* bar to begin to provide the whole population with the same legal services that the affluent presently enjoy. Even the most sanguine proponents of increased services do not contemplate expansion on this scale. The costs would be extravagant in the face of other social needs and priorities, and the development of a bulging class of professional advocates (imagine four million as compared to the present four hundred thousand lawyers) is not a very attractive or promising social vision.

Thus, there will necessarily be a permanent condition of scarcity in the availability of lawyers. The ethical dilemmas involved in deciding who will get what sort of service remain. At the same time, under present social and economic arrangements, laws will continue to be passed in response to the needs and claims of a variety of groups and interests. Given the reliance on the bar as the nation's primary enforcement institution, the gap between the law as written and existing practices will continue to widen, exacerbating what many observers of the American legal system now recognize as an enforcement crisis.

In the face of such limits, the private bar's willingness to permit the quantity, nature, and quality of service to be determined by the clients' ability to pay becomes increasingly untenable. The question of what justifies the disadvantaged getting little or no assistance might be followed with the question of what justifies the advantaged getting so much.

The problems of fairness are equally unresolvable by merely increasing the availability of counsel. The Code's ideals of partisanship and loyalty will always be inadequate to protect disadvantaged clients or to prevent harm to disadvantaged opponents, witnesses, or others. Even if legal assistance were enormously expanded, the profession's existing ethical norms offer no possibility of resolving this paradox.

The basis for this rather pessimistic assertion lies again in the social and economic context in which legal services are delivered. First, attempts to eliminate legal disadvantages in the present system inevitably generate counterpressures. Quite apart from the availability of lawyers, the "haves" invariably possess significant advantages in most of the available forums. They can (1) better withstand the delays that flow from procedural complexity; (2) invest in long-term research and preparation for recurring types of cases; (3) spend time, money, and effort influencing the framework of procedural and substantive rules; (4) take risks in individual cases and balance the losses off over time; (5) litigate uneconomic claims to protect or establish a rule; (6) invest in the implementation of favorable legal results; and (7) assure the loyalty and accountability of counsel by arranging long-term relationships. Even if a "have not" has a fully subsidized lawyer who can obtain many of these advantages (i.e., research and background preparation, potential knowledge of the system, ability to litigate uneconomic claims), others are unattainable. Public interest clients, for example, often do not have the resources to implement, monitor, or otherwise take advantage of litigation gains. Thus, parties who begin in unequal circumstances, even though they have equal access to an unbiased legal process, end up unequal.

Second, even if it became possible to enforce any existing body of rules equally, those rules would soon be changed. We are living in a time when social forces are producing expanded entitlements and lessened enforcement. If enforcement were effectively expanded, it is likely that entitlements would contract to reflect existing distributions of wealth and power. For example, when public interest lawyers were successful in suits to expand the bases of eligibility for public assistance, many states reacted by decreasing general benefit levels. In the long run, public interest lawyers alone cannot win such games of leapfrog for their clients. Political organization and activity by disadvantaged groups will be necessary to maintain, expand, and assure full implementation of any benefits and rights that lawyers might establish. If fairness is properly equated with some vision of these entitlements and the relationships they entail, lawyers can only play a marginal role in its realization.

Finally, adherence to adversarial norms becomes increasingly difficult in a system in which conflict is not mediated by a variety of other institutions. More lawyers, representing more people, more aggressively, on such controversial issues as welfare, race relations, or environmental concerns that reduce employment opportunities, could produce an unacceptable level of social conflict and division. The proponents of vastly expanded legal services have not come to terms with the extent to which our adversary system depends on widespread non-use, or avoidance. The system presently works because there is constricted access and substantial amounts of accommodation and private ordering. In the absence of these, the effective functioning of the adversary system would be possible only if there were a broad base of social harmony and cooperativeness. Unless increased access to legal services is also accompanied by a lessening of the inequalities that stand in the way of a more harmonious, accommodative society, the amount of conflict that results will either press present adjudicatory institutions beyond their capacities, or intensify the already powerful pressures against adversary behavior that operate so much to the disadvantage of the poor, the unorganized, the inexperienced, and the vulnerable.

When "more" means more courts, lawyers, and adversary relations, more may not be better at all. Such unattractive alternatives suggest that the bar as a whole might well begin to search for a different vision of its role and function.

Skepticism about expanding legal representation in an adversary system leads naturally to proposals to modify the system. Why not develop alternative, less adversary dispute processing institutions? Such suggestions, reflecting a vision of more cooperative, informal, and in some respects particularized modes of dispute processing seem very attractive. A legal system whose procedural values include inquiry and information sharing, mutuality, and the acceptance of responsibility by lawyer and client for the consequences of their actions might be much preferable to the advocate's present reliance on concealment, or the assumption in case of doubt that any other party or person is a potential enemy.

Such aspirations seem to shape the content and direction of many of the most recent proposals for reform of the legal system. Nevertheless our reaction is skeptical. The virtues of cooperation and informality notwithstanding, this vision may be as dysfunctional in the short run as the adversary model is in the long run. Without a substantial decrease in inequality and stratification, an informal, non-rule-bound system might well leave the weak and powerless more, rather than less, vulnerable. Too many proposals for changes of the sort we have just sketched are put forth as if caste and class were not formidable elements of this society. It is useful to consider carefully whether advocates and mediators are likely to remain "deprofessionalized" in such a competitive culture, and what the consequences would be of mediating a dispute between a well-funded, sophisticated party and his or her uneducated, unskilled opponent. Psychological manipulation and control are no less coercive because they are subtle. We have a similar reaction to those who believe the solution to the excesses and dysfunctions of the adversary system lies in making lawyers and clients more "sensitive," "aware," or "interpersonally competent." The competitive, aggressive behavior of many lawyers is as much a result of existing institutional arrangements, role demands, and socialization patterns as of personal proclivities. Lawyers who are more sensitive to the needs of parties other than their clients are apt to be exploited in a competitive system. Making the provision of legal services more responsive to concrete human needs, emotions, and values will require changes not only in relationships, but also in those structural features that foster undesirable patterns of behavior.

The public interest lawyer, whether serving environmental groups, the poor, or other interests, has set the stage for a different discussion of professional ethics and responsibility than has occurred thus far—one that sees increased equality, both substantive and procedural, as a legitimate and crucial concern of the bar. In so doing, these lawyers have begun to confront ethical choices for which present conceptions of the lawyer's role provide only partial answers.

The public interest practitioner is not more or less likely to solve these problems than other members of the bar who are willing to recognize the impact of social and economic inequalities on the legal system, but the problems of fairness and scarcity are daily experiences in the lives of lawyers who serve the disadvantaged. Their efforts to cope with the hard choices these problems entail may deepen our understanding of this emerging segment of the bar and, more importantly, of the moral and political issues the profession itself has too long ignored.

Contemporary Critical Approaches

Chapter 4

Clinical Approaches

In chapter 3, we observed the tension between the attorney's duty of zealous representation of her client and her duty to the public interest. We watched this tension play out in the development of one important model for public interest law practice in the United States. That model, developed by the NAACP and used again by lawyers involved in the poverty law movement of the 1960s and 1970s, seeks to develop and litigate *test cases*— or cases with the most *public impact* potential—as a way of having the most "bang for the buck," so to speak, given public interest organizations' limited litigation resources. We read an excerpt of one of the articles that defined the new field of critical legal ethics inquiry, Derrick Bell's provocative piece charging the NAACP's lawyers, in the post-*Brown* remedy phase of its school desegregation litigation campaign, with being insufficiently attentive to their clients' desires. Bell argues that it was ethically improper for these lawyers to pursue a uniform school desegregation model designed to advance certain lawyer-defined ideological goals, rather than to pursue the goals clients define in particular communities. In the Bellow and Charn excerpt we saw another example, this time from the poverty law movement, of writing exploring the legal ethics issues involved in balancing the interests of particular clients and concerns about the public interest. In this chapter, we examine how these themes play out in the development of several related contemporary lawyering movements that grew out of the historical models highlighted in chapter 3.

Section A, "Client-Centered/Collaborative Lawyering," presents several leading examples of clinical law scholarship. The clinical law movement can be characterized by its (re)turn to an emphasis on the client's proper role in shaping and defining her experience with the law. The movement challenges the dominant understanding, incorporated in ABA Model Rule 1.2, that there should be a division of labor between the lawyer and the client in planning the client's experience. Under Rule 1.2, the lawyer "shall abide by a client's decisions concerning the objectives of representation" and "shall consult with the client as to the means by which they are to be pursued" (ABA Model Rule 1.2[a]). The clinical law movement eschews this divide between client-dictated *goals* and lawyer-designed *means* of pursuing them. Its members espouse various versions of a lawyering ethics that seeks as far as possible to be *client-centered or client-collaborative* in *all* aspects of the representation process.

In his important article, Robert Dinerstein explains the client-centered lawyering model and analyzes its importance. He evaluates this approach in comparison to more traditional legal ethics models, which he argues do not go far enough in being client-centered. Finally, Dinerstein defends client-centered lawyering against William Simon's *ethical discretion* model, which we examine further in chapter 5.

Many clinical law professors have explored the client-centered model through a genre of critical writing known as *narrative scholarship*. This genre uses storytelling as a means of exposing subtle or submerged understandings inherent in stories about individuals' life experiences in the law. Clinical law professors use detailed stories about actual cases—with facts altered in an attempt to protect client confidentiality[1]—to explore the ethical subtleties of striving to develop a client-centered approach. By virtue of the kinds of clients law school clinics typically represent, these scholars most often explore stories involving clients who are poor and politically and legally disenfranchised. A major theme emerging from this literature thus explores the ethical dimensions of lawyering across social divides of socioeconomic status, race, ethnicity, and other social identity characteristics.

Section A features two such reflective narratives. In a classic example of this literature, Lucie White, a former clinical law professor (whom, you may remember, we read in chapter 1), tells the story of a client she encountered in her early days as a legal aid lawyer in the South. White reflects on the complexities of trying to be a client-centered lawyer across divides of class and race. Her client appears to agree with a legal strategy White recommends, but then takes a different direction in her welfare hearing, for complex reasons having to do with the relations of power in the community, the hearing room, and the lawyer-client relationship.

In another genre classic, Binny Miller looks at the advantages of using the client's perspectives in developing the *theory of the case*. In a twist at the end of her article, however, Miller realizes how differences between her own social identity and that of her clinic students gives her insights into the client's situation that her students do not seem to share. Miller again leaves us with questions about how to lawyer effectively across gaps in social perspective—is it possible to do so? and, if so, what kinds of practices aimed at spanning social differences are required?

Finally, Michelle Jacobs, drawing on a host of empirical literature from a variety of counseling professions (including many source citations stripped from the excerpt presented here), directly raises the question of what it takes to lawyer effectively across race and class divisions in contemporary society.

Section B turns to the "Community/Rebellious Lawyering" model, which takes issue with some aspects of the client-centered model for being too individualistic in focusing on particular clients rather than whole communities. This turn emphasizes the importance of lawyering with a deep appreciation of clients' relationships to particular communities. In an excerpt from his field-defining book, Gerald López articulates some aspects of his vision for such a community-based approach. López again uses storytelling as his primary vehicle, but in this instance relies on fictional constructs or composites designed to epitomize particular lawyering approaches.

Two final excerpts use real-life examples to pursue the insights of the community-based lawyering model from particular practice locations. Christine Zuni Cruz discusses what difference a community-based model makes in a student clinic serving native American clients. Cruz is both a member of and a lawyer providing legal services to this community, and she points out some of the advantages of possessing deep insights into its values and traditions.

Victor Hwang, a practicing public interest lawyer, describes a multifaceted campaign to restore welfare benefit eligibility on behalf of the Hmong, an Asian group that faced persecution after the end of the Vietnam War. Hwang responds to the call of the community-based lawyering movement for the development of creative lawyering strategies responsive to new views of communities' needs. The multifaceted campaign he describes involves community education, organizing, political campaigning, lobbying, and the highly strategic use of court and administrative hearing systems, all with the goal of "changing the narrative" about the Hmong's entitlement to continued welfare benefits.

Questions for Discussion and Reflection

1. Do you think that the client-centered model Dinerstein discusses is as applicable to lawyering for powerful clients as it is to lawyering for relatively powerless ones? Why or why not?

2. Is Miller's argument that the client's perspectives can and should be used to construct case theory undercut to some extent by the twist she offers at the end of her story, when she comes to understand the client's case quite differently once she meets him and realizes that she shares with him a sometimes hidden identity characteristic? Does Miller run the risk of imposing stereotypes in trying to imagine the client's experience across divides of race and class?

3. What ingredients do White and Miller seem to imply are necessary to be a *good* lawyer across social identity divides? Do you agree?

4. What does Jacobs's data about the problems of psychological counseling across race differences suggest about lawyer-client relationships in a society in which race and ethnicity often have salient significance? What does this say about the ability to provide adequate lawyering for the many members of communities whose members are disproportionately underrepresented in the ranks of lawyers and law students? (Is this an argument for the importance of affirmative action in law school admissions?)

5. Do you agree with López's arguments that "no group is ever *absolutely* powerless in any relationship" and that even relatively powerless people retain "the capacity to resist victimization and subordination and to reverse its tendencies"? Contrast this view to Bellow's and Charn's views about low-income clients and their abilities to fight the legal system. What do you think might account for any differences you see in the authors' perspectives?

6. In using many examples of privileged white lawyers doing poverty law work, López seems to be acknowledging that many legal services lawyers will come from such backgrounds. What ingredients do López, Cruz, and Hwang imply are necessary for such lawyers to be adequately prepared to be "good"—where that term means both ethically and technically competent, as discussed in the reader's introduction—lawyers in such set-

tings? Do you agree with these writers' assessments? Are they realistic? Do they leave out important ingredients or include ingredients that are not necessary?

7. Based on your reading below, do you think that client-centered or collaborative lawyering has somewhat different emphases from community-based or rebellious lawyering? If so, what are the differences? What commonalities do you see in the two approaches?

8. In taking into account considerations of the community and its future rather than the individually defined interests and desires of individual clients, as Cruz argues, aren't we returning to a version of the public interest lawyering model espoused by lawyers such as Brandeis, who wanted to act as a "lawyer for the situation"? Doesn't Cruz's model confront some of the same problems in balancing individual and community interests? What is different about Cruz's model and Brandeis's? Is it significant that the community interests Cruz considers are those of a subordinate rather than a dominant group?

9. What should a lawyer in Cruz's situation do in a case in which a client does not endorse her community's traditional values?

10. In the campaign Hwang describes, those making strategy decisions apparently defined the relevant client community as the Hmong, rather than, for example, all immigrants or all welfare recipients. Was this an ethically appropriate decision? Why or why not? Were these strategists pursuing "the public interest"? What about the needs of the broader class whose welfare benefits were cut off?

11. Does community lawyering raise the same types of conflict-of-interest questions as are raised in lawyering for individuals whose interests may conflict with the common good? Why or why not?

12. Hwang acknowledges that the lawyers involved in the community-lawyering campaign he describes violated many traditional legal ethics dictates, by, for example, "encouraging the filing of appeals without apparent legal merit, counseling masses of clients via radio and videotaped presentations, representing clients in hearings whom we had never previously

met, and allowing clients to testify without our control or objection." He states that they did so because "we felt that as political and community-based attorneys, this strategy would best serve the needs of the client community." What do you make of this view? Would your views about the ethics of swamping administrative processes with nonmeritorious appeals be different if lawyers for corporate clients were using this strategy? Why or why not?

Client-Centered Counseling: Reappraisal and Refinement[1]

Robert D. Dinerstein[2]

Traditional legal counseling reflects an absence of meaningful interchange between lawyer and client. The client comes to the lawyer with some idea about his problem. The lawyer asks questions designed to adduce the information necessary to place the client's problem within the appropriate conceptual box. At the proper time, he counsels the client by essentially conducting a monologue: the lawyer tells the client something of the nature of his actions on the client's behalf and then advises the client about the course of action he recommends. The lawyer may go into great detail about the rationale for his advice. Alternatively, she may provide a relatively terse recitation of technical advice and let the client decide how to proceed. The lawyer is concerned with the client's reaction to his advice but tends not to value client input, for he believes that the client has little of value to contribute to the resolution of his legal problem. Lawyer and client are likely to talk at, rather than with, each other. Any assurance that the lawyer provides to the client—and it could be substantial—is likely to be based on the client's perception that the lawyer is "taking care of matters" rather than on a belief that the lawyer has truly tried to understand the client as a whole, complex person.

In general, the traditional legal counseling model assumes that clients should be passive and delegate decision-making responsibility to their lawyers; that ineffective professional service is relatively rare; that professionals give disinterested service and maintain high professional standards; that effective professional services are available to all who can pay; and that professional problems tend to call for technical solutions beyond the ken of laypersons.

Client-centered counseling is a critical component of client-centered lawyering. Client-centered counseling may be defined as a legal counseling process designed to foster client –decision-making. Its goal is not only to provide opportunities for clients to make decisions themselves but also to enhance the likelihood that the decisions are truly the client's and not the lawyer's. To accomplish these goals, client-centered counselors must attend to the means they employ in the counseling process, as well as the end of client decision-making they attempt to achieve.

Clinical teachers' widespread acceptance of the client-centered counseling model has tended to submerge the debate about the desirability of the client-centered approach in general. Advocates for client-centered approaches have made a number of arguments in support of the concept, but some of these arguments have been less than fully developed. And while many clinical teachers have accepted client-centeredness wholeheartedly, legal commentators writing from different perspectives have challenged at least some of the assumptions underlying the concept.

The core argument supporting client decision-making is that it enhances the client's individual autonomy. Autonomy, or self-determination, means that a person can choose and act freely, according to her own life plan. There are many possible definitions of autonomy, but the capacity to make choices is a key component of the concept. Recognizing a person's autonomy is essential to according respect to that person; respect for autonomy is a cornerstone of liberal legal theory and of the American political system. It can be justified for its intrinsic value and on utilitarian grounds.

A person's autonomy can be compromised in a number of ways. One such way is through paternalism, which operates in counterpoint to autonomy. Pure paternalistic actions, which by definition are taken to benefit the person(s) whose will is being overborne, are problematic precisely because they deny people their fundamental right to make their own decisions in their own ways, even if those decisions could somehow objectively be shown to be wrong.

At least in American society, law plays an important function in facilitating an individual's ability to function autonomously. As mediators and interpreters of the law, lawyers are the conduits through which people can express their autonomy. By creating mechanisms that empower their clients to make their own decisions in their own way, client-centered lawyers contribute to their clients' autonomy.

Few scholars dispute the importance of autonomy as a value. The dispute is over (1) the extent to which other values, such as the moral autonomy of the lawyer or third parties, may limit the exercise of autonomy, and (2) whether a client-centered model of lawyering is the best route to maximizing autonomy. At this point, two preliminary observations are in order. First, in examining models of client counseling the question is less whether client-centeredness fosters client immorality than whether it is any more likely to do so than other client-counseling models. Second, it is not a necessary part of the autonomy argument for client-centeredness that a client's autonomy can never be overridden. Rather, if autonomy is an important value, client-centered counseling is desirable if it furthers autonomy and is especially desirable if it tends to further it more than other client-counseling models, so long as it does not unduly trench upon other important values.

Like all social relationships, the lawyer-client relationship does not exist in a vacuum. It is subject to political, social, and economic trends in society. Client-centered lawyering must be placed in the particular political and historical context in which it arose. The origins of client-centered lawyering are inextricably bound up with the development of "modern" clinical legal education itself. Modern clinical legal education developed in the crucible of the political activism of the 1960s and early 1970s. Many of the proponents of the client-centered approach were former legal services or public interest lawyers who entered academia as clinical law teachers. The experience of these lawyer-teachers with poor clients had a profound effect on their assessment of problems in the lawyer-client relationship and their proposed solutions. In particular, these teachers' goals of empowering politically disadvantaged clients provided a rationale for client-centered practice on behalf of poor people.

The political pedigree of client-centered lawyering is of more than historical interest. The realization that it arose out of a law practice that dealt primarily with poor people is essential to understanding the concept as it has developed. Yet when clinical teachers write about clinical education issues today, few stress the political underpinnings of client-centered approaches. Rather, it is Critical Legal Studies adherents and others concerned with developing more explicitly political law practices who have stressed the need for greater client participation in the lawyer-client relationship. Indeed, some of these writers, far from embracing developing notions of client-centeredness, forcefully criticize the concept. But if poor and disadvantaged clients needed empowerment in the 1960s and 1970s, it can hardly be contended that they need it less so in the 1990s.

Does its historical relationship to poverty law mean that client-centered counseling should be restricted to representation of poor people? I do not take the argument nearly that far. For one thing, middle-class clients may be significantly disempowered by the legal system. Power, after all, is relative. Middle-class white women may have a great deal of power in society at large, but may feel essentially powerless if locked into an abusive domestic situation. Middle-class white parents who are parents of children with mental disabilities may be rendered helpless trying to get a recalcitrant school system to provide statutorily required educational services. Even the businessperson may be powerless to effectuate his goals because of his adversary's personal and financial power. I do not mean to imply that these situations are all equivalent, or that they raise the same political issues as access of poor people to the legal system. But if the political argument for client-centeredness is an argument about the redistribution of power, one must recognize that power can be redistributed in any number of ways.

Certainly, to the extent that empowerment of clients provides a strong argument in favor of client-centeredness, advocates for the concept must consider the nature of the client and specifically whether the clients in question are so powerful as not to need further empowerment. For such clients, political empowerment is not a compelling argument for a client-centered approach to counseling.

Does client-centered counseling in fact contribute to empowering poor and otherwise disadvantaged clients? There are a variety of ways to approach answering this question. Clients empowered in their relationship with their lawyer might carry over that sense of power to their relationship with bureaucracies and other power structures. Furthermore, if client-centered counseling values the client's individual experience by providing an outlet for its expression within the lawyer-client relationship, clients could be expected to have more opportunities to assert themselves authentically within whatever system they are challenging (or being challenged by) by being able to insist to their lawyers that their perspective gets heard. Yet client-centered counseling is not a panacea. It does not necessarily address the concerns of some that focusing on legal rights for poor people diverts their attention from the kind of political organizing likely to provide the only hope for fundamental change in their circumstances. And it may be less effective than the critical lawyering techniques that some advocate in redressing fundamental economic and political inequities. Despite these concerns, however, the client-centered lawyer's commitment to client dialogue, non-routine handling of client problems, and the client's significant role in contributing solutions to his legal problem would be salutary developments in poverty law practice.

Some legal commentators argue that either the Model Code of Professional Responsibility ("Model Code") or the Model Rules of Professional Conduct ("Model Rules") or both solidly support a client-centered approach to lawyering. Upon close examination, these arguments are unpersuasive. At best, the Model Code and Model Rules support client-centeredness at a level of generality that is essentially meaningless. At worst, they are consistent with and therefore perpetuate fairly traditional conceptions of the lawyer-client relationship.

Model Code Ethical Consideration 7-7 provides support for client-centered lawyering insofar as it indicates that it is the client's exclusive right to make decisions except "in certain areas of the representation not affecting the merits of the cause or substantially prejudicing" the client's rights, in which case the lawyer may make decisions on his own.[3] But the kinds of decisions that EC 7-7 reserves to the client are basic to the representation; they hardly extend to the full range of decisions that the client-centered lawyer would consider to be the client's. EC 7-8's discussion of the role of the lawyer in fostering the client's decision-making also emphasizes the client's primacy in determining the objectives of the representation, even as it recognizes that the lawyer has interests in the lawyer-client relationship worth protecting. But these Ethical Considerations are aspirational, not mandatory. The mandatory Disciplinary Rules are considerably less clear on the issue of the relative authority of lawyer and client.

The only real difference between the Model Rules and the Model Code in allocating decision-making authority is that the dismantling of the dichotomy between ethical considerations and disciplinary rules resulted in an arguably stronger commitment to the decision-making priorities formerly consigned to the hortatory ECs. Surely, though, to describe the Model Rules as client-centered deprives that term of any significant meaning.

Perhaps the most that can be said is that the Model Rules' vagueness will force lawyers and clients to struggle toward accommodation of their different interests in the lawyer-client relationship. Yet it seems at least as likely that those traditional lawyers who retain benighted views of the appropriate division of decision-making responsibility between them and their clients will interpret the Model Rules as allowing them to proceed as they always have. The Model Code and Model Rules may not provide much sustenance to critics of client-centered approaches, but they also provide scant support for its advocates.

The most basic criticism of client-centered lawyering questions its underlying premise, that it is the primary duty of lawyers to foster client autonomy. William Simon is the most articulate spokesperson for the autonomy critique of client-centeredness. In his most recent article, "Ethical Discretion in Lawyering,"[4] he argues that in civil cases lawyers should have discretion to refrain from pursuing a client's legitimate, legal goals if to do so would frustrate underlying goals of justice or fairness. Of particular relevance for the client-centeredness debate, Simon asserts that lawyers should consider what he calls the internal merits of the client's goals in deciding how to represent him and what kinds of arguments to make on his behalf. But whatever the force of his critique with respect to powerful clients bent on pursuing immoral purposes, Simon fails to explain adequately how lawyers can responsibly limit the autonomy of all but the most powerful clients without imposing their values on them and denying them the opportunity at least to seek vindication of hypothetically legal interests.

The virtue of Simon's approach depends on the degree to which the lawyer's exercise of power over his client is legitimate. Simon analyzes lawyer power as if it exists solely as an independent, disconnected concept. But the lawyer's exercise of power is problematic because she is exercising power over her client. While Simon at least addressed this issue in other writings, he thus far has failed to provide a satisfactory answer to the problem of lawyer power. Simon's approach offers a great deal to those lawyers seeking justification for a more political and morally rich practice; it offers considerably less solace to the many lawyers engaged in more mundane concerns. As for clients, they appear virtually nonexistent in this latest formulation of Simon's lawyering model.

Subordination, Rhetorical Survival Skills, and Sunday Shoes: Notes on the Hearing of Mrs. G.[1]

Lucie E. White[2]

The Story

Mrs. G. is thirty-five years old, Black, and on her own. She has five girls, ranging in age from four to fourteen. She has never told me anything about their fathers; all I know is that she isn't getting formal child support payments from anyone. She lives on an AFDC grant of just over three hundred dollars a month and a small monthly allotment of food stamps. She probably gets a little extra money from occasional jobs as a field hand or a maid, but she doesn't share this information with me and I don't ask. She has a very coveted unit of public housing, so she doesn't have to pay rent. She is taking an adult basic education class at the local community action center, which is in the same building as my own office. I often notice her in the classroom as I pass by.

The first thing that struck me about Mrs. G., when she finally came to my office for help one day, was the way she talked. She brought her two oldest daughters with her. She would get very excited when she spoke, breathing hard and waving her hands and straining, like she was searching for the right words to say what was on her mind. Her daughters would circle her, like two young mothers themselves, keeping the air calm as her hands swept through it. I haven't talked with them much, but they strike me as quite self-possessed for their years.

At the time I met Mrs. G., I was a legal aid lawyer working in a small community in south central North Carolina. I had grown up in the state, but had been away for ten years, and felt like an outsider when I started working there. I worked out of two small rooms in the back of the local community action center. The building was run-down, but it was a storefront directly across from the Civil War Memorial on the courthouse lawn, so it was easy for poor people to find.

There were two of us in the office, myself and a local woman who had spent a few years in Los Angeles, working as a secretary and feeling free, before coming back to the town to care for her aging parents. Her family had lived in the town for generations. Not too long ago they, and most of the other Black families I worked with, had been the property of our adversaries—the local landowners, businessmen, bureaucrats, and lawyers. Everyone seemed to have a strong sense of family, and of history, in the town.

In the late 1960s, the town had erupted into violence when a local youth who had read some Karl Marx and Malcolm X led some five thousand people down the local highway in an effort to integrate the county swimming pool. He had been charged with kidnapping as a result of the incident and had fled to Cuba, China, and ultimately Detroit. My colleague would talk to me about him in secretive tones. Her father was one of those who sheltered him from justice on the evening of his escape. I think she expected that one day he would come back to take up the project that was abandoned when he fled.

Since World War II, the town had been a real backwater for Black people. People told me that it was a place that was there to be gotten out of, if you could figure out how. Only gradually, in the 1980s, were a few African American families moving back into the area, to take up skilled jobs in chemicals and electronics. But the lives of most Blacks in the county in the early 1980s could be summed up by its two claims to fame. It was the county where the state's arch-conservative senior senator had grown up. Locals claimed that the senator's father, the chief of police at one time, was known for the boots he wore and the success he had at keeping Black people in their place. It was also the county where Steven Spielberg filmed *The Color Purple.* By the time Spielberg discovered the county, the dust from the 1960s had long since settled, and the town where I worked had the look of a sleepy Jim Crow village that time had quite entirely passed by.

Mrs. G. and two daughters first appeared at our office one Friday morning at about ten, without an appointment. I was booked for the whole day; the chairs in the tiny waiting room were already filled. But I called her in between two scheduled clients. Mrs. G. looked frightened. She showed me a letter from the welfare office that said she had received an "overpayment" of AFDC benefits. Though she couldn't read very well, she knew that the word "overpayment" meant fraud. Reagan's newly appointed United States attorney, with the enthusiastic backing of Senator Jesse Helms, had just announced plans to prosecute "welfare cheats" to the full extent of the law. Following this lead, a grand jury had indicted several local women on federal charges of welfare fraud. Therefore, Mrs. G. had some reason to believe that "fraud" carried the threat of jail.

The "letter" was actually a standardized notice that I had seen many times before. Whenever the welfare department's computer showed that a client had received an overpayment, it would kick out this form, which stated the amount at issue and advised the client to pay it back. The notice did not say why the agency had concluded that a payment error had been made. Nor did it inform the client that she might contest the county's determination. Rather, the notice assigned the client a time to meet with the county's fraud investigator to sign a repayment contract and warned that if the client chose not to show up at this meeting further action would be taken. Mrs. G.'s meeting with the fraud investigator was set for the following Monday.

At the time, I was negotiating with the county over the routine at these meetings and the wording on the overpayment form. Therefore, I knew what Mrs. G. could expect at the meeting. The fraud worker would scold her and then ask her to sign a statement conceding the overpayment, consenting to a 10 percent reduction of her AFDC benefits until the full amount was paid back, and advising that the government could still press criminal charges against her.

I explained to Mrs. G. that she did not have to go to the meeting on Monday, or to sign any forms. She seemed relieved and asked if I could help her get the overpayment straightened out. I signed her on as a client and, aware of the other people waiting to see me, sped through my canned explanation of how I could help her. Then I called the fraud investigator, canceled Monday's meeting, and told him I was representing her. Thinking that the emergency had been dealt with, I scheduled an appointment for Mrs. G. for the following Tuesday and told her not to sign anything or talk to anyone at the welfare office until I saw her again.

The following Tuesday Mrs. G. arrived at my office looking upset. She said she had gone to her fraud appointment because she had been "afraid not to." She had signed a paper admitting she owed the county about six hundred dollars, and agreeing to have her benefits reduced by thirty dollars a month for the year and a half it would take to repay the amount. She remembered I had told her not to sign anything; she looked like she was waiting for me to yell at her or tell her to leave. I suddenly saw a woman caught between two bullies, both of us ordering her what to do.

I hadn't spent enough time with Mrs. G. the previous Friday. For me, it had been one more emergency—a quick fix, an appointment, out the door. It suddenly seemed pointless to process so many clients, in such haste, without any time to listen, to challenge, to think together. But what to do, with so many people waiting at the door? I mused on these thoughts for a moment, but what I finally said was simpler. I was furious. Why had she gone to the fraud appointment and signed the repayment contract? Why hadn't she done as *we* had agreed? Now it would be so much harder to contest the county's claim: we would have to attack *both* the repayment contract and the underlying overpayment claim. Why hadn't she listened to me?

Mrs. G. just looked at me in silence. She finally stammered that she knew she had been "wrong" to go to the meeting when I had told her not to and she was "sorry." After we both calmed down I mumbled my own apology and turned to the business at hand. She told me that a few months before she had received a cash settlement for injuries she and her oldest daughter had suffered in a minor car accident. After medical bills had been paid and her lawyer had taken his fees, her award came to $592. Before Mrs. G. cashed the insurance check, she took it to her AFDC worker to report it and ask if it was all right for her to spend it. The system had trained her to tell her worker about every change in her life. With a few exceptions, any "income" she reported would be subtracted, dollar for dollar, from her AFDC stipend.

The worker was not sure how to classify the insurance award. After talking to a supervisor, however, she told Mrs. G. that the check would not affect her AFDC budget and she could spend it however she wanted.

Mrs. G. cashed her check that same afternoon and took her five girls on what she described to me as a "shopping trip." They bought Kotex, which they were always running short on at the end of the month. They also bought shoes, dresses for school, and some frozen food. Then she made two payments on her furniture bill. After a couple of wonderful days, the money was gone.

Two months passed. Mrs. G. received and spent two AFDC checks. Then she got the overpayment notice, asking her to repay to the county an amount equal to her insurance award. When she got to this point, I could see Mrs. G. getting upset again. She had told her worker everything, but nobody had explained to her what she was supposed to do. She hadn't meant to do anything wrong. I said I thought the welfare office had done something wrong in this case, not Mrs. G. I thought we could get the mess straightened out, but we'd need more information. I asked if she could put together a list of all the things she had bought with the insurance money. If she still had any of the receipts, she should bring them to me. I would look at her case file at the welfare office and see her again in a couple of days.

The file had a note from the caseworker confirming that Mrs. G. had reported the insurance payment when she received it. The note also showed that the worker did not include the amount in calculating her stipend. The "overpayment" got flagged two months later when a supervisor, doing a random "quality control" check on her file, discovered the worker's note.

Mrs. G. had been in court a few times to get child support and to defend against evictions, but she had never been to a welfare hearing. She knew that it was not a good idea to get involved in hearings, however, and she understood why. Fair hearings were a hassle and an embarrassment to the county. A hearing meant pulling an eligibility worker and several managers out of work for a few hours, which—given the chronic understaffing of the welfare office—was more than a minor inconvenience. It also meant exposing the county's administrative problems to state-level scrutiny.

I could tell that Mrs. G. felt pressure from me to ask for a hearing, but she also seemed angry at the welfare office for asking her to pay for their mistake. I said that it was her decision, and not mine, whether to ask for the hearing, and reassured her that I would do my best to settle the matter, no matter what she decided. I also told her she could drop the hearing request at any time, for any reason, before or even after the event. When she nervously agreed to file the hearing request, I didn't second-guess her decision.

Mrs. G. brought all five of her girls to my office to prepare for the hearing. Our first task was to decide on a strategy for the argument. I told her that I saw two stories we could tell. The first was the story she had told me. It was the "estoppel" story, the story of the wrong advice she got from her worker about spending the insurance check. The second story was one that I had come up with from reading the law. The state had laid the groundwork for this story when it opted for the "life necessities" waiver permitted by federal regulations. If a client could show that she had spent the sum to avert a crisis situation, then it would be considered "unavailable" as income, and her AFDC benefits would not be suspended. I didn't like this second story very much, and I wasn't sure that Mrs. G. would want to go along with it. How could I ask her to distinguish "life necessities" from mere luxuries, when she was keeping five children alive on three hundred dollars a month, and when she had been given no voice in the calculus that had determined her "needs."

Yet I felt that the necessities story might work at the hearing, while "estoppel" would unite the county and state against us. Mrs. G. would be pointing a finger, turning the county itself into the object of scrutiny. She would accuse welfare officials of wrong, and claim that they had caused her injury. She would demand that the county bend its own rules, absorb the overpayment out of its own funds, and run the risk of sanction from the state for its error.

As I thought about the choices, I felt myself in a bind. The estoppel story would feel good in the telling, but at the likely cost of losing the hearing, and provoking the county's ire. The hearing officer—though charged to be neutral—would surely identify with the county in this challenge to the government's power to evade the costs of its own mistakes. The necessities story would force Mrs. G. to grovel, but it would give both county and state what they wanted to hear—another "yes sir" welfare recipient.

When I explained the necessities story, Mrs. G. said she might get confused trying to remember what all she had bought with the money. Why did they need to know those things anyway? I could tell she was getting angry. I wondered if two months of benefits—six hundred dollars—was worth it. Maybe paying it back made more sense. I reminded her that we didn't have to tell this story at the hearing, and in fact, we didn't have to go to the hearing at all. Although I was trying to choose my words carefully, I felt myself saying too much. Why had I even raised the question of which story to tell? It was a tactical decision— not the kind of issue that clients were supposed to decide. Why hadn't I just told her to answer the questions that I chose to ask?

Mrs. G. asked me what to do. I said I wanted to see the welfare office admit their mistake, but I was concerned that if we tried to make them, we would lose. Mrs. G. said she still felt like she'd been treated unfairly but—in the next breath—"I didn't mean to do anything wrong." Why couldn't we tell both stories? With this simple question, I lost all pretense of strategic subtlety or control. I said sure.

I asked for the list she had promised to make of all the things she bought with the insurance money. Kotex, I thought, would speak for itself, but why, I asked, had she needed to get the girls new shoes? She explained that the girls' old shoes were pretty much torn up, so bad that the other kids would make fun of them at school. Could she bring in the old shoes? She said she could.

We rehearsed her testimony, first about her conversation with her worker regarding the insurance award and then about the Kotex and the shoes. Maybe the hearing wouldn't be too bad for Mrs. G., especially if I could help her see it all as strategy, rather than the kind of talking she could do with people she could trust. She had to distance herself at the hearing. She shouldn't expect them to go away from it understanding why she was angry, or what she needed, or what her life was like. The hearing was their territory. The most she could hope for was to take it over for a moment, leading them to act out her agenda. Conspiracy was the theme she must keep repeating as she dutifully played her role.

The hearing itself was in a small conference room at the welfare office. Mrs. G. arrived with her two oldest daughters and five boxes of shoes. We took our seats across the table from the AFDC director. The hearing officer set up a portable tape recorder and got out his Bible. Mrs. G.'s AFDC worker, an African American woman about her age, entered through a side door and took a seat next to her boss. The hearing officer turned on the recorder, read his obligatory opening remarks, and asked all the witnesses to rise and repeat before God that they intended to tell the truth. Mrs. G. and her worker complied.

The officer then turned the matter over to me. I gave a brief account of the background events and then began to question Mrs. G. I asked her if she had shown the check to her AFDC worker before she cashed it. She stammered. I repeated the question. She said she may have taken the check to the welfare office before she cashed it, but she couldn't remember for sure. She didn't know if she had gotten a chance to talk to anyone about it. Her worker was always real busy.

Armed with the worker's own sketchy notation of the conversation in the case file, I began to cross-examine my client, coaxing her memory about the event we had discussed so many times before. I asked if she remembered her worker telling her anything about how she could spend the money. Mrs. G. seemed to be getting more uncomfortable. It was quite a predicament for her, after all. If she "remembered" what her worker had told her, would her story expose mismanagement in the welfare office, or merely scapegoat another Black woman, who was not too much better off than herself?

When she repeated that she couldn't remember, I decided to leave the estoppel story for the moment. Maybe I could think of a way to return to it later. I moved on to the life necessities issue. I asked Mrs. G. to recount, as best she could, exactly how she had spent the insurance money. She showed me the receipts she had kept for the furniture payments and I put them into evidence. She explained that she was buying a couple of big mattresses for the kids and a new kitchen table. She said she had also bought some food—some frozen meat and several boxes of Kotex for all the girls. The others in the room shifted uneasily in their chairs. Then she said she had also bought her daughters some clothes and some shoes. She had the cash register receipt for the purchase.

Choosing my words carefully, I asked why she had needed to buy the new shoes. She looked at me for a moment with an expression that I couldn't read. Then she stated, quite emphatically, that they were Sunday shoes that she had bought with the money. The girls already had everyday shoes to wear to school, but she had wanted them to have nice shoes for church too. She said no more than two or three sentences, but her voice sounded different—stronger, more composed—than I had known from her before. When she finished speaking the room was silent, except for the incessant hum of the tape machine on the table and the fluorescent lights overhead. In that moment, I felt the boundaries of our "conspiracy" shift. Suddenly I was on the outside, with the folks on the other side of the table, the welfare director and the hearing officer. The only person I could not locate in this new alignment was Mrs. G.'s welfare worker.

I didn't ask Mrs. G. to pull out the children's old shoes, as we'd rehearsed. Nor did I make my "life necessities" argument. My lawyer's language couldn't add anything to what she had said. They would have to figure out for themselves why buying Sunday shoes for her children—and saying it—was indeed a "life necessity" for this woman. After the hearing, Mrs. G. seemed elated. She asked me how she had done at the hearing and I told her that I thought she was great. I warned her, though, that we could never be sure, in this game, who was winning, or even what side anyone was on.

We lost the hearing and immediately petitioned for review by the chief hearing officer. I wasn't sure of the theory we'd argue, but I wanted to keep the case open until I figured out what we could do.

Three days after the appeal was filed, the county welfare director called me unexpectedly, to tell me that the county had decided to withdraw its overpayment claim against Mrs. G. He explained that on a careful review of its own records, the county had decided that it wouldn't be "fair" to make Mrs. G. pay the money back. I said I was relieved to hear that they had decided, finally, to come to a sensible result in the case.

The Terrain

Mrs. G. had a hearing in which all of the rituals of due process were scrupulously observed. Yet she did not find her voice welcomed at that hearing. A complex pattern of social, economic, and cultural forces underwrote the procedural formalities, repressing and devaluing her voice. Out of that web of forces, I will identify three dominant themes, all of them linked, sometimes subtly, to Mrs. G's social identity as poor, Black, and female. The first theme is *intimidation*. Mrs. G. did not feel that she could risk speaking her mind freely to welfare officials. She lived in a community in which the social hierarchy had a caste-like rigidity. As a poor Black woman, her position at the bottom accorded her virtually no social or political power. She depended on welfare to survive and did not expect this situation to change in the future. She was simply not situated to take action that might displease her superiors. The second theme is *humiliation*. Even if Mrs. G. could find the courage to speak out at the hearing, her words were not likely to be heard as legitimate, because of the language she had learned to speak as a poor woman of color, and because of the kind of person that racist and gendered imagery portrayed her to be. The final theme is *objectification*. Because Mrs. G. had little voice in the political process that set the substantive terms of her welfare eligibility, the issues that she was constrained to talk about at the hearing bore little relation to her own feelings about the meaning and fairness of the state's action.

If we measure Mrs. G.'s hearing against the norms of procedural formality, it appears to conform. The hearing appears to invite Mrs. G. to speak on equal terms with all other persons. Yet within the local landscape of her hearing, Mrs. G.'s voice is constrained by forces that procedural doctrine will neither acknowledge nor oppose. Each of these forces attaches a specific social cost to her gender and race identity. The caste system implements race and gender ideology in social arrangements. The "fraud issue" revives misogynist and racist stereotypes that had been forced, at least partly, underground by the social movements of the 1960s and 1970s. And the welfare system responds to gender- and race-based injustice in the economy by constructing the poor as Woman—as an object of social control. Given the power amassed behind these forces, we might predict that they should win the contest with Mrs. G. for her voice.

Yet to detect these forces, we have read the story through a structuralist lens, which shows only the stark dichotomy of subordination and social control. It is ironic that this lens, which works so well to expose the contours of Mrs. G.'s silence, also leaves her—as a woman actively negotiating the terrain in which she found herself—entirely out of focus. If we re-center our reading on Mrs. G., as a woman shaping events, unpredictably, to realize her own meanings, we can no longer say with certainty what the outcome will be. We cannot tell who prevailed at the hearing, or where the power momentarily came to rest. Rather, what we see is a sequence of surprising moves, a series of questions. Why did Mrs. G. return to the lawyer after meeting with the fraud investigator to sign a settlement agreement? Why did she depart from the script she had rehearsed for the hearing, to remain silent before her own worker, and to speak about Sunday shoes? And why did the county finally abandon its claim to cut her stipend?

Mrs. G.'s survival skills were more complex, more subtle, than the lawyer dared to recognize. There might be another meaning to Mrs. G.'s ambivalence about what she wanted to do. Perhaps she was playing with the compliance that all of her superiors demanded. By acquiescing to both of the system's opposed orders, she was surely protecting herself from the risks of defiance. But she was also undermining the value—to them— of her own submission. By refusing to claim any ground as her own, she made it impossible for others to subdue her will.

The lawyer had scripted Mrs. G. as a victim. That was the only strategy for the hearing that the lawyer, within the constraints of her own social position, could imagine for Mrs. G. She had warned her client to play the victim if she wanted to win. Mrs. G. learned her lines. She came to the hearing well-rehearsed in the lawyer's strategy. But in the hearing, she did not play. When she was cued to perform, without any signal to her lawyer she abandoned their script.

The lawyer shared with Mrs. G. the oppression of gender, but was placed above Mrs. G. in the social hierarchies of race and class. The lawyer was paid by the same people who paid for welfare, the federal government. Both programs were part of a social agenda of assisting, but also controlling, the poor. Though the lawyer had worked hard to identify with Mrs.

G., she was also sworn, and paid, to defend the basic constitution of the *status quo*. When Mrs. G. "misbehaved" at the hearing, when she failed to talk on cue and then refused to keep quiet, Mrs. G. pointed to the ambiguity of the legal aid lawyer's social role. Through her defiant actions, Mrs. G. told the lawyer that a conspiracy with a double agent is inevitably going to prove an unstable alliance.

The lawyer had tried to "collaborate" with Mrs. G. in devising an advocacy plan. Yet the terms of that "dialogue" excluded Mrs. G.'s voice. Mrs. G. was a better strategist than the lawyer—more daring, more subtle, more fluent—in her own home terrain. She knew the psychology, the culture, and the politics of the white people who controlled her community. She knew how to read, and sometimes control, her masters' motivations; she had to command this knowledge—this intuition—to survive. The lawyer had learned intuition as a woman, but in a much more private sphere. She was an outsider to the county, and to Mrs. G.'s social world. Mrs. G.'s superior sense of the landscape posed a subtle threat to the lawyer's expertise. Sensing this threat, the lawyer steered their strategic "discussion" into the sphere of her own expert knowledge. By limiting the very definition of "strategy" to the manipulation of legal doctrine, she invited Mrs. G. to respond to her questions with silence. And, indeed, Mrs. G. did not talk freely when the lawyer was devising their game plan. Rather, Mrs. G. waited until the hearing to act out her own intuitions. Although she surely had not plotted those actions in advance, she came up with moves at the hearing which threw everyone else off their guard, and may have proved her the better *legal* strategist of the lawyer-client pair.

The disarming "strategy" that Mrs. G. improvised at the hearing was to appear to abandon strategy entirely. For a moment she stepped out of the role of the supplicant. She ignored the doctrinal pigeonholes that would fragment her voice. She put aside all that the lawyer told her the audience wanted to hear. Instead, when asked to point a finger at her caseworker, she was silent. When asked about "life necessities," she explained that she had used her money to meet her own needs. She had bought her children Sunday shoes.

When Mrs. G. talked about Sunday shoes, she was talking about a life necessity. For subordinated communities, physical necessities do not meet the minimum requirements for a human life. Rather, subordinated groups must create cultural practices through which they can elaborate an autonomous, oppositional consciousness. Without shared rituals for sustaining their survival and motivating their resistance, subordinated groups run the risk of total domination—of losing the will to use their human powers to subvert their oppressors' control over them. Religion—spirituality, the social institution of the Black church—has been one such self-affirming cultural practice for the communities of African American slaves, and remains central to the expression of Black identity and group consciousness today. By naming Sunday shoes as a life necessity, Mrs. G. was speaking to the importance of this cultural practice in her life, a truth that the system's categories did not comprehend.

At the same time that Mrs. G.'s statement affirmed the church, it condemned the welfare system. By rejecting welfare's definition of life necessities, she asserted her need to have a say about *the criteria* for identifying her needs. Her statement was a demand for meaningful participation in the political conversations in which her needs are contested and defined. In the present welfare system, poor women—the objects of welfare—are structurally excluded from those conversations. When Mrs. G. insisted on her need to say for herself what her "life necessities" might be, she expanded, for a moment, the accepted boundaries of those conversations.

When Mrs. G. claimed this power, she affirmed the feminist insight that the dominant languages do *not* construct a closed system, from which there can be no escape. Although dominant groups may control the *social institutions* that regulate these languages, those groups cannot control the capacity of subordinated peoples to speak. Thus, women have evaded complete domination through their *practice* of speaking, like Mrs. G. spoke at her hearing, from their own intuitions and their own experience.

Give Them Back Their Lives: Recognizing Client Narrative in Case Theory[1]

Binny Miller[2]

In recent years the concepts of lawyering as storytelling and client voice as narrative have come into vogue. As a practical matter, lawyers have always seen their work as in part "storytelling," but only recently has legal scholarship framed lawyering in these terms. By and large, legal scholars have approached storytelling and narrative from the standpoint of theory—critical race theory, critical literary and legal theory, feminist theory, lesbian and gay theory, and ethnographic theory. In contrast, clinical theory has long grounded narrative in the actual practice of lawyering. The emerging theoretics of practice literature draws on all of these vantage points in looking at the intersection of theory and practice in legal advocacy.

Although these approaches differ in some respects, they share enough in common that they can be grouped under the rubric of "critical lawyering." These critical theorists posit that client voices have been muted by the narratives that lawyers tell on their behalf, and urge lawyers to set aside their own stories in favor of client stories. They follow in the footsteps of the client-centered movement, which has argued that clients should play a greater role in their own cases.

The critical and client-centered movements add to our understanding of the role that client voices can and should play in legal representation. But in the rush to embrace client voice, these scholars have virtually ignored the critical role that case theory can play in linking client stories to the narratives that lawyers tell on behalf of clients.

Case theory—or theory of the case—can be seen as an explanatory statement linking the "case" to the client's experience of the world. It serves as a lens for shaping reality, in light of the law, to explain the facts, relationships, and circumstances of the client and other parties in the way that can best achieve the client's goals. The relevant reality combines the perspectives of the lawyer and the client with an eye toward the ultimate audience—the trier of fact. This article is about case theory and its implications for incorporating client narratives in litigation.

The Case: Client's Story—Implying Racism

On a weekday afternoon Jay was shopping at a clothing store in a predominantly white suburb of Washington, D.C. Although he often shopped at this store, on that particular day he was bargain-hunting at the store's "Bash" sale. He purchased a pillow and washcloths and then shopped for a pair of jeans. Jay, who is black, six feet three inches tall, and weighs 260 pounds, was unable to find a pair of jeans in his size, so he decided to look for a sweater.

As Jay browsed in the sweater department on the second floor, he noticed that he was being watched by three security guards, Mr. Dirk, Ms. Deal, and Ms. Mormon. Mormon is a full-time security guard. Dirk and Deal are police officers who moonlight as security guards; because they wore store uniforms, Jay was unaware that they were police officers. Both Dirk and Deal carried guns. All three guards are white.

Jay was carrying his purchases in a bag bearing the store logo. A receipt was stapled to one corner of the bag, which was partially open because the pillow was sticking out of the top. Jay had asked for a larger bag, but none was available.

The guards followed Jay for five or ten minutes, looking down every time he looked at them. Jay approached Mormon, told her that he regularly shopped in the store, and asked her why she and her companions were following him. She denied following Jay, said she needed to "check something out," and made a telephone call on the store telephone. Jay angrily thought that Mormon was reporting him for shoplifting and rode the escalator to the first floor, planning to leave the store. He stopped at the bottom of the escalator because his "stubbornness wouldn't allow [him] to leave." Not far behind were the three security guards.

From about ten feet away, Dirk shouted, "Hey pal, what do you have in the bag?" Other shoppers and store employees were within hearing distance of this remark. Jay replied, "Well, what I have in the bag is what I purchased, and if you're accusing me of stealing, those are some strong accusations and if you are, then I will sue the fucking store." Dirk said, "Fuck you," and called Jay a "punk," and both men exchanged more profanities. Then Jay said, "You know, if you weren't wearing that gun, I'd probably whoop your ass for the degrading things that you were saying to me."

Two or three managers arrived, including Rosenholtz, an older white man with gray hair, and Thompson, a tall black man who is slightly heavier than Jay. Speaking all at once, the three guards reported that Jay had threatened Dirk with the gun. When Rosenholtz asked Jay what he wanted, he asked for a refund. Thompson put his arm around Jay and walked with him to the service counter at the front of the store. Dirk and Deal followed.

At the service counter, Jay waited while Rosenholtz began processing the refund. Dirk and Deal stood near the counter. Jay dug in his pocket for some change, sorted the pennies from the nickels, dimes, and quarters, and tossed the pennies up in the air, saying, "[M]oney is no big issue to me. . . . That's why you're following me around because you think I can't afford to buy anything." Deal suddenly moved toward Jay, urging Dirk to arrest Jay for assault and battery. Jay, who was startled by Deal's charge, heard Dirk say something in a loud and boastful voice. Dirk pushed Jay's arm and told him he was under arrest, but he did not state that he was a police officer or show any identification. Jay escaped from Dirk by backing away from the counter and toward the front exit.

A police officer arrived and Jay was handcuffed outside the store. Deal arrived in the parking lot, where she punched him three or four times, slapped him, dug her hands into his neck to grab a gold chain he was wearing, and pulled on the chain, choking him. She then ripped the chain off his neck.

Five or ten minutes passed before the police took Jay to the station and booked him. While Jay waited in the parking lot, Rosenholtz put a refund in Jay's pocket and apologized for the incident.

Supporting Stories—Seeing Racism

Perry Rodriguez, Darryl Prince, and Jimmy Williams, three other shoppers who observed Jay's encounter with the three guards, tell stories supporting Jay's view of his case. Rodriguez is Latino; Prince and Williams are black.

On the day that Jay was arrested, Rodriguez was shopping at the store with his friend Prince. Williams was shopping with his wife and three children in the pantyhose section of the store. [A discussion of the guards' stories is omitted here.]

The stories told by all three men corroborate Jay's story with respect to several key details, including the fact that Jay had a receipt for his purchases, that he threw the coins up in the air rather than at Deal, that he did not hit Dirk or anyone else, and that Deal punched Jay after he was handcuffed. Perhaps more importantly, they viewed Dirk as the hostile aggressor and the entire incident as racially charged, explaining why the security guards stopped Jay in the first place and then escalated the incident until it was out of control.

Traditional Approach

What lessons about case theory can be gleaned from the stories in Jay's case? Rather than providing a literal account of how we constructed case theory, I use the story to explore the limitations of the traditional approach; I present it as a catalyst for a different model that focuses on the client and his experience of the encounter. A traditional rebuttal theory begins with legal elements and then looks to whether the facts fit the elements of the crimes charged. Disorderly conduct is the crime of acting or speaking in a manner that "offends, disturbs, incites, or tends to incite" onlookers.

As the guards described Jay, his threats and racial epithets were offensive, disturbing, even shocking. To defeat this claim, we would have to show that the guards were either mistaken or lying. But even by Jay's account, his words were profane, loud, and possibly disturbing.

Battery is the crime of intentionally touching another person without her consent. The State must prove that Jay made physical contact with Deal using the coins as an instrument, that he intended this contact, and that she did not consent. Because none of the participants tells a story in which Deal acquiesced, the issue is whether the coins struck Deal, and if they did, whether Jay intended the contact. If either of these elements is not present, then Jay is not guilty.

Resisting arrest is the crime of refusing to submit to a lawful arrest. The State must show that Jay was arrested, that he refused to submit to the arrest, and that the arrest was lawful. A lawful arrest is one in which the individual making the arrest was authorized to do so, identified himself as an officer of the law, and had probable cause to believe that a crime had been committed. Because Jay concedes that the security guards were attempting to arrest him and that he resisted, our theory must attack the lawfulness of the arrest.

In this traditional analysis, each "crime" is treated as a separate and distinct event, rather than as part of a series of interrelated experiences. This approach does not draw a big picture of what happened or why, and it includes very little of the client, except as a source of facts about "what happened." It has a great deal of faith in the existence of an objective version of "what happened," and individuals whose stories deviate from this version are either mistaken or lying. Jay was either loud and obnoxious or not, and he either threw the coins or did not throw the coins. By the same token, Dirk either stated that he was a police officer or did not. Although the model concedes the importance of motivation and credibility in answering these questions, it provides no real framework for looking at Jay's experience of the event.

Acknowledging Client Life Experience

An alternative vision of case theory is as a phenomenon that operates at two distinct levels or layers, like geological strata. As lawyers, we must work through the first layer to get to the second layer and the possibilities of imagination.

The first level is the surface level set out in the traditional model of case theory development. This concept of case theory is hierarchical and top-down in its focus, beginning with the law, adding the facts, and finding little room for the client in the interstices. The first layer captures many aspects of a case but leaves much unsaid.

The second level is below ground and rich with almost limitless possibilities. At this level, case theory is a story that is more than the law and more than the facts. Life, or any one event in life, does not unfold in the neat boxes doctrine envisions but instead proceeds in fits and starts, with the facts all jumbled together. We start with the stories, and work the law back in. Case theory becomes a vehicle for communicating the client's story and meshing his story with the stories told by other participants. It offers images of the client and his world and creates a bridge between these images and the law.

As we think about how to frame the events at the store, race plays a prominent role in the encounter. The guards believed that Jay perceived the incident as racial but deny any racial intent, arguing that Jay made race an issue by responding to imagined racial insults with his own racial epithets. Yet the client deftly avoids either of these characterizations, never using the word "black" and admitting only to being angry. It is as if he is speaking in code by not tying the incident directly to race but obliquely conveying that only racism can explain what happened to him. By looking at the case through the lens of race, what light is shed on case theory?

At one level, the fact that Jay is black and the security guards are white makes the encounter a racial incident. We do not need case theory to see this encounter as having something to do with race, given the power of racial images in our society. But once we highlight the role of race as a critical factor, then the story comes into sharper focus. By starting with race, we can see a picture of the case that is very different from the one a traditionalist would see.

Based on what we know of Jay's story, we can create this framework:

This case is about Mr. Jay, a black man, who was shopping at a store and minding his own business until three white store security guards singled him out for surveillance and harassment because he was black. Instead of just going along quietly and playing their game, Jay got angry and shouted out the truth about racism. The guards punished him by teaching him a lesson about daring to speak out and about challenging authority. When they were proven wrong about him being a shoplifter, they got even. They charged him with disorderly conduct, battery, and resisting arrest, but the real crime was being a black man who would not stay in his place.

Thinking about the incident in the store as a racial encounter changes how we look at legal elements such as behaving in a "disorderly" manner, intending to strike another person, and identifying oneself as a police officer. It brings the dry language of the law alive and gives its words shape and meaning.

In viewing Jay's case in light of the doctrine-driven traditional approach, the key factual disputes are whether Jay was loud and used profanity, whether he deliberately threw the coins at Deal, and whether Dirk adequately identified himself as a police officer before attempting to arrest Jay. As we have seen, a race case theory makes us think anew about these legal elements and changes the relevant facts. Perhaps Jay could have been loud and profane, have thrown the coins in the direction of Deal, and have heard Dirk identify himself as a police officer, and still not be guilty of a crime. Instead, the focus shifts to the reasons Jay became so angry in his interactions with the guards, what they did to provoke him, how we might view the act of throwing the coins, and how Jay understood what Dirk said about his status as a police officer.

But case theory also gives facts meaning apart from doctrine. Case theory works at two levels, both at the enriched doctrinal level and, in an even purer way, at the level at which race is the frame, regardless of how it shapes our understanding of doctrine. This is the level at which we can say, "Now the story makes sense."

This shift, both in doctrine and in frame, forces us to look at Jay and his life experience. In this scenario, although the facts about "what happened" matter, other facts outside those parameters matter just as much. These are "life facts"—facts about the lives of the people in the case.

When race is the image that drives the case, the good life facts are that Jay is black, that he is a gentle and soft-spoken man, that he works as a janitor, that he was not stealing that day, that he has never been arrested or convicted of any crime, and that he likes to shop. While these facts might matter even if race were irrelevant, they are more powerful under our theory that the encounter was racial.

We are drawn to Jay because he makes himself vulnerable in revealing that he could not find a pair of jeans in his size in the store. We see him as cautious and hesitant to expose his own vulnerabilities, using his charges of racism as a shield, not a weapon. By removing this shield, he has exposed something of himself in telling the guards, two strangers, that race matters to him, and so does his dignity. He has put himself on the line by announcing that something as personal to him as his race could cause another person to treat him with contempt. Viewed in this light, his allegations seem less like an accusation and more like a painful query—"Are you treating me differently because I am black?"

It matters not only that Jay paid for the items in the bag but also what those items were. There is something familiar, even poignant, about his purchase of familiar household items, such as washcloths and a pillow. Who these days, besides your grandmother, uses a washcloth? We would have had a very different picture of Jay and his case if the items in the bag had been a boombox, rap music, or Nike tennis shoes. The kind of man who shops for pillows is not the kind of man who goes on a rampage in a store.

Yet this image is counteracted by the fact that Jay wore a gold chain that day. Suddenly, Jay is not a single man shopping for comforting household items such as a pillow and washcloths. He is a black man fond of flashy jewelry, like a pimp or a drug dealer. Unless we can explain the chain in a way that does not implicate these racist stereotypes, this image is at odds with the image created by other facts.

Facts from other peoples' lives also seem significant. Prince and Williams are black; Rodriguez is Latino. Prince lives with his father and sister, is a student who works part-time, and aspires to be an engineer. Williams lives with his wife and three children, with whom he goes shopping. Rodriguez lives with his aunt. These men are people like us. They have families; they go shopping; they are not troublemakers. None of these men knew Jay before his encounter with the security guards. All came to his assistance later.

As Jay's story demonstrates, thinking of case theory as life experience opens up a world of possibilities. For the lawyer, legal doctrine can change in the process; for the client, case theory fits with his experience by highlighting the importance of his life facts. This can give the client a sense of vindication and will resonate with some juries.

In looking at Jay's case, we have come a great distance from the traditional model of case theory. Once we entertain the notion that Jay might have correctly perceived that he was singled out because he was black, we can better understand why he and others acted as they did. Jay was just sick and tired of being treated badly.

My aim is to articulate a theory of case theory that is truer both to the client's life experience and to what it is that lawyers actually do. By defining case theory as an explanatory statement linking the case to the client's experience of the world, we create a context for seeing what we might not otherwise see. Case theory creates a perspective for the facts, relationships, and circumstances of the client and other parties that is grounded in the client's goals. Case theory makes actions seem quite reasonable that at first seemed unreasonable, and it allows us to accept the client's story and at the same time have a plausible explanation for other stories.

The power of race as a case theory may also be its greatest pitfall. A lawyer concerned about social justice wants to validate the client's experience of the world and, indeed, may even look for racism when a client does not identify it as a factor. An awareness of race is an important insight to possess in a case, but it cannot always control the case's direction. Rather than holding onto a race case theory with a vengeance, the lawyer must be willing to back off if the client wishes. The lawyer must strike the difficult balance of recognizing the power of a race theory and being willing not to pursue it.

Earlier, when the students asked Jay whether he wanted us to characterize the incident as racially motivated, he said a race theory made him uncomfortable. The students told me Jay was reluctant to discuss the reasons, and I did not press them further. What did his discomfort with a race case theory mean? What other options did he see? Why did he tell a story at the trial that avoided the question of race? If we had discussed these issues, Jay might have been more hopeful about his case or might have better understood the implications of a race theory.

Finally, in this process, we might also learn that much of how we as lawyers shape case theory has to do with who we are. It is not that we dominate our clients, as critical theorists argue, but rather that we are either more or less creative than our colleagues, more or less risk averse, more or less fearful of taking on the system, or have more or less life experience with the theory in question. By engaging with the client in these discussions, we might come to know more about ourselves, becoming better lawyers in the process.

Jay's case raises especially thought-provoking issues about how lawyers approach case theory based on their own life experiences and attitudes. Both the students and I are white. From the beginning of the case, I eagerly seized on the race case theory, anticipating that the client would want us to pursue this theory with abandon and feeling excited about the possibilities of putting the racist guards on trial. In contrast, the students were downbeat about the possibilities, even before they met with the client. They seemed uncomfortable talking about the case in racial terms and were quick to argue that the jury would never believe our theory. They viewed the stories of Rodriguez, Prince, and Williams as inconsistent and full of holes and, after interviewing them in person, reported that the men were not "credible" and would make poor witnesses. They found especially persuasive a conversation with the assistant public defender who represented Jay in the trial, who reported the courtroom clerk's belief that Jay's witnesses had "conspired" with him to steal from the store.

Although I pushed them hard on their assumptions, pointing out that the state's witnesses told stories that were inconsistent and irresolvable and that our theory might resonate with members of the jury who had themselves been treated poorly, they moved little from their initial judgment. Nor were they persuaded by my suggestion that the clerk's comments could themselves reflect thinly veiled racism and that our own racial biases could affect our judgment about case theory. They said they could not understand why the client had gotten so angry.

At the time, I was frustrated by our differences and was inclined to think that the students were insensitive to the pervasive power of race. They in turn probably thought that I was overly interventionist, politically correct, and dogmatic. Looking back on the case, I believe we were both wrong. We were separated not solely by differing sensitivities to race issues but instead by our ability to relate to the client's anger.

As I observed both students in the classroom and supervision meetings, they were polite, mannerly, and deferential to authority. They attended every class, and their work was meticulous. From what I knew of their backgrounds, they came from traditional families and had set their sights on law school early on. Despite the pressures of the clinic, I had never seen them express anger or even annoyance, and I could not imagine them screaming or yelling in a public place. While I do not pretend to know their inner struggles, I do not think they could imagine themselves ever acting out in a store, no matter what the provocation.

My experience was different. At some level, I felt I could understand the client's anger, even if it were the result of misperceived racism. Although, like most law professors, I lead a life that is quite conventional in many respects, in other respects it is not. I am a lesbian, and like every lesbian or gay person, I have experienced discrimination as a consequence of my sexual orientation. In response, I have gotten angry, I have cried, and I have marched in the streets. I always feel like an outsider, and as a result, I have a deep appreciation for other people who may share an outsider's perspective.

I also have been badly treated in stores. When I wear jeans and a t-shirt and store personnel are rude to me, I assume they think I am younger than my actual age, or that I have no money to spend, or both. At times, I am convinced that I have been treated rudely because I look like a lesbian. If someone asked me for proof, I could not provide it, but at a deep level I know it to be true. As a consequence, I think that I respected the client's judgment, right or wrong, about his encounter in the store.

Thinking about the case in terms of sexual orientation changes my view of the encounter between Jay and the guards and between Rodriguez and the guards. Of the three men, Rodriguez seemed to me to be the most "obviously" gay. Perhaps the guards stopped him out of overt homophobia, or out of a less conscious realization that he was somehow "different."

Although Jay's sexual orientation seemed to me more hidden, the guards could have been motivated by similar considerations. Thousands of gay men and lesbians have died as a result of individuals acting on homophobia; it is not hard to imagine that homophobia, conscious or unconscious, might lead a guard to stop someone in a store.

Sexual orientation also figured into an aspect of representing Jay even more clearly connected to case theory. Following my usual practice in the clinic, I did not meet the client or his witnesses until our court appearance on his behalf. When I met Prince and Rodriguez at the elevators outside the courtroom on the morning of court, I realized they were gay. Although a number of observations contributed to this conclusion, at bottom my intuition, not a list of "facts," led me to this realization.

We all stood together with the client outside of the courtroom waiting for the court to call our case. As I watched Jay interact with Prince and Rodriguez, it dawned on me that he also was gay. I sensed this conclusion more than I knew it. I also sensed that Prince and Rodriguez were a couple.

Since the case ended [with Jay deciding to accept a guilty plea to disorderly conduct and resisting arrest], I have thought a great deal about how my awareness of the sexual orientation of the client and his witnesses has affected how I look at the case. At the time I did not think of this awareness as a kind of case theory; I now do. While race was an obvious theme, sexual orientation resided in the background. Sexual orientation is almost always more invisible than race, yet it can have a profound effect on how we view what happened. Even when sexual orientation is not directly at issue, as it would be in a military discharge case or in a case challenging a lesbian mother's right to raise her child, it provides a lens for understanding what happened.

Sexual orientation might also explain why Prince and Rodriguez came to Jay's assistance and waited at the jail for him to be released. The state's unstated but implicit explanation for their involvement was that Jay and his witnesses were members of racial minority groups. Sexual orientation might provide an alternative explanation. So too might sexual orientation explain why the students viewed Prince and Rodriguez as unreliable.

Indeed, Jay may have reacted as he did to the guards' harassment because he perceived a homophobic slur—real or unintended. The term "punk"—the term Dirk used in hassling Jay and Rodriguez—is a somewhat dated reference to male homosexuals and is still employed by some African Americans. I was unaware of this connotation until Margaret Montoya, a Latina clinical colleague, read a draft of this article and suggested this interpretation based on her experience in the African-American community. This turn of events once again demonstrates the key role that life experience can play in lawyers' understanding of their clients and cases.

The choice between a race theory and a sexual orientation theory is not an either-or choice. Events may have transpired as they did for reasons of both sexual orientation and race—or neither.

Many questions about the possible implications of a theory based on sexual orientation remain unanswered because I did not raise the issue with the students or the client. I did not see the client again once the case ended, and I made a conscious decision not to raise it with the students. Because the client had not raised the issue of his sexual orientation with us, my guess was that he did not wish to discuss it, and for me to discuss it with the students would violate his privacy.

Had we still been developing case theory at the point when I became aware of the issue of sexual orientation, the question of whether to pursue it would have been more complicated. On the one hand, the client should have the choice about whether to argue this theory. On the other hand, the theory would not likely help the client win his case, given societal homophobia and a jury's likely inclination to see the shared sexual orientation of the three men as evidence of bias, rather than simply as a shared experience. Although a client in Jay's shoes might have noninstrumental reasons to raise the question of sexual orientation, Jay was an unlikely candidate to assert these reasons, given his absolute silence on the issue.

Moreover, there is potentially a very high cost to discussing sexual orientation issues with a client who wants to keep his sexual orientation secret.

Perhaps the most important lesson of the story is that if we are to take life experience seriously in developing case theory, we must look beyond race to other kinds of theories that may not be so immediately apparent but that are potentially relevant. Given the prevalence of racial issues in the criminal justice system, a competent lawyer should always consider the impact of race, but she must also go further. The impact of other fundamental characteristics such as gender, class, and sexual orientation may be less obvious but equally important in offering explanations in cases. Unless lawyers consciously look for these perspectives, they may miss them, even when the client's view of what happened is shaped by this perspective. The client does not look for this perspective but simply sees the world that way.

People from the Footnotes: The Missing Element in Client-Centered Counseling[1]

Michelle S. Jacobs[2]

The development of a client-centered approach to counseling was fueled by a concern that under the traditional approach to lawyering, the client came into the relationship with her lawyer in an unequal and/or subordinate position. As a result, the client was thought to be overwhelmed by the power represented in the lawyer's position and, therefore, subject to manipulation by the lawyer.

Currently, many clinical programs have adopted models of lawyer-client relationships which employ one of two prevailing client-centered models. Both models recognize the importance of lawyer-client interaction in decision-making on a non-manipulative basis. It was perceived that in a traditional lawyer-client relationship the client is manipulated into doing what the lawyer wishes, regardless of whether it was what the client actually desired. On the whole, both models provide a good framework for the lawyer (and in our realm, the law student) to learn and hone some of the skills of effective communication with his/her clients.

The irony of the models is that they were constructed to return the client to the centrality of the lawyer's work. Yet, even with the best of intentions, lawyers most concerned with preserving the autonomy of client decision-making have, by adopting the "client-centered" model of counseling, continued to place the client, especially the client of color, out at the margin.

In this article, I explore the way in which race-neutral training of interviewing and counseling skills may actually lead to continued marginalization of clients of color. I explore the empirical data gathered by social scientists operating in a counseling capacity, which demonstrate that race plays a significant role in counselor-client interaction. The data reveal that the race and behavior of the counselor can have an equally serious impact on the relationship as can the race and behavior of the client.

Proponents of neutral skills training argue that it is impossible to fully understand the world view of every single client and that any attempt to do so would destroy a lawyer's ability to represent clients effectively. If the critique of client-centered counseling presented here proposed one single approach to understanding indigent or difficult clients, the neutral skills training argument would be correct. No single theory can help a student/ lawyer anticipate the infinite number of client combinations she may encounter in her professional life. There are, however, recognized and validated methods of assisting professionals in counseling relationships to identify areas where the difficulty is engendered by race, culture, gender, etcetera.

There are parallels between medical, psychiatric, psychological, and sociological fields and the legal field. From these fields, lawyers and clinicians may seek guidance. In these fields, empirical data are routinely gathered to help assess the nature of the client relationship. Both mental health counseling and lawyering involve the development of confidential relationships with clients. The success of relationships in both of these environments is affected by the degree to which the client feels able to trust the professional. In mental health counseling and lawyering, there is an enormous potential for manipulation of the client/patient/subject because of the power differential which exists and benefits the professional. In both areas of counseling, it is common to first encounter the client when she or he is under the pressure of an impending personal crisis.

The client-centered counseling approach is itself an outgrowth of the changing therapeutic approaches in psychology. Much of the move toward client-centered counseling was influenced by comparisons of methodology in client counseling to the mental health areas. Although, as clinicians, we have borrowed heavily from the mental health field in accepting the need for a revision of the traditional lawyer-client relationship toward a more client-centered approach, we have not followed the mental health field's lead in examining other factors which may affect the lawyer-client relationship. In addressing this need, two areas I examine below are: (1) how the lawyer's unconscious racism and cultural bias may impact the attorney-client relationship; and (2) how the client's cultural experiences and internalization of microaggressions impact the client's view of the relationship with not only the lawyer, but also the law.

Lawyers, law students, and law professors, like every other member of society, carry with them preconceived notions rooted in the lawyer's own cultural background. If the lawyer in question is white, which according to statistics is the norm, and is working in a legal services, clinical, or public interest position, the client-participants are likely to be people of color and/or individuals from a lower socioeconomic background than the lawyer or law student. It is also likely that the lawyer or law student carries with him/her elements of unconscious racism. What we, as clinicians, have failed to examine is how the unconscious racism, or, in other words, the lawyer's or law student's preconceived cultural notions, will impact both the lawyer's expectations of the client and the lawyer's interpretation and understanding of the client's actions and ultimate objectives.

The potential impact of preconceived notions is demonstrated in a phenomenon known as the self-fulfilling prophecy. In this phenomenon, an originally false definition of a situation can influence the believer of the false definition to act in such a way as to bring about that situation. More specifically, the principle establishes that one person's attitudes and expectations about another may influence the believer's actions, which in turn may induce the other to behave in a way that confirms the original false definition. In [one] study,[3] the authors focused on detecting possible nonverbal mediators of this phenomenon and on the resulting performances of the interactants. The participants in the study were both black and white job applicants being interviewed by whites. The authors reported data which suggested that attitudes toward individuals are linked with nonverbal behaviors emitted toward the individual. For instance, positive attitudes led to more immediate behaviors. Discrediting characteristics were treated with less immediate behaviors. The authors sought to determine whether the white interviewers would exhibit nonverbal behavior as well as whether the target (job applicants) would be influenced by the interviewer's nonverbal behavior.

In the first study, the interviewers were naive as to the study's purpose. The "applicants," however, were not; the applicants were confederates. The authors found that the white interviewers spent 25 percent less time with the black applicants versus the white applicants. Further, the black applicants received less immediate behavior than did the white applicants. For example, the white interviewers physically placed themselves further away from the black applicants versus the white ones, which indicated negative reactions to the black applicants. Overall, the black applicants received a negative total immediacy score while the white applicants received a positive one. In the second study, the authors attempted to determine whether a white applicant, treated similarly to the way black applicants were treated, would reciprocate with less immediacy. In this test, the white applicants did not know the study's purpose. The authors found that white applicants who were treated similarly to the original black applicants had been treated in the first study performed less well, reciprocated with less immediacy, and perceived their interviews to be less adequate. The authors concluded that the actions of the interviewer could, therefore, influence the behavior of the applicant and have ramifications on the applicant's ability to secure employment. This finding is significant because issues such as black unemployment were frequently examined from the perspective of the "disposition of the disinherited" (black person), thus casting blame on the peculiarities of the victim, rather than on problematic aspects of the black-white interaction itself.

The concept of self-fulfilling prophecy can certainly provide illumination in the area of client-centered counseling. The lawyer or student unaware of her own behavior perceives the client to be exhibiting negative behavior. One of the insidious dangers of the self-fulfilling prophecy is that since individuals are seldom able to monitor their own behavior, they are more likely to attribute negative behavior from the client not to their own original nonverbal behavior, but instead to some disposition inherent in the client. Presently, except in one isolated area, skills training material devotes no attention to negative nonverbal behaviors that students and white lawyers in general might be exhibiting toward their clients. Nor do we have any idea how clients may decode and reciprocate such behavior.

One of the frequent complaints heard from the students is that the clients seem apathetic. The students feel that they care more about the client's well-being than does the client himself. Yet, the student/lawyer and the physician share the traits of high levels of education and higher socioeconomic status. These factors may be producing, in the legal services client, the same level of intimidation that the lower socioeconomic patient feels when visiting a doctor. In fact, it is generally accepted, in client-centered counseling material, that clients may be intimidated by the difference in status between the client and the lawyer. The stud[ies] demonstrate the importance of examining the impact of this status difference from the perspective of the behavior of the service provider, in our case the student/lawyer behavior, and not just from the perspective of client behavior, as is advocated by the client-centered models.

Further, enlightenment on the way race may unconsciously affect the provider of services can be gleaned from a study involving physician breaches of patient confidentiality. In this study, 628 white male physicians were asked to complete a survey which sought to determine how frequently physicians breach the confidentiality of patients who were HIV positive by reporting them to public health authorities.[4] There were eight "patients" in the study. Each patient had a different combination of sex, race, and sexual preference. The eight patient histories were identical except for the description of the hypothetical patient. The study found that white male physicians would violate the confidentiality of black homosexual and heterosexual males more often than they would hypothetical patients in other categories. While the authors would not conclusively state that the results were a result of racism, they asserted that the results were consistent with racial prejudice. The results are also consistent with studies that show, in hospital emergency room treatment situations, physicians provide different levels of service to black patients than they do to white patients.

To date, there have been no empirical studies which seek to determine how the perceptions of white law students impact on their ability to represent clients of color, especially black clients. Yet, if we can glean anything from the works in other disciplines, it is that such studies could provide lawyers and students interested in client-centered counseling with a wealth of information about how negative nonverbal behavior exhibited by the lawyer and student/lawyer expectancies can influence the nature and quality of the interaction with the client and hamper our ability to give effective representation.

One of the characteristics of the difficult client is his reluctance to participate in the interviewing process. The authors of the client-centered counseling models provide suggestions to encourage client participation. These suggestions, according to the authors, should be successful if the client is not in need of more serious psychological assistance. There are many reasons, however, why clients may be reluctant to participate in the information-gathering process.

Francis and Sandra Terrell have both authored or co-authored numerous studies concerning black clients and mental health counseling. One of their earliest works involved developing a scale to measure a black client's level of mistrust of a white counselor.[5] Later, the Terrells sought to determine whether the race of the counselor would lead black clients with a high mistrust level to prematurely terminate therapy.[6] Previous psychological studies established that ethnic differences between client and counselor were related to premature termination of counseling. One explanation for the high dropout rate among black clients was that black clients did not trust white counselors and as a result often failed to establish a therapeutic alliance with white counselors.

Client trust and self-disclosure are interrelated principles. If the client mistrust level is high, it would not, therefore, be surprising to find low level of client self-disclosure. Self-disclosure is the process of making the self known to other persons. Studies have shown self-disclosure is dependent upon the level of client trust. Trust has been found to be influenced by the counselor's attitude toward the client.

Once again, the issue of nondisclosure bears directly upon the relationship established by the student/lawyer and the client. Failure of the client to disclose completely to the lawyer, particularly after the student/lawyer has "assured" the client of confidentiality, leads the student to feel the client has been less than honest with the student/lawyer. The student/lawyer may misinterpret apparent sullenness or hostility on the part of the client as an indication that the client is unwilling to establish a relationship with the student/lawyer.

As shown by the various studies of interracial situations, empathetic listening and active responses by themselves may be insufficient to address the underlying causes. Unless the student/lawyer is adequately trained to recognize the possibilities of the underlying cause of the threat, how can s/he respond appropriately? As advocates of client-centered counseling, we have elected to borrow the terminology and approach of the social scientists in the development of our own pedagogy. Knowing this, it doesn't seem prudent to then disregard the measurements the social scientists have developed to ensure that clients of color are serviced as meaningfully as clients who are of the same cultural or racial background as the counselor.

The Rebellious Idea of Lawyering against Subordination[1]

Gerald P. López[2]

Let me tell you about Catharine. My wife and I met her through some friends. She's a twenty-four-year-old, third-year law student, from one of those Dutch-English-French-Swedish-New England families from Delaware that ended up in Washington, D.C. She's not a student at the school where I teach. But she'd fit right in with some of the best progressive students that I've had over the years. She's young, smart, industrious, unassuming, motivated, and vocationally committed to doing left activist work as a lawyer. People in law would no doubt describe her as wanting to do "public interest" law. She unashamedly describes herself as wanting to help radically change the world.

She's done well in law school and has a good deal of experience in, and demonstrated commitment to, public interest work. So she should be a prime candidate for any job she might want. It's not that simple, however. She's finding it hard to define a vision of practice for herself in the midst of all these lawyers who seem so confident about what it is they are doing.

One way to approach her dilemma, Catharine decided, is to think about the lawyers she knows, in terms of what she admires about them and their practice and, conversely, what she hasn't found so impressive. Through her work, she's certainly met a lot of different types of lawyers. Some are nationally known and widely respected in their fields; others are far less noticed, but nonetheless remarkable in the work that they do. Of these, there are five she has particularly admired. Let me describe them all to you—or at least relate what Catharine's told me. I think they'll sound like lawyers you've known, too.

Take Teresa, the director of Advocates for Justice, the public interest "impact" litigation firm where Catharine worked after her first year of law school. Teresa is an old friend of Catharine's father. They met in law school while both were serving as student volunteers in a legal services program. They worked out of the same office, he primarily with the Black community, and she with her own Latino community. Although they eventually went separate ways, they have remained friends over the years. Her dad has always upheld this woman as smart and committed—an exemplary public interest lawyer—and, during Catharine's senior year in college, urged her to talk with Teresa about career plans. Apart from their personal relationship, Catharine fought hard to get the internship with Advocates for Justice. At her school it was considered a real catch, and she was sure she'd be able to do some exciting work.

When Catharine started working at Advocates for Justice, she found that her father was right. Teresa *is* wonderful, she *has* accomplished a lot, she does care an awful lot about making the world better. Teresa is forty-six years old and remains thoroughly dedicated to winning legal rights for the poor, people of color, and other oppressed groups. She works long hours preparing and litigating cases, she enjoys mastering and presenting highly intricate legal arguments, and she often appears before prestigious federal courts. Although she used to win all the time, she has found it increasingly difficult to get decisions that really serve as landmark cases. But she hasn't stopped trying. Still, looking back on her experience with Teresa, Catharine feels somewhat unsettled by what she saw. Something struck her as not quite right.

Teresa is committed to the idea of broad-based/social change through representation of subordinated groups in the courts. Though she started out representing mainly Latino clients, Advocates for Justice now aims to secure rights and attract attention to a wide range of progressive causes. She and her colleagues facilitate group representation through class actions and other large-scale "test case" litigation, and they are justifiably proud of the numerous cases they have brought on behalf of accused criminals, welfare recipients, victims of school segregation, mentally disabled patients, women seeking abortions, and undocumented children. Catharine discovered, to her surprise (and I was surprised that she was surprised), that Advocates for Justice often seeks out litigants to fit cases it has designed in advance, cases that strategically introduce sensitive social issues into the courts. In this search, Teresa seems to assume both that client groups perceive that they suffer injuries which can be redressed and that they are willing to share these perceptions with a lawyer. In turn, she takes it upon herself to coach the client groups to frame their interests in a form the law can process. Reluctantly, she must sometimes turn away otherwise worthy plaintiffs in the interest of finding the right test case. Catharine was most taken aback when she learned that Teresa must occasionally look for facts that aren't typical of the group she hopes to represent in order to present a more appealing case.

Teresa never does any "direct service" kind of work anymore. And she repeatedly insists that, while the organizations and community groups that work with Latinos probably do good things, they're not all that useful to her legal work. Once or twice they have helped find a client for Teresa to use in a test case and, on occasion, have joined in on a press conference. But that's the only sort of interaction that goes on between them. Catharine couldn't understand why Advocates for Justice disregards groups that seemed to her fundamentally important to a lawyer's work. But then, she thought, Teresa is Latina and probably does know the community as well as she says she does. Still, when Catharine explored the community a bit herself, she found a lot going on that she believed was obviously relevant to the organization's work. She couldn't help but feel that Advocates for Justice is missing out on making some connections that could be valuable for all. Those connections, she insists, just seem to matter.

Teresa accepts educating test-case clients about their upcoming role in the litigation process as part of her responsibility as a lawyer. Once she has recruited appropriate and willing litigants, she makes certain that each wants to be a test case. Though she believes their individual lives will be affected by the result, she does not delude them. She makes plain the broad social rather than individual orientation of test cases. She explains that the cases are highly technical actions and that clients don't have to worry about investing much of their time and energy. That's the attorney's job, and that's the way it should be. She believes that most of her clients would rather defer to her expertise anyway. "After all," she told Catharine, "why shouldn't the poor have the same opportunity as the rich to have a lawyer who takes care of their legal problems for them?" Besides, involving members of the client group may cause delay and make things "too messy."

For all her admiration of Teresa, Catharine was left with a number of reservations both about Teresa's practice and that of Advocates for Justice. Of course, she couldn't really talk to her dad about any of this; even if he were receptive, she didn't feel ready to articulate what lay behind her doubts. But she did ask herself questions. Can so many fundamental societal ills really be transformed into and defined as a "case," become a litigation strategy? Is that ever a positive or optimal strategy to pursue? Given the constraints on time and resources, shouldn't more grounded progressive groups, not to mention those who are being "represented," have some say about the ways that fights get fought? And wouldn't Advocates for Justice be better off hooking its ideas into broader political strategies to achieve social change?

With all this in mind, Catharine decided to take a very different kind of job following her second year of law school, one with a small union-side labor firm. She made her first contact with the firm through one of its partners, Abe, who spoke at her school as part of a series on alternative law practices. She had been impressed by his seemingly unwavering commitment to defending the rights and expanding the power of organized labor —and, she admitted, she was more than a little intrigued by the old left labor politics that he still espoused. When she was offered a job with the firm, she looked forward most to working with a lawyer who seemed to have found a way to live out his politics in his everyday practice.

Abe is a fifty-five-year-old partner in a firm of eight attorneys and dedicated to contributing his share to the labor movement. As a child of the Depression and a son of garment workers, Abe feels real sympathy for the individuals who call his firm with employment problems. At the same time, however, he feels a constant pressure to maintain the firm's profits. His firm accepts clients based largely on the ability to pay up front and the potential for a long-term relationship with the firm, and he feels badly that he and his co-workers often have to refer needy workers elsewhere. Over the years, the firm has represented mostly local labor unions. Though the firm prides itself in taking only labor-side cases, the degree to which Abe and the other partners are insiders with union leadership— and what that connection seems to mean to them and their work—came as a surprise to Catharine.

Abe and his colleagues do nearly all the legal work that unions generate: they provide legal advice; negotiate collective bargaining agreements; represent the union in arbitration and proceedings before the National Labor Relations Board (usually against the employer, but sometimes against workers who sue the union for breach of the duty of fair representation); manage the pension fund; and litigate as it becomes necessary and if it doesn't swallow up too much of the firm's limited resources. The firm once did a fair amount of wrongful termination work for non-union workers but over the years decreased this part of the practice because it wasn't very profitable.

Everyone has his place in the labor movement, says Abe, and his is to lend his professional legal expertise. Typically, Catharine has found, Abe gets a call from the president of the union, who explains the union's problem, the union's objective, and the kind of work he'd like the firm to do. The two spend some time together working through some strategic options, and then Abe (actually, one of his associates) researches and writes the memo, brief, or proposal for negotiation. Then before a negotiation or board proceeding, Abe sits down with the union leaders to discuss the law, to fine-tune strategy, or to prepare witnesses. Occasionally Abe presses leadership on views and positions, but the structure of the relationship more routinely leaves those matters to "union discretion." When all is said and done, Abe finds himself regularly doing almost exactly what union leadership wants.

That doesn't seem to bother Abe much, though. His general philosophy is that unions *should* run the labor movement. That's their expertise and they are his clients. Nevertheless, born and raised in solidarity with organized workers, he seems to Catharine to have struggled with the conflict sometimes involved between representing the interests of union leaders and representing those of union members. He has repeatedly justified the more distasteful parts of his practice with the blanket claim that, on the whole, unions do a lot of good for workers; if he and his colleagues didn't represent them in certain "unpleasant" actions, the already beleaguered labor movement might be further weakened. Though Abe worked closely with workers and had been a proponent of rank-and-file uprisings, he told Catharine that he now sees those actions as often jeopardizing labor's place in the political world.

If the world that Abe moves in demands a comfortable relationship with labor luminaries, big pension funds, and conventional kinds of clout, the world that "poverty lawyers" move in is quite another thing altogether. At least that's what first struck Catharine when she worked with yet another lawyer, Jonathan, through a law school course centered around supervised field work. In fact, Jonathan is what Catharine has always imagined a "real poverty lawyer" to be. He works very hard under serious time constraints, and he effectively handles cases for a number of different clients at the same time. He is numbed by the repetitive nature of the problems he faces and irritated (often unconsciously) by the fact that he is not taken seriously by society or the legal community. Still, for all his good work and excellent intentions, Catharine was left with the gnawing feeling that his practice could be significantly better.

Jonathan is twenty-nine, thoroughly committed to helping poor people, and zealous in his dislike of those strongly implicated in their oppression—welfare bureaucrats, landlords, and the like. He feels overwhelmed by the number of people who come into his office with housing problems. Most of them face evictions that cannot be legally prevented: the single mother of two being evicted because she cannot pay the rent; the man of eighty against whom a default judgment has already been obtained. Jonathan has deep sympathy for all of the people who come in with housing problems. Yet, because of the sheer numbers involved, he told Catharine he has to accept clients by the "triage" method, selecting the "healthiest" cases for representation but commiserating with those who have no defense.

Jonathan sees part of his mission as educating the community about housing law. He does this in several ways. With those he cannot help, Catharine has often seen him spend time explaining in plain, lay language what has happened to them, how they can try to forestall eviction for a few days, and how to avoid having this happen to them again. With cases that he does accept for representation, he always takes time with the client (usually right before settlement) to make sure that the client understands her or his legal rights, the legal issues in the case, and what to do if faced again with an eviction (usually to get to a lawyer as quickly as possible).

Jonathan's strategy with most of the cases he accepts is to exploit every procedural tactic he can think of, and time and time again he wins on a "technicality": an error in the three-day notice or a problem with the service of the complaint. He is well aware, however, that the landlord can ultimately outlast him and find some legal reason to evict the tenant, especially if the tenant is having a hard time paying rent. So, most of the cases end in settlements, whereby the landlord agrees to allow the tenant to stay in the apartment or to reduce the rent if the apartment is a mess. Only infrequently has Jonathan actually been able to get a landlord to make substantial repairs to substandard apartments. Most clients, he says, are happy with a negotiated settlement and feel that they finally beat their landlords out of something. But to Catharine they often seemed mystified about what their lawyer actually did for them. She wondered if they weren't returning to apartments that looked very much like they did before they started complaining, and how on earth that must feel.

It's not obvious to Catharine that Teresa, Abe, and Jonathan have much in common with each other. Their philosophies on how to change the world diverge considerably. Their methods vary widely. And those with whom they work come from different walks of life, however much they all purport to help those subordinated by social and political life (though they might not use those terms). Still, it may be that these lawyers share more than she might be able to put her finger on. It may be that it is exactly those things that they share that best capture what I call the regnant idea of practice. And it may be those very commonalities that Catharine is struggling against.

Breaking Away from the Regnant Idea

Breaking away from [the regnant] idea of the lawyer for the subordinated can be daunting—as Catharine has discovered. Even when you think "something's the matter," you don't quite know what to do about it. Daily activities, office habits, and the like usually make you feel either that you're picking on too many "little things" or that you're taking on way too much in the process of resisting, much less rebelling against, what "everybody" seems to be doing and thinking. That this idea of practice (like so many things "thoroughly" known) remains so taken for granted hardly helps you to know how to order your thoughts and experiences. The culture surrounding and supporting this image of the lawyer for the subordinated makes you feel that you don't have much of a chance struggling against it.

If daunting to some, and apparently unnecessary to others, breaking away from the regnant idea presents a central challenge for all those engaged in the modern struggle against subordination. It is the challenge that Catharine herself feels she faces as she tries to build a practice for herself in the world. And she's not wrong in thinking she's got her work cut out for her. The regnant idea imposes unjustifiably limited relations between those working against subordination and those strategies available to wage the fight. It does not permit anyone in the fight, whether lay or professional, to experience others as part of a working team. And it almost laughs off anyone who wants to regard others as co-eminent practitioners.

But that's not all. The regnant idea does not acknowledge the connection between different forms of practical know-how inevitably at work in each and every person's effort to get by day to day. And it does not facilitate, much less coordinate, responses to problems that originate outside its understanding of the social world. When all is said and done, the regnant idea of the lawyer for the subordinated helps undermine the very possibility for re-imagined social arrangements that lies at the heart of any serious effort to take on the status quo. In so doing, it wastes the very excellence it sometimes displays and reduces itself to another kind of bondage to formula.

The Rebellious Idea of Lawyering against Subordination

And that's why Sophie and Amos mean so much to Catharine. They are the only two lawyers she's met, though not the only two activists, whose practices in many ways look and feel different from those of Teresa, Abe, and Jonathan. Sophie is a woman whom Catharine first met at the end of the summer when Sophie was translating for Spanish speakers at the workshop on reproductive rights. Catharine was initially intrigued by the nature of her work, and impressed by her gentle and confident manner. Continuing to work closely with Sophie over this school year, she has discovered far more about Sophie and her work that she can only describe as inspiring.

In fact, when all is said and done, Sophie is probably the lawyer whom Catharine would most like to emulate in her own practice.

Sophie works out of the neighborhood center of a legal aid organization, under the auspices of its Immigration Project. Though other attorneys are involved with the project, she is the only one housed in her particular office. She is in her mid-thirties, one of ten red-headed Irish Catholic kids in her family.

Sophie lives in the neighborhood where she works, and to Catharine that appears to make all the difference in the world. The community is a small one of predominantly low-income people, largely of color, part of the metropolitan mosaic that is Oakland. Getting stuck in the role of "permanent outsider" is a real possibility here—this community has had more than its share of so-called friends flitting in and out trying to make changes. Yet Sophie lives just a few blocks from where she works. She walks to her office each morning and gets her lunch from La Frontera (the local taco truck) nearly every day. She has been an active and interested resident throughout the three years she has lived and worked in the community. She and her husband are members of the local Tenants' Council, and they regularly attend as well as help organize and support community events. Their son is in the first grade at the local elementary school, and they participate in the school's Parent Support Network.

Living in her neighborhood is not all cheery or romantic, though. Like everyone else, Sophie has to watch out for her safety. She has to put up with a local library that is small and understaffed. She has no neighborhood park to take her son to on the weekends, no nearby recreation center where he can play with other kids. She has to travel a long way to get to the bank, or even to a sizable grocery store. With everyone else, she has to fight for more resources in local schools. She has to challenge Pacific Gas and Electric rate hikes seemingly every quarter. And she constantly has to battle with the local rent board to get the rent-control ordinance enforced.

Sophie always has things going on all burners. Even so, she is remarkably good at following through on the commitments she makes.

For Sophie, establishing opportunities for people to help themselves and others isn't limited to imaginative case processing. She keeps a constant watch, often spending a lot of time outside of her office, for news of efforts that she can learn from and contribute to. When she heard about a group of recently documented women who wanted to start a housekeeping cooperative, for example, she let them know through a mutual friend that she'd be interested in working with them—offering them what she knew from her own earlier experiences in Mexico and getting a chance to learn from this kind of entrepreneurial effort here in the United States. Such overtures don't often pan out, as Sophie herself told Catharine, but this time these women really hit it off. Together they got the cooperative started, assembled a modest handbook about cooperatives as an organizational arrangement, and put on a series of workshops sharing their own experiences with other housekeepers in the Bay Area.

Amos is a very different sort from Sophie—at least that's what Catharine thought when she first laid eyes on him. He's a large Black man with big meaty hands, a deep, resonant voice, a jowly face, wrinkly, very forty-five-ish eyes, and a few white-tipped hairs. Anything but a redheaded Irish Catholic granola head. If Sophie's the kind whose leadership skills sneak up on you, Amos is just the sort you anticipate would dominate any group. Not necessarily because he needs to, but because everyone expects him to—maybe because they don't quite know what to do with this "presence" that seems to fill every room he enters.

But whatever the apparent differences between Sophie and Amos, Catharine quickly found that their firmly held convictions and notions of practice are remarkably alike. Though he carries himself proudly and speaks confidently, Amos has a gentle, inquisitive nature that is evident when he is working. When Catharine saw him interviewing the director of the women's shelter where she was volunteering, she noticed how he was all eyes and ears—carefully assimilating new information, patiently pursuing trajectories that the director hinted at, no matter how provisional or uncertain. He didn't mechanically follow a script in conducting his needs-assessment survey of those in the community who work most closely with families and children. Rather, he seemed to have a broad and accommodating view of what he was trying to learn about. He expected his survey and his methods to be revised constantly as he met with folks such as the shelter's director.

That sort of embracing curiosity seems to inform Amos's thoughts not only about his survey but also about the whole new project he was then trying to define more concretely. When Catharine first met Amos, he had just begun as coordinator of United Help for Families (UHF), a brand new nonprofit organization in the East Bay. UHF's founders had envisioned an entity that would respond to their frustrations over the (dis)array of resources and assistance available for children and families in their community—over turf battles, gaps in and duplications of services, strategic ruts, mindless referrals, organizational mayhem. They had given the entity enough definition to raise considerable funds. But they had deliberately waited to hire a coordinator and staff whose first task would be to ground and, if necessary, reconfigure the project after a more systematic assessment of East Bay needs and of federal, state, and private support for services. They obviously thought Amos was "their man."

If you asked Sophie and Amos, they'd probably say they see themselves as only beginning to work through what their practices ought to look like. Still, if you study what they think and do in everyday circumstances, the outline of a rarely articulated idea of lawyering begins to emerge. In this idea—what I call the rebellious idea of lawyering against subordination—lawyers must know how to work with (not just on behalf of) women, low-income people, people of color, gays and lesbians, the disabled, and the elderly. They must know how to collaborate with other professional and lay allies rather than ignoring the help that these other problem-solvers may provide in a given situation. They must understand how to educate those with whom they work, particularly about law and professional lawyering, and, at the same time, they must open themselves up to being educated by all those with whom they come in contact, particularly about the traditions and experiences of life on the bottom and at the margins.

To move in these directions, those who would "lawyer rebelliously" must, like Sophie and Amos, ground their work in the lives and in the communities of the subordinated themselves, whether they work for local outfits, regional offices, or national policy-making agencies. They must, like Sophie and Amos, continually evaluate the likely interaction between legal and "nonlegal" approaches to problems. They must, like Sophie and Amos, know how to work with others in brainstorming, designing, and executing strategies aimed at responding immediately to particular problems and, more generally, at fighting social and political subordination. They must understand how to be part of coalitions, as well as how to build them, and not just for purposes of filing or "proving up" a lawsuit (as Teresa, Abe, or Jonathan might do). They must appreciate how all that they do with others requires attention not only to international, national, and regional matters but also to their interplay with seemingly more mundane local affairs. At bottom, the rebellious idea of lawyering demands that lawyers (and those with whom they work) nurture sensibilities and skills compatible with a collective fight for social change.

Clients invite lawyers to intervene in their lives, to work with them, and in so doing to help them help themselves. Asking for and providing help are central not only to professional lawyering but to everyday living—to the practice of problem-solving that consumes much of our lives. In this sense, when we say professional lawyering we necessarily refer to one dimension of getting by day to day, one way in which we make and change life, one practical knowledge among other practical knowledges, one form of all I mean when I say "lawyering." A professional lawyer's work, as Sophie, Amos, and Catharine would affirm, inevitably takes place within the larger world of problem-solving, within other peoples' lawyering, and within the client's social (not just legal) situation.

This may well be a critical insight for these women and anyone else hoping—needing, really—to challenge the status quo. We all change our world by learning to isolate (and therefore highlight) problems, and by understanding that we can act on those problems by applying familiar techniques. Realizing that we can learn to see an "experience" as a distinct "problem" that can be acted upon—as when a battered woman learns of the shared reality of other women's experiences—can often dramatically accelerate the transformation of feeling into action. We begin more regularly to see how we can take what we have and put it to work, in terms of not just intuitively getting by but deliberately taking on what we otherwise perceive as largely unchangeable.

But power—the capacity to make things the way we want them—isn't something only some people have. At least Amos and Sophie don't see it that way. And neither should we. Power necessarily runs in all directions within relationships. No person, no group is ever *absolutely* powerless in any relationship, not battered women and not low-income people of color in the East Bay. In fact, when we call a person or a group "subordinated" or "victimized," we're always describing a state of relative powerlessness. For all that they endure, battered women and low-income people of color still retain the capacity to work rebelliously with both stock and improvised stories—the capacity to resist victimization and subordination and to reverse its tendencies.

This is not to say that Amos and Sophie think (any more than we should) that groups of people find themselves persistently battered or poor simply because they lack the imagination to use their power well. Granted, no one is weaponless in a power struggle. But some of us have tanks and some of us only rocks. The relatively powerless do lose more and more often (jobs, security, lives), and the forces that shape these losses are sometimes determined in arenas largely inaccessible to most of us. That's what everybody (not just young idealists like Catharine) finds so hard about taking on the status quo. Yet nobody really believes that power comes exclusively out of a gun. Dictators themselves rely in part upon persuasion. And with good reason. We all challenge, even the weakest among us and even if admittedly on unfair terms, the ways in which power should be shared in the stories we live by.

We cannot escape the exercise of power either, certainly not through law and not even through love. Battered women and poor people probably know this as well as anyone. All of life's struggles—in the family, in the market, in the courtroom, in the street—occur through exercises of power that shape and respond to our relationships.

This is not to say that any of us ever "chooses" in any simple sense how things will turn out. Just ask Amos and Sophie or, for that matter, Teresa, Abe, and Jonathan. Choice suggests both a sharp separation between who's choosing and what's chosen and a set of well-defined and stable options. It conjures up images of unconfused and unconfusing transactions—of a world in which we are of a single mind about ourselves, about others, and about our environment. It evokes visions of uncoerced and uncoercive transactions—of a world in which we select our individual and collective identities free from constraints imposed by social institutions and practices.

To help us remember how our everyday lawyering is inescapably a part of the power we all inevitably exercise, try picturing things the way Sophie and Amos must. Think of social life as networks of competing power strategies. Think of every social situation as the convergence of particular power strategies. These strategies frequently take the form of stories and arguments. That's right, the very same stories and arguments we all use to move things along. We tell ourselves stories about the situations in which we find ourselves in order to understand them, to reach desired outcomes, and to give life meaning. And through what we call argument we talk about or debate the very meanings of the stories we tell and live by. These stories and arguments (in both stock and improvised form) together constitute important strategies through which we help establish meaning and distribute power (if only temporarily).

Along with the many informal strategies we daily use, law provides more formal strategies to understand and shape our relationships. Contrary to popular belief, law is not a set of rules but a set of stories and storytelling practices that describe and prescribe social reality and a set of conventions for defining and resolving disputes. Law is not a collection of definitions and mandates to be memorized and applied but a culture composed of storytellers, audiences, remedial ceremonies, a set of standard stories and arguments, and a variety of conventions about story-writing, storytelling, argument-making, and the structure and content of legal stories. Rooted in the larger culture and daily sharing the larger culture's norms and conventions, the legal culture nonetheless generates over time its own way of doing things and injects that way back into the larger culture. Like the practice of everyday living, "law" delineates something we learn how to do.

A professional lawyer's practice, however ambitious, generally parallels the practice we all engage in as problem-solving lay lawyers. In representing people, both professional and lay lawyers learn from and deploy story/argument strategies to exercise power in necessary or desirable ways.

The Challenge of Working Together

As much as lay and professional lawyering share, and as much sense as working together makes for subordinated people and professional lawyers, tension inevitably pervades this collaboration. Amos, Sophie, and all those who work within the rebellious idea of lawyering labor to appreciate this tension, to identify its terms, and to negotiate its traps.

Yet these ensembles of problem-solvers never feel entirely confident of their success in working through these tensions; instead, they typically see themselves as "plugging along," alert to some dynamics, blindsided by others. Along the way, these people become acutely aware of the role that forgiveness and patience must play in their mutual efforts to reconstruct their work as together they confront the problems entailed in fighting subordination.

Were these left-lawyers to see through the eyes of Amos or Sophie, they would discover just how often subordinated people do deploy story/argument strategies, some remarkably ingenious and resourceful, to contest the roles others would assign them. They would notice how often the help that subordinated people seek from lawyers results from the operation of just such a strategy, a strategy that importantly interrupts daily life and calls attention, in the form of a dispute, to life that is unacceptable as it is. A lawyer need not romanticize subordinated people, nor treat them all as transcendently clever or immune to hoodwinking and resignation, nor downplay her or his own ability to help with certain sorts of problems in order to respect and trust their resourcefulness. The lawyer need only treat them as capable, with a will to fight, and with considerable experience in resisting and occasionally reversing subordinated status.

[On the] Road Back In: Community Lawyering in Indigenous Communities[1]

Christine Zuni Cruz[2]

I am a member/citizen of the Pueblo of Isleta, one of the nineteen pueblos and one of the twenty-two tribal nations located in the state of New Mexico. I am also of San Juan Pueblo descent. Since leaving college I have had only one goal, and that has been to return "home" to use my education for "the people": an easy thing to say, but not an easy thing to accomplish. First of all, I had to travel what I like to call the "road back in," not an easy road to find, nor an easy road to travel. It seemed like all the roads leading out of the reservation were paved, many by the federal government, but you had to look long and hard for that road leading back in. The temptation of the "brain drain expressway" overcomes a lot of people, and they find themselves hurtling down that road to big cities and bright lights, some detoured for years, and others never to return. I found that, as you travel that road back in, you find yourself critically appraising and then discarding some of the baggage you acquired when you were outside the community, perhaps because the road back in is a hard road, and you find that a lot of what you acquired is just heavy, useless baggage which is actually impeding your journey.

As a native person, a practitioner, and an instructor of Indian law, my view of community is profoundly affected by the uniqueness of tribal community and native identity. This includes both the attributes of a community or nation of native peoples and an individual's connection to that community.

The three voices I speak in—native, lawyer, and clinician—provide different perspectives. As native, I speak as a native person living within my native community; as lawyer, I speak from my experience in working within the community; as clinician, I speak combining the above voices, seeking to improve the lawyering done in the name of, on behalf of, for, and with native peoples and native nations. These voices inform my discussion of community and culture. The basis of my ideas stems from my experience of being part of a distinct native community, long served by lawyers and a profession external to the community. My perspective on community comes from my work within my own pueblo, and within other pueblos both as a lawyer and a judge. My perspective on culture is closely related to community, but it is also informed by the work I engaged in over several years to revise the New Mexico Children's Code to provide greater cultural protection for native children and youth.

Lawyering which respects those who comprise the community as being capable and indispensable to their own representation and which seeks to understand the community yields far different results both for the community and the lawyer. Self-determination is important to lawyering which benefits the community and the people within that community. If the lawyer cannot respect a peoples' culture, which means understanding a peoples' goal toward self-determination, then the people will not be well represented.

However, the means by which the end is obtained are all important. Successful community lawyering has just as much to do with process as it does with outcome, and when one values community, process becomes critical. Process is critical because for native peoples community lawyering is about self-determination, both for the community and the individual, about recognizing traditional norms and practices, and about valuing relationships.

This paper looks at lawyering for and within distinct communities and at the responsibility lawyers have to understand how culture, both their own and their clients', impacts their lawyering. More specifically, I will discuss lawyering for and within distinct native communities and how clinical instructors and students can prepare to enter distinct communities and practice across cultures.

Indian community emanates first from those relations created by blood ties and tradition. Generally, an Indian person's community is the tribe they are born into and tied to by membership and by participation. Thus, community includes a person's nuclear and extended family, and all who are tied by other relationships to the nuclear and extended family, by religious, marital, or other societal bonds. Community may also be defined in relation to land. For Indian people, community may be defined as "the people" within certain territorial landmarks, boundaries of the reservation, or specific areas within those landmarks and boundaries. These definitions work for describing tribal-land–based communities, but not necessarily for describing the urban-based Indian community. Thus, community may also include the participatory groups of which one is a part, which expand those which arise from blood, custom, or societal obligation, and which arise as a result of some commonly shared bond, whether it is geographic or racial, religious or political identity.

The recognition of the right to one's culture, or cultural rights, as a basic human right is a critical matter to native peoples, particularly because destructive or assimilative practices aimed at indigenous culture have been the norm applied to eradicate or absorb native peoples historically. The recognition that culture is a pronounced, valued, and integral component of lawyering on behalf of native individuals and communities is of no small significance to native peoples.

I use culture broadly to include all that gives us a cultural identity: language, race, ethnicity, religion, land, worldview, foods, and music, for example. Culture, and hence cultural identity, impacts lawyering. For example, the culture of our client influences how our client speaks to us; the culture of the lawyer also influences how the lawyer speaks, what the lawyer hears, and how she listens.

Initially, I saw the opportunity to teach students with a specific interest in Indian law in a clinical setting as an opportunity to improve the overall delivery of legal services to Indian peoples. I would say now that I also see an opportunity to expose students to the receipt of legal services from the various perspectives of native clients with the hope of influencing students' awareness of how their own consideration of culture and community directly impacts the quality of the legal service delivered to native peoples. The first time I heard a student say she, for the first time ever, "saw" her own culture and considered how her own culture and background impacted her and therefore, her lawyering, as a result of her clinical experience, I felt everything up to that point, and still feel that everything beyond it, has been worth it.

Perhaps because of my own native background, when I look at communities I cannot separate them from the cultural markers which make them distinct communities. A discussion of community lawyering which does not include cultural considerations is incomplete because of this impact of culture on all aspects of the attorney-client relationship. Cultural influences are not always so apparent, nor easily understood, which is precisely why it is important not to lose sight of the tremendous influence culture can have on clients from distinct communities.

Many lawyers cross cultural boundaries in their work, and are astute about this fact; fewer, however, seem to grapple with their need to understand the influence of the client's culture on the client and the legal issue or problem faced. Even less recognizable is the influence the lawyer's own culture has on the lawyer him/herself, his/her lawyering style, approach, and problem-solving technique and their impact on the client. In crossing cultural boundaries, one is most acutely aware of the culture entered; equally important, however, is the awareness that one is viewing the "entered" culture from one's own particular cultural perspective. Keeping in mind that crossing cultural boundaries is a two-way process is critical; it requires the lawyer to consider his or her own cultural view as well as the cultural view of the client.

For example, a lawyer representing a client with a difference in language faces multiple issues. From the initial interview to trial or other resolution of the matter, each of the basic lawyering skills must be modified to accommodate the difference in language. From the competency of the interpreter, the interjection of a third party into an interview, the language skill of the attorney who does not make use of an interpreter, the questioning, the language itself, to the politics surrounding the use of a language other than English, language difference can greatly challenge the lawyering skills of the average attorney and raise issues of the competent representation of the client by the lawyer.

Even if lawyer and client speak the same language, whether it is English or another language, differences in cultural values and worldview can affect the quality of understanding. This is where self-awareness of one's own cultural trappings, coupled with an awareness of the differences in cultural values and worldview of the client, can help an attorney.

In seeking to address the relationship between culture and lawyering, there are many challenging issues encountered in both the classroom and the real world. The most difficult of these include issues of self-identity, cross-cultural communication and understanding, cognizance of place, outside/insider issues, and assuming responsibility for understanding the impact of lawyering choices on the client, the community, or both.

It is much more meaningful to discuss issues of community and culture in concrete rather than abstract terms. The following sections are intended to provide more of an idea of how considerations of community and culture operate in the real world of lawyering for specific native communities. It is also intended to show some of the difficulties that arise in seeking to introduce considerations of community and culture in a profession long cast in terms of individuality and an acultural approach to the law.

Community lawyers do more than represent individual clients. They represent clients in definable communities. They learn about the cultures, values, and beliefs of the people in the community. They see problems of individual clients in the context of the community. Individuals in communities may face all sorts of problems, but lawyers engaged in community lawyering go beyond individual cases to develop and implement communitywide solutions that will benefit others in the community who may face similar problems. Community lawyers grapple with the tension between "zealous representation"[3] of individual clients and community concerns. Community lawyers are also aware of the impact that their work may have on the community. Consequently, community lawyers seek to help the community take advantage of the legal system in light of the culture, values, and beliefs of the people in the community.

Many of the challenging questions which present themselves in community lawyering stem from the relationship of the individual (as client or as lawyer) to the community. Many clinics and private practitioners represent individuals from distinct communities, such as tribal rural communities or urban neighborhoods; some also represent the community as a whole or groups from within the community. Whether representation is undertaken of individuals, of the community as a whole, or of a specific group within the community, a number of questions arise regarding the relationship of the individual to the community.

Several examples come to mind, but I will use one which I believe illustrates how knowledge of community standards and even knowledge of a community's physical features can help to understand client decision-making and improve the understanding and therefore the representation of the client.

I received a call from an attorney who was quite perplexed by resistance she received from a client, a friend of the attorney, after having given what she thought was great advice to a legal issue he had confronted. She thought I could shed some light on his unexplained reaction to the advice. The attorney had suggested that her client engage in a legal fiction regarding his residence in the community. The client had informed her that he owned a home within the community, and the attorney suggested he claim that home as his legal residence. However, the client rejected the advice outright, leaving the attorney without an explanation and feeling quite uneasy. Because I was familiar with the community she asked me to suggest why the advice would be so soundly rejected. I gave her two related possibilities: one, there is a high premium placed on accountability within the community. To say you live in the community, when in fact you don't, would be known to all within the community to be untrue, and would be shameful to the individual who could and undoubtedly would be called on by the small community to account for the "legal fiction", once [its members] became aware of it. Two, there are many "homes" in the community which are old and uninhabitable. It was possible that her client owned one of these homes, which would make it more of an untruth, rather than a legal fiction, to say his legal residence was in that home. She reported later that the "possibilities" proved to be correct.

The community lawyering approach situates and considers the client both within the context of the community and as an individual. In the example above, knowledge of the community's physical features and of the community's values helps explain the client's reaction. Perhaps this information would be obtained from the client himself, under a client-centered approach to lawyering. Under a community lawyering approach, however, which situates the client in the context of his/her community, it is expected that proposed solutions and their impact on the client as an individual and in relation to community will be queried. Should the client not volunteer this information, the community lawyer would be expected to independently raise and explore solutions in the community context with the client. In addition, the community lawyer would be concerned with community values and would become acquainted with the community's physical features as a result of visiting and spending time in the community. The difference between the community lawyering approach and the client-centered approach is primarily one of challenging the individualistic approach embedded in client-centered lawyering. The premise of community lawyering is that cultural influences and the client's position in relation to the community must be understood by the lawyer as impacting the client and that the lawyer has a responsibility for recognizing this.

Crossing tribal boundaries in our work makes us acutely aware of how much we learn by respecting differences and working with them; we pursue different methods of obtaining information as the cultural, political, and governmental structure of native communities dictates.

An attorney, bothered that a tribal court would not treat a court order involving a client like a public document and release it to her on behalf of her client, sent out a letter to the court questioning why the court would not release the public court order to her. The judge reminded the attorney that tribal courts are different from state courts and warned against expecting tribal courts to do things in the same manner as state courts. The judge did release the order to the client, but only after ascertaining her approval because it involved a family matter. It provided a tremendous learning opportunity to the attorney, underscored a basic principle and reminded the attorney how easy it is to take the wrong approach, even when trying to integrate community and culture into lawyering.

It is also important to be respectful of the information obtained and how it should be used.

> We have many particular things which we hold internal to our cultures. These things are spiritual in nature. . . . They are ours and they are not for sale. Because of this, I suppose it's accurate to say that such matters are our "secrets," the things that bind us together in our identities as distinct peoples. It's not that we never make outsiders aware of our secrets, but we—not they—decide what, how much, and to what purpose this knowledge is to be put. That's absolutely essential to our cultural integrity, and thus to our survival as peoples. . . . Respect for and balance between all things, that's our most fundamental spiritual concept.[4]

The corollary to the point raised above is the extent to which a community client is considered in the context of his/her individuality. Just as it is important to carefully consider and explore with clients the community context in which their legal issue may be situated, it is also important to consider a client's relationship to the community, how a client is situated in the community, or how a client may wish to operate within the context of the community. This raises three issues. One is the need to be aware of stereotypes and overgeneralizations, which arise either as a result of general information about a community or as a result of specific information acquired about a community in the course of work within or with particular communities. One attorney assumed a client was familiar with traditional indigenous dispute resolution simply because the client was from a particular tribe. When the attorney discovered the client had no knowledge of the process, the attorney immediately recognized that he was operating on an unchecked assumption and saw it as a valuable lesson regarding his underlying generalizations about both the client and the process. When stereotypes or overfamiliarization with both problems and people from a community begin to drive the lawyering of individuals, there is significant danger in the failure to see viable solutions that may be available or problems with the "standard" approach and its applicability to an individual's unique circumstance.

One illustration of the above is currently surrounded in some controversy. Individual clients residing on Pueblo reservations have sought divorces from state courts for years in situations where both husband and wife reside on the reservation. Attorneys serving Pueblo clients have accepted these clients and obtained divorces in state court. The Pueblos currently do not provide an action for divorce within their tribal court systems; the greatest relief individuals can obtain is a legal separation. The approach [the clinic] has taken in handling these cases is based on two premises: one, that clients obtain the greatest relief possible, a legal separation, from the tribal forum; and two, that the only relief sought from the state court be the dissolution of marriage itself. The clinic also seeks to file not only a divorce petition, but a petition to domesticate the tribal court's legal separation decree, thus affirming the tribe's exclusive jurisdiction over all other matters related to the separation including child custody and support, alimony, and division of personal and real property. The practice of filing a petition to domesticate tribal court domestic relations orders was brought to the clinic from my private practice in other family law cases and applied to the divorce cases we accept to reinforce state recognition of tribal court orders. This approach allows the individual to obtain the narrowest legal relief from state court, with the greatest respect being accorded to exclusive tribal jurisdiction. At a recent continuing legal education seminar, however, the practice of seeking divorces from state court by individuals residing on Pueblo reservations was challenged as contrary to tribal sovereignty and as outside the state's jurisdiction. It was asserted that the state lacks jurisdiction over domestic relations and other matters involving tribal residents. From the individual Pueblo perspective, however, the unfortunate reality of divorce leaves seeking dissolution of state-licensed marriages in state court as the only recourse to severing a legally recognized status which otherwise affects both parties and their ability to remarry, their tax status, and their debt obligations. The Pueblo stance on not providing for divorce is deeply imbedded in religion, yet the need for individual relief cannot be ignored. It presents a classic conflict of community and individual interests, which is further complicated by jurisdictional and sovereignty concerns.

Of the work that I have engaged in at the community level, success has only been possible due to the strengths of the community itself; the technicalities of the law were only a part of the picture. To see so clearly that the law and the lawyer were secondary, tools in the hands of those represented, helped me to see the role of the lawyer as being side by side with the client and sometimes behind the client, and rarely out in front. Serving as counselor and advisor were as critical as serving as mouthpiece.

In representing a tribe on a request (which was denied) made to the state for a stoplight at an intersection of two state highways located on the reservation, easements for which had been granted by the tribe to the state, three extra-legal factors influenced the outcome: the resolve of the leadership and council, their participation in the negotiations, and the detrimental impact of external commuters on the safety of the tribal population. Each of these, while considered by the attorney, were not considered in quite the same way in the initial analysis of the issue. Were the attorney to have devised the approach, it would not have been the same approach ultimately used and influenced by the council and the leadership. The influence of community, the dynamics put into play when the client is a tribe, the willingness of the attorney to be directed as opposed to being directive, and to respect and understand the decision-making process of the tribe were important to the attorney's ultimate approach to the issue. Considering the community impacts and changes the lawyering approach.

In the practice of Indian law, community representation entails the representation of Indian nations. Oren Lyons, Faithkeeper of the Turtle Clan of the Onondaga Nation and spokesman for the Six Nations Iroquois Confederacy, in commenting on the attorney-client relationship in an address on the legal representation of Indian nations, stated, "When you talk about client relationships, you're talking about the future of nations. It's a great responsibility. I sure would not like to be a lawyer."[5]

The Hmong Campaign for Justice: A Practitioner's Perspective[1]

Victor M. Hwang[2]

There existed a chasm between the rhetoric of equal justice and the reality of people of color. The chasm was clearly seen in the justice system especially for Asian Pacific Americans and we felt an urgent need to do something about it.

—Attorney Dale Minami, on the impetus for the creation of the Asian Law Caucus[3]

Why the disjuncture? Why the dissociation? And what might be done? Put another way: In post–civil rights America, how might theories, lawyers, and activists bridge both the "gap of chasmic proportions" between progressive race theory and political lawyering practice and the growing divide between law and racial justice?

—Professor Eric Yamamoto, raising the question of the divide between practitioners and theorists[4]

So why do we not bridge this chasm between progressive thought and action? The reasons are varied. Progressive academics have explained that they are too much under attack within their profession, that they have little experience with political activism and community struggles, and that their jobs are simply to produce theory for theory's sake. Civil rights practitioners, on the other hand, have countered that their failure to engage in progressive race theory results from such factors as inertia on the part of attorneys, the lag time on the part of academia in producing relevant analysis, a lack of energy to read difficult critical theory, and impracticality. While these excuses certainly have a ring of truth, they do not explain the successful alliance between neoconservative attorneys, politicians, and theorists.

But of even greater concern than the practical barriers, some progressive academics have raised the philosophical and ideological question of whether they should cooperate with frontline attorneys at all. This school of thought contends that social change can come only when there is a convergence of interests between the needs of the minority and the will of the majority, and therefore any momentary victory through the courts is only fleeting in substance and more likely to arouse a majority backlash.

The problem is that while we can debate the intangible but real harms caused by the chasm between progressive theorists and practitioners, we cannot ignore the daily injuries done to our communities by orchestrated assaults on their rights and by barriers to the pursuit of legal recourse. Families that are being unlawfully evicted, working in hazardous sweatshops, facing deportation, or being denied basic life-sustaining benefits do not care whether the change is temporary or systemic; they are concerned with the realities of food, shelter, health, and employment. Life must go on even in the absence of an alliance with the academics; that is, a true critical race praxis combining "critical, pragmatic, socio-legal analysis with political lawyering and community organizing."[5] Frontline community advocates have turned instead to their clients and their communities for centering and direction. While academics continue to question the value of "regnant lawyering," many frontline attorneys have evolved into "rebellious" and "political" lawyers, engaging in legal advocacy which is "grounded in the lives and in the communities of the subordinated,"[6] and utilizing a multi-pronged strategy of media, organizing, and litigation.

Unlike regnant lawyering, which has been criticized for placing too much emphasis on the attorney and the legal system, or even traditional civil rights lawyering, which some believe places too much emphasis on the rule of law, political and rebellious lawyering perceives the law as only one of many tools in the campaign for social change. This approach treats the client as a partner in the struggle and engages in an "everything at once" strategy.[7] The practice of political and rebellious lawyering not only involves a client in the attorney's legal case, but also integrates the attorney's legal case into the client's campaign for justice by conducting a simultaneous and coordinated attack in the courts of law, media, and public opinion. Thus, while many would acknowledge the wisdom of scholar

Derrick Bell's interest convergence theory,[8] political lawyers have adapted by expanding their attack to include not only the legal cases, but also the very will of the majority.

Since rebellious lawyering is grounded in the lives and history of the communities being served, this paper will begin by introducing both the Asian Law Caucus and the Hmong in order to set the context for their coordinated campaign against a particular provision of welfare reform. The Asian Law Caucus ("Caucus") was founded in 1972 by a small group of recently graduated attorneys and law students as an outgrowth of the Third World Strike movements at San Francisco State University and the University of California at Berkeley. Its founding members envisioned the Caucus as a community law firm organized "to exercise law with a political emphasis—defending 'political' cases, attacking racism in institutions, highlighting society's neglect of Asian American concerns, and supporting the work of progressive community organizations," and "to be responsive and accountable to the Asian American communities, using law to promote and protect their interests."[9]

Attorneys at the Caucus approach their work through a three-pronged strategy: 1) conducting multilingual community outreach, education, and organizing; 2) providing direct legal services to indigent clients; and 3) engaging in impact work such as class-action litigation or policy advocacy. Each of these components is seen as critically related and dependent upon the others.

The Hmong are a distinct ethnic minority group of Asia whose oral histories trace their roots back four thousand years to parts of northern China. Originally called the "Miao" or "Meo" by the Chinese (a term reportedly connoting barbarians or the sound a cat makes), the term "Hmong" first became popularized in 1972, denoting free people. It is a fitting term because throughout their history, the Hmong have maintained a fiercely independent existence and culture, resisting all attempts to conquer and assimilate them.

The Hmong, who had earlier earned a reputation as courageous warriors while fighting alongside the French during World War II, were recruited by the CIA along with several other ethnic minorities living in the mountains of Laos. These soldiers defended American bases and airstrips, guided and flew bombing sorties, ambushed convoy lines along the Ho Chi Minh Trail, and worked behind enemy lines to gather military intelligence. In particular, the Hmong served as a key element in the covert nature of the war by rescuing (or recovering the bodies of) downed American pilots who had been shot down while on bombing runs against the Vietnamese. In order for the United States plausibly to maintain its denial of military involvement, hundreds of Hmong were routinely dispatched behind enemy lines to take on the dangerous task of rescuing downed American pilots. Often less than half would return, successful in their mission of carrying out one or two American servicemen through enemy fire.

Armed with inferior and outdated weapons, the Hmong distinguished themselves through their military prowess and apparent willingness to serve in dangerous situations where they were both outmanned and outgunned. As the Hmong soldiers of military age were quickly killed, younger and younger boys were conscripted into service so that by 1968, 30 percent of the Hmong ground troops were under the age of fourteen years old. Though the details of this promise vary from account to account, the Hmong claim that the CIA promised them a homeland if the United States won in Laos and pledged that the United States would care for the Hmong even if it were to lose the war. The CIA has never denied that such promises were made. In light of the centuries of persecution by the Chinese and the nomadic lifestyle of the Hmong, it is not difficult to understand why the Hmong agreed to fight under those terms.

In early 1973, despite the entreaties of many of its Southeast Asian allies, the United States negotiated a peace agreement with North Vietnam and began the withdrawal of all American troops and supplies from Laos and South Vietnam. The Hmong who had honorably served under American command were told to report to the Long Chieng airbase on May 11, 1975, where they would be flown out to safety. Though thousands of Hmong soldiers and families reported to the airfield, only two airplanes were ever sent to rescue the top military officials. As Communist forces overran the airfield in the ensuing weeks, thousands of Hmong were massacred and forced to flee into the jungles, where they were hunted down, starved, and subjected to chemical warfare.

According to some studies, Hmong survivors witnessed, on average, fifteen "major trauma events" involving killing or torture. Several Hmong families reported to us either aborting pregnancies in order to conserve food during their flight to Thailand, or killing their own young babies while hiding from communist patrols. Although there are no precise statistics, it is estimated that between one-tenth and one-half of all Hmong refugees died during this period from starvation, execution, or exposure to lethal chemicals.

More than 50,000 Hmong initially escaped to Thai refugee camps, where they lived for years under subhuman conditions until the United States and other nations finally admitted them as refugees. In 1975, the United States was willing to admit fewer than 300 Hmong refugees, mainly high-ranking army officers and their families. The Hmong in the refugee camps suffered under inhumane conditions for up to a decade before they could be sponsored to Western nations.

Between 1980 and 1996, 130,000 Hmong refugees eventually resettled into the United States, mostly from the Thai refugee camps. The actual Hmong population in the United States is estimated to be much higher at present due to their high birth rates, with the majority of the population living in the Central Valley of California and in Minnesota and Wisconsin. The community is one of the poorest amongst the Asian ethnicities and stands out as an extreme under all common socioeconomic indicators.

Many Hmong accepted government welfare as part of the "promise" that had been made to them in exchange for their military service. Others viewed welfare as part of the only life they knew, having grown accustomed to daily handouts in the Thai refugee camps. Many others relied on welfare because they were unable to find employment due to racial discrimination; language, cultural, and social barriers; and the high incidence of depression and post-traumatic stress disorder within the community.

On August 22, 1996, in the midst of a heated election year, President William J. Clinton signed into law the Personal Responsibility and Work Opportunity Reconciliation Act of 1996, commonly known as the Welfare Reform Act. Even as he committed to "ending welfare as we know it," President Clinton publicly acknowledged during the signing ceremony that the Act went too far in unfairly punishing lawful permanent residents of the United States.

Even in the midst of one of the longest periods of economic boom in the history of this nation and while the number of welfare recipients was already declining, the Welfare Reform Act proposed to "save" $54.2 billion in spending from the federal budget over a five-year period by eliminating the safety net for many of our nation's most vulnerable populations. Nearly half of this total cut, or $23.8 billion, would be saved by denying basic food, shelter, medical care, and old age and disability benefits to lawful immigrants even though they constituted only 5 percent of the total population of welfare recipients. Under the purported goals of "promoting self-sufficiency" and "deterring illegal immigration,"[10] the Welfare Reform Act proposed to slash $13 billion in Supplemental Security Income (SSI) benefits and nearly $4 billion in food stamps, cutting off aid to more than half a million senior and disabled immigrants and more than a million families.

The only immigrants exempted from these harsh cuts were those who were somehow deemed either morally worthy or blameless for their economic situation. These groups included: 1) recent refugees and political asylees within seven years of their entry into the United States, 2) immigrants and their families who could be credited with forty quarters (or roughly ten years) of work history in the United States, and 3) immigrants and their families who had served in the United States armed forces.[11]

As of August 22, 1996, when the Welfare Reform Act was signed, all legal immigrants falling outside one of these three exempt categories were immediately barred from applying for any federal public benefit. Thus, for example, a lawful permanent resident who had worked for a number of years at a gas station but was subsequently rendered quadriplegic during an armed robbery of the station was statutorily disqualified from applying for any federal aid normally provided to severely disabled citizens.

By removing the safety net for our nation's most fragile and vulnerable populations in the course of ending "welfare as we know it," the government threw large segments of the immigrant community into a state of panic, shock, and depression. In spite of the stated purposes of the Act, which were to deter illegal immigration and to promote self-sufficiency, the overwhelming majority of the immigrants targeted for these "savings" were lawful permanent residents rather than illegal or undocumented immigrants, who had never been statutorily eligible for most federal public benefits in the first place. Moreover, often because of their age or disability, those groups of immigrants targeted by the Act were also those least likely to be able to achieve self-sufficiency.

Many public interest, social service, immigrant rights, and community groups responded to the grave threat posed by this clear political scapegoating of the immigrant community. Foreseeing the impact of the Act upon the Asian Pacific American population in the Greater Bay Area, the Caucus drastically realigned the priorities of the office, suspending or curtailing the practice of law in areas not directly related to welfare or immigration law, such as hate crimes and affirmative action. Through our three-pronged strategy of organizing and educating the community, providing direct legal services, and engaging in impact work, we strived to play a role in local, state, and national arenas.

As a community law firm, we moved to respond to welfare reform as early as 1995, long before there was sufficient "injury" or legal "standing" to respond through litigation. Locally, the Caucus responded as a triage unit, conducting an intensive multilingual community education and outreach campaign at senior meal sites, public libraries, community fairs, churches, community centers, Chinese language schools, hospitals, ESL classrooms, and other familiar community gatherings throughout the Bay Area. Following each presentation on the new law of welfare reform, we used trained social workers and senior volunteers to screen the hundreds of welfare recipients in the audience to see who might be saved through one of the legal exceptions and who could be naturalized prior to the cutoff date. Through this process, we eventually represented hundreds of clients through the SSI administrative process and helped hundreds more naturalize before the termination date.

On a more regional level, we produced weekly community bulletins updating social service providers, community groups, and ethnic media on the ongoing changes and implementation of the new welfare laws and produced multilingual handouts for clients outlining appellate rights and timelines. In order to counteract some of the confusion and misunderstanding generated by the English-only Social Security mailings, the Caucus held press conferences with ethnic media in advance of government mailings to explain the changes and released its own translations of forms to assuage community fears. It also conducted in-service trainings for social work staff and other legal service providers, as well as for government agencies, which ironically had difficulties in understanding their own directives.

The incongruity between the stated purposes of the Act and the populations it affected should not be overlooked because in many ways, welfare reform was less an attack on welfare recipients than an attack on legal immigrants and immigration. Similar in logic to the policy of the Thai government in providing less-than-minimal food and water to Hmong refugees in its camps, the true and openly stated purpose of welfare reform was to discourage future immigration by punishing those immigrants already lawfully present. This call for "welfare reform" was initiated by neoconservative scholars and assisted by think tanks and politicians, who fed off of public narrative and stereotypes such as the "black welfare queen" and the "rich Asian cheating the welfare system" to propagate a conservative agenda to limit immigration.

On this level, the Caucus worked extensively with its Washington, D.C. counterpart during this period not only to amend the law, but also to attempt to change the narrative of the welfare debate and the public's view of immigrants. Sadly, by maintaining a file of recorded deaths at the hands of welfare reform—a folder which media and legislators frequently requested—the Caucus played a key role in changing the face of welfare reform in the public eye. In place of the stereotypical images of welfare cheats and abusers, the public began to hear of hardworking senior and disabled immigrants who took their own lives out of fear while living in the richest nation in the world.

Through a combination of direct services, impact litigation, community education and organizing, and a coordinated public and media advocacy campaign, the coalition of advocates was surprisingly successful at changing the rhetoric of welfare reform. Within a year of the overwhelming passage of the Act, Congress had moved to amend many of the harshest provisions. Before the scheduled cuts against immigrants were to take effect in August 1997, Congress passed the Balanced Budget Act of 1997, which allowed those senior and disabled immigrants who were already receiving SSI to continue receiving benefits. In many states with large immigrant populations such as California, supplemental programs such as the California Assistance Program for Immigrants (CAPI) and state food stamps were implemented to assist those falling through the cracks of federal coverage.

As the Caucus sent out our weekly fax alerts to more than a hundred community agencies explaining the changes in the law, we began to receive calls from people named Xiong and Her in the remote parts of northern California inquiring about the proposed cuts in the food stamp program. As the first calls came into the Caucus welfare reform hotlines, we gave legal advice over the phone and apologized that we could do no more due to the geographic distance and our commitment to the Bay Area. However, as the calls continued to mount from Marysville, Chico, and Yuba City, we decided to drive north one weekend to give a presentation on welfare reform for residents there and to gain a better understanding of what was in store for the future.

On an early Saturday morning, Sally Kinoshita, an extern from U.C. Davis, and I drove to a church in Marysville, approximately two and a half hours northeast of San Francisco. We arrived a little early, but as we pulled up, we realized based on the overflowing parking lot that there were hundreds of people already inside. The church was filled to capacity with more than five hundred Hmong men, women, and children eager to learn about their rights under the Welfare Reform Act. As Sally began to set up for our presentation, I ran out to purchase a disposable camera in order to photograph the over-capacity audience. The community group sponsoring our event, the California Statewide Lao/Hmong Coalition, asked us for permission to videotape the event.

The Hmong were angry about their predicament and viewed this as yet another instance in a long series of betrayals of their people. Were it not for the illegal American involvement in Southeast Asia and the Hmong willingness to assist in rescue operations for United States personnel, the Hmong would never have faced the degree of genocidal persecution by the Laotian government that had required them to flee their homes. Their subsequent difficulties with adapting to American society, their inability to secure employment, and the ongoing trauma of their persecution and refugee experience were all direct byproducts of their unassailable loyalty to the United States. To now terminate them from food stamp programs because of a popular sentiment that they were morally unworthy of support was simply too much for the Hmong to accept.

As we listened, it became clear to us that the real issue was as much about honor and recognition as it was about the food stamp subsidy. While most families would suffer a loss or reduction in their household food stamp benefits under the Welfare Reform Act, those most affected spoke equally of the wrong done to their community by the government's refusal to acknowledge their service to the United States. While as legal advocates we had approached the issue in terms of how to legally protect the Hmong from food stamp cuts in October, the Hmong viewed the problem and its causes more broadly in terms of both time and scope. Their struggle was not simply a question of losing a few hundred dollars a month but rather the continuing American failure to recognize the Hmong history of sacrifice and contribution. Thus, while many seemed wary at first, the audience quickly warmed up to the idea of filing legal appeals once we reframed the appeal as a method by which the community would have another opportunity in their ongoing campaign to educate the American people about the Hmong. The audience also responded well to the concept of a coordinated group action, which would tie up the administrative process and force the government to scramble and locate sufficient judges, courtrooms, and Hmong interpreters to deal with the mass of appeals.

Instead of responding within the narrow confines of the black-letter law, we decided collectively to challenge the spirit behind welfare reform and to attack the discourse claiming that immigrants were morally undeserving of benefits because they had not contributed enough to the system. Both from a strategic "political lawyering" viewpoint and from the community's perspective, what was critical was not necessarily winning the immediate legal appeal, but rather advancing a long-term campaign that would allow the counter-narrative to emerge. Notably, due in part to the strong moral claim in this case, we consciously chose to engage in a strategy of political and rebellious lawyering rather than impact litigation. Our goal was to mobilize and empower the Hmong community to file individual appeals in mass in order to publicize their claims and stories to the rest of the American community. We did not want to have lawyers simply control the case by choosing class representatives, drafting sterile legal briefs, and litigating the case in a vacuum through the courts. The process of fighting back and raising a voice was as important as the substance of the fight itself.

The Hmong community began organizing soon after the passage of the Welfare Reform Act in order to protect their community from the proposed cuts, to seek eased naturalization requirements, and to push for full veterans' benefits. Through a number of public rallies and demonstrations, where thousands of Hmong marched in combat fatigues, the Hmong sought to educate federal and state elected officials on their history of service. In February 1997, a delegation of Hmong from Fresno traveled to Washington, D.C. to lobby federal officials. "A lot of people in Congress still don't know about the Hmong history, so we plan to introduce ourselves and our issues," said one of the principal organizers. In May 1997, 3,000 Hmong from Minnesota traveled to Washington, D.C. to be honored by various Congressmen in a public ceremony and to receive the Vietnam Veterans National Medal.

In California, more than 2,000 Hmong joined other immigrants in two rallies that took place in Sacramento in March and May of 1997. Carrying signs that read "I rescued your son in the jungles of Laos, now what?" and "Paid the price, 40,000 Hmong dead for America," the Hmong effectively brought their plea to the forefront of the media's attention. The contrasting images of military sacrifice and disabled veterans in the fight against Communism effectively undermined the narrative of undeserving immigrants living off welfare.

The Hmong community's public advocacy persuaded Congress to include in the Balanced Budget Act of 1997 a "sense of Congress," which made a number of significant factual findings, even though it failed actually to amend the Welfare Reform Act on behalf of the Hmong. Specifically, the "sense of Congress" recognized that "[t]housands of Hmong . . .

fought in special guerrilla units on behalf of the United States during the Vietnam conflict" and many "sacrificed their own lives and saved the lives of American military personnel." The Congressional statement also indicated that it was the legislative body's "sense" that the Hmong should be considered as veterans for the purposes of the Welfare Reform Act's exemptions.

The Caucus began intensive research on both legal and historical matters in order to prepare for the Hmong community's administrative defense. It drafted a short legal memorandum based primarily upon the Balanced Budget Act's "sense of Congress," arguing that the legislative intent should be given weight as law. Copies of the brief were circulated to the Hmong community through their internal social networks and to advocacy groups in most major areas of concentration of Hmong including Fresno, Stockton, Sacramento, and parts of Wisconsin and Minnesota. Following the circulation, several thousand Hmong households in California filed appeals requesting that they be allowed to appear before an administrative judge in pro per to argue against the reduction or termination of their benefits.

Recognizing the community's high illiteracy rate coupled with the lack of a widely used Hmong written language, Caucus staff working with volunteer Hmong social workers took to popular Hmong radio shows to notify the community of their legal rights and of what to expect from the process. Copies of the videotape from our initial training at the Marysville church were also distributed and viewed by hundreds of Hmong at home and in group settings. Contrary to the tradition of intimate and confidential one-on-one meetings between attorney and client, we counseled hundreds of unseen clients via radio, third-party intermediaries, and duplicated videotapes. Working with a group of volunteer second-generation Hmong American undergraduates and Asian American law students in the Greater Bay Area, the Caucus engaged in an intensive effort to assist the Hmong clients in preparing their cases in advance. Using portable computers and printers, the students set up a number of traveling clinics in areas accessible to the community and worked with the Hmong veterans to translate and draft declarations outlining their cases.

Concurrently with our community organizing, media, and legal campaigns, our affiliate lobbying office in Washington, D.C., the National Asian Pacific American Legal Consortium (NAPALC), had been holding frequent meetings with the Department of Agriculture and other federal officials for the purpose of convincing them to reverse their positions on welfare reform. The D.C. groups at the time were not only attempting to pass new legislation to reverse certain provisions of the Welfare Reform Act, but were also lobbying various federal departments to interpret and implement the new welfare laws in a manner that would least impact our communities.

Armed with the declarations and questionnaires that we had collected directly from the Hmong community, NAPALC infused the voices and causes of the community into the general platform of demands by its D.C. counterparts. In meetings with various federal bureaucrats, they plied them with the compelling stories of Hmong sacrifice and American betrayal. The effect was to both advance the cause of the Hmong and soften the opposition's general attitude towards immigrants as a whole. In addition, NAPALC contracted with a well-respected law firm inside the Beltway to issue a favorable legal interpretation analyzing the "sense of Congress" regarding the Hmong. Lawyers from this firm, Hmong grassroots activists, and NAPALC attorneys met with the White House Counsel, the Office of Management and Budget, the White House Domestic Policy Council, and the Undersecretary and General Counsel's Office of the Department of Agriculture, armed with a legal memorandum in an attempt to obtain a political remedy. We hoped that this memorandum by a "political law firm" might be persuasive political lawyering of a different stripe.

On June 23, 1998, President Clinton signed into law the Agricultural Research, Extension and Education Reform Act of 1998, which, among many provisions, amended 402(a)(2) of the Welfare Reform Act to add an exemption for "certain Hmong and Highland Laotians."[12] Notably, the amendment provided for a food stamp ineligibility exception for any Hmong and Highland Lao legal permanent resident who "was a member of a Hmong or Highland Laotian tribe at the time that the tribe rendered assistance to United States personnel by taking part in a military or rescue operation during the Vietnam era," as well as his or her spouse and children. Working with both local organizers and Washington, D.C. lobbyists, the Caucus also helped secure the passage of the Hmong Naturalization Act, a change in law that would make it easier for many of the older Hmong and Laotian veterans finally to become United States citizens. Most recently, in 2001, the Caucus continued to work with many of the Hmong organizers with whom it had collaborated, to address broader issues of educational equity, hate violence, police misconduct, census, and political representation.

Conclusion

The Caucus's work with the Hmong community was ultimately significant not only because it succeeded in raising the concerns of a small minority to the highest levels of government, but also because it changed the overall narrative regarding immigrants and welfare and diminished support for the immigrant-targeted provisions of welfare reform.

From a practitioner's point of view, this victory demonstrated the power and possibilities of a political and community-based lawyering campaign. Despite remarkably limited resources and the seeming weight of both the law and public opinion against our success, we were nevertheless able to wage a war in the courts of law and public opinion to help build the momentum for change. Although the legal issues appeared to be insurmountable on their face, we were able to obtain the legal remedy we sought through a combination of litigation, community organizing, political lobbying, and media advocacy.

Perhaps as important as the result was the process by which we proceeded. In engaging in this form of community lawyering, we hoped to assist in empowering a community that had previously been denied both a voice and access to the courts. Although we violated many traditional rules of lawyering by encouraging the filing of appeals without apparent legal merit, counseling masses of clients via radio and videotaped presentations, representing clients in hearings whom we had never previously met, and allowing clients to testify without our control or objection, we felt as political and community-based attorneys that this strategy would best serve the needs of the client community.

In partial answer to the interest convergence theory advanced by some critical race theorists, the Hmong case offers a more optimistic alternative in an era of changing demographics. It cannot be denied that hard-fought legal victories may be fleeting in the face of a hostile majority sentiment, but in this new millennium in which demographics are rapidly changing, there is no reason that we cannot also win over the majority view. We no longer face a hostile monolithic majority that is opposed to all forms of social change; our issues and potential constituencies are no longer solely black and white. Moreover, just as the conservatives have advanced their agenda in the 1990s by creating temporary alliances to divide and conquer our communities, so must we on the frontlines respond by building coalitions, whether permanent or temporary, to defend our communities. Through a strategic campaign of political and community-based lawyering, effective use of the press, working with elected officials with compatible interests, aligning with groups beyond the usual suspects, and mobilizing communities, we can forge the majority opinion.

It must be noted, however, that this form of political community-based lawyering does not completely address the chasms of need because it is by nature a defensive and reactive weapon based on the immediate needs of the community. It does not portend to offer a proactive vision of social justice beyond the limits of our work with the Hmong and immigrant communities or supplant the call for a true critical race praxis. It is simply what must be done to answer the attacks upon our community.

As frontline practitioners, we sorely need the assistance of academic allies for the building of a true critical race praxis. We need to build a proactive agenda; we need theories in our litigation, research, and amicus briefs, as well as allies who will draft editorial opinions and appear before the media to help influence public opinion. From a larger perspective, it could be argued that the progressive Asian American voice in the affirmative action cases was sacrificed as a result of our defensive commitment of resources to the Hmong campaign. Yet, there is another gap, that is, the chasm between academics and community, that must be bridged even as academics and practitioners join together in conferences and in litigation. While we need vision from the academics, it must also be a vision based on the view from the ground and not one that looks at a utopia beyond the hills and from the tower.

Chapter 5

Critical Theories

This chapter examines the development of several different lines of critical theory in legal ethics scholarship. First, we will read two representative pieces from the critical legal studies (CLS) movement, which had its apex in the late 1970s and early 1980s. The CLS movement was led primarily by left-leaning law professors angry about the placid, noncritical approaches of mainstream law schools in the face of upheavals such as the Vietnam War and Watergate.[1] Many CLS scholars concentrated on doctrinal subjects, but a few focused on legal practice and legal ethics. Indeed, quite a few CLS leaders either had prior experience in legal services or were practitioners experimenting with new forms of progressive legal practice. The excerpt from professor Peter Gabel and public interest activist Paul Harris reflects an alliance between these two sides of the movement. Their piece exudes optimism and energy, calling on progressive lawyers to implement new practices that would reinvent lawyering as part of a broader political transformation.

William H. Simon's excerpt sounds in a different tone. Simon, as we shall see, remains one of the leaders of the critical turn in legal ethics thought. In this excerpt and many other articles, Simon argues that lawyers not only should, but inevitably must exercise independent ethical discretion in their lawyering decisions. Simon argues that this ethical discretion should be directed to concerns about the public good, much as Pearce and Gordon did in chapter 2.

CLS now stands more as a historical moment than a continuing school of thought; most of its leaders have moved on to new projects and self-definitions. CLS nevertheless remains the direct intellectual ancestor of many other contemporary critical movements in law, including critical race theory and feminist legal theory. In sections B and C, we look at examples of scholarship exploring the intersections of these two movements and legal ethics inquiry.

Section B presents several examples of work that explores the intersection of race and legal ethics. First, Angela Davis, a professor and former public defender, examines the role of race in the exercise of prosecutorial discretion. Davis shows how, at many steps of the criminal process, prosecutors' decisions can, often in unintended and/or unconscious ways, exacerbate or perpetuate racism. Davis argues that prosecutors' ethical duty to see that justice is served, rather than simply to obtain convictions, includes the affirmative duty to reduce racism in the criminal justice system. She argues for the use of racial impact studies as a means of monitoring whether prosecutors are living up to this ethical responsibility.

Prosecutors perhaps present the clearest case of a category of lawyers whose ethical duties include furthering the interests of justice. Bill Ong Hing, however, examines the ethical duties of *non*-government lawyers on matters involving race, and concludes that *all* lawyers have overriding ethical duties to further the interest of justice over the interests of their clients in representations that raise race issues. Drawing on examples from the news, Hing shows how legal cases stand as public narratives that define racial meanings. He explores from this perspective the importance of lawyers' decisions about how to handle race-charged issues in their cases. Applying Simon's ethical discretion theory, Hing argues that an important aspect of the public good lawyers should take into account in making decisions about lawyering tactics is avoiding appeals to racial conflict and affirmatively promoting racial harmony. Indeed, Hing asserts, this duty should be explicitly added to existing legal ethics codes.

Tony Alfieri has much the same goal as Hing. Like Hing, Alfieri seeks to expose the racial implications of conventional legal ethics doctrines. Alfieri, however, reaches somewhat different conclusions about the adequacy of Simon's proposals as a template for how to incorporate race concerns into lawyers' ethical understandings of their roles. Alfieri, a prolific writer on race and legal ethics issues, is sometimes difficult to understand because the reach of his ideas is quite abstract; for the same reason, it is difficult to give full justice to his ideas in a short excerpt. Nevertheless, studying his ideas is well worth the effort. He hails from the clinical law movement, and his work sometimes sounds reminiscent of the client-centered/community lawyering approach we explored in chapter 4. But Alfieri is also critical of client-centered ethics, especially where clients' wishes contravene the fostering of better images surrounding race. Readers interested in further exploring Alfieri's ideas may start with the many articles listed in the Appendix. The Appendix also offers some leads for readers interested in more fully exploring critical race theory in general.

Section C looks at the development of a feminist legal theory literature focused on the intersection of feminism and new ethical visions for law practice. Carrie Menkel-Meadow makes some provocative preliminary suggestions about possible connections between feminist theory and the transformation of lawyers' ethics. Among other ideas, Menkel-Meadow questions the contemporary emphasis on adversarialism, a question we saw raised from a historical perspective in chapter 2. Many other feminist theorists have proposed other versions of a feminist legal ethics, and still others have focused on a nongendered *ethics of care* as an ethic for lawyers, as summarized in the Appendix.

An excerpt from Angela Harris's classic article criticizing feminist essentialism raises questions concerning the intersections among gender, race, and other social identity attributes in relation to personal value formation. Harris warns against equating more powerful voices in the legal academy—usually those of educationally privileged middle-class white women—with the perspective of *all* women. Other feminist scholars have raised similar points in disputing the idea of a feminist lawyering style. Some of the highlights of this debate are summarized in the Appendix.

Lani Guinier examines the connections between the adversarial ethics of the legal profession and methods of teaching in law schools. Guinier reflects on the legal ethics implications of an empirical study she and others conducted at the University of Pennsylvania Law School. That study found higher levels of alienation and lower indices of achievement among women than among men, as measured by grades and other factors, despite equal or higher credentials among entering women. Guinier begins to envision a model of a law school inspired by an alternative, less adversarial approach.

Finally, Phyllis Goldfarb pursues the insights that might be gained from studying still another intersection: that between feminist theory and the clinical practice movement. Goldfarb sees in both movements a focus on developing a rich, detailed, experientially based and contingent ethics of practice very different from the universalistic, rule-bound approach of conventional legal ethics thinking.

Questions for Reflection and Discussion

1. Which, if any, aspects of Gabel's and Harris's proposals for transforming law practice according to the political vision of the 1970s do you see in use

today? What factors do you think account for your observations? Which, if any, aspects of their proposals still seem viable?

2. Simon discusses how a lawyer for a defendant in a personal injury case should handle a situation in settlement negotiations in which her opposing counsel is poorly prepared and does not realize that there has been a change in the law that significantly benefits her client's ability to recover for her injuries. What do the current rules call on a lawyer to do in this situation? What does Simon argue a lawyer should do? Which approach do you think is more ethically appropriate? Why?

3. Simon's call for lawyers to exercise discretion in such a manner as to serve the interests of justice in handling their clients' claims harks back to Brandeis's Progressive-Era model of "lawyering for the situation," which we studied in chapter 2. Do you agree with Simon's argument? Why or why not?

4. Do you agree with Davis's argument that prosecutors have an ethical duty, above and beyond the limited constitutional requirements enunciated in the U.S. Supreme Court's opinions, to prevent racial disparities in the criminal justice system? Why or why not?

5. Do you agree with Hing's argument for imposing special ethical duties with regard to race matters on non-government lawyers? Why or why not? What do you see as your own ethical duties with regard to race matters in practicing law? As noted in the literature discussed in the Appendix, Wilkins argues that lawyers of color have special ethical obligations to their communities of origin. Do you agree? Why or why not?

6. Alfieri worries that Simon's approach may lead a lawyer to "simply reenact his own private moral preference at the expense of a client-community participatory resolution." Do you agree with Alfieri? If so, how do you think a lawyer might or should go about obtaining "client-community participatory resolution"? What if the client and/or community is in favor of fanning the flames of racial animosity?

7. Menkel-Meadow argues that the infusion of traditional "outsider" voices in law can lead to the development of creative new ideas, both about substance and philosophy in law and about practice norms. Can you think of any examples of such development occurring?

8. In your view, is the character of Portia in *The Merchant of Venice* a good model of how a lawyer might practice a transformed feminist ethics of lawyering? Why or why not? Do you see connections between Portia's social position as a woman and her rhetorical strategies, as Menkel-Meadow suggests?

9. What similarities, if any, do you see between the ethics of care to which Menkel-Meadow refers and other legal ethics models we have explored? Are there differences between such an ethics of care and these other models? What are these differences? Which, if any, model(s) do you find most appealing as alternatives to the status quo? Why?

10. Harris warns against generalizing, or *essentializing,* "women's" experience across race, class, and other differences in social location, while also acknowledging that some categorization of experience is necessary. What are Harris's suggestions about how to avoid essentializing experience while at the same time continuing to appreciate and examine social difference?

11. Harris does not directly address a legal ethics vision. What might a legal ethics vision informed by Harris's analysis look like? How, if at all, might it be different from Menkel-Meadow's?

12. Do you agree with Guinier's thesis that there are important connections between lawyers' general ethical stances in practice and the ethical predispositions they learn in law school? If so, what connections do you see?

13. Guinier is careful to emphasize that not all female law students she studied were uncomfortable with a law school atmosphere of adversarialism, nor were all male law students comfortable with such an environment. Instead, she argues, students of both sexes could benefit from a transformation of law school teaching methods along the lines she envisions. What changes does she argue for, and what is your own assessment of whether these changes would make you and your classmates *better* lawyers, in both the ethical and the proficiency senses of this term?

14. What are the similarities Goldfarb sees between feminist legal theory and clinical pedagogy? How are these related to alternative conceptions of lawyers' ethics?

15. Goldfarb argues for building legal ethics from concrete experience and detailed, contextual understandings. How is this perspective like, and how is it unlike, Wilkins's call in chapter 1 for context-specific ethics regulation?

16. Menkel-Meadow, Harris, and Goldfarb all draw heavily from literary classics in developing their arguments. Why do you think they do so?

Building Power and Breaking Images:
Critical Legal Theory and the
Practice of Law[1]

Peter Gabel and Paul Harris[2]

Most lawyers on the Left have a pessimistic view of their own political role in bringing about fundamental social change. Some think that the law is simply a tool used by the ruling class to protect its own economic interests, a view which by definition means that no important gains can be won in the legal arena. Those who believe this tend to relegate themselves to the role of protecting oppressed people against the worst abuses of an unjust system while awaiting the development of a revolutionary movement "at the base." Others graduate from law school believing that meaningful reforms can be won through legislative and judicial action, and often devote several years of hard work for little pay to the goal of getting people more rights. But they then discover that the expansion of legal rights has only a limited impact on people's real lives, and that even these limited gains can be wiped out by a change in the political climate. The consequence is that by their mid-thirties many lawyers have either lost their early idealism or have had their original cynicism confirmed. And even the most committed find themselves at a loss as to how to integrate their politics with their everyday work as lawyers.

In this article we present a more optimistic approach to radical law practice that is based on a view of the legal system different from those described above. We reject both the orthodox Marxist view that the law is simply a "tool of the ruling class" and the liberal-legalist view that powerless groups in society can gradually improve their position by getting more rights. Instead we argue that the legal system is an important public arena through which the state attempts—through manipulation of symbols, images, and ideas—to legitimize a social order that most people find alienating and inhumane. Our objective is to show the way that the legal system works at many different levels to shape popular consciousness toward accepting the political legitimacy of the status quo, and to outline the ways that lawyers can effectively resist these efforts in building a movement for fundamental social change. Our basic claim is that the very public and political character of the legal arena gives lawyers, acting together with clients and fellow legal workers, an important opportunity to reshape the way people understand the existing social order and their place within it.

Our perspective on the nature of the legal system has been strongly influenced by the work of the Conference on Critical Legal Studies, which over the last five years has been developing a new critical analysis of the role of law and legal institutions in maintaining the status quo. The actual legal strategies that we propose, however, have emerged principally from the efforts of practitioners within the National Lawyers Guild who have struggled to discover new forms of legal practice that would go beyond a purely defensive or reformist stance. This article is a first attempt to link the theoretical advances made by the Conference with the accumulated practical experience of creative Guild attorneys, and in so doing to outline a new theory of practice that can be of value to lawyers who often lack the time or opportunity to situate their work within a broad political context.

A Power-Oriented Approach to Law Practice

A first principle of a "counter-hegemonic" legal practice must be to subordinate the goal of getting people their rights to the goal of building an authentic or unalienated political consciousness. This obviously does not mean that one should not try to win one's cases; *nor* does it necessarily mean that we should not continue to organize groups by appealing to rights. But the great weakness of a rights-oriented legal practice is that it does not address itself to a central precondition for building a sustained political movement—that of overcoming the psychological conditions upon which both the power of the legal system and the power of social hierarchy in general rest. In fact an excessive preoccupation with "rights-consciousness" tends in the long run to reinforce alienation and powerlessness, because the appeal to rights inherently affirms that the source of social power resides in the state rather than in the people themselves. As Karl Klare and Alan Freeman have shown so clearly in their respective studies of the labor and the civil rights movements, the long-term effects of a legal strategy based primarily on the acquisition of legal rights tends to weaken the power of popular movements because such a strategy allows the state to define the terms of the struggle.[3] By granting new legal rights that seem to vindicate the claims of the individuals and groups asserting them, the state can succeed over time in co-opting the movements' more radical demands while "relegitimizing" the status quo through the artful manipulation of legal doctrine.

A legal strategy that goes beyond rights-consciousness is one that focuses upon expanding political consciousness through using the legal system to increase people's sense of personal and political power. As we will show, this can mean many different things depending upon the political visibility of any given case and the specific social and legal context within which a case arises. But in any context, a "power" rather than a "rights" approach to law practice should be guided by three general objectives that are as applicable to minor personal injury cases as to major cases involving important social issues. First, the lawyer should seek to develop a relationship of genuine equality and mutual respect with her client. Second, the lawyer should conduct herself in a way that demystifies the symbolic authority of the state as this authority is embodied in, for example, the flag, the robed judge, and the ritualized professional technicality of the legal proceeding. Third, the lawyer should always attempt to reshape the way legal conflicts are represented in the law, revealing the limiting character of legal ideology and bringing out the true socio-economic and political foundations of legal disputes. Reaching these objectives may have a transformative impact not only upon the lawyer and client working in concert, but also upon others who come into contact with the case, including the client's friends and family, courtroom participants such as jurors, stenographers, and public observers, and, in some cases, thousands or even millions of people who follow high-visibility political cases through the media. Of course, any particular lawyer's actions in a single case cannot lead to the development of an anti-hierarchical social movement; we believe, however, that if lawyers as a group begin to organize themselves around the realization of these goals, their impact on the culture as a whole can be much greater than they currently believe is possible.

Counter-Pressure in High-Visibility Political Cases

Although a central objective of this article is to argue that all legal cases are potentially empowering, the classic political case remains one which receives widespread public attention because it emerges from a social conflict that has already achieved high visibility in the public consciousness. Examples of such cases in recent years include the political trials that arose out of the student and antiwar movements, and the many Supreme Court cases that have emerged from the civil rights and women's movements. Such cases contain unique possibilities and also difficulties for the lawyers and clients involved in them, because the aim is not only to win on the legal issues raised by the case, but to speak for the movement itself. Precisely because the State's objective is in part to defuse the political energy that has given rise to the case, the legal issue is often one which deflects attention from and even denies the political nature of the conflict.

The Chicago Eight Trial

Perhaps the clearest example of this "deflection" was the so-called "conspiracy" trial of the Chicago Eight, in which the issue as defined by the prosecutor was whether the defendants who had helped to organize the antiwar demonstrations outside the Democratic National Convention in 1968 had conspired to cross state lines with the intent to incite a riot. The political meaning of the demonstrations was to challenge the morality of the Vietnam War and the political process which served to justify it, but this meaning was, of course, legally irrelevant to the determination of whether the alleged conspiracy had taken place.

Using a case like this to increase the power of an existing political movement requires a systematic refusal to accept the limiting boundaries which the state seeks to impose on the conflict. Had the lawyers and clients in the Chicago Eight trial presented a legal defense in a normal professional way, they would have deferred to the authority of Judge Hoffman and politely tried to show, perhaps with success, that the defendants did not "intend" to incite a riot or did not "conspire" to cross state lines to do so. But the lawyers and clients understood very well that even a legal victory on these terms would have meant a political defeat for their movement. They understood that the prosecutor's real purpose was to channel the political struggle in the streets into an official public chamber, to recharacterize the protestors as hooligans, and to substitute a narrow and depoliticized legal description of the meaning of the Chicago events for their true meaning. In this context state power consists not so much in the use of direct force, but in the use of the sanctity of the legal process to recast the meaning of the disruption that took place.

In concert with their courageous clients, William Kunstler and Leonard Weinglass were able to reverse the government's strategy and cause it to backfire, seizing upon the media's coverage of the trial to strengthen the resistance that had begun in the streets. By openly flaunting the hierarchical norms of the courtroom and ridiculing the judge, the prosecutor, and the nature of the charges themselves, they successfully rejected the very forms of authority upon which the legitimacy of the war itself depended. As Judge Hoffman gradually lost the capacity to control "his" room, he was transformed on national television from a learned figure worthy of great respect into a vindictive old man wearing a funny black tunic. In the absence of an underlying popular movement, the tactic of showing continuous contempt for the proceedings might simply have been an unproductive form of "acting out." But within its concrete historical context, this tactic was the most effective way to affirm to millions of supporters following the trial that their version of the meaning of the Chicago protests was right and could not be eroded by the state's appeal to a mass belief in authoritarian imagery.

Counter-Pressure in "Nonpolitical" Cases

The advantage of overtly political cases is that they provide opportunities to dramatize the real basis of existing social conflicts and to challenge the state's efforts to control the way that these conflicts are portrayed within existing legal categories. The lawyers and litigants can both speak for oppositional groups that are already partially constituted and actively contribute to the formation of such groups through the politicizing of the lawsuit itself. Thus, as yet uncommitted but sympathetic supporters can see the courage of the participants in the case and may internalize this courage as a source of power in themselves, furthering their own willingness to identify with the movement's goals and perhaps to take action in support of them.

The vast majority of legal cases do not, however, have this immediate potential for public impact. Ordinary divorce, personal injury cases, or unemployment hearings are political in that they involve the influence of large social forces upon individual lives, but they are not normally experienced as such; rather, they appear simply to be minor ruptures in a "private" personal life. A divorce may provoke intense anxiety about economic security, emotional isolation, and the time and expense of childcare. These are all social problems that call for social solutions. But as a result of the fragmentation produced by the existing social order, each isolated divorce client experiences these problems as personal in nature and sees the legal process solely as something that must be paid for to make the break-up official and to protect property and custody rights. How is it possible to politicize such cases?

Finding an answer to this question is among the most important tasks facing attorneys, for several reasons. First, these minor cases comprise the bulk of every community lawyer's practice. If the lawyer perceives these cases as routine and politically meaningless, he or she will increasingly perceive his or her work in this way. Maybe this is a principal reason why so many lawyers eventually give up their radical aspirations, if they don't quit legal work altogether. Second, the legal system itself contributes to social fragmentation by treating conflicts as isolated cases arising in each person's private life. One way that the dominant ideology contributes to alienation and powerlessness is by generating a false distinction between public and private life, a distinction that translates collective social problems into individual personal matters. Unless lawyers find a way to counter this perception, they cannot help but reinforce it by relating to their clients through this ideological framework. Third, the experience of minor lawsuits is one of the few times that most people actually encounter the public sphere directly, and the experience almost always intensifies the alienation they already feel. The degrading and manipulative way that these cases are routinely processed in the adversary system only increases people's sense of hopelessness about politics and about human nature in general.

We propose three principal approaches to politicizing nonpolitical cases which we believe will enable both lawyers and clients to begin to overcome this alienation. They are: 1) the disruption of the state's attempt to individualize and isolate such cases by discovering the inherent political content of common types of cases, and using this political content to build community organization; 2) the politicization of local courtrooms and other "legal" public spaces that are currently colonized by government officials; and 3) the de-professionalization of the lawyer-client relationship at a widespread level. The unifying objective of all these approaches is to utilize legal conflict as a tool to increase the experienced power of all those affected by the conflict, including lawyers themselves, their clients, and the communities to which they are naturally linked.

Here are some examples of potential alternative practices that would have as their objective the politicization of non-political cases:

1. A family law practice might be organized with the aim of politicizing issues the state currently characterizes as purely private or personal in nature. Such a practice could include any or all of the following elements: (1) creating new legal forms to support nontraditional relationships that challenge the idea that lasting love and intimacy are available only within isolated "family units" (this is perhaps the most political aspect of the gay-rights movement); (2) developing a holistic multi-service center providing medical and psychological assistance to families breaking down under the strain of such social forces as stress at the workplace, unemployment, and the privatization of personal life; (3) developing new approaches to traditional divorce and child-custody cases which make the process of separation as educational and empowering as possible (including, for example, the use of face-to-face mediation instead of lawyer-to-lawyer adversary proceedings, and group-forming strategies like the pro se divorce clinic in which women and/or men can discover their common experience of being imprisoned within traditional family roles while working together to change their status).

2. A low-level criminal defense practice might concentrate on breaking the routinization of "criminal control" in a particular section of an urban area. The aim would be to link certain types of crime that repeatedly occur in a given area—e.g., small drug sales by addicts—with their socioeconomic roots, and working with existing neighborhood groups to build consciousness about the way the defendant's problem is actually the community's problem as an oppressed area within the socioeconomic structure. The guiding principle here would be to penetrate the right wing's appeal for law and order and crime control by seeking to reduce crime through increased community solidarity and resistance to the socioeconomic destruction of the area. One aspect of such a practice might be the development of progressive community arbitration projects that would be designed to educate both "criminals" and the group to which they belong about the social causes of their own activity.

3. An entertainment law practice could strengthen the political base of community artists, not only by helping them gain legal protection for

their work, but also by helping them organize to resist exploitation by publishers, galleries, and the networks, and by discovering alternative methods of financing neighborhood cultural centers where groups of artists could both live and work.

4. In a landlord-tenant practice which primarily consists of fighting evictions on a case-by-case basis, lawyers can politicize cases by encouraging organizing efforts among tenants and by simply suggesting that people discuss their common difficulties *as tenants*. Such a suggestion helps reveal that the political issue at the root of landlord-tenant conflicts is not whether tenants "need more rights," but rather what the destructive effects of the housing market itself are on people's communities and home lives. Moreover, if efforts are made to link newly formed groups of tenants to an existing local tenants' organizing committee, it becomes easier for people to overcome the isolation and frustration that is brought about by the sense that they alone face eviction lawsuits or have trouble with their landlord. The more that such organization takes place in the private sphere, the more possible it becomes to articulate political claims in the courts, and the more difficult it becomes for local government officials to ignore such claims as legally irrelevant. By politicizing a common set of human problems that the legal system would turn into a series of isolated cases involving the static categories of "landlord" and "tenant," these efforts expose an arena of social conflict and thereby expand and deepen the political meaning of a dispute.

Obviously, these examples are both simplistic and overly utopian if conceived as isolated attempts by individual lawyers. But if hundreds of lawyers begin to form networks that make the development of this kind of practice their self-conscious aim, they will have a real impact, not so much from the instrumental gains that they will make in individual cases, but from their contribution to the development of an authentic politics. If *every* dispute is founded ultimately upon conflicts and contradictions within the system as a whole, every such dispute raises the potential for thematizing in both reflection and collective action the relationship between private life and public totality. The activity of engaging in this politicization of legal practice is the activity of realizing the liberating politics of a future, more humane society in the present. It is the experience of engaging in this form of politics that is the true source of its transformative power.

Ethical Discretion in Lawyering[1]

William H. Simon[2]

Lawyers should have ethical discretion to refuse to assist in the pursuit of legally permissible courses of action and in the assertion of potentially enforceable legal claims. This discretion involves not a personal privilege of arbitrary decision, but a professional duty of reflective judgment. One dimension of this judgment is an assessment of the relative merits of the client's goals and claims and those of other people who might benefit from the lawyer's services. Another is an attempt to reconcile the conflicting considerations that bear on the internal merits of the client's goals and claims. In both dimensions, the basic consideration should be whether assisting the client would further justice.

This article argues that lawyers should have such discretion. The argument differs from more prevalent approaches to legal ethics in rejecting the premise that the legal permissibility or enforceability of a client's course of action or claim is an ethically sufficient reason for assisting the client. It also differs from many critiques of prevalent legal ethics doctrine that appeal to moral concerns outside the legal system against values associated with the legal role. The argument here is that ethical discretion would best vindicate our legal ideals and contribute to a more effective functioning of the lawyer role.

The argument focuses on the issues of legal ethics that are usually understood as arising from conflicts between the interests of the client and those of third parties and the public, although it suggests that these conflicts are better understood in terms of competing legal ideals. The analysis considers only civil practice. Although it has relevance to criminal practice, defending its application there would require qualifications and elaborations that would take it too far afield.

The Discretionary Approach

The basic maxim of the approach I propose is this: the lawyer should take those actions that, considering the relevant circumstances of the particular case, seem most likely to promote justice. This "seek justice" maxim suggests a kind of noncategorical judgment that might be called pragmatist, ad hoc, or dialectical, but that I will call discretionary. "Discretionary" is not an entirely satisfactory term; I do not mean to invoke its connotations of arbitrariness or nonaccountability, but rather its connotations of flexibility and complexity.

The discretionary approach incorporates much of the traditional lawyer role, including the notion that lawyers can serve justice through zealous pursuit of clients' goals. Although it assumes a public dimension to the lawyer's role as well, that dimension is grounded in the lawyer's age-old claim to be an "officer of the court" and in notions about the most effective integration of the lawyering role with other roles in the legal system.

The discretionary approach does not ignore considerations of institutional competence. It does not assume that the full responsibility for a proper resolution rests on the lawyer alone. It is compatible with the conventional understanding of the role of judicial and administrative officials in law enforcement. The discretionary approach is distinctive, first, in treating the premises of that understanding as rebuttable presumptions that do not warrant reliance when they do not apply, and second, in imposing a more flexible and demanding duty on the lawyer to facilitate official decision when the premises do apply.

Substance versus Procedure. One manifestation of the substance-versus-procedure tension is the lawyer's sense of the limitations both of her individual judgment of the substantive merits of the dispute on the one hand and of the established procedures for resolving it on the other. We could tell the lawyer to work only to advance claims and goals that she determined were entitled to prevail. The most important objection to this precept is not that the lawyer's decisions about the merits would be controversial—the decisions of judges, juries, and executive officials may also be controversial. Instead, the most important objection is that judges, juries, and executive officials acting within the relevant public procedures are generally able to make more reliable determinations on the merits than the individual lawyer. But the qualification "generally" is crucial. The lawyer will often have good reason to recognize that the standard procedure is not reliably constructed to respond to the problem at hand, and she will often be in a position to contribute to its improvement.

The basic response of the discretionary approach to the substance-procedure tension is this: the more reliable the relevant procedures and institutions, the less direct responsibility the lawyer need assume for the substantive justice of the resolution; the less reliable the procedures and institutions, the more direct responsibility she need assume for substantive justice.

This means, to begin with, that the lawyer needs to develop a style of representation that will, in the general procedural context in which she practices, best contribute to just resolutions. This will normally be the regulatory "on the merits" style, but it may incorporate some elements of the libertarian "arguably legal" style. The distinctive feature of the discretionary approach is that the lawyer must treat this style as a set of weak presumptions. Once the lawyer formulates her general style, she must watch for indications that some premise underlying her judgment that the style is a good one does not apply in the particular case and, when she finds them, revise the style accordingly.

The most common reasons why some premise will be inapplicable are an unusual degree of aggressiveness or vulnerability on the part of another party or an unusual incapacity on the part of official institutions. The lawyer should respond to such circumstances by taking reasonably available actions that help restore the reliability of the procedure. By directing the lawyer to attempt first to improve the reliability of the procedure, the discretionary approach respects the traditional premise that the strongest assurance of a just resolution is the soundness of the procedure that produced it. But to the extent that the lawyer cannot neutralize or repair defects in the relevant procedure, she should assume direct responsibility for the substantive validity of the decision. She should make her own judgment about the proper substantive resolution and take reasonable actions to bring it about.

Consider a well-known scenario involving two lawyers negotiating a personal injury case.[3] The plaintiff is an indigent who has suffered severe injury as a result of the undisputed negligence of the defendant, but he may have negligently contributed to his own injury. During negotiation, the insurance company lawyer conducting the defense realizes that the plaintiff's lawyer is unaware that a recent statute abolishing the contributory negligence defense would apply retroactively to this case. The plaintiff's lawyer is negotiating under the assumption that there is a substantial probability that his client's negligence will entirely preclude recovery when in fact there is no such probability. The defense lawyer proceeds to conclude the negotiation without correcting the mistaken impression.

In the personal injury case, the critical concern for the defense lawyer should be whether the settlement likely to occur in the absence of disclosure would be fair (in the sense that it reasonably vindicates the merits of the relevant claims). On the facts given, it seems probable that the settlement would not be fair. The plaintiff's lawyer probably set her bottom line well below the appropriately discounted value of the plaintiff's claims because of her mistake about the law. Here the defense counsel's responsibility is to move the case toward a fair result, and the best way to do this is probably to make the disclosure and resume the negotiation. This duty is triggered by the fact that, without some assistance from defense counsel, the procedure cannot be relied on to produce a just resolution. The plaintiff's counsel's mistake is a major breakdown in the procedure, and since the case is headed toward pretrial settlement, there will be no further opportunities for counsel, judge, or jury to remedy the breakdown.

The defense counsel should also assess the likelihood that disclosure will backfire and lead to a less fair result because the plaintiff's counsel takes this information and then tries to get more than she is entitled to through some aggressive tactic of her own. But this risk seems small if, as the scenario suggests, the defendant's lawyer is more experienced than the plaintiff's, the latter has not been aggressive, and the matter seems likely to be wound up before the plaintiff has an opportunity to make new maneuvers.

Now consider a case in which the breakdown arises from incapacity on the part of official institutions. Suppose an experienced tax practitioner has conceived a new tax avoidance device. She herself is convinced that it is improper, but there is a nonfrivolous argument for its legality. The lawyer might believe that the Internal Revenue Service and the courts are best situated to resolve such questions. She might reason that the agency and the courts have greater expertise than she, that they are better able to resolve issues in a way that can be uniformly applied to similar cases, and that they are subject to various democratic controls. However, such arguments are plausible only to the extent that the agency and the courts will in fact make an informed decision on the matter. The arguments do not warrant the lawyer using the device in a case where the agency and the courts will never effectively review it. This might happen because the agency lacks sufficient enforcement resources to identify the issue or to take the matter to court. In such a situation, the lawyer should respond to the procedural failure. She can do so by trying to remedy it, for example, by bringing the issue to the attention of the IRS. If that course is not possible (for example, because the client will not permit it), or if it will not be sufficient to remedy the procedural deficiencies (for example, because the agency is so strapped that it cannot even respond to such signals), then the lawyer has to assume more direct responsibility for the substantive resolution. If she thinks that the device should be held invalid, she should refuse to assist with it. In these circumstances, she is the best situated decision-maker to pass on the matter.

In situations in which the procedure is sufficiently reliable that the lawyer need not assume direct responsibility for the substantive merits, she retains a duty to take reasonably available actions to make the procedure as effective as possible and to forgo actions that would reduce its efficacy. When she need not consider the substantive merits herself, she should do what she can to facilitate the adjudicator in doing so.

Take an issue of deceptive impeachment tactics. Is it appropriate for the lawyer in cross-examining a handwriting expert surreptitiously to substitute a writing with a signature different from the one the witness has identified in the hope that the witness will not notice the substitution and continue to insist on what will then be a demonstrably mistaken identification? The libertarian "arguably legal" standard tends to permit such tactics; the regulatory "on the merits" standard tends to condemn them. Under the discretionary approach, the matter requires an inquiry into whether the tactic is likely to contribute to the adjudicator's ability to decide the case fairly. To the extent that the lawyer has no knowledge that will not be presented at hearing, the ethical issue will not be urgent because, to the extent the tactic fails to contribute to a fair understanding of the issues, the adjudicator can discount it appropriately. But if the lawyer has knowledge or insight that will not be formulated as admissible evidence, the ethical issue may be important. Suppose that the lawyer's extra-record knowledge indicates that the witness is highly competent and the identification is correct but that the tactic might be effective because the witness is prone to nervousness and distraction in public appearances. Here the tactic is likely to detract from, rather than to enhance, the adjudicator's ability to decide fairly. On the other hand, suppose that the lawyer has extra-record knowledge suggesting that the witness is not competent and the identification is mistaken. Here she might plausibly decide that the tactic would contribute to a fair decision.

In this case, the ethical concerns arise from the fact that, even in a relatively reliable procedure, the lawyer typically has some opportunities to improve her client's chance of success in ways that, were she required to consider the matter, she would acknowledge do not facilitate decision on the merits by the adjudicator. The libertarian approach relies on the judge to check such moves at the prompting of opposing counsel, but the judge, even after hearing from both sides, is often less well informed about specific factual issues than counsel. In such situations, counsel should not defer responsibility to the judge for tactics she does not believe contribute to a fair decision. Since she has an advantage in assessing the matter, she should exercise her own judgment and, when appropriate, self-restraint.

Thus, far from collapsing the lawyer's role into the judge's, ethical discretion suggests a lawyer role that complements the generally accepted understanding of the judge's role. The lawyer assumes substantial responsibility for vindicating substantive merits to the extent that the judge cannot be expected to do so. In other situations, her responsibility is to facilitate the judicial role.

Of course, one can imagine a procedural context that is so reliable as to make superfluous the type of discretion urged here: the dispute will be determined promptly, through an adjudication by a competent decision-maker able routinely to identify and neutralize obfuscation and excessive aggressiveness, after a hearing at which both sides are ably represented and adequately financed, governed by rules and procedures that ensure full development of the evidence and issues, and where effective relief is available.

It is ironic that conventional discourse about legal ethics should often treat this ideal situation as paradigmatic. Not only is the situation rare at best, but ethical issues are here unimportant. Since, by hypothesis, relevant information is fully available and each side can counter the aggression and deception of the other, ethics collapses into strategy. No ethically questionable practice would be likely to benefit the client. Ethical issues arise because actual procedures fall short of the ideal. One of the strengths of the discretionary approach is that it acknowledges and responds to procedural imperfection.

The Limits of Role and Legality

The discretionary approach is grounded in the lawyer's professional commitments to legal values. It rejects the common tendency to attribute the tensions of legal ethics to a conflict between the demands of legality on the one hand and those of nonlegal, personal, or ordinary morality on the other.

The specious law-versus-morality characterization is used most frequently to privilege client loyalty. For example, in the hypothetical discussed above involving a personal injury negotiation in which the plaintiff's lawyer underestimated the value of the claim because of a mistake about the law, the defense counsel's client loyalty option is often seen as the "legal" one and the disclosure option as a "moral" alternative. In fact, of course, concern for the plaintiff is strongly grounded in the belief that without disclosure the plaintiff will be deprived of a substantive legal entitlement to recover for negligently inflicted losses. Thus, both options are equally "legal" in the sense that they are grounded in important legal values.

Prosecution and Race: The Power and Privilege of Discretion[1]

Angela J. Davis[2]

> For everyone to whom much is given, from him much will be required; and to whom much has been committed, of him they will ask the more.[3]

At every step of the criminal process, there is evidence that African Americans are not treated as well as whites—both as victims of crime and as criminal defendants. And because prosecutors play such a dominant and commanding role in the criminal justice system through the exercise of broad, unchecked discretion, their role in the complexities of racial inequality in the criminal process is inextricable and profound.

In this article, I examine prosecutorial discretion—a major cause of racial inequality in the criminal justice system. I argue that prosecutorial discretion may instead be used to construct effective solutions to racial injustice. Prosecutors, more than any other officials in the system, have the power, discretion, and responsibility to remedy the discriminatory treatment of African Americans in the criminal justice process. Through the exercise of prosecutorial discretion, prosecutors make decisions that not only often predetermine the outcome of criminal cases, but also contribute to the discriminatory treatment of African Americans as both criminal defendants and victims of crime. I suggest that this discretion, which is almost always exercised in private, gives prosecutors more power than any other criminal justice officials, with practically no corresponding accountability to the public they serve. Thus, I maintain that prosecutors, through their overall duty to pursue justice, have the responsibility to use their discretion to help eradicate the discriminatory treatment of African Americans in the criminal justice system.

Courts have consistently upheld and sanctioned prosecutorial discretion, and make it increasingly difficult to mount legal challenges to discretionary decisions that have a discriminatory effect on African American criminal defendants and crime victims. These challenges are usually brought as selective prosecution claims under the Equal Protection Clause, requiring a nearly impossible showing that the prosecutor intentionally discriminated against the defendant or the victim. One reason this standard is so difficult to meet is that much of the discriminatory treatment of defendants and victims may be based on unconscious racism and institutional bias rather than on discriminatory intent. Another reason is the exacting legal standard for obtaining discovery of information that would help to prove discriminatory intent when it does exist.

In this article, I suggest a solution that would promote equal protection of the laws through the electoral process and help address the difficult legal challenges to discriminatory treatment. I propose the use of racial impact studies in prosecution offices to advance the responsible, nondiscriminatory exercise of prosecutorial discretion. The crux of the racial impact studies is the collection and publication of data on the race of the defendant and the victim in each case for each category of offense, and the action taken at each step of the criminal process. This data would then be analyzed to determine if race had a statistically significant correlation with various prosecutorial decisions. The studies would serve a number of purposes. First, they would reveal whether there is disparate treatment of African American defendants or victims. Second, they may reveal the discriminatory impact of race-neutral discretionary decisions and policies. Third, they would help prosecutors make informed decisions about the formulation of policies and establish standards to guide the exercise of discretion in specific cases. Finally, the publication of these studies would inform criminal defendants, crime victims, and the general public about the exercise of prosecutorial discretion and force prosecutors to be accountable for their decisions. Publication of the information would help inform the general public about prosecutorial practices so they could more effectively hold prosecutors accountable through the electoral process. Publication might also help criminal defendants alleging race-based selective prosecution to overcome the strict discovery standard set by the Supreme Court in *United States v. Armstrong*.

Racial impact studies may reveal illegitimate differential treatment based on unconscious racism or class bias, or legitimately different outcomes based on disproportionate offending and uninterested or uncooperative victims. The studies may also reveal that there is no differential treatment, thereby invalidating misperceptions of unfairness. In any case, the availability of the information would be invaluable in improving the overall administration of criminal justice. As Justice Brandeis said, "Sunlight is said to be the best of disinfectants."[4]

The Prosecution Function

Like the decisions of many officials in the criminal justice system, prosecutorial decisions often have a discriminatory effect on African Americans. The decisions and actions of prosecutors—and thus the discriminatory effect of these decisions—have greater impact and more serious consequences than those of any other criminal justice official. This great influence and its consequences stem from the extraordinary, almost unreviewable discretion and power of prosecutors.

The Charging Decision

The first and "most important function exercised by a prosecutor" is the charging decision.[5] Although police officers decide whether to arrest a suspect, the prosecutor decides whether he should be formally charged with a crime and what the charge should be. This decision is entirely discretionary. Even if there is probable cause to believe the suspect has committed a crime, the prosecutor may decide to dismiss the case and release the suspect. She may also file a charge that is either more or less serious than that recommended by the police officer, as long as there is probable cause to believe the suspect committed the crime. Other than a constitutional challenge by a criminal defendant, there is very little process for review of these decisions.

Some states require that felony charges be formally instituted by a grand jury, but the grand jury process is controlled entirely by the prosecutor. The grand jury can be as small as five members and as large as about two dozen. Grand jurors hear the testimony of witnesses, ask questions, and decide whether and with what offenses the suspect should be charged. The prosecutor, however, usually decides which witnesses will be called, directs the questioning of those witnesses, interprets the law, and makes a recommendation to the grand jury. Neither the target of the investigation nor his counsel may be present during the grand jury proceedings, nor may they or any member of the general public be informed of the substance of the witnesses' testimony or any other details of these proceedings.

The charging decision is one of the most important decisions a prosecutor makes. In conjunction with the plea bargaining process, the charging decision almost predetermines the outcome of a criminal case, because the vast majority of criminal cases result in guilty pleas or guilty verdicts. The charge also often determines the sentence that the defendant will receive, particularly in federal court, where criminal sentences are governed by the federal sentencing guidelines, and in state cases involving mandatory sentences. Because the sentencing guidelines and mandatory sentencing laws virtually eliminate judicial discretion, the prosecutor often effectively determines the defendant's sentence at the charging stage of the process, if the defendant is eventually found guilty. The charging decision's effect on the outcome of a case is felt to a lesser degree in state court. Although some state courts have some form of sentencing guidelines, most states give judges more discretion in determining the sentence for a convicted defendant. Nonetheless, the range of penalties is set by the initial charging decision.

The gravity of the charging decision is epitomized by a prosecutor's decision to seek the death penalty. No state's laws require that the death penalty be sought in any particular case, and all thirty-eight states that currently provide for the death penalty leave the decision to the discretion of the prosecutor. Most state death-penalty laws allow the prosecutor to seek the death penalty in cases involving specific aggravating factors. The decision to seek the death penalty, like all charging decisions, can only be challenged on constitutional grounds, and these challenges are extremely difficult to sustain.

Plea Bargaining

Most criminal cases end in a guilty plea. The typical plea bargain arrangement involves an agreement by the prosecutor to dismiss the most serious charge or charges in exchange for the defendant's guilty plea to a less serious offense. The defendant gives up his right to a trial and avoids the possibility of being convicted of a more serious offense and being imprisoned for a longer period of time. Sometimes, the plea bargain offers the possibility of avoiding imprisonment entirely. Although the judge must approve plea bargains in most jurisdictions, judges routinely approve these agreements because they expedite the process by disposing of criminal cases without the time and expense of a trial.

Like the charging decision, the plea bargaining process is controlled entirely by the prosecutor and decisions are entirely within her discretion. A criminal defendant cannot plead guilty to a less serious offense unless the prosecutor decides to make a plea offer. While the defense attorney may attempt to negotiate the best possible offer, the decision is ultimately left to the prosecutor's discretion.

Although prosecutors make important, influential decisions at other stages of the criminal process, the charging and plea bargaining stages provide the most independent power and control and allow the least opportunity for counterbalancing input from the defense. Prosecutors do not control the trial stage of the process and defense attorneys are theoretically on equal footing at this stage, as judges control the pace and content of the trial through their rulings. The sentencing hearing also provides for participation by the defense attorney and is controlled by the judge, unless mandatory sentencing laws are involved. In mandatory sentencing cases, which are increasingly common, the prior charging and plea bargaining decisions of the prosecutor often determine the sentence the defendant will receive, making the input of the defense attorney and the judge almost irrelevant.

Racism in the Prosecutorial Process

Because prosecutors are arguably the most powerful decision-makers in the process, their decisions potentially have the greatest discriminatory impact. No discussion of the impact of prosecutorial discretion on racial disparities in the criminal justice system would be complete, however, without a discussion of the discretionary decisions of police officers. Prosecutors typically do not become involved in a criminal case unless and until a police officer makes an arrest. If race is a factor in the decision to arrest a suspect, the police officer has infused the process with a layer of racial discrimination even before the prosecutor has an opportunity to exercise her discretion.

Racial impact studies in prosecutor offices may reveal racial disparities in law enforcement. These studies may demonstrate that police are arresting African Americans and presenting them for prosecution at disproportionately higher rates than their similarly situated white counterparts. If such evidence is revealed, police should be compelled to explain or remedy the disparities. The available literature suggests that such racial disparities frequently exist in the arrest stage of the criminal process.[6]

Race and Police Discretion

Police officers often act in a discriminatory manner in the performance of their official duties when they disproportionately stop, detain, and arrest African American men, with or without probable cause, and with or without articulable suspicion. In fact, courts have upheld race as a legitimate factor in the decision to stop and detain a suspect.[7]

One factor that contributes to discrimination at the arrest stage is the discretion afforded police officers in deciding whom to stop and whether to make an arrest. Despite the requirement that a police officer's decision to stop a suspect must be based on an articulable suspicion, the Supreme Court has shown increasing deference to the judgment of police officers in its interpretation of this requirement. The practical effect of this deference is the assimilation of police officers' subjective beliefs, biases, hunches, and prejudices into law.[8] Because police officers are not required to make an arrest when they observe conduct creating probable cause, their discretion may result in the failure to detain or arrest whites who commit acts for which their African American counterparts would often be detained or arrested.[9]

Police officers engage in discriminatory conduct in numerous forums. Traffic stops provide a particularly egregious example. Police officers use alleged traffic violations as an excuse for stopping and detaining motorists they suspect of other criminal conduct. Once the driver is stopped, the police officer will use the opportunity to observe the interior of the car for any items that might be in "plain view."[10] The officer may also obtain the consent of an intimidated driver to conduct a full search of the car. Even if the driver refuses to give the officer consent to search the car, the police officer often may arrest the driver, rather than simply issue a citation, as long as there is probable cause to believe that a traffic violation has been committed. Once an arrest is made, the officer is justified in conducting a full-fledged search of the person and the surrounding area. Police officers may use minor traffic violations as an excuse to stop individuals they would otherwise have no legitimate reason to detain. These so-called "pretextual stops" allow police officers to use any traffic violation, no matter how minor, as a justification for a stop and possible arrest. Because police officers do not stop motorists every time they observe a traffic violation, the stops can be used in a discriminatory manner. The Supreme Court has unanimously upheld the constitutionality of pretextual stops, despite studies showing that they are disproportionately used to stop and detain African Americans and Latinos.

The racial impact of discretionary arrest decisions is particularly significant for drug offenses. Although whites use drugs in far greater numbers than African Americans, African Americans comprise a disproportionate percentage of drug arrests, convictions, and imprisonments. Law enforcement agents concede that drugs are used and sold in middle- and upper-class neighborhoods and business districts, but they have focused their law enforcement efforts in urban and inner-city areas which are populated primarily by African Americans and other people of color. These decisions have obvious racial effects.

Race and Prosecutorial Discretion

Although some prosecutors are involved in the investigatory stage of the criminal process, most prosecutors enter the process after an arrest is made. A prosecutor may not know about racial considerations in the arrest process, and in most instances, does not have jurisdiction or control over the police department or other law enforcement agencies. If a prosecutor is aware of the inappropriate or illegal consideration of race at the arrest stage of the process, she may legitimately decide to exercise her discretion to decline prosecution. The consideration of race in the arrest process is usually not obvious, however, and unless a prosecutor is intentionally attempting to ferret out such decisions, she may not discover them. Additionally, because prosecutors must rely on police officers to prosecute their cases successfully, they are not motivated to confront them with accusations of racism and discrimination.

Prosecutors should bear the brunt of the remedial responsibility to eliminate racism in the criminal process, even though inappropriate or illegal considerations of race may occur at the arrest stage, often before prosecutorial participation in the process. Although police officers may and should take steps to discover and eliminate the inappropriate consideration of race, their power to affect and influence the criminal process begins and ends at the arrest stage. Prosecutorial power affects every stage of the process, including the arrest stage.

Like police officers, prosecutors often make decisions that discriminate against African American victims and defendants. These decisions may or may not be intentional or conscious. Although it may be difficult to prove intentional discrimination when it exists, unintentional discrimination poses even greater challenges. Prosecutors may not be aware that the seemingly harmless, reasonable, race-neutral decisions they make every day may have a racially discriminatory impact. This discriminatory impact may occur because of unconscious racism—a phenomenon that plays a powerful role in so many discretionary decisions in the criminal process— and because the lack of power and disadvantaged circumstances of so many African American defendants and victims make it more likely that prosecutors will treat them less well than whites.

Unconscious Racism

If one acknowledges that African Americans experience both disparate and discriminatory treatment in the criminal justice system, the discussion ultimately turns to the issue of blame. Whose fault is it? Who has committed the invidious act or acts that have caused African Americans to experience this discriminatory treatment? It is this intent-focused analysis, sanctioned by the Supreme Court in its equal protection findings, that has stymied legal challenges to discrimination in the criminal context. Instead of focusing on the harm experienced by African Americans as a result of actions by state actors, the Court has focused on whether the act itself is inherently invidious and whether the actor intended to cause the harm. In addition, the Court has placed the burden of proving intent on the shoulders of the victim. If the victim is unable to prove the actor's bad intent or, in certain contexts, if the actor can establish a nondiscriminatory explanation for his behavior,[11] the Court offers no remedy for the harm experienced by the victim.

The main problem with this intent-focused analysis is that it is back-ward-looking. Although perhaps adequate in combating straightforward and explicit discrimination as it existed in the past, it is totally deficient as a remedy for the more complex and systemic discrimination that African Americans currently experience. When state actors openly expressed their racist views, it was easy to identify and label the invidious nature of their actions. But today, with some notable exceptions, most racist behavior is not openly expressed. More significantly, some racist behavior is committed unconsciously, and many who engage in this behavior are well-intentioned people who would be appalled by the notion that they would be seen as behaving in a racist or discriminatory manner.

Unconscious racism, although arguably less offensive than purposeful discrimination, is no less harmful. In fact, in many ways it is more perilous because it is often unrecognizable to the victim as well as the perpetrator. And the Court, by focusing on intent rather than harm, has refused to recognize, much less provide a remedy for, this most common and widespread form of racism. By focusing on blame rather than injury, the Court serves to satisfy the psychological needs of the uninjured party while leaving the victim without relief.

Professor Charles Lawrence defines unconscious racism as the ideas, attitudes, and beliefs developed in American historical and cultural heritage that cause Americans unconsciously to "attach significance to an individual's race and [which] induce negative feelings and opinions about nonwhites."[12] He argues that although America's historical experience has made racism an integral part of our culture, most people exclude it from their conscious minds because it is rejected as immoral. Professor Lawrence's definition of unconscious racism provides a useful framework in which to examine the discriminatory impact of prosecutorial decision-making.

The Discriminatory Impact of Race-Neutral Prosecutorial Decision-Making

Most prosecutors today would vehemently deny that they have ever discriminated against African American defendants or victims or that they take race into account in any way in the exercise of their prosecutorial duties. Prosecutors exercise a tremendous amount of discretion without governing rules and regulations and are not legally required to exercise their discretion in any particular way. Nonetheless, many prosecutors informally consider nonracial factors in making charging and plea bargaining decisions. Factors that prosecutors frequently cite as reasons for making certain charging and plea bargaining decisions are: the seriousness of the offense, the defendant's prior criminal record, the victim's interest in prosecution, the strength of the evidence, the likelihood of conviction, and the availability of alternative dispositions. These otherwise legitimate, race-neutral factors may be permeated with unconscious racism.

The seriousness of the offense is certainly a legitimate factor in making a charging decision. A prosecutor may decide to dismiss a case involving the possession of a single marijuana cigarette while charging and vigorously prosecuting a case involving distribution of a large amount of cocaine. Few would question this decision regardless of the race of the defendants. The more difficult issue arises when two cases involving the same offense but defendants or victims of different races are charged differently. If two murder cases involving similar facts with victims of different races are charged differently, the issue of unconscious racism becomes relevant. If a defendant in a case involving a white victim is charged with capital murder while a defendant in a similar case involving a black victim is charged with second-degree murder, questions arise about the value the prosecutors unconsciously placed on the lives of the respective victims. A prosecutor may unconsciously consider a case involving a white victim as more serious than a case involving a black victim. This unconscious view may influence not only the charging decision, but related decisions as well.

For example, if a prosecutor deems a particular case to be more serious than others, she will tend to invest more time and resources in that case, both investigating and preparing for trial. Such an increased investment would consequently yield more evidence and stiffen prosecutorial resolve. The likelihood of conviction is also obviously increased by the additional investment in investigation. Thus, although the strength of the evidence and the likelihood of conviction are facially race-neutral factors, they may be influenced by an unconsciously racist valuation of a case involving a white victim.

The victim's interest in prosecution is another legitimate factor that prosecutors consider in making charging and plea bargaining decisions. If the victim of a crime informs the prosecutor that he has no interest in the prosecution of his case and no desire to see the defendant punished, the prosecutor may legitimately dismiss the case based on the victim's feelings, especially if she believes that the defendant does not pose a danger to society and there are no other legitimate reasons for pursuing the prosecution. Few would question this decision, especially if the victim of the crime considered the prosecution process too onerous and difficult.

On the other hand, should a prosecutor pursue a prosecution in a case that she would otherwise dismiss for legitimate reasons simply because the victim wants to see the defendant punished? Or should a prosecutor assume that a victim is not interested in prosecution when the victim does not appear for witness conferences or respond to a subpoena? These questions demonstrate the significance of the intersection of class and race in the criminal process. They also raise fundamental questions about the duty and responsibility of the prosecutor to seek justice for all parties— defendants as well as victims—and to assure that all parties receive equal protection under the law.

The prior record of the defendant is another legitimate, seemingly race-neutral factor considered by prosecutors in the charging/plea bargaining process. Defendants with prior records are more likely to be charged and less likely to receive a favorable plea offer. Prosecutors consider both arrest and conviction records; defendants with recidivist tendencies are arguably more deserving of prosecution. Race, however, may affect the existence of a prior criminal record even in the absence of recidivist tendencies on the part of the suspect.

As previously noted, race plays a role in the decision to detain and/or arrest a suspect. Some courts have even legitimized this practice. In addition, policy decisions about where police officers should be deployed and what offenses they should investigate have racial ramifications. The fact that a white defendant has no criminal arrest or conviction record may not be a reflection of a lack of criminality on his part. If he lives in a neighborhood or attends a school that resolves certain criminal offenses (drug use, assault, etc.) without police intervention, he may be a recidivist without a record. Likewise, a black defendant who lives in a designated "high crime" area may have been detained and arrested on numerous occasions with or without probable cause. Thus, the existence or nonexistence of an arrest or conviction record may or may not reflect relative criminality in black and white defendants. A prosecutor without knowledge of or sensitivity to this issue may give prior arrests undue consideration in making charging and plea bargaining decisions.

Another factor that prosecutors sometimes consider is the availability of alternative dispositions. For some less serious offenses, prosecutors may be willing to consider dismissing a case based on the existence of alternative resolutions that serve the overall interest of justice. For example, if a defendant who has stolen is able to make restitution and the victim is satisfied with this resolution and would be burdened by numerous court appearances, dismissal of the case may be the best disposition for all parties. The dismissal would also have the added benefit of eliminating the time and expense of trying another case for the prosecutor, the defense attorney, and the court. As with all of the otherwise legitimate considerations, however, this issue also has class and racial ramifications.

Prosecutorial Discretion—Power, Privilege, and Ethical Responsibility

As members of the executive branch and highly specialized officials in the criminal justice system, prosecutors are in the unique position to use their discretion to eliminate many of the racial disparities in the criminal justice system.[13] No other official is empowered to effect such change. The elimination of race discrimination is totally consistent with the role of the prosecutor. It is the responsibility of the prosecutor to seek justice, not simply to win convictions.[14] The prosecutor's duties and responsibilities to the criminal justice system as a whole stem from her dual role as an advocate for the government and as an administrator of justice. As administrator of justice, the prosecutor represents the interests of society as a whole, including the interests of the defendant as a member of society. The prosecutor often experiences tension and conflict in her attempt to implement these dual roles.

The prosecutor's duty to combat discrimination in the criminal justice system exemplifies the conflict in the implementation of these dual responsibilities. On the one hand, the prosecutor has a duty as both an advocate for the government and a representative of society to protect the community through the enforcement of the criminal laws. On the other hand, she has a responsibility to ensure that victims and defendants in the criminal justice system are treated fairly, equitably, and in a nondiscriminatory manner. The latter responsibility is owed to individual victims and defendants and to society as a whole; society has an interest in a fair and nondiscriminatory criminal justice system. The two responsibilities do not present an insurmountable conflict. The simple answer is that the prosecutor must protect the community through the fair, equitable, and nondiscriminatory enforcement of the laws.

Prosecutors currently use their discretion not only in the prosecution of individual cases, but also in the implementation of general policies. United States attorneys or state's attorneys may implement formal or informal general policies regarding the prosecution of certain types of cases. For example, a chief prosecutor may have a policy of prosecuting all cases involving firearms possession, domestic violence, or some other criminal behavior that may be particularly widespread in his community. Likewise, a prosecutor may institute a policy of dismissing cases involving small quantities of marijuana or of seeking a probationary sentence for the defendants in these cases. Each of these policies may reflect the attitudes, values, and priorities of the prosecutor and/or the community about certain criminal behavior.

The interest and responsibility of both the prosecutor and the community in the nondiscriminatory treatment of defendants and victims in the criminal justice system should also be the basis for the implementation of general prosecutorial policies. As with most criminal justice policies, they would reflect a balancing of all of the interests at stake. The goal of the prosecutor's office should be the implementation of policies in a manner consistent with the overall administration of justice.

Conclusion

The biblical quote cited at the beginning of this article has a simple meaning: from whom much is given, much is expected. Prosecutors have been given more power and discretion than any other criminal justice official, so they have a greater ability to effect change where it is needed. The Supreme Court has not required much of prosecutors, but the Court's standards should serve as a floor rather than a ceiling, as a base rather than a goal. Prosecutors can, and should, seek to eliminate racial disparities regardless of blame and intent. They can, and should, set a higher standard of performance for themselves than the requirements set by the Supreme Court. They have both the power and privilege to do so. The publication of racial impact studies will help to assure that they do.

In the Interest of Racial Harmony: Revisiting the Lawyer's Duty to Work for the Common Good[1]

Bill Ong Hing[2]

The image of armed Korean American merchants atop the roofs of their stores defending their property against rioting African Americans was shocking. Plastered across the front pages of major newspapers and featured on television news programs throughout the country following the Rodney King verdict, this picture epitomized the racial conflict between African Americans and Korean Americans in south central Los Angeles.[3]

The days following the April 29, 1992, acquittal of the Los Angeles police officers who beat African American motorist Rodney King could be described as an uprising of the "have nots." But refusing to acknowledge the racial and ethnic dimensions would be an imprudent oversight. Sister Souljah expressed at least a partial view of the racial undercurrents at work:

> I think that we have to look at the fact that black people didn't just run outside and burn up their houses because they were angry. The Beverly Center was wrecked and that's in a white area. Korean businesses were targeted because that Korean woman shot and killed Latasha Harlans [*sic*] and she was convicted of the crime and she did not [get] one day in jail and we've got 25 percent of our black male population behind bars doing exorbitant sentences for small crimes and we don't get justice. These are the reasons why people were attacked.[4]

The racial motivation of many of the protestors did not go unnoticed by Asian Americans. Just a few weeks after South Central erupted in violence, I attended an Asian American Leadership teleconference sponsored by AT&T. Although the event had been scheduled well before the Rodney King verdict, much of the discussion revolved around the victimization of Korean merchants in South Central. Some of the conference participants expressed a sense of outrage on behalf of the Korean merchants. One respected participant suggested prosecuting the arsonists and looters for hate crimes.

Most of the conference participants were Chinese Americans, Japanese Americans, and Filipino Americans interested in expressing support for the Korean merchants, though it was not clear how many of them supported the hate violence theme. I cringed at the suggestion to prosecute. Certainly I was not blind to the fact that some looters and arsonists acted against Korean merchants out of racism. But beyond the lack of economic justice in South Central, my interest was in healing racial wounds. Pushing a hate violence prosecution struck me as counterproductive to that purpose.

The turmoil in South Central brought other racially charged legal conflicts to the fore. African Americans boycotted certain Korean American–owned businesses and accused Korean American merchants of race discrimination in their hiring practices. A few construction companies that hired minority workers as required by set-aside provisions attempted to satisfy those requirements by hiring Latino and/or Asian workers, but no African Americans. And even before the uprising, African Americans had organized to limit the number of liquor stores in their neighborhoods, many of which are owned by Korean Americans.

The method of dealing with cases involving racial conflict supported by conventional client-focused ethics may not be in complete harmony with the broader public interest. For example, the movement to close liquor stores in south central Los Angeles by using land use and nuisance theories has heightened racial animosity between Korean Americans and African Americans. African Americans have expressed resentment over the lawsuit brought by Chinese Americans in San Francisco challenging admissions policies to the local academic high school. And the African American boycotts of Korean American merchants in Flatbush, New York, which featured legal counsel on both sides, exacerbated racial friction and led to more violence. Yet in all of these situations, lawyers used strategies that were neither unethical nor adversarially out of bounds.

Lawyers called to work on issues such as these, having the potential to exacerbate racial conflict, are well positioned to work to improve race relations. I wonder if these lawyers should be required to work constructively on matters involving racial tension.

This article rests on the premise that racial harmony is a critical, normative goal for all of us—including lawyers. Improving race relations must become a high national priority. I thus question the use of aggressive, adversarial legal strategies in the first instance in conflicts arising between different racial and ethnic groups. The lawyer can and should play a central role in working for the common good by lawyering in a manner that promotes better race relations. I urge a reconsideration of what Louis Brandeis termed the "lawyer for the situation," or the functionalist-progressive vision of lawyering. And I urge that this role of the lawyer be a matter of duty rather than simply one of aspiration—a duty which may in fact conflict not only with the values of the client, but also with those of the lawyer. In my view, racial harmony is so vital to bettering society as its complexion becomes increasingly multicultural that lawyers must elevate the goal of racial harmony above their clients' and their own personal values, and in short, above adherence to the adversary ethic.

Racial Harmony as a Preeminent Societal Goal

The general proposition that racial harmony is a societal goal elicits little debate. Many community, religious, and political leaders speak of the need to put aside racial differences and work collectively for the good of our communities and the nation. Those engaging in such work receive admiration and honors. The roots of such a goal rest on religion, moral philosophy, and basic concepts of humanity. Although some mainstream statements or actions appear insensitive to race relations or even racist, I think we would be hard pressed to find mainstream advocacy against promoting racial harmony. While views may differ about the precise contours of a "racially harmonious" society, avoiding racially charged conflicts like those in South Central forms the baseline on which at least most of us can agree.

Striving for racial harmony is more than just another societal goal. It stands out as a particularly urgent and compelling priority. Racial and ethnic tension and violence damage the psyche of our nation, thereby hampering social and political progress. The violence in south central Los Angeles highlights the urgency of this priority. The quest for better race relations must become one of our nation's chief societal goals.

We therefore need a new commitment to improving race relations in our increasingly diverse society. We need to promote constant awareness of interethnic group relations and strive to eliminate conscious and unconscious racism. We must reach a new level of consciousness, develop a new, inclusive vocabulary, and recognize the variety of racial and ethnic issues confronting our society. We must urge one another to judge people by the "content of their character" and not the "color of their skin."[5]

Lawyers can and should play a crucial role in achieving these goals. The progressive/functionalist approach to lawyering, however, has been criticized for naively assuming a single, uncontroversial vision of the public interest to guide decision-making. William Simon notes that in most situations of ethical conflict, the dictates of justice and legality are unclear.[6] Thus, the goal of racial harmony becomes controversial when it leads to the subordination of the interests of one side in a legal dispute.

Accordingly, Simon argues that ethical discretion in lawyering should be regarded as a legitimate judgment—one with which people may disagree, but which nevertheless represents a "good faith attempt to apply the norms and practices of the culture." People will differ about what the public interest is, but lawyers should continue to struggle in good faith to achieve their competing visions of the public interest and not passively defer to articulated client goals. By this reasoning, labeling the interest in racial harmony a goal is a political judgment, but a legitimate one.

The lawyers of the civil rights movement, for example, sought equality and equal treatment of all individuals by public as well as by private entities. Many saw their roles as consistent with a duty of lawyers to engage in public functions or to help make the legal system more accessible to the disadvantaged. Although we do not generally associate the lawyering style of civil rights attorneys with this goal, their work also manifests a desire to work toward racial harmony. Ending racial oppression is, after all, one important facet of promoting better race relations.

The goal of racial harmony and peaceful coexistence in a multicultural society derives in part from the quest for equality. My purpose here is to urge that this goal influence the lawyering method not just in civil rights cases but in all cases involving racial tension at the heart of our diverse communities.

My purpose in this article is to encourage the legal profession to consider adopting a specific set of rules and guidelines that lawyers would be obligated to follow in cases involving, or potentially involving, racial and ethnic tension. My assumption is that the manner in which lawyers handle cases can affect race relations negatively, positively, or not at all. Actions that intentionally or unintentionally define the dispute in terms of race or ethnicity can divide communities or deepen existing tension. On the other hand, the use of community-minded resolutions to end disputes involving racial groups at odds with one another can favorably affect race relations. My point is to demand that the legal system show leadership by forcing parties in conflict to sit down and do their best to define their conflict in nonracial, nonethnic terms before proceeding to more hostile postures.

I suggest rules that would apply in three different, but perhaps overlapping, scenarios: (1) When the case involves explicit racial conflict within a community. Examples include situations where African Americans accuse Korean American merchants of discriminating against them in hiring, or where African American tenants harass or violently attack southeast Asian tenants in public housing. (2) When one party acts in what she believes to be a racially neutral manner, but the other party construes her actions as racially or ethnically motivated. For instance, a largely African American community-based group in south central Los Angeles has been working to close liquor stores on the theory that they are detrimental to the community. Many Korean Americans feel that they have been racially and ethnically targeted by this crusade. (3) When the initial dispute does not implicate racial differences, but the two parties or interest groups are of different racial or ethnic groups.

These three scenarios are not mutually exclusive. For example, cases involving robberies or destruction of Korean American stores by African Americans can be classified in any of the three categories. There are also situations where the potential for conflict is less direct. Construction companies, for instance, could set out to fill minority hiring requirements by hiring only Asian American and Latino workers, and African Americans might contemplate a responsive action against these companies. As these situations arise, the lawyers involved should be required to invoke certain procedures.

Formal rules could simply require lawyers to first attempt to settle disputes through nonadversarial procedures, such as alternative dispute resolution (ADR), mediation, or simple discussion. In theory, court-annexed nonbinding arbitration programs that exist in some jurisdictions can be applied in any type of noncriminal case. California's requirement of nonbinding mediation in domestic violence cases, for example, rests on the premise that couples can do a better job of resolving the conflict than judges. Alternatively, when a civil suit falls into one of the three identified categories, the rules could require attorneys to complete a form and questionnaire indicating whether less antagonistic options exist and describing these options. Perhaps lawyers could submit something analogous to an environmental impact statement before proceeding with a lawsuit. Such a statement indicates an awareness of the potential impact on race relations and documents the good faith efforts made to pursue alternatives to the proposed action. If after these steps are taken the case proceeds, the lawyer should continue to pursue the societal goal of better race relations and object to the use of racially inflammatory strategies that the client may want to pursue.

The purpose of these proposals is to require the lawyer to sit down and discuss with the client the possible negative effects on race relations that the immediate pursuit of certain options may have. Ideally, the lawyer will exercise nonadversarial options first, and as a result, the posture and demeanor of the client's case will be calculated to minimize the threat to race relations. Even if the initial options do not achieve the client's legitimate, nonracial goals, the postponed use of more aggressive options will result in less damage to race relations. By then, the initial expression of good faith has established a track record of more sensitive, nonracial approaches, and the process may have clarified that the issues are not race related or perhaps framed the issues in nonracial terms.

These procedures recognize that today the phrase "I'll see you in court" (or its procedural manifestations) constitutes a belligerent challenge. The procedures I suggest seek to avoid these symbols until efforts have been made to frame the dispute in nonracial terms. The requirement to pursue alternatives does not preclude reaching the most aggressive option at some point. But at least the process reduces the chance that exercising the final option will result in a racial explosion.

In taking this approach, lawyers should not remain neutral to the client's morals if those morals are racist or have a high likelihood of inciting racial and ethnic tensions. Rather, the lawyer should appeal to the client with broader notions of consciousness and public welfare.

Certainly, I recognize that the goals of a client in any of the situations posited may not be illegitimate in the sense that they are fraudulent or illegal. The public importance of the lawyer acting as a "buffer who mediates"[7] between the client's goals and social interests, however, is not solely to avoid illegality but to contribute to society's betterment.

What I am proposing goes beyond but does not preclude the common approach of issuing a demand letter. I conceive of a more expansive duty, however, requiring the attorney and client to demonstrate good faith efforts to minimize potential negative racial ramifications. A perfunctory demand letter for purposes of notice or minimal good faith is simply insufficient. The duty I propose requires serious efforts such as formally requesting a meeting or conference that will allow parties to at least sit down together. This duty means seriously pursuing options to reach an accord without first resorting to racial claims. It also means following these guidelines as part of our earnest quest for racial harmony.

If we are serious about working toward racial harmony, the current rules do not live up to the task. The provisions of the Model Rules, Model Code, and the Canons of Professional Ethics may be construed to allow, and perhaps even encourage, the lawyer to point out social, moral, or political considerations in cases involving racial conflict. In all of these provisions, however, the client appears to have the final word. The language encouraging the lawyer to take responsibility is couched in terms of aspiration, rather than professional duty. As long as the client makes the final call, this approach to lawyering remains relatively uncontroversial. We need rules that obligate lawyers and clients to attempt to settle disagreements through nonadversarial procedures first.

(Er)race-ing an Ethic of Justice[1]

Anthony V. Alfieri [2]

For several years, I have pursued a project devoted to the study of race, lawyers, and ethics in the American criminal justice system. Building on the evolving jurisprudence of Critical Race Theory, the project spans a series of case studies investigating the rhetoric of race, or race-talk, in the prosecution and defense of racially motivated violence.

The purpose of this ongoing project is to understand the meaning of racial identity, racialized narrative, and race-neutral representation in law, lawyering, and ethics. To that end, the case studies serve as a means to develop working hypotheses regarding the sociolegal experience of subordination: specifically, the subordinating discourse and imagery of race trials, the nature of client and community harm caused by such subordination, the color-coded partisanship of purportedly race-neutral ethics regimes that countenance such subordination, and the legitimacy of alternative race-conscious ethical regulation. The process of reworking these hypotheses, one hopes, will not only reveal the sociolegal structures of racial violence in American history, but also reconstruct dominant visions of racial dignity and community in American law.

The reconstructive nature of this project derives in part from the teachings of Critical Race Theory and the emerging voices of color in Asian-Pacific and LatCrit scholarship. Unlike traditional canons of colorblind or color-coded representation, the vision of practice underlying this growing jurisprudential movement implies an ethic of good lawyering based on a color-conscious, contextual approach to civil and criminal advocacy. Still formative, the approach strives to accommodate the identity interests of client dignity and community integrity and, at the same time, to heed the injunction of effective representation.

The centrality of context to this approach lends added significance to the celebrated publication of William Simon's *The Practice of Justice: A Theory of Lawyers' Ethics*. Together with the new wave quartet of Robert Gordon, David Luban, Deborah Rhode, and David Wilkins, Simon stands among the preeminent scholars in legal ethics, singular in his deft integration of critical theory into the study of the legal profession. Simon's trenchant critique of the profession and its jurisprudential underpinnings gives direction to second wave projects like the one at hand. Indeed, *The Practice of Justice* provides a normative framework for designing race-conscious, community-regarding duties of legal representation. Instead of simply rehearsing Simon's critique and casting objections against it, this essay endeavors to put Simon's book to work in the service of fashioning an ethic of representation in race cases.

Liberal Visions: Dominant and Contextual

Like his new wave, post-realist compatriots, Simon treats law and the animating force of legal consciousness as ideological artifacts produced by normative contest and political conflict. He explores the ideology of the profession by interrogating its prevailing habits of mind, speech, and conduct. His inquiry begins with the introduction of the Dominant View,[3] an ideological stance rooted in state bar codes, disciplinary doctrine, and professional responsibility literature.[4] Attributing both moral anxiety and ethical disappointment to this Dominant View, Simon searches for an explanation of popular and professional disenchantment with the social role and moral aspiration of lawyers. He locates this explanation in the norms of professional responsibility that govern a lawyer's commitment to legality and justice. The core of that commitment, according to Simon, is loyalty to the client. Pointing to the structural tension between client interests and third-party or public interests, Simon observes an anxious profession struggling with hard moral decisions.

Simon's observation of moral anxiety is widely shared. Yet, for Simon, the instant anxiety signals a greater deterioration in the "moral terrain of lawyering."[5] He traces this anxiety to the jurisprudential foundation of the Dominant View and its core principle of client loyalty. That categorical imperative, Simon explains, carries crucial assumptions about the nature and purpose of law and the legal system that extend beyond the Dominant View. Here, the reach of jurisprudential logic extends through a common style of decision-making that Simon calls categorical. Ethical judgment driven by categorical injunction entails a style of decision-making that "severely restricts the range of considerations the decisionmaker may take into account when she confronts a particular problem."[6] Under this style, Simon notes, "a rigid rule dictates a particular response in the presence of a small number of factors."[7] Hence, he adds, the "decisionmaker has no discretion to consider factors that are not specified or to evaluate specified factors in ways other than those prescribed by the rule."[8] Both the American Bar Association's *Model Code of Professional Responsibility* and its *Model Rules of Professional Conduct,* Simon concludes, "legitimate the lawyer in pursuing any arguably lawful goal of the client through any arguably lawful means."[9]

Even competing visions of practice, Simon laments, suffer from the infirmities of this categorical style of judgment. The altruistic Public Interest View, for example, adheres to the basic maxim "that law should be applied in accordance with its purposes, and litigation should be conducted so as to promote informed resolution on the substantive merits."[10] More conventional perspectives on ethics and professional responsibility suffer in the same way. To Simon, for instance, a rule-focused approach emphasizing mechanical, positive law compliance quickly degenerates into the folly of moribund formalism. A role-morality perspective underscoring nonlegal value commitments and personal moral autonomy, by comparison, strains the bounds of professional role and legal obligation to an untenable degree. A contrasting personal-relations approach stressing the friendship-based extralegal values of loyalty, trust, and empathy unwittingly denigrates norms of legal merit and justice. Last, a prudential approach heralding the "lawyer-statesman" ideal of practical reason derived from common law modes of decision-making badly underestimates the moral quality of practice.

Overcoming the reigning preference for categorical styles of judgment, Simon advances a contextual approach to ethical decision-making that urges vindication of the underlying legal merits of a matter. For Simon, this approach involves "a judgment that applies relatively abstract norms to a broad range of the particulars of the case at hand."[11] His Contextual View imagines a legal ethics regime contingent on a lawyer's discretionary judgment exercised in a manner likely to promote justice. On this view, the promotion of justice is neither inconsistent with the rational, vigorous pursuit of a client's private goals nor inconsonant with the procedural and adversarial public norms of the legal system. Both private and public values, Simon contends, may be served in the particularized circumstances of a case to uphold the aspirational tradition of legal professionalism.

Jurisprudentially, then, Simon steers a delicate course. He seeks to maintain a sense of fidelity to law and to the norms of liberal legalism while he struggles to temper the radical excesses of possessive individualism through discretionary appeal to a greater ideal of public justice. Unfortunately, even a scholar of Simon's elegance and skill must fail in such an enterprise. The weight of liberal foundational norms—moral agency, radical individualism, contractarian commodity exchange, and public-private separation—condemns the project of ideological reparation. Consider, for example, Simon's overbroad concept of client agency. Construed either as an isolated individual or as a corporate entity, Simon's client often seems to possess an unchecked free will, a power of agency unfettered by material constraints in counseling or in the political economy. Consider as well his crabbed notion of the "public dimension" of client-group loyalty and client-community nexus outside the legal system. Narrowly defined, client loyalty operates to exclude the competing values of family, group, and community. Simon confesses as much but offers little guidance in the effort to reintegrate those values into a richer conception of other-regarding loyalty relevant to the support of "third-party and public interests."[12] More troubling, his underdeveloped notion of a larger, public community reinstates the private alienation of liberal individualism. Equally frustrating, the vitality of liberal legalism enjoys reinvigoration under his prescription of discretionary judgment. Because the prescribed act of discretion is itself ungrounded in community or some other public-regarding principle, Simon's lawyer may simply reenact his own private moral preference at the expense of a client-community participatory resolution. The next part ponders whether a race-informed, post-liberal vision of ethical lawyering might fare any better.

Post-Liberal Visions: Race-Consciousness and Racial Community

Critical Race Theory offers a battery of post-liberal visions embracing race-consciousness and racial community. Both liberal and postmodern in nature, the visions offer conflicting interpretations of racial identity, racialized narrative, and race-neutral representation. Several contemporary trials illustrate this conflict and the interpretive violence that binds racial discourse and symbol together in the harmful experience of client and community subordination. Consider, for example, the recent trials of Damian Williams and Henry Watson, the Alabama-based United Klans of America, and Lemrick Nelson and Charles Price. Careful scrutiny of these trials shows racial identity to be mutable in character, racialized narrative to be unstable in form, and race-neutral advocacy to be color-coded in content. The shifting circumstances of procedural and substantive laws, judges and juries, parties, victims, attorneys, and sociolegal culture add to this variability, creating cross-cutting lines of racial demarcation within law and the legal system. Surprisingly, what emerges out of this racial vortex is a relatively fixed set of status boundaries implying a system of moral hierarchy. The upshot is seen in the spectacle of the American race trial where identity, narrative, and representation shift in an ongoing contest of accommodation and resistance to well-entrenched racial hierarchy.

Racial identity is deeply embroiled in the moral hierarchy of the American race trial. It is expressed in lawyer speech and conduct, in the discourses of constitutionalism, in legislation, and in the common law. The colors of black and white, in fact the categories of blackness and whiteness, dominate those discourses, naturalizing color-coded inferences and color-conscious stereotypes about racial identity. The heart of both inference and stereotype is race-infected moral inferiority.

The precept of inferiority is rhetorically encoded in the racialized defense. Color-coded claims that overtly or covertly appeal to demeaning racial stereotypes shape the form and substance of the racialized defense. Pervasive in American law, culture, and society, the claims disclose the historical linkage connecting the past defense of antebellum slave rebellion and the contemporary defense of deprivation-fueled insurrectionist violence. The strength of that link hinges on moral character.

The prevalence of racial identity judgments of moral inferiority in criminal lawyer narrative and storytelling follows in part from the basic presuppositions of traditional criminal defense advocacy (partisanship and moral nonaccountability) and in part from the liberal premise of freely exerted client subjectivity. On these bases, racialized narratives appear contingent on instrumental lawyer strategy and voluntary client self-construction. Although contingent, advocacy narratives in race cases sound determinate themes of a natural or a necessary racial order. These themes resonate in historical proclamations of a naturally defective black moral character and courtroom declarations of the necessary portrayal of a deprivation-induced black moral deficiency. Clothing strategic argument in the natural and necessitarian rhetoric of racial inferiority legitimates subordinating constructions of moral character and conduct under a claim of race-neutral representation. The stance of race-neutrality cloaks the color-coded practice of advocacy.

Consider the rhetoric of race in cases of black-on-white racially motivated private violence, specifically in the assault and attempted murder trial of Damian Williams and Henry Watson. To win acquittals, the Williams-Watson defense attorneys challenged and ultimately refuted substantial evidence of intent and voluntary conduct available to prove criminal liability for attempted murder and aggravated mayhem in the beating of Reginald Denny and others. Their main defense rested on a "group contagion" theory of mob-incited diminished capacity. Marshaled as a partially exculpatory defense, the theory holds that young black males as a group, and the black community as a whole, share a pathological tendency to commit acts of violence in collective situations. Both Williams and Watson are young, male, and black. Among the victims, Denny is white, and the others are of mixed ethnic and racial backgrounds.

The rhetorical structure of criminal defense stories of black-on-white racial violence embedded in the Williams-Watson trial record reflects the sometimes dissonant incorporation of competing narratives of deviance and defiance. The narratives construct the identity of young black males in terms of both bestial pathology and insurrectionist rage. That dissonance produces racialized narratives of "good" and "bad" young black men, thus reducing racial identity to a dichotomy of virtue and sin. Under this dichotomy, blackness itself resembles an act of original sin fatal to moral character. Distilling male racial identity into objective, universal categories of unalterable human nature distorts the meaning of racial identity and the image of racial community. The tendency of white and black criminal defense lawyers to privilege deviance narratives and to subordinate defiance narratives in storytelling magnifies that distortion, inscribing the mark of bestial pathology into the sociolegal texture of racial identity and community.

Next consider racial rhetoric in the context of white-on-black private violence, particularly in the 1981 lynching of Michael Donald by the Ku Klux Klan. The legal defense of lynching displayed in the Alabama Klan trials demonstrates the identity-making function of legal narrative in the context of race and community bias. Specifically, the defense captured a white community-minded imagination infusing the most ordinary individuals with racial invective and hatred. Several lynching defenses—jury nullification, victim denigration, and diminished capacity—embody a distinct narrative form of the racialized defense. Both the defense of jury nullification and that of victim denigration erect moral hierarchy by overt use of racialized narrative. Nullification rhetoric trumpets white racial supremacy. Denigration rhetoric intones black racial inferiority. The defense of diminished capacity, by contrast, reproduces hierarchy by covert reference to the normative value of segregated community.

The moral hierarchies implanted in the racialized narratives accompanying the lynching defenses of nullification, denigration, and diminished capacity denote difference in sociolegal status. The defense of jury nullification, for example, invokes community commitment to racial difference and subordination. Propounded as an expression of community moral sentiment, nullification seeks to rectify or to reinforce perceived inequalities of racial status. For the white defender of black lynching, the criminal jury trial provides a forum for citizen political participation aimed at curing the problem of white disenfranchisement.

The racialized defense of victim denigration rests on the obfuscation of racial identity behind the image of deviance. Criminal defense lawyers employ deviant imagery in elevating the status of the white lawbreaker and degrading the worth of the black victim. The denigration defense centers on the racially subordinate status of black victims. Renewing this status bolsters claims of black moral, physical, and mental inferiority, thereby providing the moral rationale for lynching and segregation.

The racialized defense of diminished capacity combines commitment, community, and delusion to free white lawbreakers of moral and criminal culpability. Proponents of the defense contend that the extreme nature of white commitment to broad racial supremacy induces a delusional state of mind. Caught up in the emotion of populist resistance to arguably unlawful state mandates (desegregation and affirmative action), white lawbreakers engage in acts of racial violence without individual or collective remorse. Overcoming the image of white savagery, the defense offers the sympathetic impression of white innocence and empowerment.

Consider as well the racialized defense of Lemrick Nelson and Charles Price in the 1991 murder of Yankel Rosenbaum. A bundle of racialized narratives attend the Nelson-Price state and federal trials, infecting both prosecutorial and defense tactics. The dueling narratives generate race-contaminated opening statements, witness examinations and closing arguments replete with claims of white hierarchical bias allegedly manifested in the acts of police officers and prosecutors, and widespread assertions of black deviant pathology demonstrated in family dysfunction, juvenile delinquency, and drug abuse. Moreover, the narratives spawn pretrial motion strategies, such as recusal and adult transfer, that hinge on the contention of the defective, indeed irredeemable, state of white and black moral character. Apparently, for blacks at least, this original defect seals the criminal fate of both adults and children.

Dominant ethics rules tolerate the above color-coded criminal defense strategies under neutral accounts of liberal theory. Two principal accounts stand out in this respect, circulating through the great bulk of ethics rules. The first, loosely based on the contractarian strand of liberalism, draws on the familiar presuppositions of moral agency, radical individualism, commodity exchange, and public-private separation. In this code-ratified account, the client reaches independent moral decisions concerning the private objectives, and even the means, of representation.[13] Formulated under market conditions, the decision seeks to maximize client commodity value in economic exchange relationships, including welfare state interchanges. In this way, the contractarian account treats deviance-specific racialized strategies as the rational and voluntary decision of an autonomous client.

A second account, founded on an enlarged communitarian strand of liberalism, relies on the understated deliberative and third-party elements woven into the often overlooked texture of liberal theory. In this similarly rule-sanctioned account, the client approves deviance-enhanced strategies that result from lawyer-client colorblind deliberative counseling. Deliberation, of course, may be inclusive or exclusive of the public at large. Public-inclusive deliberation ensures some recognition and accommodation of third-party individuals or groups. Conversely, public-exclusive deliberation affords little cognizance of or solicitude toward third-party interests. In this sense, advisory-directed forms of lawyer-client deliberation in no way guarantee an outcome favorable to third-party or public interests. Code-encouraged dialogue may be confined simply to economic and political deliberative factors without mention of higher moral or wider social considerations.

The Model Rules and the Model Code countenance the deformity of client and community racial identity constructions by allowing color-coded, racial-deviance–based criminal defense strategies to survive unregulated on the presumption that a client may freely adopt a self-subordinating narrative as a function of either independent moral decision-making or lawyer counseling. Ethical legitimacy in this context rests in part on the rhetoric of colorblindness and in part on the belief that the discourse of the public sphere of law and society is somehow separate from the self-conscious identity-making imaginings of the private sphere of family and community. To the extent that ethics rules reinforce racial status boundaries in law and society, reformers must treat advocacy narratives as a kind of status-preserving discourse fostered by laws, legal agents, and legal institutions. Effective code reform, therefore, must be undertaken against the practical backdrop of laws, legal institutions, and the sociolegal relations of lawyers, clients, and legal administrators and adjudicators.

Portia Redux: Another Look at Gender, Feminism, and Legal Ethics[1]

Carrie Menkel-Meadow[2]

In 1985, I wrote an article entitled, "Portia in a Different Voice: Speculations on a Women's Lawyering Process."[3] In that article I attempted to explore how gender differences might affect the ways in which lawyers performed their tasks, structured their work, made ethical decisions, and interpreted and enforced the law. The article was a speculation on, and application of, the then very popular theories of a noted educational psychologist, Carol Gilligan. Gilligan's book, *In a Different Voice: Psychological Theory and Women's Development,* was at that time both soundly embraced and criticized by American, British, and Australian feminists. Her argument posited a male mode of moral reasoning referred to as the "logic of the ladder" because of its vertical hierarchy of values. This male mode of reasoning was based on abstracted, universalistic principles applied to problematic situations to create an "ethic of justice." Opposed to male moral reasoning was the female "ethic of care," based on the structure of the "web." This female ethic was grounded in a relational, connected, contextual form of reasoning that focused on people, as well as the substance of a problem.

Carol Gilligan and I used the character of Portia from Shakespeare's *The Merchant of Venice* to illustrate the oppositional ethics that exist in any problem of justice or moral reasoning. Both of us inscribed in our reading of Portia—disguised as a male jurist and alternately interpreted to be a lawyer, judge, legal envoy, or law clerk—a lawyer who appealed to the equitable, contextual, merciful sides of law, rather than to the draconian certainty of rules and universal principles.

A great deal has happened since 1985, and I welcome this opportunity to reexamine the arguments that I and others have made in our claims of feminist ethics based on an ethic of care.

Empirical research seeking to assess these differences in women's lawyering is quite mixed and often depends on the frame of reference of the researcher. Thus, sociologist Cynthia Fuchs Epstein, after a full career of studying women lawyers, suggests that those seeking difference will find it, while those who seek to establish women's "equality" to men may be more likely to find more overlap in behavior than difference.[4] In short, Epstein maintains there may be more variation among individuals within a particular gender in their legal behavior, than differences across gender. While some studies support the notion that women may have different motives for studying and practicing law, other studies report that whatever differences were previously present are diminishing over time, either because the greater number of women entering law reduces the stark motivational differences or because students in general have become more conservative over time. Still other studies report that there are no gender differences in motivation to study or practice law at all.

Contributions to the development of law go beyond some of the process claims about practice referred to above, and suggest areas where women or other excluded groups in the profession have had or will have an impact on the substantive law. Women lawyers have adopted a variety of strategies or patterns of arguments in advocating legal and doctrinal change. These arguments range from utilizing conventional categories to protect women's interests, such as claims for privacy and equality, to re-crafting old categories, such as the defense of consent in rape. Women lawyers are also creating new categories of analysis, such as sexual harassment and pornography, and exposing male and white bias. They challenge assumptions of male experience in defining legal categories, such as freedom from connection in defining liberty, and they argue that women's difference will produce different legal theories and constructions thereof, such as the recognition of additional compensable wrongs in the tort arena. Finally, feminist scholars and lawyers are exposing how law disadvantages women, even when framed in "neutral" terms, and exposing how arguing from a woman's perspective may transform the legal emphasis from one of rights to one of needs. Like critical race theorists, feminists argue that their position as outsiders, and as the "acted upon" in law, allows them to see other possibilities of legal regulation and definition. Recently, women theorists and lawyers have moved from analyzing "traditional" women's issues to more conventional legal doctrinal areas. This move is an attempt to illuminate how corporations, labor unions, organizations, and bankruptcy proceedings might be reconfigured to include women actors.

Claims that women might begin to think of legal categories in different ways do not require adherence to an essentialist position about women's natures. If only a few women think of legal categories in different ways or shift the perspective from which the larger community analyzes legal problems, then women will have contributed to a broadening of our thinking about law. Just as "two heads are better than one," the inclusion of both genders will increase the number and quality of ideas available to solve legal problems and to revise conventional, and often taken-for-granted, categories. In my view, this analysis also provides a forceful argument for the inclusion of other groups traditionally excluded from the law, including visible and invisible minorities, the physically challenged, gays, and racial and ethnic minorities. Any disruption of conventional and dominant group thinking must improve the quality of legal decision-making.

As noted by my constitutional law colleague, Kenneth Karst, the key to an ethic of justice is a rights consciousness that is located in the right not to be interfered with, in other words, personal and individual liberty. From this we can see the foundational aspects of the Anglo-adversary system: "I take care of my side and you take care of yours and almost anything we do to win our 'rights' is justified."

Juxtaposed against this philosophy of liberal individualism is the ethic of care that struggles with rules, prefers to make decisions in contexts, tries to keep the parties in relation, and conceives of a responsibility to others. An ethic of care suggests concern for others and reduction of harm. It suggests a shift in focus from converting the negative sum games of law, in which the lawyers benefit, to a more positive sum game, in which the parties benefit, might transform the adversary system. The difficult question in analyzing these themes in practical legal ethics is, do they produce different principles or processes for resolving ethical dilemmas?

Before I return to the question of what women lawyers' legal ethics might be, let us consider how the character of Portia in *The Merchant of Venice* illuminates both the complexities of the rule and morality of law and the ambiguities of gender in legal role-playing. *The Merchant of Venice* places discussions of ethics, morality, and right-doing at its center. Complicated for modern readers by the controversial aspects of its anti-Semitism, the play still deals with important modern moral and legal ethical dilemmas—contracts, commercial bonds, fidelity, marriage, friendship, loyalty, justice, the spirit versus the letter of the law, legal remedies, and choice. Portia has become an evocative figure primarily because of the "mercy speech" she delivers in Act IV, and it is her role upon which I will focus. Nonetheless, the deeper meaning of Portia's character must be derived from her behavior in other scenes of the play as well.

During the trial scene of *The Merchant of Venice,* Portia, disguised as a male jurist, comes to "save" the fate of her lover Bassanio's friend, Antonio, against the demands of enforcement of the bond of Shylock the Jew. The recompense is a "pound of flesh" for failure to honor a debt. Over the years, many literary critics and legal commentators have read this scene as central to one of the major themes of the play, that "mercy should season justice." Portia is seen as the symbol of mercy and Shylock the symbol of "justice, judgment and Law." The source of much of this commentary is Portia's first main speech in the scene where she sets the stage by asking Shylock to consider the virtues of mercy:

> The quality of mercy is not strain'd,
> It droppeth as the gentle rain from heaven
> Upon the place beneath: it is twice blest,
> It blesseth him that gives, and him that takes,
> 'Tis mightiest in the mightiest, it becomes
> The throned monarch better than his crown.
> His sceptre shows the force of temporal power,
> The attribute to awe and majesty,
> Wherein doth sit the dread and fear of kings:
> But mercy is above his sceptred sway,
> It is enthroned in the hearts of kings,
> It is an attribute to God himself. . . .

In this passage, which is evoked by feminists and others seeking the feminine side of mercy and justice, Portia tries to persuade Shylock that power is the possession of earthly kings who inspire fear and dread, rather than the attribute—mercy—that brings kings closer to God by feeling it in their hearts. Portia is appealing to Shylock to give up his legal claim, with a powerful reference to the contrast between state and earthly power and religion. In the context of the play, such a reference is distinctly ironic.

Shylock's God is not Portia's God, and Shylock sees the law as a source of equal treatment in Venice—at least until other Venetian laws are conveniently uncovered—even if he is an outsider Jew. In addition to her appeal to the sacred, Portia asks Shylock to be empathetic, to recognize that only when others impose the law upon us are we likely to ask for mercy. When we are the actor imposing the law or demanding justice of others, we want the law to operate exactly according to text. By reminding Shylock that we all want salvation, she asks him, in effect, to "do unto others as you would have them do unto you." It is from this famous and evocative speech that Gilligan and I have argued that Portia represents a feminine, mediating force in law, calling for the tempering of justice with mercy and appealing to hearts as well as scepters.

Yet it is important to examine the rest of the scene to fully understand the complexity of Portia's role as lawyer. Shylock rejects Portia's pleas. "I crave the law," he says, "the penalty and forfeit of my bond." At that moment, Portia becomes an extraordinary, albeit conventional, lawyer. She recognizes that the law must be followed and the bond enforced because precedents must be obeyed or "many an error by the same example will rush into the state,—it cannot be."

Having decided that the law must be enforced, Portia demands to see the document, the contract of debt. She gives Shylock his judgment—a pound of flesh, closest to the heart of Antonio. Then, in an act of clever lawyering and language manipulation, Portia proceeds to read the text of the law quite literally. She reports that Shylock had better find a skilled surgeon, for the bond grants him a pound of flesh, but "this bond doth give thee here no jot of blood, The words expressly are 'a pound of flesh:' Take then thy bond, take thou thy pound of flesh, But in the cutting it, if thou dost shed One drop of Christian blood, thy lands and goods Are (by the laws of Venice) confiscate Unto the state of Venice." Portia shows Shylock the law and tells him that if he urges justice, he shall have justice and, thus, must live by the law himself. Shylock capitulates and asks for the previously offered "settlement" of three times the money owed. Yet, Portia, the masterful lawyer, recounts still another Venetian law in response. Because Shylock will have "justice," interpreted as the letter of the law, he must contemplate how those laws affect him as well; according to the law, any alien—Jew—who seeks to tamper with the life of a citizen shall lose his property, half to the citizen harmed and half to the state. Furthermore, his life shall be at the discretion of the Duke. The Duke and Antonio, however, show Shylock their mercy. They allow him to live, but only as a

Christian, forcing him to give up his faith and identity. They condition their mercy on Shylock's promise to leave his property to his Christian son-in-law.

Has mercy triumphed over justice? No. Portia has played a clever lawyer's game and shown that she can be as manipulative of language and the law as any of her brethren. Can we, as others have argued in their commentaries, try to read the feminine back into her plea for mercy because she is dressed as a male when she plays the judge? Does Portia demonstrate the need for women to conform to conventional legal rules when they become lawyers, in a sort of professional form of cross-dressing? In this argument we have to see her plea for mercy, also made while disguised, as expressing her real, more female self. We must also acknowledge that the actual acts of "mercy" in this act are committed by men, Antonio and the Duke.

I think Portia's "disguise" is an important metaphor. Portia's judge's robes are those of the professional role and "mantle" she must take on. She tries to use non–rule-based measures of morality and justice—mercy, heart, feeling, concern for others—to appeal to Shylock, but when forced to resort to law and rules, she shows herself as capable as any male lawyer. Perhaps it is Shylock's unwillingness to accept her offer of mercy that pushes Portia into the literal reading of the contract—demonstrating how hard it is, even for judges, to dislodge the desire of litigants from their self-interested "justice." Disentangling implications of gender in this play is further complicated by the fact that Portia, in Shakespeare's time, was actually played by a male disguised as a female while playing Portia. Of course, all the words were written by a male. And, as some commentators have suggested, Portia's "justice" is correct—Shylock would, after all, be a murderer or at least have murderous intent. Should punishment be meted out for the consequences it would deter or should punishment be sensitive to the rehabilitative possibilities of particular wrongdoers?

Portia is a complex character, able to slip back and forth between both gender and professional roles; she demonstrates what sociologists term "role virtuosity" and flexibility. Sophisticated feminists now know that we cannot make claims for "women" based on a universalistic attribution of generalized characteristics of womanhood. Thus, Portia's variegated behavior demonstrates that not all women act from some essentialist place called "womanhood." Indeed, the treatment of Jews as cruel, usurious, and evil in Shakespeare's essentialist world should remind us of the danger of attributing individual qualities to whole groups of people.

Yet Portia's role virtuosity is not without purpose: she comes to save her husband's friend. Thus, posed as a judge, she is not impartial—she has a purpose. Consider the difficulties of partiality and purpose in the roles of judges and lawyers as they seek both to represent and rule on particular clients, parties, and laws. As judges, would women play their roles with more emotional partiality or concern for the Other? Portia's effort is to save someone, a noble goal. But, she "disguises" herself as an impartial judge and clearly, in a modern context, would be disciplined for her bias and lack of disclosure in the case. Are those who represent good causes to be forgiven the means that they employ? This remains a heated issue in legal ethics, as elsewhere in moral philosophy, and there is no clear answer.

What are we to make of Portia's brilliant lawyering to save her husband's friend whose debt in fact helped finance her marriage? What are we to make of the fact that Portia, like any advocate, has taken the short-term, immediate gratification approach, rather than the long-term view? Are we concerned that Portia, like others in the play, is racist and does not see the humanity of the Jew, while nonetheless asking him to see the humanity of Antonio? Hell hath no fury like a woman advocate advancing her own cause! Portia's behavior warrants the frequent criticism that accompanies "strident" feminist law reformers who blindly see all men as the enemy.

Yet Portia's actions in Act IV must be read together with her action in Act V, as well as with her prior big scenes—scenes in Acts I and II in which she comes to terms with the patriarchal "rules" established for the choice of her mate. Ultimately, Portia is a learner and a harmonizer. She accepts the rules of her father, and she teaches her husband a lesson or two about marital fidelity and loyalty in the concluding "rings" scene, while still making room for her husband's friend. Thus, Portia adopts the rules and ways of men, yet simultaneously extracts promises of love and fidelity, and suggests other roles for law and justice by stressing our connections to one another as members of humanity.

Asking students and lawyers to think about the effects of their work on others and on themselves, the wear and tear of conventional adversary practice, and working through legal ethical hypotheticals together with collective, multi-personed groups are some of the ways that the conventional justice system modeled on individual autonomy could be affected by women's and other voices in the law. Collective grappling with ethical problems as they are happening has always seemed far more enriching to me than resolving difficult problems through a priori rules that one can then argue do not apply or can be distinguished. I know we will have to agree on some first principles for our legal communities, but it seems to me that before we finalize our rules we need to hear more conversations with more Portias and others who have new, if complex, suggestions for how we should determine legal morality.

Thus, broadly defined "legal ethics"—leading our lives as lawyers, making decisions about our clients, our opponents, ourselves, and our families, searching to be "good lawyers" as well as "good people"—in my view is enhanced by taking account of the values of "others," those previously outside the profession. Whether the character Portia, or the real Portias who currently practice law, are actually the representatives of alternative values, we cannot yet say. But it seems to me that both legal education and law practice should look for ways to allow a broader range of values to be expressed, while acknowledging that debate and discussion will be difficult. We are at the first stage, acknowledging and arguing about whether mercy has a place in a rule-bound system of justice, trying to figure out what it means to be a caring lawyer. The second stage will seek to define these terms more rigorously, to apply them to particular situations, and to let the moral philosophers and legal ethicists debate their validity. We will try to educate new lawyers to be sensitive to these additional values, and then we will have to measure if they are, and if it makes any difference in what they do. For me, Portia may have more value as a symbol than as a reality. But, as a foil, or as an alternative to a rigid system of rules and justice, she provides a metaphor for at least one critique of law that I look forward to following in the years to come.

Race and Essentialism in
Feminist Legal Theory[1]

Angela P. Harris[2]

In *Funes the Memorious*, Borges tells of Ireneo Funes, who was a rather ordinary young man (notable only for his precise sense of time) until the age of nineteen, when he was thrown by a half-tamed horse and left paralyzed but possessed of perfect perception and a perfect memory.

After his transformation, Funes knew by heart the forms of the southern clouds at dawn on the 30th of April, 1882, and could compare them in his memory with the mottled streaks on a book in Spanish binding he had only seen once and with the outlines of the foam raised by an oar in the Rio Negro the night before the Quebracho uprising. These memories were not simple ones; each visual image was linked to muscular sensations, thermal sensations, etc. He could reconstruct all his dreams, all his half-dreams. Two or three times he had reconstructed a whole day; he never hesitated, but each reconstruction had required a whole day.

Funes tells the narrator that after his transformation he invented his own numbering system. "In place of seven thousand thirteen, he would say (for example) Maximo Perez; in place of seven thousand fourteen, The Railroad; other numbers were Luis Melian Lafinur, Olimar, sulphur, the reins, the whale, the gas, the caldron, Napoleon, Agustin de Vedia."[3] The narrator tries to explain to Funes "that this rhapsody of incoherent terms was precisely the opposite of a system of numbers. I told him that saying 365 meant saying three hundreds, six tens, five ones, an analysis which is not found in the 'numbers,' The Negro Timoteo or meat blanket. Funes did not understand me or refused to understand me."[4]

In his conversation with Funes, the narrator realizes that Funes's life of infinite unique experiences leaves Funes no ability to categorize: "With no effort, he had learned English, French, Portuguese and Latin. I suspect, however, that he was not very capable of thought. To think is to forget differences, generalize, make abstractions. In the teeming world of Funes, there were only details, almost immediate in their presence."[5] For Funes, language is only a unique and private system of classification, elegant and solipsistic. The notion that language, made abstract, can serve to create and reinforce a community is incomprehensible to him.

In this article, I discuss some of the writings of feminist legal theorists Catharine MacKinnon and Robin West. I argue that their work, though powerful and brilliant in many ways, relies on what I call gender essentialism—the notion that a unitary, "essential" women's experience can be isolated and described independently of race, class, sexual orientation, and other realities of experience. The result of this tendency toward gender essentialism, I argue, is not only that some voices are silenced in order to privilege others (for this is an inevitable result of categorization, which is necessary for both human communication and political movement), but that the voices that are silenced turn out to be the same voices silenced by the mainstream legal voice of "We the People"—among them, the voices of black women.

This result troubles me for two reasons. First, the obvious one: as a black woman, in my opinion the experience of black women is too often ignored both in feminist theory and in legal theory, and gender essentialism in feminist legal theory does nothing to address this problem. A second and less obvious reason for my criticism of gender essentialism is that, in my view, contemporary legal theory needs less abstraction and not simply a different sort of abstraction. To be fully subversive, the methodology of feminist legal theory should challenge not only law's content but its tendency to privilege the abstract and unitary voice, and this gender essentialism also fails to do.

In accordance with my belief that legal theory, including feminist legal theory, is in need of less abstraction, in this article I destabilize and subvert the unity of MacKinnon's and West's "woman" by introducing the voices of black women, especially as represented in literature. Before I begin, however, I want to make three cautionary points to the reader. First, my argument should not be read to accuse either MacKinnon or West of "racism" in the sense of personal antipathy to black people. Both writers are steadfastly anti-racist, which in a sense is my point. Just as law itself, in trying to speak for all persons, ends up silencing those without power, feminist legal theory is in danger of silencing those who have traditionally been kept from speaking, or who have been ignored when they spoke, including black women. The first step toward avoiding this danger is to give up the dream of gender essentialism.

Second, in using a racial critique to attack gender essentialism in feminist legal theory, my aim is not to establish a new essentialism in its place based on the essential experience of black women. Nor should my focus on black women be taken to mean that other women are not silenced either by the mainstream culture or by feminist legal theory. Accordingly, I invite the critique and subversion of my own generalizations.

Third and finally, I do not mean in this article to suggest that either feminism or legal theory should adopt the voice of Funes the Memorious, for whom every experience is unique and no categories or generalizations exist at all. Even a jurisprudence based on multiple consciousness must categorize; without categorization each individual is as isolated as Funes, and there can be no moral responsibility or social change. My suggestion is only that we make our categories explicitly tentative, relational, and unstable, and that to do so is all the more important in a discipline like law, where abstraction and "frozen" categories are the norm. Avoiding gender essentialism need not mean that the Holocaust and a corncob are the same.

The notion that there is a monolithic "women's experience" that can be described independent of other facets of experience like race, class, and sexual orientation is one I refer to in this essay as "gender essentialism." A corollary to gender essentialism is "racial essentialism"—the belief that there is a monolithic "Black Experience" or "Chicano Experience." The source of gender and racial essentialism (and all other essentialisms, for the list of categories could be infinitely multiplied) is the second voice, the voice that claims to speak for all. The result of essentialism is to reduce the lives of people who experience multiple forms of oppression to addition problems: "racism + sexism = straight black women's experience," or "racism + sexism + homophobia = black lesbian experience." Thus, in an essentialist world, black women's experience will always be forcibly fragmented before being subjected to analysis, as those who are "only interested in race" and those who are "only interested in gender" take their separate slices of our lives.

Beyond Essentialism: Black Women and Feminist Theory

Our future survival is predicated upon our ability to relate within equality. As women, we must root out internalized patterns of oppression within ourselves if we are to move beyond the most superficial aspects of social change. Now we must recognize differences among women who are our equals, neither inferior nor superior, and devise ways to use each others' difference to enrich our visions and our joint struggles.[6]

—Audre Lorde

In this part of the article, I want to talk about what black women can bring to feminist theory to help us move beyond essentialism and toward multiple consciousness as feminist and jurisprudential method. In my view, there are at least three major contributions that black women have to offer post-essentialist feminist theory: the recognition of a self that is multiplicitous, not unitary; the recognition that differences are always relational rather than inherent; and the recognition that wholeness and commonality are acts of will and creativity rather than of passive discovery.

The Abandonment of Innocence

Black women experience not a single inner self (much less one that is essentially gendered), but many selves. This sense of a multiplicitous self is not unique to black women, but black women have expressed this sense in ways that are striking, poignant, and potentially useful to feminist theory. bell hooks describes her experience in a creative writing program at a predominantly white college, where she was encouraged to find "her voice," as frustrating to her sense of multiplicity.

It seemed that many black students found our situations problematic precisely because our sense of self, and by definition our voice, was not unilateral, monologist, or static, but rather multidimensional. We were as at home in dialect as we were in standard English. Individuals who speak languages other than English, who speak patois as well as standard English, find it a necessary aspect of self-affirmation not to feel compelled to choose one voice over another, not to claim one as more authentic, but rather to construct social realities that celebrate, acknowledge, and affirm differences, variety.

This experience of multiplicity is also a sense of self-contradiction, of containing the oppressor within oneself. In her article "On Being the Object of Property,"[7] Patricia Williams writes about herself writing about her great-great-grandmother, "picking through the ruins for my roots." What she finds is a paradox: she must claim for herself "a heritage the weft of whose genesis is [her] own disinheritance."[8] Williams's great-great-grandmother, Sophie, was a slave, and at the age of about eleven was impregnated by her owner, a white lawyer named Austin Miller. Their daughter Mary, Williams's great-grandmother, was taken away from Sophie and raised as a house servant.

When Williams went to law school, her mother told her, "The Millers were lawyers, so you have it in your blood."[9] Williams analyzes this statement as asking her to acknowledge contradictory selves:

> [S]he meant that no one should make me feel inferior because someone else's father was a judge. She wanted me to reclaim that part of my heritage from which I had been disinherited, and she wanted me to use it as a source of strength and self-confidence. At the same time, she was asking me to claim a part of myself that was the dispossessor of another part of myself; she was asking me to deny that disenfranchised little black girl of myself that felt powerless, vulnerable and, moreover, rightly felt so.[10]

The theory of black slavery, Williams notes, was based on the notion that black people are beings without will or personality, defined by "irrationality, lack of control, and ugliness."[11] In contrast, "wisdom, control, and aesthetic beauty signify the whole white personality in slave law."[12] In accepting her white self, her lawyer self, Williams must accept a legacy of not only a disinheritance but a negation of her black self: to the Millers, her forebears, the Williamses, her forebears, did not even have selves as such.

Williams's choice ultimately is not to deny either self, but to recognize them both, and in so doing to acknowledge guilt as well as innocence. She ends the piece by invoking "the presence of polar bears"[13]: bears that mauled a child to death at the Brooklyn Zoo and were subsequently killed themselves, bears judged in public debate as simultaneously "innocent, naturally territorial, unfairly imprisoned, and guilty."[14]

This complex resolution rejects the easy innocence of supposing oneself to be an essential black self with a legacy of oppression by the guilty white Other. With such multilayered analyses, black women can bring to feminist theory stories of how it is to have multiple and contradictory selves, selves that contain the oppressor as well as the oppressed.

Strategic Identities and "Difference"

A post-essentialist feminism can benefit not only from the abandonment of the quest for a unitary self, but also from Martha Minow's realization that difference—and therefore identity—is always relational, not inherent.[15] Zora Neale Hurston's work is a good illustration of this notion.

In an essay written for a white audience, *How It Feels to Be Colored Me,*[16] Hurston argues that her color is not an inherent part of her being, but a response to her surroundings. She recalls the day she "became colored"—the day she left her home in an all-black community to go to school:

> I left Eatonville, the town of the oleanders, as Zora. When I disembarked from the river-boat at Jacksonville, she was no more. It seemed that I had suffered a sea change. I was not Zora of Orange County any more, I was now a little colored girl.[17]

But even as an adult, Hurston insists, her colored self is always situational: "I do not always feel colored. Even now I often achieve the unconscious Zora of Eatonville before the Hegira. I feel most colored when I am thrown against a sharp white background."[18]

As an example, Hurston describes the experience of listening to music in a jazz club with a white male friend:

> My pulse is throbbing like a war drum. I want to slaughter something—give pain, give death to what, I do not know. But the piece ends. The men of the orchestra wipe their lips and rest their fingers. I creep back slowly to the veneer we call civilization with the last tone and find the white friend sitting motionless in his seat, smoking calmly. "Good music they have here," he remarks, drumming the table with his fingertips.
>
> Music. The great blobs of purple and red emotion have not touched him. He has only heard what I felt. He is far away and I see him but dimly across the ocean and the continent that have fallen between us. He is so pale with his whiteness then and I am so colored.

In reaction to the presence of whites—both her white companion and the white readers of her essay—Hurston invokes and uses the traditional stereotype of black people as tied to the jungle, "living in the jungle way."

Yet in a later essay for a black audience, *What White Publishers Won't Print*,[19] she criticizes the white "folklore of 'reversion to type'":

> This curious doctrine has such wide acceptance that it is tragic. One has only to examine the huge literature on it to be convinced. No matter how high we may seem to climb, put us under strain and we revert to type, that is, to the bush. Under a superficial layer of western culture, the jungle drums throb in our veins.

The difference between the first essay, in which Hurston revels in the trope of black person as primitive, and the second essay, in which she deplores it, lies in the distinction between an identity that is contingent, temporary, and relational, and an identity that is fixed, inherent, and essential. Zora as jungle woman is fine as an argument, a reaction to her white friend's experience; what is abhorrent is the notion that Zora can always and only be a jungle woman. One image is in flux, "inspired" by a relationship with another; the other is static, unchanging, and ultimately reductive and sterile rather than creative.

Thus, "how it feels to be colored Zora" depends on the answer to these questions: "'Compared to what? As of when? Who is asking? In what context? For what purpose? With what interests and presuppositions?' What Hurston rigorously shows is that questions of difference and identity are always functions of a specific interlocutionary situation—and the answers, matters of strategy rather than truth."[20] Any "essential self" is always an invention; the evil is in denying its artificiality.

To be compatible with this conception of the self, feminist theorizing about "women" must similarly be strategic and contingent, focusing on relationships, not essences. One result will be that men will cease to be a faceless Other and reappear as potential allies in political struggle. Another will be that women will be able to acknowledge their differences without threatening feminism itself. In the process, as feminists begin to attack racism and classism and homophobia, feminism will change from being only about "women as women" (modified women need not apply) to being about all kinds of oppression based on seemingly inherent and unalterable characteristics. We need not wait for a unified theory of oppression; that theory can be feminism.

Lessons and Challenges of
Becoming Gentlemen[1]

Lani Guinier[2]

There are many lessons to be learned from the experience of those women law students for whom law school is a hostile learning environment. These are lessons that men as well as women, law students as well as lawyers, might take from the study Michelle Fine, Jane Balin, and I conducted at the University of Pennsylvania Law School.[3] Within these lessons is also a challenge to all consumers and producers of legal education: can we use the negative experience of some women in law school to initiate fundamental changes in legal education generally?

Our study of the academic performance and quality of life for women at this one law school reveals many institutional failings that actually affect everyone. Many of the problems we identify reflect the shortcomings of a one-size-fits-all approach to pedagogy and the correspondingly single-minded focus on adversariness as the dominant professional norm of good lawyering. These problems, which suggest troubling deficiencies in the educational enterprise, became visible as they converged around a particular group. The experience of women in law school, in other words, is not necessarily about gender per se. Not all women experience law school as a hostile learning environment. Moreover, some men do. Gender may mask bureaucratic choices and organizational inertia that adversely affect the learning experience of many consumers of legal education. At stake is not only how we educate women. We need to rethink how we admit, train, and acculturate all lawyers to the demands of a changing profession.

Our survey suggested that many, though not all, women felt alienated. For instance, many of the women respondents had entered law school full of self-confidence, one-third of them eager to practice public interest law after graduation; by contrast, only 8 percent of their first-year male counterparts intended to practice in public interest. Yet, only 10 percent of the third-year women and 5 percent of the third-year men reported that they still expected to practice public interest law. Something seemed to happen between the first and the third year that affected only the women. The men entered the Law School with particular ambitions and held onto them, while the women matriculated with aspirations that they relinquished over time.

We also detected a gender difference in rates of participation. In comparison with the men who responded to our survey, women law students were significantly more likely to report that they "never" or "only occasionally" asked questions or volunteered answers in class. Even more alarming than the gender disparity, however, was the fact that only the first-year women expressed discomfort with their low rate of participation —the third-year women were no longer distressed by their virtually unchanged level of class participation.

We soon discovered that our findings were replicated by other researchers. A recent study of law school teaching at eight different law schools across the country found that male students speak disproportionately more in all classes taught by men, and that gender disparities are more apparent in elite schools regardless of the gender of the professor.[4] As Catherine Krupnick found in her study of Harvard undergraduate classrooms, professors allowed those with the quickest response time to dominate classroom discussion; even with a female instructor, men still participated more than women.[5]

The women who reported that they did not speak in class also did not feel comfortable initiating conversation with professors after class; they were waiting for friendliness cues. In contrast, the men did not express such hesitation in approaching professors. This was true whether the professors were women or men.

The survey revealed another disparity in the qualities students reported to most admire in a law school professor. Although both women and men identified "knowledge of subject matter" and "enthusiasm for teaching" as their top two selections, for their third most-valued quality, the men chose "expresses ideas clearly," whereas 93 percent of the women specified "treats students with respect." After inspecting this survey data, we asked seminar students if they could explain this difference; they responded that men already feel respected and therefore do not esteem that quality as much.

To gauge the impact of these gendered dynamics on women's grades as well as on their attitudes, we looked at the academic performance of 981 law students at the University of Pennsylvania over a period of three years. We found that men and women entered with virtually identical credentials: same LSAT, same GPA, same rank in class. But by the end of the first year, men rose to the top of the class, and women sank to the bottom. In the aggregate, men students were almost three times more likely in the first year and two times more likely in the second and third years to be in the top tenth percentile than women. In addition, they were one-half times more likely to be in the top fiftieth percentile than women; this difference was sustained over the course of three years.

To give perspective to both the survey and the academic performance data, we arranged focus groups in which we asked people to talk informally about their experience at the law school. We concluded that the women's experience was not simply a complaint that law school was too hard or too tough. They were vocalizing a fundamental critique about the way in which those of us committed to legal education perform our jobs. They were signaling a problem with law school as a learning institution that was potentially affecting everyone.

As my colleague Susan Sturm explains in her article "From Gladiators to Problem-Solvers," legal education is modeled after the notion that lawyers are gladiators.[6] To deal with a legal problem, a conflict, or any controversy in this model, one fights to win. Thus, legal education is premised on the idea that lawyers are adversaries who must be trained how to be tough to win. Students who do well often do so because they see the most aggressive version of the Socratic method as a game or contest in which they play to win by fighting quickly and aggressively.

Those who defend the emphasis on speed and aggressive interventions rely on conventional assumptions about what constitutes good lawyering. A common contention is that women are in law school to become lawyers —professionals whose job it is to make money for their clients and who are not particularly nice, friendly, or empathetic. One law school professor has described the stereotypical Socratic approach at its worst as learning how to ask rude questions. Most people ask a question because they would like to know the answer; lawyers are trained never to ask a question unless they already know the answer. Questions are asked to put someone on the spot; to demonstrate how little that person knows; to extract outside information; and to use others as examples of a particular policy or its implications. There is a sense that the conversation contains a covert agenda. My students often say, "Well, I think what you're trying to get at is . . ."

instead of "What I think is. . . ." The requirement to perform in a particular way in law school encourages some students to parrot rather than to think. It is also particularly alienating to those intending to pursue careers in government or public service, whose mission is not just to learn to think like a lawyer but to do "justice."

Beyond socializing students to a single, hierarchical view of lawyering and dominating first-year classes to the exclusion of other constructive pedagogy, the use of the Socratic method in the large traditional law school classroom may obstruct the formation of a "learning community" for all those students (not just women) who learn better through collaborative and non- adversarial methods. Interestingly, the preference of some women students for cooperative (rather than competitive) styles of learning parallels their classroom-participation dynamics. They often learn better in informal peer groups that integrate social and academic experiences, not only in terms of learning information, but also in terms of developing leadership skills.[7]

If individualized combat were essential to lawyering, then the concerns or preferences of some women for collaborative learning environments would easily be dismissed. However, many researchers are finding that the skills involved in lawyering are complex and are not captured in a one-size-fits-all pedagogical method that presents lawyering as a contest. Many suggest that the litigious mode of pedagogy is outdated, since many lawyers do not litigate. In fact, most lawyers now do not go to court. Most lawyers do not even work at large firms. For those who are employed as in-house counsel or are engaged in transactional lawyering, negotiation contrasts starkly to the classic notion propagated by the Socratic method of advocating one side of a dispute before an appellate court.

Moreover, collaboration and teamwork are increasingly valued within the profession. Those who are good collaborators use crucial lawyerly traits of compromise, role flexibility, proffering questions as well as criticisms, and group problem-solving. Problem-solving is listed by the American Bar Association's MacCrate Report task force as the "fundamental lawyering skill." Professional schools in business and in medicine utilize the problem method of instruction to achieve training for the actual situations their graduates will tackle; indeed, the Wharton School at Penn has rearranged its classrooms to emphasize group-based problem-solving as integral to its instruction.

Viewed from the perspective of training students to become lawyers in the settings where they will be practicing, conventional pedagogy may not be up to the task. Similarly, we may find that conventional assessment techniques are not predictive of the kinds of work lawyers actually do. Measures of qualifications such as the LSAT or a single, timed, issue-spotting examination are efficient and purportedly objective, but this does not mean that they are fair or functional for the purposes for which they are used. Applying these very domain-specific measurements in contexts for which they never were intended undermines their validity.

For example, we examined criteria used in Penn's admissions process: undergraduate GPA and class rank; LSAT; Lonsdorf index (which is computed by a formula weighing LSAT score, median LSAT score at undergraduate institution, and undergraduate GPA), and the undergraduate institution. Men and women entered the Law School with quite comparable records. For example, women's LSAT scores were not statistically different from men's, and their undergraduate GPAs were slightly higher than those of males.

Then, we investigated whether there was a correlation between selection criteria and performance in the Law School. Various explanations were proffered to justify women's under-performance in grades. A few colleagues reasoned that we were admitting the wrong women. One even suggested that men's collegiate GPAs were stifled due to their varsity sports participation (a variable which law school eliminated). Others thought that women's underperformance was related to majoring in less challenging undergraduate areas. We found that there was no statistically significant difference between the undergraduate majors of the men and the women students. Finally, we found that the LSAT is a very weak predictor of performance at Penn for both men and women, with virtually no correlation to first-year grades for scores falling anywhere in the uppermost quartile.

Rather than finding that the Law School was admitting "the wrong women," we found that the wrong credentials are being used to surmise who will do well in law school and what is expected of those students once they become lawyers. We discovered that our admissions criteria and our Socratic pedagogy have been functioning as efficient quantitative measures to ease the burden of processing admissions files, but that those same measures function independently of the real goal of legal education: to prepare students to do the multifaceted work of lawyers.

Thus, the invitation issued by our research is to rethink legal education by strategizing backwards from what we want students to learn so that it prepares and trains everyone, not just women, to meet the challenges of serving as tomorrow's lawyers for Bovis, for other corporations, or for a community group lacking the funds to go to court. For many students, a teaching style that legitimizes alternative forms of participation, respects all perspectives, and broadens the educational dialogue makes them better advocates by deepening their knowledge of the world around them as well as enhancing their understanding of the implications of their claims. Concededly, in the short term, maybe women must become "gentlemen" in order to succeed within the present system. But for the long-term, this is a chance not for women to think like men, but for men to start thinking with women about how to solve America's problems, bringing a fresh perspective to a profession suffering from public dissatisfaction. Changing legal pedagogy can help us educate all students using multiple approaches that stimulate, not stifle, intellectual curiosity and that will enable them to be creative problem-solvers as attorneys.

The lessons of "Becoming Gentlemen," in other words, are that problems that may converge around women are often located in the institution of legal education and not in the women. The challenge is to find a way to begin a much larger conversation about the role of lawyers as twenty-first-century private and public problem solvers, and about the kind of legal education most capable of preparing our students—all of our students—to meet those challenges.

A Theory-Practice Spiral: The Ethics of Feminism and Clinical Education[1]

Phyllis Goldfarb[2]

This article concerns the relationship between theory and practice in legal academia. In particular, it examines the relationship between theory and practice from the standpoint of two movements within law's academy: clinical education and feminist jurisprudence. Although the former is often thought of as a practical movement, and the latter a theoretical movement, I hope to demonstrate the fundamental methodological similarity of the two movements, and hence, the problematic nature of the theory-practice label. Ironically, the methodological similarity of the two movements is found in their responses to the problematic nature of the theory-practice relationship.

This article also examines the ethical impulse that sparks clinical education and feminism. I suggest that each movement's perceptions of the theory-practice relationship are embedded in ethical concerns and have far-reaching ethical implications.

The ethical import of the theory-practice relationship also explains why works of classical literature can contribute to an understanding of the feminist and clinical enterprises. This article begins with the reading of a text, Sophocles' *Antigone*,[3] from the perspective of each of these intellectual movements. Which aspects of this Greek drama draw a feminist thinker's particular attention? To which aspects would a legal clinician pay special notice? The responses to these questions are obviously different. A feminist's reading would center on issues of gender; the focus of a clinician's reading is not immediately apparent.

Despite this difference, I have chosen to begin in this fashion in order to test—or more accurately, because I will declare the outcome of the test, to demonstrate—my claim of methodological similarity between the two movements. If the two have similarity, their approach to a situation in context will likely reveal it. I have chosen the text of *Antigone* as the context, in preference to a hypothetical constructed specifically for my purposes, because of its likely familiarity, its rich interpretive landscape, its ethical significance, and its ultimate epistemological message, which foreshadows the themes of this article. I have also chosen it because of the powerful human conflict it describes. If the methods of feminism and clinical education are sound—that is, if they have breadth and depth—they will apply to any human conflict, not just human conflicts ordained as legal conflicts. Moreover, if the medium is at least part of the message, then delving deeply into a particular context to extract and examine a more general idea is an appropriate way to manifest my primary contention: that the two readings converge in their shared challenge to the popular understanding of theory and practice as separate undertakings.

Reading Antigone

Sophocles' *Antigone* opens in the midst of crisis. Antigone and her older sister Ismene have suffered the loss of their brothers, Polynices and Eteocles, who have killed one another while fighting for the throne of Thebes. Having assumed the throne, their uncle Creon has issued an edict declaring that Eteocles, the ruler whom the Theban people had favored, would be given an honorable state funeral, while Polynices, who had returned from expulsion to forcibly seize the throne, would be denied all last rites. The edict forbade anyone to bury Polynices on pain of death.

As the curtain lifts, Antigone is informing Ismene that she has decided to defy Creon's edict. In a previous conversation in which Antigone had tried in vain to dissuade Polynices from doing battle, Polynices had asked his sisters to bury him when he met his death. Antigone now declares that her obligation lies with her dead brother and with the holiest laws of the gods, which impose an obligation to bury one's deceased kin, not with the law of the king. Frightened by Antigone's defiance, Ismene insists that because they are only women, they are too weak to resist men and the state. When Ismene refuses to assist Antigone in defying the decree, informing her that she is "bound to fail," Antigone speaks harshly to her. Ismene responds by assuring Antigone that she loves her.

This conversation shapes Antigone's central conflict, and the drama unfolds toward its somber conclusion. Among its many themes, the play seeks to unravel the complex relationship between law and morality. This philosophical inquiry is captured in the struggles of its characters. Antigone elevates her religious responsibility to her deceased brother over her responsibility to obey the law. Polynices' rejection of Antigone's pleas that he not go to war has not affected the primacy of her responsibility to their relationship. This choice is consistent with her previous behavior in insisting on the primacy over her own life of her responsibility to her relationship with her exiled father, Oedipus, whom she had cared for until his death. In contrast stands Creon's insistence until near the play's end that his duty to consistently apply law and policy outweighed his familial relationships with Polynices or Antigone.

A Feminist's Reading

A feminist reader of *Antigone* might note that, although only Ismene explicitly evokes gender to support her stance, tying her refusal to resist the state to her womanhood, the genders of the other characters are more than incidental features. In staking out their positions, Antigone and Creon are evocative of Amy and Jake, the eleven-year-old representatives of the two distinct modes of moral reasoning explored by Carol Gilligan in *In a Different Voice*:[4] a morality based on responsibility and care in relationships versus a morality based on a logical hierarchy of rights and principles. Through Amy and Jake, Gilligan sought to demonstrate that in a world where males and females are socialized differently, and arrive at adulthood with different interpersonal orientations and a different set of social experiences, gender can influence the process of moral reasoning.

Gilligan sees different partial truths in these different moral ideologies and recognizes a need for dialogue between them. *Antigone* supports Gilligan's view by revealing the disastrous folly of both Creon's and Antigone's rigid morality, displayed in their mutual refusal to consider the merits of each other's position. At the same time, however, the play challenges the possibility of transforming moral discourse by including both voices when the power to declare truth is so unevenly distributed. Because Creon commanded the force of law, his truth could officially annihilate Antigone's truth, casting it as deviant and dangerous. If not for the depths of tragedy that befell his family, Creon was unlikely to have recognized the partiality of his view. *Antigone,* then, underscores the reasons that feminists value double vision: they acknowledge the need for genuine dialogue across differences while remaining sharply cognizant of the societal structures that impede its accomplishment.

A feminist reader might also note that although, as a woman, Antigone was an outsider to the political machinations of her male relatives, the course of her life was determined by her male relatives, particularly by their moral choices. In King Oedipus, the first play of the Sophocles trilogy, Antigone's fate is set in motion by Oedipus' violence—his slaying of a man after a quarrel, and his self-mutilation, resulting in blindness, on the discovery of his father's and mother's true identity (his father the man he had slain, his mother the mother of his children)—Creon's banishment of Oedipus for his unintended offenses of incest and patricide, and Antigone's brothers' approval of their father's banishment stirred by their desire for the throne. These acts lead Antigone to sacrifice her own needs and desires to care for her father as he wanders in exile, shunned by all who learn his identity. Later, her brothers' violence against one another provokes Creon's edict against Polynices' burial, which, in turn, leads to her disobedience of the edict, and inevitably to Creon's violence when he orders her death as the price of her disobedience.

Lacking the political or social power exercised at various times by the men in her family, but directly affected by the manner in which they exercised their power, Antigone's experience of the state was undoubtedly different from that of her father, uncle, and brothers. Although she chose her course of action pre-reflectively, had she elaborated the moral reasoning process by which she confronted her perceived legal, filial, and religious responsibilities, she might have asked herself a version of the questions Catharine MacKinnon asks in her recent book, *Toward a Feminist Theory of the State*:

> What is state power? Where, socially, does it come from? How do women [in my situation and in other situations] encounter it? What is the law for women [in my situation and in others]? How does law work to legitimate the state, [privileged] male power, itself? Can it do anything for women [in my situation and in others]? Can it do anything about . . . [the] status [of women in my situation and in others]? Does how the law is used matter?[5]

Thinkers addressing questions such as these are developing a feminist theory of the state that "comprehend[s] how law works as a form of state power in a social context in which power is gendered."[6]

Antigone, or any of a number of other lived or vicariously lived situations, readily provides the impetus for such a theoretical project. Feminist theorizing begins with the concrete experiences of particular women, such as Antigone, whose situations crystallize the relationship of their needs and interests as they view them to state authority as they encounter it. These experiences are then questioned, probed, examined, explored, and analyzed, a process that produces tentative theoretical conceptions. Once formulated, these theories are continually held up to the light of new experiences for evaluation, refinement, modification, and development. In short, feminist thinkers view concrete situations as containing strong theoretical potentialities. Theory then circles back to guide future behavioral choices, which, in turn, test and reshape theory. This method of analysis is an essential feature of feminism.

A Clinician's Reading

Examining whether a clinical educator would bring any special perspective to a reading of *Antigone* is an effort less obvious than the above. Legal clinicians, having drawn in the past on a variety of theoretical foundations for their work, are likely to have a more diffuse focus than feminist readers focused on gender. Nevertheless, clinicians might find in *Antigone* a justification of clinical methods. They might compare the possibilities for insight immanent in study and deliberation alone with the possibilities for insight immanent in Antigone's situation.

Some teachers are drawn to clinical settings due to a deeply held belief that experiencing a conflict between one's personal morality and a prescription of law or law practice provides a bone-deep entryway into exploring the relationship between law and morality, or constructing a theory of state power and how it operates. Confronting such a situation, clinicians believe, brings the values at stake and the potential consequences of various courses of action into sharp relief. Thus, a person facing an actual conflict is more likely to notice and contemplate the breadth and depth of the concrete consequences that may flow from the situation. Experience strengthens the motivation for inquiry, enlivens the critical issues, and provides a sound basis for examination and analysis. Theory forged in experience is likely to be thick and rich, and to relate directly to the important features of that experience. In other words, clinical education is rooted in the notion that theory formed through a clinical process is more likely to be useful and more likely to be right.

The stories underlying the cases that find their way into law school clinics may resemble Greek tragedies: their characters confronting trying circumstances and behaving wisely or foolishly, nobly or ignobly. The complexity, richness, and texture of these cases do not easily lend themselves to simply stated understandings or moral summaries. Clinic students, as well as clients, may find themselves standing in Antigone's position, experiencing distaste, perhaps even a powerful visceral resistance, toward the prescribed form or custom of law practice. They may also find themselves standing in Creon's position, uncritically accepting the practices of law without attention to consequences. Alternatively, they may feel, like Ismene, a deep ambivalence about their personal and civic responsibilities. The value of clinical methods depends on using Antigone's, Creon's, Ismene's, and others' standpoints as starting points for inquiry.

A clinician might observe that Antigone's starting point was all too literally her ending point as well. Antigone had neither the inclination nor the opportunity to examine her experience, both internal and external, to consider the full range of alternative courses of action available, to assess carefully the competing perspectives implicated in her situation, and then to elaborate the principles that would guide her. On the other hand, Creon's simple starting theories are dramatically altered by the play's end. Reflection on his tragic experiences leads Creon to reconsider the principles of living that he once firmly held and to recognize a "more complicated deliberative world."[7] This interaction between theory and experience, enabled by conscientious reflective practices, is the epistemological model that animates clinical education.

Ultimately the play *Antigone* supports such an epistemology. Had Antigone adopted such a model, or had Creon adopted it sooner, perhaps tragedy could have been averted. As Martha Nussbaum observes, the play is "unusually full of words for deliberation, reasoning, knowledge and vision,"[8] equating flexibility with good deliberation, and concluding with the assertion that wisdom is the most important component of happiness. Creon learns a hard-won lesson about "changing one's vision of the world, about losing one's grip on what looked like secure truth and learning a more elusive kind of wisdom."[9] Antigone, then, subtly advocates a process of continuous attention to, and reflection on, the particularities of a situation as the route to the interpretations and reinterpretations that are the source of wisdom. This theme embodies a clinical perspective on the role of concrete experiences and practices in the process of making and remaking theory.

Summarizing Comparisons

In the foregoing description of clinical methods, one hears the echo of feminist methods. This section moves beyond awareness of the echo and elaborates more systematically the hints of resemblance and distinction contained in the respective methodological descriptions of each movement. First and foremost, the methodologies of feminism and clinical education both emphasize, as the reading of *Antigone* illustrates, direct personal experience as theory's starting point, as well as its returning point for testing and rebuilding. To reiterate the methodological premise of both movements, each conceives of the relationship between explanation and experience, theory and practice, in the shape of a spiral.

Clinical education has a predominantly pedagogical identity, generating considerable attention to the learning process. In the interest of effective learning, clinical students engineer and participate in events that they carefully analyze, soon thereafter, and others who observed or participated in the same events may join in the examination. Feminists, on the other hand, though concerned with the learning process, generally do not identify with pedagogy in the same way as clinical educators. Without the demand of short-term learning objectives, feminists rely on the delayed retelling of experience to those who may or may not have shared analogous events, but who rarely shared the actual events.

Feminists rely on the consciousness-raising process of storytelling about a broad range of life experiences as one source of experiential data. Clinic educators and students rely on a narrower band of experience, their own engagement in professional work, as their primary source of data. Clinic students, for purposes of learning, deliberately choose this band of experience, which they could otherwise avoid or postpone. Feminists, on the other hand, generally examine their own and others' unavoidable, everyday experiences for purposes of learning.

Because experience contains both cognitive and affective content, exploring an experience fully requires exploring not only its cognitive, but also its affective dimensions. Feelings often provide windows to thought, and analyzing the causes and consequences of particular affective reactions often is a valuable step toward comprehending experience. When feminism and clinical education claim that experience precedes explanation, and that explanation must remain open to experience, they are tacitly recognizing the role of affect in experience and, therefore, in human understanding. Feminists and clinicians, in their respective settings, devote time to bringing this role to the surface, rather than submerging it, in order to facilitate understanding.

Contextual Reasoning

The Aristotelian practical reasoning process employed by each movement, moving as it does from specific to general, links the particulars generated and examined by clinical and feminist methods to the conceptual insights of many disciplines. Moreover, Aristotelian-style reasoning links these particulars to each movement's normative concerns. Clinicians and feminists worry, as did Aristotle, about the outcomes produced by applying principles to a limited factual context rather than developing a full contextual understanding before rendering judgment.

Attention to context means that feminists and clinical participants must explicitly acknowledge as relevant pieces of the context the norms they bring to the details of events. As feminists and clinicians have indicated, only by examining their normative structures can people truly comprehend and evaluate their behavioral choices. Acknowledging one's normative inclinations as a facet of the exercise of judgment conforms with the feminist's concern for candor in decision-making and for persistent appraisal of the soundness of one's judgment. This self-conscious examination also conforms with the clinician's concern for vigilant attention to the ethics of lawyering practices.

Critical Inquiry

Critique is inherent in the feminist enterprise. Feminists closely scrutinize the norms and ideologies embodied in institutional arrangements and compare these norms to their own ethical values. Although fewer clinical scholars have risen to this challenge, such scrutiny is inherent in the clinical project as well. No one concerned with the power allocations in legal process can avoid such critical institutional assessment. Taking this obligation seriously frees thinkers to envision and implement better institutional choices.

For feminists and clinicians, the need to consult the subtleties of varied experiences and a broad array of knowledge sources emerges from the urgency of knowing. Both clinicians and feminists find more at stake in this quest than intellectual integrity alone. The quality of living itself is the weight in the balance. Clinicians are deeply concerned with the conditions that trigger the legal process, with the consequences of legal process for their clients, and with the effect of legal process on all who encounter it. Feminist legal thinkers are concerned with these issues as well, because they are issues that implicate trenchant questions of fairness, justice, and equality. The concern with consequences, and with concepts that may generate better consequences, is an animating force of each movement.

Moral Judgment

From an Aristotelian perspective, feminist methodology and clinical methodology each represent a species of activist moral philosophy. Both movements view engagement in an ethically conscious practice as a prerequisite to the knowledge and development of judgment. Although the practices of each movement are not equivalent, each conceives of an ethical practice as involving engagement in activity in which one learns reflectively from and with others. Although perhaps eliciting and attending to somewhat divergent details, each views reasoning from the details of real events to principled resolution as the appropriate manner of engaging and developing moral judgment.

Insistence on contextual development does not undermine the capacity of feminists and clinicians to make moral judgments. Rather, this is the feature of feminist and clinical methods that makes moral judgment possible. It is in this sense that feminists and clinicians, while ethically scrupulous, are the opposite of ethical relativists. They have made a moral judgment that moral judgments must be as carefully and flexibly tailored as possible to actual lived situations. In other words, feminists and clinicians require elaborate knowledge of the many-faceted realities and novelties of a situation before passing judgment and taking action. Feminists and clinicians do not use their sensitivity to the harm that faulty judgments can unleash to evade making judgments, but to highlight the importance of taking extraordinary care in developing the requisite knowledge from which to undertake the task of judgment.

Reexamining Ethics

The methodologies of the feminist and clinical education movements suggest that the story of *Antigone*, a case in a law school clinic, or other richly specified narratives represent promising springboards for inquiry into broad questions about law and morality. The considerable and sundry details of such narratives express the subtleties and complexities of the morally charged situations in which humans find themselves. Unlike many children's tales, a single lesson does not surface readily from these narratives. Rarely do these real-life or lifelike contexts provide easily grasped answers to obvious questions. Rather, they suggest multiple interpretations and analyses. The narratives contain painstaking renderings of competing viewpoints that check our natural tendencies to oversimplify and overlook details and perspectives that unsettle the neat conclusions that we desire. We must actively engage the full breadth and depth of these narratives to honestly and effectively further our analysis. What we will come to know as a result of this inquiry will be altered by the contextualized process through which we have come to know it.

I have sought to demonstrate that such a theory-building practice is a distinctly ethical project. Clinical and feminist methods represent possibilities for rescuing the morally significant details that are systematically excluded from the culture's storehouse of standard stories. Acute empirical sensitivity—foregrounding the stories of those whom cultural structures have generally relegated to the background, and supporting the voices often rendered barely audible—can help to accomplish this goal. Working through the cognitive dissonance created by the infusion of these previously neglected perspectives expands our understanding and promotes both a critique of the societal structures that obscured such knowledge and an interest in dismantling these knowledge-distorting structures. From the feminist-clinician-prophet-philosopher's vantage point, the distinction between epistemology and ethics collapses.

From feminists' and clinicians' relentless demand for elaborate concrete detail and for special attention to the data provided by those whom society frequently disempowers comes a reconceived notion of what qualifies as ethical inquiry. This notion of ethical inquiry is a process grounded in our experiences of social and institutional interactions and concerned with the way people actually respond to the moral choices presented by everyday life and work. The focus of ethical theory is no longer the justification of actions affecting the "generalized others" of traditional philosophy, but the justification of actions affecting the "concrete others" with whom we are enmeshed. Ethical systems emerge from this network of relationships when we seek to resolve and explain our resolutions of the quotidian dilemmas that we encounter in the complex, nuanced, temporal context in which they arise. This ethical theory, then, responds to the experiences central to daily personal situations and requires reflection on such situations to develop moral consciousness. In the hands of feminists and clinicians, ethics becomes a sustained practice of empirical attention and reflection on the actions of people in actual situations. Ordinary life expresses and creates ethical theory, which is understood as having an inescapably social character. The better our context-sensitive empiricism, the better our moral deliberations, and the more precise the articulation of our ethical principles will be.

Chapter 6

Legal Ethics Exploration through Literature, Myth, and Popular Culture

In chapter 5 we noted some examples of feminist theorists drawing on literary classics to develop new visions of feminist ethics. As we explored there, the use of literature in studying lawyers' ethics can be a way of tapping into wise and subtle ideas embodied in various historical and cultural traditions, as well as detecting possibilities for creative transformation of those ideas into new visions or practice possibilities. The study of cultural products can also uncover deep-seated stereotypes or tensions in our understandings of lawyers' roles. In this chapter, we continue an examination of work whose central purpose is to explore the intersection between representations of lawyers in literature and popular cultural forms such as film and the study of legal ethics.

Paul Bergman explores images of redemptive law practice in a variety of older and more recent films. Note that some of his analytic categories resemble models of good lawyering explored in previous chapters. For example, Bergman sees in the movies he analyzes models of lawyers whose redemption comes in realizing the satisfactions of being *client-centered* (compare with Dinerstein, Miller, and White); *justice-centered* (compare with Pearce, Gordon, Simon, Hing, and Alfieri); and a *problem-solver* (compare with López on lay lawyering). Other themes Bergman discusses that we have encountered in other works include the satisfactions of returning to one's community of origin (compare *Counsellor at Law* and *Lawyer Man* with Cruz), and of connecting one's passion in lawyering to personal experiences of injustice or discrimination (compare *Philadelphia* with McNeil on Houston's life). Still another is the conflict between an ethic of justice and an ethic of care (compare *An Act of Murder* with Menkel-Meadow on *The Merchant of Venice*).

The 1930s movies Bergman describes also reflect some of the historical themes explored in chapter 2, such as the movement of Jewish lawyers from immigrant neighborhoods into gentile culture and the ambivalence produced by leaving one's community of origin (*Counsellor at Law* and *Lawyer Man*); and the legacies of discrimination on the basis of race, class origin, sexual orientation, and disability that linger in the profession (*Philadelphia*).

Rob Atkinson explores still other themes we have encountered previously in this reader. He explores the parallels between Japanese novelist Kazuo Ishiguro's story of an English butler in *Remains of the Day* and the current debate between legal ethicists who place lawyers' loyalty to their clients first and legal ethicists, such as Gordon, Pearce, Luban, and Simon, who embrace a *moral activist* view, which emphasizes lawyers' ethical duties to attend to the public interest. Atkinson ends his piece by reflecting on the value of stories in shaping the ethical lives of communities, including professional communities, and in closing emphasizes the special power of religious stories, which are considered in more detail in chapter 7.

Questions for Reflection and Discussion

1. What additional themes emerging in the Bergman and Atkinson excerpts parallel themes we have explored in prior chapters? You may wish to list these themes and the appropriate comparisons.

2. What other analyses of lawyers' ethics could be pursued by drawing on your own favorite depictions of lawyers' conduct in novels, film, cartoons, or other cultural artifacts?

3. Were Maggie Ward's actions in *Class Action* acceptable under the current Model Rules? Why or why not? What alternatives did she have under the Model Rules in dealing with client deceit? Would you have handled Maggie's ethical dilemma the way she did? If not, how would you handle such a problem? Is your plan more like that envisioned under the Model Rules or like the layperson's conception reflected in *Class Action*?

4. Was it permissible under the Model Rules for Maggie to join her father's firm, which represented the opposing party in a case she handled at her old firm? Why or why not? Was it permissible for her to talk to her father about the report she found? Was it permissible for her to litigate against her father? What steps would be required in this situation under the Model Rules?

5. Can you think of examples of lay depictions of lawyers exhibiting good ethical conduct that contradict the requirements of the Model Rules? What does this say about the fit between lay persons' moral intuitions and lawyers' professional ethics obligations as they are currently conceived? For each of the examples you thought of, do you think the lay conception or the professional conception was better? Why? What would you have thought before attending law school?

The Movie Lawyers' Guide to Redemptive Legal Practice[1]

Paul Bergman[2]

The Chinese use two brush strokes to write the word "crisis." One brush stroke stands for danger; the other for opportunity. In crisis, be aware of the danger—but recognize the opportunity.[3]

An enduring film image is the "moment of crisis" that produces the "moment of truth." Ships about to sink or brakeless cars plummeting down steep mountain roads often provide the impetus for dramatic revelations. In such settings, and in line with the policy behind the "dying declaration" exception to the hearsay rule,[4] characters are prone to revealing long-hidden truths. In Filmland, crises can also be very good medicine. Characters who are fortunate enough to survive moments of crisis often emerge with improved happiness and moral values. Forced by crises to confront suppressed realities, movie characters may choose to redeem their lives by committing their futures to performing what audiences are likely to perceive as good works. Thus, filmmakers may use crises as a tool for sending powerful normative messages about what constitutes a morally good and personally satisfying life.

This essay examines films in which movie lawyers are redeemed by moments of crisis. Just as crises may serve as tools for sending normative messages about what constitutes a morally good and satisfying personal life, so too may crises lead movie lawyers to "redemptive lawyering," or morally good and personally satisfying professional lifestyles. The essay examines images of redemptive lawyering for reel lawyers and compares those images to the attitudes of real lawyers.

Redemptive lawyering in films occurs when sudden, dramatic, or even catastrophic events jolt movie lawyers into adopting morally good and personally satisfying professional lifestyles. Images of redemptive lawyering can convey powerful normative images of lawyering ideals, and of what lawyers can be and can do to emerge from frustrating, unsatisfying, and even unethical careers. The subsections below describe three forms of redemptive lawyering that movie lawyers have adopted in response to crises.

Problem-Centered Lawyering

"Problem-centered lawyering" is one form of redemptive lawyering. Redemption occurs when a crisis enables a lawyer to realize that ultimate professional satisfaction consists of using legal knowledge and legal experience to craft satisfactory solutions to clients' problems. The idea is that a life devoted to problem-solving is personally satisfying. Moreover, because most of us tend to believe that helping people in need is a socially valuable activity, audiences are likely to perceive devotion to clients' problems as morally good.

Counsellor at Law[5] presents an archetypal example of a movie lawyer who finds redemption in problem-centered lawyering. George Simon (John Barrymore) is an up-from-the-gutter Jew who has become one of New York City's most successful lawyers. Simon's office, where the entire movie takes place, is a jumble of frantic activity. Simon is in his element, juggling a stream of legal and personal problems brought to him by clients, his mother, his partner, his wife, an investigator, various office employees, and others. However, what matters most to Simon is not his law practice, but his non-Jewish trophy wife, Cora (Doris Kenyon). He brags about Cora constantly, and is so concerned with preserving Cora's social status that he turns down a case that would have produced a lucrative fee, but that Cora felt would embarrass her in the eyes of her friends. Thus, when Simon finds out that Cora has been unfaithful, the moment of crisis is at hand. For Simon, because law practice was but a means to acceptance by what he considered the social elite, Cora's unfaithfulness robs his practice of its meaning. Simon opens the window of his suddenly dark, quiet office and prepares to jump to his death. But like many a prizefighter, Simon is saved by the bell—in this case, the bell of his telephone. Simon's adoring secretary, Regina Gordon (Bebe Daniels), was supposed to have left for the day, but she returned to the office because she was worried about him. Regina answers the phone and tells Simon that the caller is the president of a steel company whose son is in serious trouble. At first, Simon remains in suicide mode; he orders Regina to hang up. In moments, however, Simon reverts to the confident, energetic lawyer we have seen throughout the movie. He excitedly grabs the phone, shouts instructions to the president, and rushes out of the office with Regina to his client's aid.

The moment of crisis enables Simon to achieve redemption by becoming a problem-centered lawyer. In crisis, Simon recognizes that chasing after Cora and her elite society friends is unimportant compared to the personal satisfaction and even the exhilaration of confronting and overcoming challenging legal problems. Moreover, Simon's commitment to problem-solving is morally good, as he places himself in the immediate service of a client who, although the president of a steel company, is at bottom a father worried about his son. The film's final scene symbolizes Simon's redemption. As he leaves his office for the first time in the film, so he sheds his old self and what he had falsely valued in law practice. *Counsellor at Law* conjures a strong image of commitment to problem-solving as a lawyerly ideal, and suggests that devotion to problem-solving is both professionally satisfying and morally good without regard to the status of the client.

Client-Centered Lawyering

"Client-centered lawyering" is a second form of redemptive lawyering. Redemption occurs when crisis enables a lawyer to realize that the ultimate source of a satisfactory professional career is bonding with clients. This image depicts clients as weak and in desperate need of protection. It suggests the need for lawyers to empathize with clients in order to provide them with the legal help they deserve. An empathic lawyer is both professionally happy and morally good.

Lawyer Man[6] is an early and somewhat general example of client-centered redemption. Anton Adam (William Powell) has a small but successful practice serving the largely immigrant population on New York's lower east side. Olga Michaels (Joan Blondell) is Adam's standard-issue adoring secretary. After a significant courtroom victory, Adam closes his storefront office and joins a powerful uptown practice, where he prospers. To Olga's disgust, Adam seems to have turned his back on his former clients. Economic success for Adam comes with a price, however—the mob wants him to do its bidding. When Adam refuses, the mob sets him up and the ensuing criminal charges ruin his lucrative career. Adam's specific moment of crisis emerges when the mob boss offers Adam a judgeship. While this probably would not be a crisis for most lawyers, it is for Adam because he understands that the offer was made with the idea that, because he has been publicly disgraced and has nowhere to turn, the mob will expect to dictate Adam's decisions. Adam does have a place to turn, however—the lower-east-side practice where he started his career. Arm in arm, Adam and Olga happily walk through streets teeming with the politically powerless population to which Adam will devote the remainder of his career.

Adam's bond is not with a specific client, but with a population with which he shares common roots. More typically, personal redemption for movie lawyers comes from the plight of a specific client. In *The Verdict*,[7] Frank Galvin (Paul Newman) is a boozed-out personal injury lawyer who tries to scratch out a living by soliciting clients in funeral parlors. Galvin has one case of real value, a medical malpractice case against two anesthesiologists and the hospital that employed them. The complaint, which had been filed by Galvin's mentor, Mickey Morrissey (Jack Warden), alleged that the doctors administered an improper anesthetic to a young woman who entered the hospital's emergency room to have a baby. The improper anesthetic left the young woman comatose. Unfortunately for his clients, the comatose woman's guardian, Galvin, has done nothing on the case. It's hard to prepare for trial when you're dead drunk most of the time.

Galvin's moment of redemption occurs when he decides to visit the comatose woman in the hospital. As he takes photographs of her lying helplessly in a hospital bed, kept alive by a respirator and feeding tube, he bonds with her though she cannot speak, hear, see, or offer him a drink. For the first time, Galvin realizes the woman's helplessness and his responsibility to bring to justice the doctors who ruined her life. Significantly, Galvin tells the nurses who want to know why he is in the hospital room, "I'm her lawyer." Thereafter, Galvin works relentlessly for his client. Further evidence of Galvin's redemption occurs when he engages in pretrial settlement negotiations with defense lawyer Ed Concannon (James Mason) in the chambers of Judge Hoyle (Milo O'Shea). Judge Hoyle chides Galvin for turning down a large settlement offer, commenting, "your client could walk out of here with a lot of money."

"She can't walk," is Galvin's reply. Galvin is so personally connected to his client that he takes the judge's figurative comment as a personal slight.

The film's conclusion further signifies Galvin's redemptive transformation. Though the jurors have no legal basis for doing so, they return a huge verdict in favor of the comatose woman. Galvin later receives a phone call from Laura Fischer (Charlotte Rampling), whom Concannon had employed as a sexual spy to report on Galvin's trial strategy. Galvin's refusal to answer the phone suggests that he has renounced his former habits and will devote himself to his clients.

Joe Miller (Denzel Washington) in *Philadelphia*[8] becomes a client-centered lawyer when he connects discrimination against homosexual AIDS sufferer Andrew Beckett (Tom Hanks) to discrimination against African Americans. Miller is an African American lawyer with a small but successful neighborhood personal injury practice. At the start of the film, Beckett is an up-and-coming star attorney with one of Philadelphia's largest and most prestigious law firms. However, by the time he asks Miller to represent him in an employment discrimination lawsuit against the law firm, Beckett is deathly ill with AIDS. Beckett claims that he was illegally fired because of his illness. Miller initially refuses to take the case, partly because he thinks it unwinnable, but primarily because he wants nothing to do with the AIDS virus or homosexuals.

Some weeks later, Miller and Beckett are doing legal research at adjacent tables in a public law library. Miller's moment of crisis emerges when he notices a white patron staring at him. The patron's disdainful look suggests that as an African American, Miller could only be a client and therefore should not be in a section of the library reserved for lawyers. Miller then observes a librarian rudely trying to convince a noticeably ill Beckett to move to a private research room. At this redemptive moment, Miller recognizes that both he and Beckett are targets of discrimination. After Beckett holds his ground, Miller asks him about the status of his employment discrimination claim. Beckett calls Miller's attention to a portion of a case establishing that Beckett's claim is legally valid. Miller reads the last portion, in which the court refers to discrimination against AIDS sufferers as the equivalent of "social death," and comparable to any form of illegal discrimination in which prejudice is based on the presumed characteristics of a group rather than individual merit. The language cements the personal bond between Miller and Beckett as targets of discrimination. In the next scene Miller is representing Beckett; he serves the senior partner of Beckett's former law firm with a complaint for employment discrimination.

The film suggests the redemptive power of client-centered lawyering. Miller had been anti-gay, and his practice seemingly consisted of going through the motions on behalf of clients in whom he had no personal interest in order to earn a good, steady income. After taking on Beckett's case, Miller becomes aware that homosexual relationships are much like his own, and he views gay rights as an important civil rights issue. He tries the case with a zeal that demonstrates that he has a personal, as well as an economic, stake in its outcome. Thus, *Philadelphia* suggests that lawyers can redeem themselves by personally bonding with clients.

The Accused[9] offers a final example of client-centered redemption. Sarah Tobias (Jodie Foster), who scrapes out a meager living as a waitress, is raped by three men in a bar. Numerous barflies cheer the rapists on. Prosecutor Kathryn Murphy (Kelly McGillis) initially seeks the maximum punishment. However, she soon finds out that Tobias has a spotty past and that just before the rape, Tobias had been drinking heavily and dancing provocatively. Fearful of losing, Murphy agrees to guilty pleas to a lesser, nonsexual charge.

As it did for Frank Galvin in *The Verdict*, Murphy's moment of redemption occurs bedside in a hospital. Shortly after Murphy has plea-bargained away her case, Tobias is in a parking lot when she is taunted by one of the barflies. She furiously rams her car into his truck, and sustains serious injuries which result in her being hospitalized. Murphy's moment of crisis arrives when she visits Tobias in the hospital. Tobias accuses Murphy of treating her no better than did the barflies—both, Tobias says, treated her "like a piece of shit." Recognition of the truth of Tobias's statement produces Murphy's moment of redemption. Murphy insists on prosecuting the barflies for contributing to the rape, over the vehement objections of her boss, the district attorney. Murphy identifies with Tobias personally and tells him, "I owe her." The case goes to trial. Tobias describes what happened, a key witness comes forward to support her story, and the barflies are convicted.

The Accused suggests how easily what may be "business as usual" for lawyers can appear contemptuous to the outside world. After all, Murphy's conduct prior to her redemptive moment is in no way unusual or improper. Prosecutors routinely offer plea bargains when they face weaknesses in proof. From Tobias's perspective, however, Murphy abandoned her and implicitly denied Tobias's worth as a human being. By personally bonding with Tobias, Murphy derives personal satisfaction and punishes immoral behavior.

Justice-Centered Lawyering

"Justice-centered lawyering" is a third form of redemptive lawyering. Redemption occurs when crisis enables a lawyer to realize that ultimate professional satisfaction consists of pursuing justice. Like client-centered lawyers, justice-centered lawyers typically represent politically powerless clients. For the latter group of lawyers, however, personal satisfaction and moral goodness result from the positions they advocate rather than from personal attachments to individuals.

In *An Act of Murder*,[10] Calvin Cooke (Fredric March) is a strict, letter-of-the-law judge known in the community as "Old Man Maximum" for his harsh sentencing policies. Off the bench, Judge Cooke is devoted to his wife, Cathy (Florence Eldridge). Judge Cooke's moment of crisis occurs when he learns that Cathy has a terminal illness. Judge Cooke crashes his car with the intention of killing Cathy in order to spare her a long and painful death. Although the authorities are prepared to assume that Cathy's death was the result of an accident, Judge Cooke confesses that he intentionally killed her. He is charged with murder, and insists on pleading guilty. Over Judge Cooke's objection, the trial court judge appoints defense attorney David Douglas (Edmond O'Brien) to represent Judge Cooke so as to ensure that a factual basis for the plea exists. Douglas asks for an autopsy, which produces surprising evidence: Cathy was dead from lethal poison before the crash occurred. Additional evidence shows that Cathy also knew of her illness, and that she ingested poison before taking the fatal car ride. After hearing this evidence, the judge dismisses the case. The experience redeems Judge Cooke. Acknowledging his moral guilt, Judge Cooke states that if he is allowed to remain a judge, he will have an enlightened view of justice. To do justice, he must look not only at a person's behavior, but also the person's circumstances and the reasons for that behavior. Henceforth, in his court, "a man shall be judged not only by the law, but by the heart as well." Thus, Judge Cooke's personal crisis allows him to recognize that a uniform application of black-letter rules will not necessarily produce justice. Moral application of rules demands that judges holistically evaluate people's backgrounds and circumstances.

A yearning to do justice also characterizes the redemption of Maggie Ward (Mary Elizabeth Mastrantonio) in *Class Action*.[11] Maggie is an associate in a large civil defense firm, hungry for partnership. As second chair to Michael Grazier (Colin Friels), Maggie defends Argo Motors against a lawsuit filed by her father, Jedediah Ward (Gene Hackman), a crusading plaintiff's personal injury lawyer. Jedediah's complaint alleges that design defects in a car manufactured by Argo, the Meridian, caused numerous deaths and injuries. Maggie learns of a "smoking gun": Dr. Pavel (Jan Rubes), an Argo engineer, had submitted a report stating that the Meridian's design would cause it to explode under certain conditions. Argo disregarded the report, figuring that defending a few wrongful death cases would be cheaper in the long run than retrofitting thousands of cars. Rather than turn the report over to Jedediah in response to his legitimate discovery request, Maggie accedes to her firm's plan to mislabel the report and bury it in a truckload of Argo documents given to Jedediah. Her moment of crisis emerges when she realizes that the law firm duped her. The report was not turned over to Jedediah at all, and even the copy that Maggie had in her desk was removed. Maggie redeems herself by responding to her law firm's deceitful conduct with some trickery of her own. She tells Jedediah about the report, tricks Grazier into denying under oath that the report existed, and provides an Argo witness who testifies to having seen the report. Argo's defense collapses and it has to settle Jedediah's claims for millions of dollars. Maggie then joins Jedediah's law firm, happily dancing and reuniting with her father.

An Act of Murder and Class Action manifest markedly different conceptions of justice. For Judge Cooke, justice is a process, a method of evaluating individual responsibility. For Maggie, justice requires choosing sides. Automobile manufacturers and the corporate law firms that represent them are evil; individual consumers and the solo and small firm practitioners who represent them are good. Nevertheless, both Judge Cooke and Maggie experience crisis, and both react by committing to justice.

How the Butler Was Made to Do It: The Perverted Professionalism of *The Remains of the Day*[1]

Rob Atkinson[2]

I have chosen as the text for my professionalism homily a passage from Kazuo Ishiguro's *The Remains of the Day.*[3] *The Remains of the Day* depicts the tragic consequences of flawed professional visions. Closely analogous visions figure prominently in the contemporary debate on the professionalism of lawyers. In the two contexts, there are parallel dangers. On the one hand is the risk of embracing, individually or collectively, flawed perfectionist ideologies of professionalism, mirages that seduce us with the promise of either moral nonaccountability or easy moral answers. On the other hand is the risk of discarding all forms of professionalism as discredited ideology or hypocritical cant, thus despairing of meaningful professional lives. A careful analysis of *The Remains of the Day* reveals a mediating, tragic vision of professionalism, somewhere between the perfectionistic and the nihilistic. It is a professionalism that accepts the imperfection —indeed, the imperfectability—of both individuals and institutions without rejecting the possibility of virtuous professional lives and cultures.

   In this essay, I add my voice to the voices of those who believe that professionals, and perhaps even professionalism, can be redeemed, though never perfected. A principal means of that redemption, Ishiguro shows, lies in the inseparable and almost saicramental acts of telling one another stories and analyzing them together. *The Remains of the Day* is a story about professionalism with a protagonist and narrator who explicitly insists on moral analysis. That story implicitly invokes its complement, a moral analysis of the professions that accounts for their members' need to tell stories.

The Story

The larger story is about an English butler looking back over his career in one of the great English country houses. The butler's name is Stevens, and he has been in service for most of his professional life to the fictitious but typical Lord Darlington. His retrospective is set in 1956, when the great era of the country house is over, and with it the age of the classic English butler. The Labor Government's wealth transfer taxes have begun to break up the ancestral estates of people like Lord Darlington. Members of the aristocracy are now opening their houses to throngs of tourists or, worse still, conveying them to the National Trust or, worst of all, selling them to foreign, even American, millionaires. This last indignity has befallen Lord Darlington's house.

Even for those with the money, like Darlington Hall's new owner, things are not what they were. In Stevens's words, "finding [staff] recruits of a satisfactory standard is no easy task nowadays."[4] Even in the old days, as Stevens frequently laments, the less ambitious often opted out of domestic service to marry and raise families of their own. Stevens himself, however, has no children; he has never been married. For that matter, he has never taken a vacation.

When Stevens's new American employer learns of this, he insists that Stevens take the estate's Ford out for a week's holiday in the late summer when he is himself away in the United States. Stevens eventually assents, but only when he is able to convince himself that the trip has a professional purpose. He has just received the first letter in a long while from a former head housekeeper at the Hall, Miss Kenton, and he interprets this to mean that she may be ready, after twenty years of married life, to leave her husband and return to domestic service. He recalls "her great affection for this house . . . her exemplary professionalism."[5] His taking a trip to her home in the West Country, he persuades himself, may convince her to return in her former professional capacity. But we begin to suspect that he has been interested in more than her exemplary professionalism, and that her affection was not always limited to the house.

In the course of his trip, Stevens reflects that social life in the country house is not all that has suffered since the war; the personal reputation of the recently deceased Lord Darlington is at a low ebb as well. In the mid-1930s, he had hosted several "unofficial" meetings between the British Foreign Secretary and German Ambassador von Ribbentrop, in an effort, as we would now say, to reanchor Germany in the West. In recognition of his good offices, he had been rather graciously received in the reconstituted Reich. Stevens is at pains to point out that many entirely loyal English aristocrats were initially inclined to trust the new German leadership, and that Lord Darlington was not the last to realize the true nature of Nazism. More ominously, Stevens admits, Darlington had flirted, intellectually and otherwise, with a female member of the British Union of Fascists and had entertained that organization's leader, Sir Oswald Mosley, at the Hall. But Stevens tries to minimize Darlington's association with the Black Shirts, reducing it to a very few incidents over a very brief time. It is on one of those incidents that I want to focus.

One summer afternoon Lord Darlington calls Stevens into the study, and, after the usual pleasantries, asks whether there are any Jews on the house staff. When informed that there are two Jewish housemaids, Lord Darlington tells Stevens, "'Of course, you'll have to let them go.'"[6] Apparently prompted by Stevens's barely perceptible surprise, Lord Darlington explains: "'It's regrettable, Stevens, but we have no choice. There's the safety and well-being of my guests to consider. Let me assure you, I've looked into this matter and thought it through thoroughly. It's in all our best interests.'"

Because the two maids are under Miss Kenton's direct supervision as housekeeper, Stevens thinks it appropriate to inform her of their dismissal. He brings the matter up that very night at their routine meeting for cocoa in her parlor. Stevens offers Miss Kenton the opportunity to speak with the maids herself before sending them along to his pantry for their dismissal the next morning. Miss Kenton expresses outrage and warns Stevens that if the maids are dismissed, she will leave as well. But Stevens carries out the order, and Miss Kenton does not leave.

Before examining the incident in more detail, I want briefly to reassure the skittish, those who are beginning to wonder how this tale can possibly relate to the practice of law other than perhaps to imply a deprecating comparison between lawyers and domestic servants. Thus, for those of you who think the assertedly parallel lines are diverging, let me offer a brief aside. Suppose Lord Darlington, punctilious in all his affairs, had called his London solicitors to confirm that his firing of the maids was legally proper. He might have asked for a written opinion on the subject and for carefully drafted dismissal papers to effect their discharge. Predictably, Lord Darlington would have rung up a senior member of the firm, and that member might well have assigned the research and drafting to a junior associate. The subordinate would have discovered that, under traditional common law notions of employment, the Jewish maids could be dismissed for even immoral reasons. I suspect, however, that both he and his senior would have been troubled by the prospect of playing a part in that morally sordid but perfectly legal action. It thus takes no great stretch of the imagination to see the dilemma of the butler and the maid played out in perfectly parallel fashion in a law firm of their day—or of ours.

As the next part shows, the responses of Stevens and Kenton are typical of two competing approaches open to contemporary American lawyers in such a situation. Either answer, standing alone, is inadequate, and the story itself presents a more satisfactory, but by no means perfect, response. The medium in which Stevens and Kenton give their answers—a story—reveals not only the relative merits of the alternative answer, but also why Stevens and Kenton failed to choose that alternative, and at what cost. The factors influencing their choices operate on us as well, and we are at risk of incurring similar costs. To shift from the terminology of economics to the language of literature, we are in danger of suffering the same fate.

Perverted Professionalism

Whenever someone serves another, that service poses a question: should the service be limited by anything other than the principal's will? Modern society imposes one obvious set of constraints: the outer bounds of the state's positive law. But are there other limits? That is a fundamental question of professional ethics: should a professional always do all that the law allows, or should the professional recognize other constraints, particularly concerns for the welfare of third parties? This question divides scholars of legal ethics and thoughtful practitioners into two schools: those who recognize constraints other than law's outer limit, and those who do not. Mr. Stevens and Miss Kenton, in their treatment of the maids and in their professional lives generally, fall on opposite sides of this divide. The course of their lives suggests not so much that one answer is wrong and the other right, but that each poses distinct dangers to moral integrity and that each is the beginning, rather than the end, of moral analysis.

Mr. Stevens's Neutral Partisanship

Stevens's position closely parallels what students of the legal profession call "neutral partisanship." The second of these two correlated principles, partisanship, entails advancing client ends through all legal means, and with a maximum of personal determination, as long as the ends are within the letter of the law. The first principle, neutrality, lets the professional claim personal disinterest in, or even antipathy toward, client ends and moral nonaccountability for helping to advance them. So it was with Stevens's firing of the Jewish maids. Looking back on the incident, he sees it this way: "My every instinct opposed the idea of their dismissal. Nevertheless, my duty in this instance was quite clear, and as I saw it, there was nothing to be gained at all in irresponsibly displaying such personal doubts. It was a difficult task, but as such, one that demanded to be carried out with dignity." When Miss Kenton expresses her outrage, he reminds her that "our professional duty is not to our own foibles and sentiments, but to the wishes of our employer."[7]

For Stevens and the neutral partisans, the ultimate decision, in matters of morality and public policy, is the client's to make. Furthermore, this has an important corollary: the professional's job is essentially technical. In the words of a prominent academic proponent of neutral partisanship, the client is like an "individual facing and needing to use a very large and very complicated machine (with lots of whirring gears and spinning data tapes) that he can't get to work."[8] In Stevens's words, "Let us establish this quite clearly: a butler's duty is to provide good service. It is not to meddle in the great affairs of the nation."[9] Neutral partisanship tends to reduce the human dimensions of one's professional life, to deal with its unpleasantries in abstract and impersonal terms. Thus, for example, Stevens speaks of the "particular contracts to be discontinued," and refers to the maids as "the two employees concerned."[10] And as neutral partisanship reduces professional service to technical assistance, so it tends to reduce moral concerns to matters of individual taste, if not idiosyncrasy. We have already heard Stevens dismiss his moral qualms as "foibles and sentiments."[11]

This is not to say, however, that Stevens's position is totally divorced from morality, any more than is the contemporary justification of neutral partisanship as practiced by lawyers. Rather, Stevens firmly grounds his position in morality, in very much the same way today's neutral partisan lawyers do. Stevens insists that the moral dimension of one's professional role as a butler derives from the moral standing of one's employer:

> The question was not simply one of how well one practised one's skills, but to what end one did so; each of us harboured the desire to make our own small contribution to the creation of a better world, and saw that, as professionals, the surest means of doing so would be to serve the great gentlemen of our times in whose hands civilization had been entrusted. . . . A "great" butler can only be, surely, one who can point to his years of service and say that he has applied his talents to serving a great gentleman—and through the latter, to serving humanity.[12]

Unlike earlier generations of butlers, Stevens insists, his generation did not see the world as a ladder descending from the houses of royalty through the nobility and gentry to the merely wealthy, with the professional status of servants running along the same scale. Rather, according to Stevens, his generation saw the world as a wheel revolving around the hub of great country houses. There, affairs of state were debated and often resolved before being discussed in official fora like Parliament and formal diplomatic conferences. In that world, one's professional status as a butler turned on how close one was to the hub, and on how active one's employer was in "furthering the progress of humanity."[13] The key to professional status in Stevens's more idealistic generation was, accordingly, "the moral status of an employer." This attitude, he maintains, had significantly influenced the course of his career, particularly his decision to work for Lord Darlington.

Defenders of neutral partisan lawyering are also at pains to show how the professional role they prescribe serves the public good. In contrast to Stevens, they do not focus on the humanitarian impulses, or even on the moral status, of the client. Rather, the reverse is true: they are at pains to show that whenever the lawyer helps a client exercise legal rights, even in an immoral way, the lawyer has acted well as a professional. Yet this professional probity, like Stevens's, is grounded in an ethical good. In the case of neutral partisan lawyers, that ethical good is the client's exercise of moral autonomy as authorized by the law. Society recognizes individual autonomy as a good of the highest order, so the argument runs, and carves out a sphere in which individuals can exercise that autonomy without interference. By helping lay folk operate within that envelope—sometimes even by pressing its edge—the lawyer is accomplishing a moral and social, not just professional, good. When, accordingly, proponents of neutral partisanship describe their model as amoral, they are not referring to its ultimate grounding, which is emphatically moral. They are referring, rather, to the lawyer's immunity from the task of scrutinizing the morality of particular client acts. Theirs is morality at the wholesale but not the retail level; a morality of the long run, not the particular case; a morality of fidelity to role obligations, not attention to particular acts.

In this sense, it is quite reminiscent of Stevens's professional morality. Just as the neutral partisan's moral inquiry ends with a determination of the legality of the client's act, so Stevens believes that the butler's moral inquiry ends when he convinces himself that "this employer embodies all that I find noble and admirable."[14] Just as the neutral partisan is not concerned with the morality of particular acts within the law, so Stevens does not take it upon himself to question the particular judgments of employers of the right general character. Rather, Stevens condemns in no uncertain terms "the sort of misguided idealism which . . . suggested that any butler with serious aspirations should make it his business to be forever reappraising his employer—scrutinizing the latter's motives, analysing the implications of his views," with the implied threat of leaving.[15] Similarly, defenders of neutral partisanship condemn withdrawing from cases on grounds of moral disagreement with the client.

Both of these laissez-faire attitudes—that of Stevens the butler on the one hand and that of neutral partisan lawyers on the other—rest on varieties of moral skepticism. Stevens's skepticism is the less radical. For him, it is a matter of expertise, a division of labor. As we have seen, Stevens deeply believes that butlers should choose employers who serve lofty public ends. But he also believes that people of his station, unlike their employers, cannot keep up with the more subtle refinements of what he calls high affairs of state, what we would call matters of public policy. As a general matter, he says, "The fact is, such great affairs will always be beyond the understanding of those such as you [the reader] and I."[16] Thus, in the case of the maids, he tells Miss Kenton that "'there are many things you and I are simply not in a position to understand concerning, say, the nature of Jewry. Whereas his lordship, I might venture, is somewhat better placed to judge what is for the best.'"[17]

The skepticism at the root of neutral partisanship in lawyering generally takes a less personal, and more radical, form. It has been traced to the Hobbesian, positivist notion that "ends are natural, individual, subjective, and arbitrary."[18] On that view, the only ends individuals share are the desire to be free to pursue their private ends and the corollary desire for security in that pursuit. The legitimate function of law is to define limits within which individuals can exercise autonomy without impinging upon each other. The lawyer's job is to advise the client, faced with a bafflingly complex legal order, about where the outer edge of this sphere of autonomy lies. Not to assist the client in exercising autonomy up to the very margin allowed by law would be to usurp the role not just of judge and jury, but of the legislature as well. Ultimately, it would undermine the legitimacy of government itself. Thus, though the moral skepticism of neutral partisan lawyers is more global and less self-effacing than that of Stevens, it produces the same result: deferring to clients on moral judgments within the letter of the law. Thus, moral skepticism, somewhat paradoxically, is the foundation of Stevens's and the neutral partisan lawyer's faith in the rightness of fidelity to clients' ends.

Miss Kenton's Moral Activism

Miss Kenton's reaction to the firing of the maids offers a striking contrast to Mr. Stevens's response, and it implies a vision of professionalism quite different from neutral partisanship. She recoils from the technocratic, antiseptic attitude of Stevens, his treatment of the dismissals "'as though [he] were discussing orders for the larder.'"[19] In contrast to his references to "contracts" and "employees," she persistently refers to the maids by their first names, Ruth and Sarah, and invokes her long, personal relationship with them. And she does not dismiss deeply held personal aversions as "foibles and sentiments." She says she's outraged, and she puts her position in unmistakably moral terms: "'Does it not occur to you, Mr Stevens, that to dismiss Ruth and Sarah on these grounds would be simply— wrong? I will not stand for such things.'"[20] A bit later, she refers to the dismissals as "'a sin as any sin ever was one.'"[21] Most significantly, she takes direct moral responsibility for the immediate consequences of her actions, rather than insulating herself within her role. She will not be a partisan for what she believes to be a moral wrong, because she cannot be neutral professionally toward what she opposes personally.

In all of these respects, and most fundamentally in the last, Miss Kenton implicitly anticipates the growing ranks of scholarly critics of neutral partisanship in the legal profession. Although they differ on details, these critics all agree that, with narrow exceptions like criminal defense work and other David-versus-Goliath analogues, lawyers cannot claim moral absolution for unquestioningly assisting their clients in unjust acts, however legally proper. In their view, lawyers should not merely decline to assist in such acts; they should also act affirmatively to promote justice in their representation of private clients. Accordingly, following one of its chief proponents, I will call this position "moral activism."[22]

Conclusion: The Moral Significance of Stories

Stories—especially long stories like novels and biographies, the stories of whole lives—are important to the study of virtue. Such stories remind us that moral decisions have cumulative weight, that action over time shapes character, produces virtue or vice. They hold up for us examples of moral success and failure, virtuous and vicious lives. At the same time, they hold up a counterbalancing reality, the mutability of moral life. They warn us that, to the end, we are at risk of falling from grace, and they console us that, even at the eleventh hour, we can hope to find it.

Stevens astutely points out that his father's generation was given to telling stories about professional excellence, whereas Stevens's own generation preferred general theorizing. What his own story marvelously illustrates, however, is the way the two must fit together. Stevens's signal lapse was his failure to interpret adequately the stories from which he derived his fundamental values, to apply those values in the moral dilemma he faced, and to see how they fit into a coherent whole, a viable whole—in a word, a life.

Our most fundamental values, like those of Stevens, come to us in the form of stories—stories of our parents and grandparents, stories of our cultural heroes. Beyond that, our most cherished moral heroes tend to be those who told and interpreted stories. The prophecies of the Old Testament and the sermons of Jesus are filled with stories; so are the dialogues of Plato. Curiously and significantly, our accounts of these moral teachers come to us in the form of stories about their telling stories, as metastories about reciprocally learning and teaching: one day Jesus and his disciples went out in a boat on the Sea of Galilee to a lonely place by themselves; one day Socrates walked with some friends home from the Piraeus; in the cool of the day, God sought out Adam and Eve in the Garden of Eden. From the bedrock of such fellowship, we are told in our most cherished stories, come both the cornerstone and the capstone of the moral life.

Stevens's story, finally, tells us something about whose stories we listen to and who gets to tell them. The stories I have alluded to just now, you will have noticed, all come from the Western humanist tradition. But the story I have been interpreting was written by a young, university-educated, Japanese-born man about an aging English butler. The dialogues in that story are hard to maintain because they involve others. Much of what made it difficult for Stevens to speak to Darlington was that Stevens was working-class; perhaps Stevens did not listen to Kenton in part because she was both a woman and a subordinate professional. Because they were Jewish, the maids were not merely ignored, but affirmatively dismissed. Ishiguro's story and the Western humanist tradition as a whole hold out the prospect that such lines can be crossed and the imperative that they should be crossed. If we are to learn from that story, if we are to be faithful to that tradition, we must try to cross them.

We Western humanists take openness to the other to be essential to our own moral lives. It comes as no surprise to us that lawyers have something to learn from butlers and maids; that we all can learn from a living English novelist of Japanese descent and from a dead peasant poet of Scotland; that we may learn as much from the louse on a lady's Sunday bonnet as from her minister's Sabbath sermon. We are saddened to be told, not that we have much to learn, but that we have little to teach. For we covet the epitaph of Chaucer's student cleric, reflecting as it does the inseparable reciprocity of Socratic dialogue: "And gladly wolde he lerne, and gladly teche."

This faith that dialogue—openness to others—offers redemption, personal as well as professional, also has, of course, its religious expression. Come, prayed a prophet greater even than Burns, in a canon older than the West: And let us reason together; though our sins be as scarlet, they shall be as white as snow.

Chapter 7

Legal Ethics and Religious Commitment

In this chapter we turn to the growing literature examining the connection between legal ethics and lawyers' religious commitments. This has been the topic of a number of recent symposia, as described in the Appendix. Here we sample just a few representative perspectives. Stephen Carter's contribution is an excerpt of remarks delivered at a symposium titled "Rediscovering the Role of Religion in the Lives of Lawyers and Those They Represent." Carter suggests that lawyers and persons of faith share a stance of *resistance* against the dominant culture. Echoing ideas we have encountered before but arriving at them from a different starting point, Carter argues that lawyers should resist the dominant cultural idea that lawyers' primary ethical duty is to get clients what they want. He suggests that religious principles might change a lawyer's view of her professional obligations in other ways as well, and he discusses the influence of faith on former NAACP litigator and U.S. Supreme Court Justice Thurgood Marshall and others.

Writing from a Jewish perspective, Russell Pearce (whose work we also read in chapter 2) explains that his faith commitments lead him to reject the separation of professional from religious morality and, much like Carter, to reject an adversarial legal ethic.

Finally, Thomas Shaffer, one of the most distinguished contemporary legal ethics scholars to focus on the connections between religion and legal ethics, applies a religious perspective in examining the moral questions involved in lawyers' representation of guilty clients. Focusing on both Judaic and Christian teachings, Shaffer sees an important, religiously based moral principle underlying a lawyer's willingness to represent those he terms "repulsive," such as murderers and rapists. He argues that the same moral principle does not hold sway in representing white-collar, corporate criminal defendants, and reasons that this moral distinction lies in part in the fact that lawyers who represent white-collar criminal defendants are likely to be defending ongoing conduct.

Questions for Reflection and Discussion

1. Do you think lawyers' religious commitments should affect the way they practice law? Why or why not?

2. Do your own religious or personal ethical views influence your vision of how you will practice law? Do you anticipate conflicts between your personal values and the role morality of lawyers? If so, what are your thoughts at present about how you may resolve these conflicts?

3. Do you buy Schaffer's distinction between serving as a lawyer for murderers and rapists and serving as a lawyer for white-collar criminals? Aren't serial rapists engaged in ongoing conduct, and might not white-collar defendants have committed a one-time-only act? Do you see any other relevant distinctions between representing a rapist and representing a white-collar criminal? Does a difference in the ability of the two types of defendants to find alternative legal representation figure into your analysis? Do you agree with Shaffer that there is an important moral intuition embedded in the concept of helping or representing the "repulsive," i.e., those who are shunned by general society?

Panel Discussion: Does Religious Faith Interfere with a Lawyer's Work?[1]

Stephen Carter[2]

What I do want to do is begin with what I hope is a respectful inversion. That is, an interesting question for me is less whether trying to lead a faithful religious life interferes with the work of a lawyer, but rather whether trying to be a lawyer interferes with leading a faithful religious life.

I speak not on behalf of all religions. I speak as a Christian, but of course I do not speak on behalf of all Christians. I am going to speak mainly about my own faith commitment and how that interacts with my work, although I will make some general claims about religions, or at least about Christianity, and some about religions generally, which my co-panelists are free to refute and point out errors.

In order to talk about the subject, I need to begin with a couple of very rough definitions. The first, and in a way the hardest, is "what is a lawyer?" That is, we are accustomed to thinking we know what a lawyer is, and I wonder if that is really true. We tend to think of the people practicing law as lawyers, maybe judges or law professors.

The question, then, is, if they are all lawyers, what exactly is it they have in common? One thing they have in common is they have all been trained in the law—that is, they have been through a professional training program in a law school of some kind—and they all, at least in theory, are bound by a set of prescriptive norms of their profession. Some of those norms are set out, as in the Model Rules and in other canons that bind lawyers; some of them are not. Some of them are simply general expectations of the profession.

But the idea that I am trying to get across is this: being a lawyer is being a member of a profession. It is more than simply knowing something about the law. It also suggests being bound somehow by a professional ethic, and I will come back to that point because the professional ethic that binds lawyers is an important part of what I want to talk about.

Now, I said that was the hard question, which means you must think that I think that "what is a Christian?" is the easy question. But I do not think it is an easy question at all. I just do not think it is a question capable of being answered.

When I say "Christian," I am thinking of perhaps a subset of the sociological Christian; namely, those who have a stake in Christianity, those who feel called in important ways to be different, those who will sometimes find themselves—maybe even often find themselves—in tension with various aspects of the culture they inhabit, even in tension with sometimes the requirements of the vocational roles they might play in society. So I am bypassing the definition of Christianity to try to explain the category of Christians I am thinking of. A lot that I say will be generalized and go beyond Christianity to other faiths. I just want to emphasize that I am not making any strong claims there.

Now, in order to come to my subject about this conflict, this question of interference, I need to say a couple of things about the nature of a democratic society and about the nature of both religion and law in the democratic society.

Weber, as many of you know, linked religion and law as the two great sources of legitimate authority, and I think that it is no accident that we continue to link them today. When we talk about their conflicts, when we talk about areas where they work together, I think we do so, in part, because we recognize that for a very long time, and certainly in a democratic society, that, while based on law, society nevertheless has a healthy respect for religious freedom, which means in part the religious flourishing of each individual. Are you going to have conflicts as each of these, law and religion, makes competing claims of the allegiance of members of society?

What religion and lawyering have in common in my vision, however, is only partly to do with authority. It is really to do with social role in a narrower, but in some ways a more important, sense. The role I have in mind is the role of resistance; that is, the role of resistance of the individual or resistance of a community to that which a dominant culture seeks to impose on it.

It has become very common in the literature on religion, both in theology departments and in law schools, to talk about religions as communities of resistance. I think that is a healthy discussion, a healthy direction in which to move.

Democracies, after all, need their communities of resistance because democracies thrive not on voting but on dialogue, on discussions among citizens. That is what the process of self-government requires.

If we are going to have discussions, we must first begin with the notion that we are going to have some differences. That is not to say we would have no commonalities—here I agree with John Courtney Murray that before we can disagree, first we must figure out what we agree on—and yet, there are going to be sharp differences in any democratic society, and we should welcome those differences. We should embrace them. We should hope that we never try to standardize our citizens to the point where everybody thinks the same way, values the same things, or has the same ideas.

One of the great and important features of religion in a democracy is precisely its ability to spark in its adherents different visions of the meaning of life, different understandings of what is important.

Now let me drop a footnote. I am not saying that the reason to be religious is to get a different understanding of the world. I am not saying that the only reason to value religion in a democracy is because of its ability to spark resistance. I am saying that the ability to spark resistance is one important reason, and a very important reason, to value religion in a democracy.

Because religions making their own claims of truth will then potentially put themselves at variance with the claims made by a variety of dominant forces in the culture, whether government or nongovernmental forces, religions tend to resist, at least at their best.

Christianity, in particular, has been at its best when it has resisted and at its worst when it has decided to make itself a pillar of the status quo. It has been, you might say, more purely Christian when it is recognized itself as creating a different set of meanings than those that others might prefer.

What does all this have to do with religion in the life of a lawyer? Well, I would argue that lawyering—and this is why I define lawyering as the lawyering profession—can potentially play a similar role, a similar resisting, subversive role in a culture. I am not referring to law as playing this role, law being simply the product of governance. I am referring to lawyering, the activities day-to-day of the members of the legal profession.

You see, it strikes me that in order for a profession to be a profession, to be a group with distinct norms and a strong claim to self-governance, the profession itself must be willing to say, "We are different; being a lawyer makes me a different person than I would be were I not a lawyer."

That is not to say that it is easy to predict exactly the ways in which I will be different, but it strikes me that it is important for lawyers to assert that difference. It is important for lawyers, it seems to me, to assert allegiance to a morally admirable ethic that makes a strong claim on us, that in turn makes us different from other people.

The alternative for lawyers is to not resist, to yield to the same cultural forces that buffet everybody else. There is a line from one of my favorite theologians, controversial though he may sometimes be, David Tracy, who has written:

> The strange embrace of modern science, technology, and industrialism throughout the world has helped to render the present time for many an empty time, bereft of memory, free of hope, powerless to resist. The consumerism of our age is a relentless attack on the soul of every individual and every tradition.[3]

Now, Tracy was writing this particularly in the context of the religions. But think for a moment about law. When we think of the consumerism of our age, I think particularly about the pervasive ethic of our time, the ethic of "I ought to be able to get what I want and you ought not to be able to stop me."

I am fond of saying—I do think it is true—that Democrats and Republicans today tend to run for office on exactly the same platform. The platform is: "Vote for me and I will give you exactly what you want, make sure the people you do not like do not get what they want, and it will cost you nothing either way." That is the platform of both political parties pretty much today. Political parties do not ask us to do anything hard, anything sacrificial, anything to divert us from this dominant cultural norm of "I ought to be able to get what I want."

Lawyers are in the client service business, and so many lawyers conceptualize the role as "my goal is to help the client get what the client wants." We learn this in law school. I certainly heard this in the practice of corporate law. "Carter," I was told by a partner who was relentlessly trashing one of my memos—which was not a very good memo and deserved to be trashed, but he could have left off before he got to this point—"the problem is you are not thinking like a lawyer. It is not your job to throw up obstacles in the client's path. It is your job to identify potential obstacles and help the client figure out how to get around them. The lawyer's job is to say 'yes' to the client, not to say 'no' to the client."

Well, that did not scare me at the time as much as it should have, but it scares me a lot now to think that I am in a law school teaching students who will go out and encounter a partner who will tell them "your job is to help the client get what the client wants."

The lawyers will often point to the rules, the ethical rules, where we discover—and we could all recite it, almost from our first days of law school—that the lawyer's job is "zealous advocacy within the bounds of the law." But what is interesting about that ethic is how recent a vision of lawyering it is. This is not the traditional vision of the lawyer. This is a middle-of-the-twentieth-century, bureaucratic definition of the lawyer that can be identified very closely with the rise to power of the American Bar Association as an entity.

If you go back to the nineteenth century, when there were no ethical rules, lawyers were writing treatises about legal ethics to try to figure out what the rules were. The treatises, if you look at them, are quite striking. What is striking about them is how far down the list of ethical responsibilities is what the client wants, often no further up that fifth or sixth, and nowhere any higher than third or fourth, among the lawyer's responsibilities.

The lawyer who says, "My job is to help the client get what the client wants" is, in principle, not different from the breakfast cereal maker who says, "My job is to help people who are eating breakfast get the cereal they want," or the automobile manufacturer who says, "I make the cars people want to drive"—not part of a profession, not giving any kind of adherence to a morally admirable norm, and not entitled in any interesting sense to self-regulation.

Now, in the field of legal ethics there is a story that I tell to try to explain this. It is a story about morality. The story goes like this: "Well, in a liberal democracy, the norm is freedom and what diverts us from the norm is regulation. And so, my job is to assist my clients in maximizing their autonomy. And so, when you think my clients are wriggling through technicalities, I am simply working to maximize the autonomy of clients, and that is a moral good."

That is the story in the legal ethics literature to explain why this basically consumerist ethic of modern law is morally good.

But what I would suggest to you, as a Christian who is also a lawyer, is that I find this deeply dissatisfying. As a Christian who is also a lawyer, it is not possible for me to give my ultimate fealty to a set of principles that say that what life is principally about is people getting what they want. Now, I quite recognize that to say such a thing is to cut against the grain of what modern America seems to be about, but religions have cut against the grain before, and I assume—I hope—will continue to do so.

It seems to me the Christian lawyer's responsibility is a higher one than simply to say, "My job is to help the clients get what they want."

Now, what are the distinctions in the rules? Let me first set out a plan for discovering those distinctions.

It seems to me that, for me as a Christian and for anyone who is a believing member of a faith, conflicts actually should arise often. There should often be situations in which I have trouble reconciling my duties to God with my duties to the service of my clients. The reason you should have them often is not a claim I am making about the substantive content of any religion; it is simply that if we live in a society that is not organized around the principles of any particular religion, as this one is not, and if it is important for religionists to be made different by the faiths that we profess, as I believe that it is, then there should be moments when these rub up against one another in ways that are uncomfortable, and it would be astonishing if the legal profession were the one place in the world that was exempt from this. I think it probably is not.

To understand the "not," let me give you a couple of concrete examples. I would say, first, there is a lot of literature now—it is a burgeoning subject—about lawyers and their religious faith, and does that interfere or not interfere. It is wonderful and very interesting literature. I am not going to take the time to poke into all of it, but I cannot resist poking into some of it.

In particular, I cannot resist, although I told the moderator I was going to leave it out—there is an article, which many I am sure have read, about being a Christian lawyer by Ken Starr. I want to read part of what he says because, whatever you may think of Ken Starr—and I know there is probably a mixture of views in the room on that subject—what he says is quite striking. Starr writes: "Above all, Christian lawyering means treating one's colleagues and adversaries with a profound sense of respect for human dignity"[4]—which I agree with. He continues:

> It means civility and kindness in interpersonal relations, even toward one's
> adversaries, even when they do not reciprocate. Turning the other cheek
> translates into not stooping to engage in sharp or questionable practices. It

means respect for truth and a singleminded commitment not to play fast and loose with the truth.[5]

I think all of these propositions are correct, beginning with the point about human dignity and moving on to the point about how we treat our opponents.

There has been a big movement recently in legal circles, the civility movement, where various states have been appointing commissions to talk about how more lawyers can be more civil to one another, and there has been some sharp opposition in some of the journals to this movement, saying basically "do not regulate me; this is how I do business; this is the most effective way to serve my client."

Now, I am unpersuaded that this is the most effective way to serve my client—it is an interesting moral argument—but I am also unpersuaded that you can really effect civility through regulation. But it does seem to me that in the concern about lawyer civility, there is room for lawyers from faith traditions that teach respect for others, as most do. There is room for lawyers to step forward and say, "It seems to be correct that we as a profession ought not to be engaging in activities that diminish human dignity, whether in the causes we represent or in the way in which we conduct our day-to-day affairs."

I was a law clerk for Supreme Court Justice Thurgood Marshall. Those of you who knew Thurgood Marshall, or know about him, know that he was a wonderful storyteller. And, as I assume you know, before he was a Justice of the Supreme Court, he was a litigator of civil rights cases, a very successful one for many years—he won twenty-nine of forty-two cases before the Supreme Court—and he litigated his cases at a time when there was considerable personal risk involved.

Thurgood Marshall was also a Christian and was deeply affected by his Christianity in his dealings with other people. Even when I knew him, and I knew him quite well toward the end of his life when he was watching the slow chipping away of his work by other justices with whom he had sharp disagreements, I never heard him say a harsh, negative word about anybody. When I say "anybody," here is an interesting point.

In 1954, when it became time to argue *Brown v. Board of Education,* the states that wanted to continue segregating shopped for what they considered the best lawyer in America, and that lawyer was John W. Davis of Davis, Polk, and Wardwell, an enormously successful litigator. He probably, by most calculations, not only won more, but argued more, cases than anyone in the history of the Supreme Court bar by far. Plus, he was no mere hired gun. He had a moral commitment here. He did believe in segregation.

So when I arrived to be Thurgood Marshall's law clerk at the ripe age of twenty-six, fresh out of law school, therefore knowing everything, I said to him, because he likes to tell stories, "What do you think of John W. Davis?" I waited for the fire and brimstone because this was the style of the 1970s, and I figured that was the way that we talked about those with whom we had sharp disagreements. To my dismay, what Justice Marshall said was, "John W. Davis? A great man, a decent human being, who just happened to believe in segregation." Now, this seems to me a splendid, almost sublime example of Christian love in action in the lawyer's office.

I told that story at a conference a couple of years ago, and somebody said to me, "Yeah, but what did he say in 1954 about John W. Davis?" which is a fair question. I was not there. I was born in 1954, so I was not there when that happened. I would like to think that the stories in the various Marshall biographies are true and that this civility really was a part of his everyday dealings with other people.

One of the rarely told stories about that era is how much good work got done because of back-room deals that Thurgood Marshall and some other lawyers swung with some of the worst segregationists, governors and senators of the era who would condemn the National Association for the Advancement of Colored People in the morning and go in the back room and make a deal in the evening—because, as Justice Marshall liked to say, "You could do business with them." He could do business with them, in part, because of Marshall's own enormous caution in not vilifying his opponents, in refusing to participate in that activity.

But this seems to me, in a way, to be the easy part—dealing with your adversaries and not lying. This is the easy part of asking how religion and lawyering, and Christianity in particular, intersect.

Let us deal with the hard part for a minute. Let us deal with substance. It strikes me that once we decide not to accept client service as the highest ethic, then it matters deeply to the lawyer what the client is doing and how the client is doing it. One of the hardest things for a lawyer in private practice to do is to say to a client, "You are wrong"—not "you are wrong on the law," not "you are wrong on the facts," but "you are morally wrong."

The textbooks about legal ethics are full of explanations, some of them very powerful ones, of why lawyers should not say to clients, "This is morally wrong." As a Christian, I find those explanations ultimately unpersuasive. That is, more to the point, what I find unpersuasive is the claim that lawyers have an obligation to participate in the client's wrongness without speaking up or trying to change it. It strikes me that it simply cannot be, for me as a Christian, that what Christ requires of me is to give my service to whomever will bid for it without regard to what they are actually doing.

The great legal ethicist Tom Shaffer has a story that he tells about this. Shaffer tells a story of his own days as a young lawyer in private practice. This was in the early days of the Kennedy administration, shortly after the president had issued the executive order banning racial discrimination in entities receiving federal contracts.

Shaffer says a partner called him into the office and said to him, "We have a client who is concerned with this Executive Order. The client says, 'I receive federal contracts in one division of my business. Do I have to desegregate the other divisions? I realize I have got to desegregate the one getting the contracts, but do I have to desegregate the other ones?'" The partner said to young Tom Shaffer, "Go research this and come back with an answer."

Shaffer comes back eventually and says, "I have researched the law and I think that under the Executive Order the client does not have to desegregate the other businesses."

In Shaffer's presence, the partner calls up the client and says, "I have got an answer to your question. The answer is that the law does not require you to desegregate all your other businesses, but morally you should because it is the right thing to do."

Now, this account has always been controversial in legal ethics classrooms. One of the questions that remains asks: Is this a right or a wrong thing to do? My suggestion is that this is actually the minimum, the very minimum, that at least a Christian lawyer, and I think a lawyer of a strong faith, ought to do. If you are going to take on the case, at least be willing to say something to the client.

But perhaps consider nonparticipation itself. Why? Because lawyering ought to be a resisting activity. Lawyering, like religion, ought to be an activity willing to stand apart from the rest of what society values—not trying desperately to say, "I fit in, I am the same as everybody else," but it would not be hard to say, "I am different from everybody else; I have a different set of commitments because I give my allegiance elsewhere."

This is particularly pertinent to the lawyer whose ultimate allegiance is not to simply a moral professional ethic, but is ultimately just to God.

If my ultimate allegiance is to God, my ultimate allegiance is not to my client. And when there is a conflict between the two, how can I possibly choose my client and still say I am a child of God?

This seems to me the conflict that a Christian lawyer and that most lawyers with strong religious commitments will face. But it strikes me that there is only one resolution to it. It does not mean a lawyer cannot be in law practice, it does not mean lawyers cannot make a lot of money, but it does mean that what lawyers must never do is say to themselves, "All that matters is what my client wants, because if what my client wants is wrong in the eyes of my faith, it is quite unclear how I can justify helping my client go out and get it."

The Jewish Lawyer's Question[1]

Russell G. Pearce[2]

In his essay "The Holy Way: A Word to the Jews and to the Nations,"[3] Martin Buber declares the "modern thinking" embodied in professionalism's separation of the religious self from the professional self to be "totally un-Jewish."[4] In contrast to the professional ideal, "the world of true Judaism is the world of a unified life on earth." Buber observes that "man can do justice to the relation to God that has been given to him only by actualizing God in the world in accordance with his ability and the measure of each day, daily."[5] The separation of work from religion, like the separation of "holiness-through-works from holiness by grace," is "alien" to Judaism.[6]

In this regard, Buber's observation has roots in traditional Jewish thinking. Godly actions have been a necessary part of being a religious Jew. The portion of the Torah called The Life of Holiness enjoins Jews to be holy as God is holy,[7] and requires, among other things, that you leave "the gleanings of your harvest . . . for the poor and the stranger,"[8] "love your neighbor as yourself,"[9] and treat "the stranger who resides with you . . . as one of your citizens."[10] Similarly, the prophets remind us that faith and prayer alone are not sufficient service to God. The prophet Isaiah, for example, told the people that God would not listen to their prayers until they began to "devote yourselves to justice; aid the wronged; uphold the rights of the orphan; and defend the cause of the widow."[11]

The understanding of Judaism as a way of life is common to the diverse strains of modern Jewish thought. According to eminent Reform Jewish theologian Rabbi Leo Baeck, a Jew "directs him[- or her-] self toward God in such a way that no part of his [or her] life is without this center, without this contact."[12] The great Conservative theologian Rabbi Abraham Joshua Heschel similarly taught that "the meaning of redemption is to reveal the holy that is concealed, to disclose the divine that is suppressed.

Every person is called upon to be a redeemer, and redemption takes place every moment, every day." The eminent Orthodox scholar Rabbi Joseph B. Soloveitchik also instructed that the Halakhah "penetrates into every nook and cranny of life. The marketplace, the street, the factory, the house, the meeting place, the banquet hall, all constitute the backdrop for the religious life."[13]

Jewish tradition therefore contains the framework for a version of Jewish lawyering radically different in premise from that underlying the professional project.

Within the Jewish community, I take an expressly pluralist perspective. As a Reform Jew, I respect "the right of individual Jews to make the final decision as to what constitutes Jewish belief and practice for them."[14] In that spirit, and following the teaching that Judaism is a way of life, I offer my own answer-in-progress to the Jewish question. The answer is at once both directly contrary to, and substantially compatible with, the prevailing conception of the lawyer's role.

In the epigram to this essay, the Baal Shem Tov reproaches his student the Maggid of Mezeritch for reading without "soul." If one can read with soul, one can surely lawyer with "soul." As Abraham Joshua Heschel taught, "it is not enough to do the mitzvah; one must live what he does. . . . When the soul is dull, the mitzvah is a shell."[15] Heschel describes the integration of soul into act as Kavvanah, "direction to God. . . . It is the act of bringing together the scattered forces of the self; the participation of heart and soul, not only of will and mind." Interestingly, Heschel expressly calls for us to bring God into the legal system. He writes that "God will return to us when we shall be willing to let Him into all parts of our lives, including into our courts."

Such a kavvanah of lawyering demands a rejection of the professional project's separation of the professional from the religious self. As a Jewish lawyer, I would direct my heart toward God in every moment of my legal practice. This task requires study and prayer, but it also requires conduct. As Rabbi Leib, son of Sarah, taught, a Jewish lawyer (like all Jews) "should see to it that all his [or her] actions are a Torah."[16]

But how exactly to fulfill this goal is far from clear. As discussed above, this lack of clarity results in part from Jewish tradition's hostility to a lawyer's zealous representation of a client. As a result, those who try to derive a Jewish ethic for a modern lawyer have to look beyond legal ethics to construct explanations of why adversarial legal conduct is appropriate. For example, in two of the few articles discussing Jewish approaches to legal ethics, Rabbis Alfred Cohen[17] and Gordon Tucker[18] examine the extent of a professional's duty of confidentiality when a client poses threat of harm to a non-client. Both applied the principle that halakhah requires putting the interests of the community above that of the individual. In the application of this principle to the problem of confidentiality, their analysis diverged. Rabbi Tucker argued that the good of the community requires revealing confidences to protect a non-client from physical or financial harm even though the individual client will suffer detriment. In contrast, while advising consultation with halakhic authority, Rabbi Cohen asserted that "it may be that maintaining professional secrecy is so absolutely integral to the proper function of that profession and the profession so essential to the welfare of society that the halacha would decide that the practitioner must maintain his professional secrets."

In legal ethics, therefore, as in many modern moral questions, the Jewish response is not self-evident. For the Jewish lawyer, legal ethics becomes a subject for Jewish study and reflection. But while recognizing the vital importance of further study, we can find in our tradition foundational principles that on their face not only harmonize with, but require dedication to, the best aspirations of our legal system. Recognizing the risk of oversimplifying our often complicated and sometimes contradictory tradition, I will tentatively suggest two such principles.

One principle is equal justice under law. The Torah's command "justice, justice, shall you pursue" requires the creation of a just legal system.[19] While the Torah was not speaking of a political system like our own, it does suggest attributes of justice that are applicable today. One such principle is equal justice under law. Decisions should "not favor the poor or show deference to the rich."[20] The "stranger who resides with you shall be to you as one of your citizens."[21] Another such principle is concern for the poor and powerless. Proverbs instructs judges to "open thy mouth for the dumb"[22] and "plead the cause of the poor and needy."[23]

These principles suggest that the conduct of the Jewish lawyer in upholding the rule of law and in serving the poor could be quite consistent with professional ideals. What differentiates this perspective from the simple equation of Jewish and professional values is that its foundation is Jewish values that may overlap with professional values, but will not necessarily do so.

So long as the Jewish lawyer seeks equal justice under law from a religious perspective, she will reject the professional project but not equal justice under law. As I have argued elsewhere, religious lawyering's rejection of the professional project does not necessarily undermine rule of law. Acceptance of personal identity rather than a professionally neutral role suggests a different way to think about realizing the goal. Instead of trying to "bleach out" difference, we should try to "create community" by speaking frankly about how to realize a legal system that results in equal justice given our differences and our similarities.[24] This indeed is very much the task of the Jewish lawyer. As Buber teaches, "holiness is true community with God and true community with human beings, both in one."[25]

Should a Christian Lawyer
Serve the Guilty?[1]

Thomas L. Shaffer[2]

People who teach or practice law are in some ways like public executioners or the Air Force officers who watch over the buttons that will send nuclear missiles into action: other people, ordinary people, want to know what we do to overcome what seem to ordinary people to be moral obstacles to doing what we do.

What ordinary people say to lawyers, and what my students say when they first come to law school, when they are still more ordinary people than they are law students, is this: how can lawyers lend their skills and talents to the representation of people who harm society?

The reason that question keeps coming up is that the answers given to it by the American legal profession are not sensible. An example: at least since about 1850 the American legal profession, when asked why lawyers represent guilty people, has said that guilty people aren't really guilty. "Guilt" is a lawyer's word; it means the judgment pronounced by the state on someone accused of crime. In our system, it means the judgment pronounced by a judge and jury after the accused person has been given what we call a fair trial.

One of the things "fair trial" means is a trial at which the accused person has a lawyer on his side. Therefore, this answer goes, no one is guilty until he has been found guilty after he has had a lawyer's help. So one of our official professional ways of answering the old, old question is to say that the person who asks the question doesn't understand what guilt means. The problem with this traditional answer is that ordinary people who are not easily intimidated by lawyers will say that they do know what guilt is. They don't have to wait for the state to certify it. Dirty Harry knows what guilt is. So did Captain Furillo of *Hill Street Blues.* So do you. There are cases of doubt, of course, but in cases that cause ordinary people to ask lawyers the old, old question, there is not doubt. Someone has murdered an old woman or raped a child or poured noxious poison into the river. It is obvious that the deed was done, and obvious who did it. You can tell because the first thing the guilty party says to himself is, "Gee, I am in trouble. I better get myself a good lawyer." Good lawyer means clever, resourceful lawyer, "someone who can get me off."

And so the guilty person gets a clever lawyer, and the clever lawyer does his best, and the culprit avoids being certified as guilty by the state, which means that he is restored to civilized society, there no doubt to continue his evil career. Ordinary people know what they're talking about when they ask law teachers: how can lawyers help guilty people?

Another of our official professional answers says that lawyers may serve the guilty because the state, the "system," needs them to do it. You can't punish the guilty if you don't give them a fair trial first. You can't have a fair trial unless the guilty person has a lawyer to help him. Therefore you need lawyers. The state needs lawyers. Lawyers do not, after all, serve guilty people; they serve the state. As I once argued to myself, when I defended a member of the American Nazi Party,[3] I am not lending my skill and talents to organized hate: I am not serving evil; I am serving the Constitution.

I decided later that that answer won't do. Service to the state—even service to the Constitution—will not excuse service to evil. Surely that is clear in terms of ordinary morality. Ordinary people understand ordinary morality; that's why they are not persuaded by this second official professional answer to the old, old question.

To say, though, that the legal profession's official answers to the old, old question are fatuous is not to say that there is no answer. My concern for most of the last twenty years has been to see if I can work out sensible answers to old, old questions in legal ethics, and particularly to see if I can do this within the context of the story of Israel and of the Cross—the story of Jews and Christians.

On this question of guilty clients, which is the oldest of the old, old questions for lawyers, I have found it useful to make some distinctions. I make distinctions because I am a Roman Catholic. My peculiar branch of the Hebraic tradition includes the medieval Scholastics, who have taken a lot of grief for their hair-splitting and counting angels on the points of pins, but the Scholastics had a useful canon for argument: never deny, they said; seldom affirm; always distinguish. I have some distinctions I want to make, now, on this old, old question of lawyers serving the guilty.

The first distinction is between being guilty and being repulsive. The second is between being guilty and being punished. And the third is between being faithful and being loyal.

The Distinction between Being Guilty and Being Repulsive

The first thing you notice when you think about repulsive people, as distinguished from guilty people, and when you do this thinking in the light of the Gospel, is that Jesus of Nazareth seemed to prefer the repulsive. He went to parties with tax collectors, who were the first-century equivalents of twentieth-century bosses of organized crime. He was generous to prostitutes, thieves, Samaritans, and Roman army officers. He seemed always to turn toward the repulsive—for his meals, when he took a drink of water, when he wanted to give a lesson about prayer to his fellow Pharisees, and even while he was being tortured to death in the name of the law. That fact from the Gospel and parallel curiosities one could assemble from the moral teachings of the Rabbis don't answer the question of how a lawyer who is also a Jew or a Christian can serve the guilty—but those images from Scripture give us fair warning that the answer is not as simple as either lawyers or ordinary people think.

It is not a bad thing that society regards certain people as repulsive. No human institution or community could exist unless we did. All of our communities define themselves by excluding repulsive people. Our institutions—institutions such as the criminal law, the courts, the legal profession—serve this elementary and essential need that the community has: they assist in locating and identifying in a public way those who cannot be members of the community.

In this way the Torah and the priesthood excluded from the community those who harmed society, from murderers and thieves to adulterers and people who had contagious skin diseases. Jesus of Nazareth did not quarrel with such legal institutions in his community. He honored them. The rules said that you should not touch a leper, for example—that if you did you became a leper. When Jesus cured the leprous man, he chose to do so by touching him. That meant, as St. Mark's Gospel says, that Jesus could no longer go into the town. It also meant that the cured leper should go to the priests and have his cure checked out, and that is what Jesus told him to do.

In the same way, Jesus honored the rigorous rule of the Torah that an adulterous woman was to be stoned to death. He did not dispense with that rule either, or disregard it; what he did was call for the witnesses that the Torah required before the stoning could take place. What he did in both cases was to turn toward the repulsive, to take their side, to be with them. If we take the Gospel stories as moral models, Jesus says to us, his followers, that we should turn to the repulsive, to those our communities tell us, for good reason, to avoid. The lesson says to separate the condition of being guilty from the condition of being repulsive. The Gospel gives no warrant for turning away from repulsive people, even though there are sound moral, social, and legal reasons for doing so.

The distinction between the repulsive and the guilty gives comfort to a lawyer. It doesn't answer everything that comes up when you think about serving the guilty, but it helps. I think, for example, of the time I was appointed by the United States District Judge to represent a prisoner who had been convicted of raping a five-year-old child. Guilt was certainly an issue in that assignment, but revulsion was a more serious problem for me. It was a problem for other lawyers, too. I asked a colleague of mine, an expert in criminal law, for some advice on the case. The first thing he said to me was, "Well, if you get him out, I hope he moves in next door to you."

Revulsion is an issue when it is absent, too. The best guilty clients—the ones we lawyers most like to work for—are not repulsive. They are college-educated, pleasant people who eat well, drive fine automobiles, take vacations without regard to cost, and are generous to their neighbors. They are guilty not of rape or armed robbery but of such things as price-fixing, securities fraud, water pollution, oppression of the poor in the Third World, and making illegal political contributions. These activities get a person into trouble, but they don't make him repulsive. In fact, the guilty who are not repulsive avoid getting into trouble more often than the repulsive guilty do. They understand, as the repulsive guilty do not, that lawyers are most helpful when they keep you out of trouble.

The case of the unrepulsive guilty is one we have to return to later, when we discuss the distinction between being faithful and being loyal; for present purposes their situation perhaps shows that being guilty is not the same thing as being repulsive.

The Distinction between Being Guilty and Being Punished

The interesting thing about the legal profession's second official answer to the problem of serving the guilty was that it involved turning to power, turning to the state, serving not the person of the guilty, but, as I once told myself, serving the Constitution. The interesting thing that the Gospel says about revulsion, as distinguished from guilt, is that the moral thing to do is to turn toward the repulsive person, to reach out to that person, to reach through his repulsiveness. It is fairly evident that we are in the presence of a radically different approach to a professional problem; but, even so, the scriptural approach to revulsion does not reach the question of guilt.

The second distinction I am provoked to by my Scholastic forebears is the distinction between guilt and punishment. Let's concede that the person the lawyer is serving is a guilty person, in the sense that ordinary people know him to be guilty. Assume a not-doubtful case of guilt and ask whether it is a moral thing for a lawyer to use her efforts in such a case to avoid the law's punishment for the guilty person.

I suppose the clearest case in the Gospel is, again, the woman taken in adultery. The Torah prescribes death by stoning in such a case. Jesus was asked by some law professors if they should follow the Torah and execute the punishment. Guilt was not at issue—not, at any rate, guilt in the ordinary person's sense of the word.

Jesus said, "Let him who is without guilt cast the first stone."[4] The story is often told as if its meaning was that we are all guilty, so why should she be punished when we are not? The professors were wrong to judge the woman. That meaning is sentimentally attractive, but it cannot be the meaning of the story. A civil order in which no offender was punished would be a chaotic civil order—no order at all. And, besides that, in this case, Jesus and the law professors were dealing with a bit of law that had been given to them by the Creator of the Universe. It is unlikely, even if it is sentimentally attractive, that Jesus was saying: "Oh, come on, fellows (wink, wink)—let her go."

Nor was Jesus saying that the punishment was out of all proportion to the offense. To a modern reader it seems to be, but a first-century rabbi would not have said that, because the punishment as well as the offense is in the Torah, and it is not possible to repeal the Torah. The Jewish tradition does deal with the problem of punishments being excessive. Jews, then and now, place an almost absolute value on human life. But you have to be a good lawyer to honor both Torah and tradition. And Jesus' professional ancestors, the rabbis who preserved and taught the Torah, were very good lawyers indeed. What they had done was to ponder the will of God in the Torah so thoroughly as to make capital punishment unlikely.

In capital cases, the Torah requires two eyewitnesses. That and other requirements made it unlikely—virtually impossible, in fact—that an adulterous woman would be stoned. What Jesus was doing, when he said, "Let him who is without guilt cast the first stone," was calling for the application of the law requiring two witnesses (who would be called upon to cast the first stones). When the law professors turned away, they were saying to him, and to the woman, that no one was there to be a witness. They had failed to prove their case.

Then, as you will recall, Jesus pointed out to the woman that no one remained to condemn her. And, he said, he would not condemn her either. She was free to go. She had had a good lawyer. She had been found not guilty.

And there, I think, you have a distinction between being guilty and being punished. There is no doubt that the woman was guilty; the story assumes that. But a lawyer, invoking legal requirements, stepped between her guilt and her punishment, and she went free.

The Distinction between Being Faithful and Being Loyal

I said I would need to return to the case of the unrepulsive guilty—the pleasant and generous people who are guilty of exploiting the poor, polluting the environment, fixing prices, and corrupting public officials.

It is possible to pursue this situation fairly far—to include business and financial activity that is apparently well within the law. It is not hard to imagine entirely legal exploitation of the poor; the history of industrial America until about 1940 is primarily a history of such exploitation. Most forms of environmental pollution have been legal, and many of them are still legal. The corruption of public officials is usually not a matter of overt bribery; one of Philip Marlowe's powerful antagonists once said, when Marlowe accused him of bribing police officers: "Don't go around thinking that I buy politicians or law enforcement officers. I don't have to."[5]

There is a lot of interesting ethical territory in there, but I am not proposing to get into it at first. I want at first to get into cases of the unrepulsive guilty: the commercial employer who has a tough time making a profit and who needs lawyers to help him figure out how to pay less than the minimum wage, or how to avoid his employees' legal right to organize and bargain collectively—have a union—and not get caught at it; or who, having evaded the law on wages or unions, wants to avoid punishment. The polluter who has undoubtedly polluted but who would like his lawyer to show him how to hold the public authorities at bay until he can make another year or two of profit—and then he will obey the law.

What makes these cases different is that they are continuing enterprises. The clients of mine that I told you about were like the woman taken in adultery or the thief on the cross: their crimes were in the past. The thief on the cross was dying; Jesus told the woman to go and sin no more, and I'm sure she did as she was told; my rapist had committed the crime [he was] accused of committing, or not. But not so the exploiter, the polluter, the price fixer, or the corrupter of public officials. They want lawyers to assist them in continuing to do what they are doing. The moral issue that is raised here has less to do with frustrating retributive justice than with complicity. The question is whether a lawyer should lend his assistance to wrong that has yet to occur.

The disagreement between ordinary people and lawyers on this question is the clearest of all. The ordinary, decent thing to do when you seem to be getting into murky moral territory—and I'm just sure your mothers told you this—is to get out. When in doubt, don't. Our capacity for self-deception is infinite; mothers understand that. If we stay in the murky territory, even for a little while, we will manage to persuade ourselves that it is all right to be there. The safe moral thing to do is to get out while the still small voice that is whispering in your ear is the voice of your guardian angel and not the voice of the fallen angel on the other shoulder.

The American lawyer's official answer is just exactly the opposite. Our official answer says that we are not responsible for what our clients do. We need not be concerned about what they do with the learning and skill they buy from us, nor for what we think they plan to do with what they ask us to do for them. As long as we ourselves stay within the bounds of the law—that is, we do nothing illegal ourselves—and do not advise our clients to break the law, we are being professionally moral. Our clients may use our advice to cheat the poor, poison the consumer, and ruin society. But we claim—and the law gives us—a license not to have to answer for our clients.

Here is where I want to distinguish between loyalty and faithfulness. If I am faithful to you, I may sometimes decide to risk your being annoyed with me and tell you what I think will make you a better person. It may not be what you want to hear, or even what you are prepared to do. But I would argue—as a teacher of lawyers who sees as relevant the scriptural morality of Jews and Christians—that it is part of the job. Another way to put this is to notice the way Aristotle defined the virtue of friendship. Friends are people who seek to make one another better; they are collaborators in the good. They are faithful to one another in their mutual interest in being good people. This is more than loyalty: loyalty takes the friend's side, regardless. Loyalty hates those whom the friend proposes to hate. Faithfulness is willing to risk disloyalty. Faithfulness is willing to try to influence the friend. Faithfulness is what makes it possible to negotiate the problem of the guilty client who wants my legal services in order to do something disgusting.

Chapter 8

Future Challenges: Corporate Power and Lawyers' Counseling Role

In this final chapter, we return to the ethical questions raised by lawyers' roles in counseling powerful corporate entities whose activities can affect both the physical and the financial well-being of large numbers of individuals. The two pieces included here both offer critical perspectives on the current legal ethics approach to corporate counseling. Both authors write in the wake of the collapse of energy giant Enron, Inc., which inflicted enormous financial harm on investors and the general economy. Lawyers were involved in several aspects of Enron's demise. For example, lawyers for the many law firms Enron used, including Vinson and Elkins (V and E), had drafted true sales letters for many transactions that turned out to be shams designed to bolster Enron's financial picture. V and E lawyers also conducted what appeared in retrospect to be an extremely cursory internal review in response to whistleblower Sherron Watkins's letter warning that Enron was about to "implode" as a result of these bookkeeping shenanigans. And a lawyer for Arthur Andersen, Enron's accounting firm, wrote an email that seemed to encourage—and in fact led to—the destruction of massive quantities of relevant documents after Arthur Andersen learned that the Securities and Exchange Commission had commenced an investigation.

David Luban and Robert Gordon both use the lessons of Enron as the starting point for critiquing current conceptions of lawyers' ethical responsibilities in counseling corporate clients. Each, however, takes quite a different perspective in his analysis. Luban, who is by training a philosopher rather than a lawyer, finds the source of lawyers' ethical wrongdoing at Enron in certain characteristics of human nature—namely, the tendency of people to derive their moral stances from the conduct and attitudes of the people around them. Luban points out that socialization into an ethical culture occurs incrementally, and he urges law students to write a memo to themselves describing their "bottom line" on legal ethics questions, to which they can later refer when involved in the pressures of practice.

Luban, as noted in the Introduction, is one of the founders of the movement in legal ethics scholarship toward a more morally activist approach to client counseling. His classic book, *Lawyers and Justice*, takes as a central case study the conduct of lawyers for the Ford Motor Company, who advised their client to go ahead with the manufacture of the Ford Pinto, even knowing that a design defect in this model would lead to scores of painful injuries and deaths each year. These harms would occur as the result of gas tank explosions when the Pinto was involved in rear-end collisions at speeds as low as 21 miles per hour.[1] An expense of approximately $11 per car could have repaired this defect, but cost/benefit calculations balancing Ford's likely liability costs against $11 multiplied by the millions of Pintos Ford had manufactured led lawyers and others within Ford to the conclusion that it should not take steps to fix the gas tanks. Luban argued, to the contrary, that lawyers' ethical obligation in this scenario was, in his words, "to put your lips together and blow"[2]—in other words, to serve as whistleblowers exposing the company's internal secrets in order to prevent serious bodily harm to consumers. In the new piece offered here, which has never before been published and is therefore presented in its entirety, Luban continues to develop themes concerning lawyers' personal ethical responsibility for the morality of the projects their clients pursue.

Robert Gordon, on the other hand, places his focus on the social-structural conception of lawyers' roles as corporate counselors rather than on their personal ethics in this role. Gordon first lays out the various arguments in support of the status quo conception that corporate lawyers should play a combined advocacy and counseling role. One of these is the *libertarian* view—i.e., that helping clients avoid regulation helps the economy. Another is the *risk-management* approach, which sees law as a neutral business obstacle rather than as the expression of normative commitments to which corporations ought to comply. Neither of these justifications was available to the lawyers involved in the Enron collapse, however; certainly, Enron's avoidance of legal regulation helped neither the general economy nor Enron's long-term business success. Instead, Enron's lawyers relied on the justifications of being mere *limited-function bureaucrats,* who knew little about the corporation's overall soundness, or being *client advocates,* who were ethically obligated to pursue their client's self-defined goals.

Gordon argues that none of these justifications can hold sway given the special characteristics of corporate entities. Returning to the historical models of corporate lawyers as statesperson-advisors or wise counselors he championed in chapter 2, Gordon proposes that a new, specialized ethics role be defined for corporate counselors—that of *Independent Counselor.* Such counselors would give advice from a sympathetic perspective to further corporations' long-term aims, but would adopt a more independent, objective view of corporations' conduct than corporate lawyers typically do today. Such counselors would assume that corporations wish to be good citizens and comply with both the rule of the law and its underlying spirit or public purposes. Independent corporate counselors' advice would thus be aimed at satisfying rather than subverting the law and would disapprove maneuvers such as Enron's borderline accounting practices, which had the opposite aim.

Questions for Reflection and Discussion

1. On the basis of what you have learned in the course of your legal ethics course, write yourself the kind of memo Luban describes. What kinds of ethical dilemmas do you anticipate you will face in the practice context in which you are most likely to end up? What today are your "bottom lines" —i.e., the lines you will not cross—with respect to these issues? (You may want to put this essay away in a place in which you can find it several years from now, so that you can go back and compare your ethical compass today to that you will have acquired after several years of immersion in a practice context.)

2. The issue of lawyer confidentiality in the face of client wrongdoing involving physical and financial harm to others was one of the most controversial issues throughout the ABA Ethics 2000 Commission process. After much debate and several votes, the ABA House of Delegates in 2003 approved a new version of Model Rule 1.6, proposed by the ABA Task Force on Corporate Responsibility, that creates a discretionary exception to a lawyer's duty of confidentiality to prevent "reasonably certain death or substantial bodily harm" and to prevent "the client from committing a crime or fraud that is reasonably certain to result in substantial injury to the financial interest or property of another and in furtherance of which the client has used or is using the lawyer's services" (ABA Model

Rule 1.6[b][1] and [2]). Would this new language have permitted V and E or their Enron lawyers to expose the accounting practices that eventually led to Enron's demise? Why or why not? Would this new version of Model Rule 1.6 permit Ford Company lawyers to blow the whistle on their client for its decision not to fix the Pinto gas tank design defect? Why or why not?

In your view, do the revisions to Model Rule 1.6 go far enough? Too far?

Making Sense of Moral Meltdowns

David Luban[1]

Every legal ethics teacher knows that the sexiest issues for the classroom are the classic problems of litigation ethics, especially in criminal law. What if an innocent person has been sentenced to death for my client's crime? What about brutally cross-examining the rape victim to make her look like a liar when I know she is telling the truth? What about prosecuting a capital case when the prosecutor has personal doubts about the eyewitness? Each of these cases presents a dramatic setting, with what seems like a clear moral choice confronting a lawyer. Do I or don't I? Should I or shouldn't I? The options are few and easy to understand; the information I need to make the decision is there in front of me. It's just me and my conscience—and, of course, my client, but in the end I am the lawyer who either will or will not take the fateful step.

The only trouble with focusing on cases like these is that they don't have a whole lot to do with the professional lives of most lawyers. Few lawyers ever see a courtroom; fewer still prosecute or defend criminals. Most American lawyers work in business settings, doing the legal work of business clients—work that has more to do with transactions than lawsuits. Once we turn from the criminal law cases to the world of transactional lawyers, things start to look much different.

Different, but not necessarily less dramatic, and certainly not less important. The fact is that, just as the criminal defender lives with a chronic source of moral difficulty—the guilty client whose interest is hiding the truth—business lawyers also face a chronic source of moral difficulty. For them, it is the client whose business needs require skating near the edge of the law, putting other people's money at risk to gain a competitive edge. Sometimes, these clients insist on skating over the edge of the law. We live in an era in which the name "Enron" may become as much an icon as "Watergate" did thirty years ago. Names like Enron, Worldcom, Tyco, Arthur Andersen—and, now, Parmalat—dominate the headlines. Business pages of newspapers have become crime news—almost as much as the sports pages have. Corporate giants crater the landscape around us. And the dilemma is, in the words of Geoffrey Hazard, that "honest lawyers can suffer the misfortune of having crooked clients."[2] The trick is how to avoid becoming a crook yourself. You may think that the answer is easy: just don't do anything crooked! This morning, I want to suggest that just not doing it is harder than it sounds.

Business lawyers work in organizations and represent organizations. When the clients are big companies, their lawyers work in large organizations, either big law firms or something the size of Enron's general counsel's office, with 250 lawyers. And, morally speaking, practicing law in a big organization is radically different from the criminal lawyer in the law-school hypotheticals.

Let's see why. To start with, the criminal lawyer knows that she is standing at a crossroads and facing a choice. Do I destroy that rape victim on the stand or don't I? The lawyer knows what's at stake, and even if her own mind is torn, she knows what options it's torn between. She also knows when the decision has to be made: discrete decisions come in discrete time frames. Not only that, the consequences of her action are reasonably clear, whichever way she chooses. And, in an important way, she owns the decision. Obviously, she has a client, so she isn't deciding entirely on her own. But once the client has said his piece, matters are up to the lawyer.

In short: she knows *that* she faces a moral choice. She knows *when* she faces it. She knows *what choices* are available. She knows *what the consequences* of those choices are likely to be. And she knows *whose responsibility* it is.

In organizational settings, things aren't like that. Decisions get parceled out among many people, and every piece of work is the product of many hands. Information filters in piecemeal, a little at a time. As a result moral moments aren't nearly as obvious. They aren't really moments at all. They don't scream out "You've reached the crossroads!" Changes come gradually, like walking in a very large circle. Not only that, the consequences of decisions are often nearly unfathomable. And, working in teams, it really isn't all that obvious whose responsibility any choice ultimately is. It may be everyone's or nobody's at all. All in all, the situation is incredibly ambiguous, far more than in the criminal defense dilemmas.

No one had a keener eye for the moral ambiguity of bureaucratic entities like big businesses than C. S. Lewis. Some years ago, giving a talk not unlike this one, Lewis warned his student audience, "To nine out of ten of you the choice which could lead to scoundrelism will come, when it does come, in no very dramatic colours. Obviously bad men, obviously threatening and bribing, will almost certainly not appear."[3] Instead, the problem starts the first time that your supervisor asks you to bend a rule for the company's good.

> Next week [Lewis tells us] it will be something a little further from the rules, and next year something further still, but all in the jolliest, friendliest spirit. It may end in a crash, a scandal, and penal servitude; it may end in millions, a peerage and giving the prizes at your old school. But you will be a scoundrel.[4]

And, if I'm right, you may never even notice.

Suppose, for example, that a CFO calls in an in-house lawyer, and a consultant, and an accountant, and says that he'd like to structure some deals that will help push accounting losses off the books. (Think Andy Fastow.) The lawyer may not know off the top of his head whether there is a legal way to do it, but that is what he gets paid the big bucks to figure out. The last thing the lawyer is thinking about is that an ethical rule forbids him from counseling or assisting in a client fraud. No one is talking about fraud. They're talking business goals. The lawyer, accountant, and consultant accept the business goal—making business losses vanish from the balance-sheets—and reason backwards to whatever complicated structure it will take to achieve it. So what if the law requires a proper business purpose other than sanitizing an annual statement? The whole lawyering problem is figuring out some way to package the client's goal as a proper business purpose, although that might require you to start drifting into the gray zone at the margin of the law. Transparency avoidance feels to the lawyer like little more than a formalistic game, not much different from tax avoidance.

The trouble is that transparency is what the law requires, and transparency avoidance bears an uncanny resemblance to fraud. By the time the smoke clears, the CFO may be looking at ten years in jail and the *Wall Street Journal* will be doing exposes of the deals. Or maybe not, as Lewis says. Maybe you'll all get rich. You'll still be a scoundrel. But, rich or poor, while the deals are under construction, from the lawyer's point of view it all looks like an interesting challenge, nothing more. Chuck Davidow, a

Washington lawyer involved in the Powers Committee's investigation of Enron, reports that when he talked with the lawyers about all the special-purpose entities that Fastow created, they were proud of their handiwork, not ashamed. Yet Neal Batson, the Enron bankruptcy examiner, has found legal malpractice and violations of fiduciary duty on the part of Enron's general counsel and two Houston law firms. All of it is documented in his final report, 200 pages spent unraveling transactions of such incredible complexity that even the lawyers who papered them admitted that they didn't understand what they were doing. Or maybe they were simply saying they didn't understand because it's better to admit that you were malpracticing than that you *did* know what you were doing and were committing fraud.

Enron isn't the first modern case of massive client wrongdoing. As a matter of fact, every decade for the past forty years has produced at least one scandal that lives on eternally in the ethics casebooks. In some of these cases, the clients were uncomplicated crooks who embroiled their lawyers in fraud simply by fooling them. But the current raft of corporate scandals seems to be rather different. In these, I suggest, lawyers went along with their clients because, fundamentally, they bought into their clients' moral world. They accepted their values, they shared their assumptions, and they fell into the same traps. If I'm right about this, the only way we can understand the Enron-era ethical meltdowns is by understanding the moral world that produced it. That's what I want to explore this morning. As I see it, there are four main dimensions that we need to examine: ethical, cultural, economic, and psychological.

Start with the ethical. At its simplest what we seem to have witnessed in Enron, WorldCom, Global Crossing, Arthur Andersen, Merrill Lynch, and the other high-profile cases of the last two years is an epidemic of dishonesty, self-dealing, cheating, and even outright theft—an incredible failure to honor the most basic rules of Sunday school morality by executives who people trusted to know better than that and to do better than that. Obviously, it's not the first such epidemic: we all remember the insider trading scandals of the 1980s followed by the savings-and-loan catastrophe. It won't be the last, either.

But what conclusions do you draw from pandemic business scandals? That is likely to depend on your overall outlook on business regulation. Those who think that our economy works best when executives have lots of power and discretion to make innovative, high-risk decisions are likely to favor tough enforcement over new regulation. Their view is that the fraudulent executives are bad apples in a basically sweet barrel. Whatever we do, let's make sure we don't kill the apple tree with a regulatory chain saw. Other people argue that the problem isn't a few bad apples but a system that allows gross conflicts of interest and cries out for regulation. Their view is that the rottenness goes a lot deeper into the barrel than the notorious bad apples on top. With a system that makes self-dealing so easy and so profitable, it's no wonder that basic honesty goes out the window.[5]

I take a different outlook from both of these. My proposition is that most of the people who brought us these scandals mostly have ethical belief-systems that aren't much different from yours and mine. I suspect that if you asked them whether they think lying and cheating are okay they would answer with an indignant "no!"—and if you gave them a lie-detector test when they said it, the needle wouldn't budge. I don't pretend to see into people's brains, but I'd be willing to bet that virtually none of the architects of these scandals—not the executives, not the accountants, not the lawyers—really thinks he did anything wrong. In that case, you might be asking what planet these people come from, but the answer, of course, is that we're standing on it. In their basic moral outlook, most won't turn out to be that much different from anyone else.

The fact is that everyday morality doesn't have settled principles for hyper-competitive, highly adversarial settings. For example, when the other guy fights dirty, can you fight dirty too? On this issue, most people's moral intuitions are conflicted. Even Sunday school sends a double message. On the one hand, we say that two wrongs don't make a right, and tell ourselves to turn the other cheek. On the other hand, we say that turnabout is fair play, we say an eye for an eye, we say you have to fight fire with fire. Take a legal example that I suspect litigators in this audience know all too well: discovery abuse. If the other side does it, can you retaliate? The legal answer is no. Rule 26 doesn't have a "they started it!" exception. But we all know lawyers who think that if the other side starts playing discovery games, you're hurting your client if you turn the other cheek. The legal rules may be clear, but the moral rules are anything but.

All this applies to business settings, because business is as competitive as it gets outside war. Take an example, the old Second Circuit case, *U.S. v. Regent Office Supply.*[6] This case presented the question whether it's fraud for salesmen to lie their way past secretaries so they can make their pitch to a purchasing agent, if the goods they're selling are high quality and the prices are honest. In *Regent Office Supply,* the government and the defendant companies stipulated the facts in the mail fraud indictment, and in effect asked the court for an advisory opinion on lies told by salesmen to get their foot in the door. The court made no secret that it was annoyed to be asked, as the opinion puts it, "to give approval or disapproval to the myriad of sales pitches used for various purposes in the diversified world of commerce." It was an awkward, embarrassing question. The court didn't want to condone lying, but it also didn't want to put the discount stationery industry out of business. It found the Solomonic solution: it held that deceit by itself doesn't necessarily amount to fraud, but then proceeded to denounce deceit as "repugnant to 'standards of business morality'." I suspect the judges on the panel understood very well that the evidence before them showed the opposite: that these lies were actually an accepted part of business morality.

I'm not suggesting that "everyone does it" is a legitimate moral excuse. Rather, I'm suggesting that there are very few consensus moral rules for highly adversarial, competitive settings. That implies a lot of moral uncertainty and ambiguity in a culture as addicted to competition as ours is.

This takes me to my second point, the cultural obstacles to dealing with Enron-type ethical meltdowns. The fact is that our culture loves the Fastows and Skillings of the world as long as they succeed. The explanation of success worship goes all the way back to Max Weber's classic study of the Protestant ethic and the spirit of capitalism. According to Weber, capitalism flourished in religious climates that emphasized the idea that business is a secular calling, just as much a part of the divine plan as religious callings. And in these religious traditions, worldly success was a sign of divine approval. Now I don't mean to put too much weight on the Protestant origins of American capitalism: 400 years and millions of non-Protestant immigrants have pretty much made that history a dead letter. But the residue remains, and it's hard to deny that Americans still tend to worship success and love winners. The lawyers who work for them are no exception.

More than that: I think it's undeniable that American culture has always had a soft spot in its heart for bad boys who break rules to get results, as long as they do it in style. A favorite Hollywood genre is movies whose heroes are a gang of thieves pulling off an intricate heist—*The Sting*, *Oceans 11*, all the way down to last summer's offering, *The Italian Job*. True, they're usually stealing from other bad guys, or going after the idle rich with more jewelry than is good for them. But they're still crooks— and we kind of like them. Almost as popular is the Hollywood good guy who breaks rules to get results, from John Wayne in *The Man Who Shot Liberty Valance* to Stallone in *Rambo* to *My Cousin Vinnie*. The main thing is that they have to be winners, and they have to do it in style. We're willing to forgive a lot when it comes to flamboyant rascals who also happen to be winners. Jesse Ventura parlayed a bad-boy image into a governor's mansion. And there's no denying that Enron reveled in a kind of high-octane flamboyant aggressiveness, where top performers got million-dollar bonuses and then joined Skilling for Land Cruiser racing in Australia.[7]

Having a soft spot for bad-boy winners seems harmless enough, but the flip side is a little uglier. As a culture, we don't have much patience with losers. If they did something wrong, we don't cut them the same slack we do for winners. Even if they were blameless, we aren't likely to find them all that appealing. In a fascinating series of experiments, a social psychologist named Melvin Lerner discovered that the worse someone is treated, the more likely observers are to rate the victim as an unattractive, flawed person.[8] Lerner suspects this is an unconscious attempt to ward off the scary thought that if unfair stuff can happen to her, it can happen to me. We unconsciously disparage the victim in order to find a distinction, some distinction, between her and us in order to reassure ourselves that *we* won't get shafted next.[9] I find this explanation pretty plausible. Whatever the explanation, though, the experiment shows unmistakably that we don't tend to find losers beautiful.

Instinctively, I think, everyone understands this, and the implications for business ethics are disturbing. Given the choice between breaking rules and winning, and being a law-abiding loser, you're more likely to win friends and influence people if you break the rules—especially if you can portray the rules as red tape crying out to be cut. No wonder that Enron executives took the most aggressive accounting positions they possibly could. Pushing rules as hard as you can in order to be a winner is arguably what our culture wants.

Now, this phenomenon helps explain the executives, not the lawyers. Except for a few celebrated personal injury lawyers, the bar isn't known as a haven for flamboyant bad boys. Of course, business law has its share of tough guys who would rather be feared than loved, like the famous New York City bankruptcy lawyer who sometimes grabs other lawyers by the necktie to pull their faces into convenient screaming range. But he isn't really a flamboyant bad boy. He's just a jerk.

The transactional lawyer's job is to keep the flamboyant bad boys out of trouble. The problem is that when a successful client is flying high, as high as Enron flew, you don't want to be the doom-sayer who puts on the brakes. A hundred years ago, Elihu Root, one of the founders of Cravath,

Swaine, and Moore, said, "The client never wants to be told he can't do what he wants to do; he wants to be told how to do it, and it is the lawyer's business to tell him how."[10]

So far, I've called attention to two important facts: first, the ethical fact that the basic rules of everyday morality don't have a lot of traction in adversarial or highly competitive settings; second, that our culture is more willing to tolerate stylish scoundrels who come out on top than honorable, rule-following losers. Hold on to those thoughts. We'll see their significance once we turn to the third major challenge to reform.

This is the economic fact that a capitalist economy always produces losers. In one way, this is obvious: competition means that some people win and others lose. But I'm pointing to something a bit less obvious. One of the fundamental puzzles of economic theory is why corporations exist in the first place. For a century, economists have pointed out a paradox: corporations are little islands of central planning at the very heart of the market system. Corporations are miniature command economies. Managers gather and process information, set targets, and give their employees instructions. That's perfectly obvious. What makes it puzzling is that we know command economies don't work very well compared with market economies. Why do big corporations exist, then, instead of dissolving into a federation of small independent contractors?

Nobel Prize winner Ronald Coase, the granddaddy of law and economics, answered the question in 1937.[11] Coase's explanation was simple and elegant. Even if free-market theory says that it would be more efficient to structure corporations as internal markets, setting up markets costs money. Sometimes they're worth it, but sometimes it's cheaper and more efficient to settle for a command structure inside the firm. And that's why corporations exist.

So far, so good. But the fact remains that centrally planned economies have built-in infirmities. The reason that market economies beat planned economies is that they're better at processing information and responding to change. The world changes faster than the planners can gather and process information. They're perpetually behind the curve. A central planning system simply can't respond the way that a decentralized pricing system does.

That's the lesson we have to keep in mind, because it's an iron law of economics that applies to corporate executives just as much as it applied to commissars in the dinosaur socialist economies of yesteryear. It doesn't matter how smart executives are, or how fast on their feet. The world around them is faster. Inevitably they set their quarterly targets based on information that's inadequate or obsolete. And sometimes reality catches up with them. The economy goes south just when they've placed their bets on a few more golden quarters of going north.

The problem is that a manager who's set an impossible target has usually put his boss and employees on the line as well. The sociologist Robert Jackall, who conducted one of the best studies ever on the moral world of corporate managers, points out that corporate hierarchies are almost feudal in structure. Ask a manager what his job is, and he's likely to answer, "I work for Joe Smith." Corporate hierarchies are networks of personal patron-client relations. Managers offer perks and protection in return for loyalty and performance. A manager extracts targets and promises from subordinates, and on the basis of those numbers makes promises to his own boss, who does the same with her own boss. When one of those promises fails, it runs the risk of taking down not just yourself but the people above and below you as well.[12] In a weird way, executives fighting desperately to hide their losses and stay in business probably do it in part out of a warped sense of fiduciary obligation to other people in the company. The moral pressure to meet your numbers, combined with self-interest, is overwhelming.

Jackall studied old-economy companies: textile manufacturers and chemical giants. How different are the new-economy companies like Enron? The details are different, but the pressure to set extravagant targets and meet them by hook or by crook was, if anything, even more intense. Enron was structured as a perpetual tournament. New employees picked ten other employees to rate their performance, with all the gamesmanship possibilities that that implies. In addition, management kept a database where any employee could comment on any other. At the end of the year, all the ratings were put on a bell curve, and those at the bottom were ruthlessly fired. Winners went hiking in Patagonia with Skilling.[13] The heat was on full-blast.

What do you do when you can't keep your promises and meet your targets? Fundamentally, you have four choices. One is to pin the blame on someone else. Claiming you didn't know what others were doing is the simplest way, but more subtle methods exist as well. For example, Jackall discovered a system of milking factories in the chemical giant he studied. A manager struggling to meet his numbers short-changes essential maintenance on the equipment. Eventually, the equipment goes kablooie in a very expensive way, but by that time the manager has been promoted and the meltdown happens on someone else's watch. Top management had little interest in tracking accountability, because in Jackall's company everyone knew that the boss got to the top the same way.[14]

If you can't pin the blame on someone else, a second option is to arrange things so the losses fall on your customers, your shareholders, your employees—anywhere but on yourself. Michael Lewis's classic memoir of his years as a 1980s Wall Street bond trader recalls that whenever it came down to a choice between absorbing a loss yourself and blowing up your customer, traders blew up their customers without thinking twice about it.[15] Enron's management dumped their own stock while locking their employees' stock in soon-to-be-worthless 401(k) plans.

Option three, Enron's main strategy, is to smear on the cosmetics, cover up the losses as long as possible, and hope for a miracle turnaround to pull your bacon out of the fire. Rational managers *should* know better than to rely on miracles. But look at the character traits that make for successful entrepreneurs: boundless optimism, big egos, a taste for risk, unwillingness to take no for an answer. Exactly these traits predispose executives to bet the farm on one last roll of the dice and assume that Lady Luck will smile on them. Surely the economy will rebound and grow you out of your troubles. Only sometimes it doesn't.[16]

These are the three dishonest strategies: blame someone else, shaft someone else, or cover up and hope against hope. The fourth strategy, obviously, is to accept that you've lost, take your lumps, and move on.

It isn't always fatal. During the heyday of the dot-coms, a failed E-business was a badge of honor on your resume, like a Purple Heart. If you were twenty-five years old and hadn't burned through your investors' money at least once in some failed E-business, it just showed you weren't ambitious enough.[17]

But E-business never-never land is obviously the exception. In real business, big business, new economy or old, failure is failure. In that case, given the choice between cheating, covering up, or watching your career evaporate, it's fanciful to think that executives will seriously entertain the last option; and unfortunately, the others are dishonest. Remember our previous arguments: a powerful strain in our culture admires rogue winners more than honest losers, and in hyper-competitive settings everyday morality doesn't give firm guidance. What we've now learned is that the failures that drive executives to cheat and cover up are built into the very nature of a corporation, which is a planned economy that can't avoid placing high-risk bets. Put these three factors together and you have a recipe for scandals. The conclusion seems unavoidable: the crooks, like the poor, will always be with us.

But none of this explains our original puzzle of why the crooks continue to think they aren't crooks. It also doesn't explain the puzzle of why their advisors, lawyers, and accountants were proud of their deals even after the collapse. Here, I think, social psychology offers an answer. The basic reason is cognitive dissonance. Whenever our conduct and principles clash with each other in a way that threatens our self-image as an upstanding person, the result is a kind of inner tension—dissonance. And dissonance theory tells us that wired into us is a fundamental drive to reduce dissonance. How do you accomplish that? Well, you can't change your past conduct. Instead, you change your beliefs. That's what fifty years of research have taught. In situation after situation, literally hundreds of experiments reveal that when our conduct clashes with our prior beliefs, our beliefs swing into conformity with our conduct, without us ever noticing that this is going on.

In one classic dissonance experiment, subjects were asked to perform a boring, repetitive task—rotating screws in holes of a pegboard. Afterwards, they were paid to tell the next student waiting to perform the same task that it was really very interesting. This is "counterattitudinal advocacy," known more colloquially as "lying." You might predict that the higher the pay, the more likely the subjects were to start believing what they told the other students. But dissonance theory makes the opposite prediction. Deceiving your fellows for little or no benefit to yourself creates dissonance, and so it was the low-paid advocates who internalized the belief they were advocating. That's what the experiments confirmed.[18] Apparently, when my own behavior makes me, in Saint Augustine's words, "a great riddle to myself," I solve the riddle in the simplest way: *if I said it, I must believe it; if I did it, I must think it's right.* All this, I want to emphasize, goes on unconsciously.

How can this happen? The answer, as any psychiatrist will tell you, is that we don't automatically know our own beliefs. Instead, we figure them out by looking at our own behavior. If I ate that piece of chocolate cake, I guess that means I like chocolate cake. If I covered up losses with smoke-and-mirrors accounting, I must think that smoke-and-mirrors doesn't really count as a cover-up. And what if this contradicts what I've always been taught and always thought I believed in the past? Well, I tell myself that only a fanatic refuses to learn from experience—and I'm no fanatic.

One surprising result follows. Most of us are inclined to think that the big problem in the ethics scandals is lack of integrity on the part of the principals. But if integrity means doing what you think is right, these men and women had integrity to burn. They got it the cheap way: once they did things, they believed those things were right. Integrity doesn't help very much when you're in the grips of self-deception.[19]

The problem is not simply that we unconsciously adjust our moral beliefs so they inevitably make us look good. Psychologists have also shown that our judgment is deeply affected by the people around us. Show a group of people two lines, and if eleven of them say that the shorter line is longer, the twelfth is likely to see it that way as well.[20]

The same thing is true with moral judgment, and that is the special problem that lawyering in organizational settings creates: you are always in the room with eleven other people. In the 1960s, a young woman named Kitty Genovese was assaulted and murdered in Queens, New York, with dozens of people in their apartments witnessing the assault. Not a single person called the police. The media were filled with dismay at this sign of social indifference. But two social psychologists had a different explanation. They conjectured that groups of people are usually less likely to help out in emergencies than single individuals are. To test their hypothesis, they had subjects fill out questionnaires in a room. While a subject worked on the questionnaire, a staged emergency happened, either the sound of crashing equipment and screams from the next room, or else smoke billowing into the room where the subject was sitting. The results were remarkable: When subjects were by themselves, most responded quickly to the emergency. But when another person sat next to them and failed to respond, they mimicked the other person and did nothing themselves. Evidently, we respond to unusual situations by first checking to see how other people respond. And of course, just as we take cues from the other person, he takes cues from us. We reinforce each other, sometimes in disastrously wrong beliefs. Pedestrians stepping around the body of a homeless man collapsed in the street may not be heartless or callous. They may simply be taking their cues from each other. The evidence suggests that if they were alone when they encountered the unconscious man, they would stop to help.[21]

The conclusion is disturbing. Our moral compass may point true north when we are by ourselves; but place us next to a few dozen other compasses pointing east, and our needle falls into line with theirs—and contributes to the magnetic field influencing the needles of other people's compasses.

The Kitty Genovese effect goes a long way toward explaining why no one blew the whistle on the corporate scandals. Insiders simply took their cues from each other. They saw everyone else acting as though everything was copacetic—and they acted that way themselves. But it's also important to realize that cognitive dissonance and the social nature of perception fit together. Both ideas are variations on a single theme: that the human conscience has a tendency to take its cues from the situation we're in, a situation defined partly by our own past actions and partly by the actions of the people around us. No doubt being wired this way served some important purpose for our evolutionary ancestors in the dawn of time. But it can lead to tragic results when we stumble into a social situation that seems to demand morally compromising behavior.

Nothing demonstrates the power of situations to distort conscience more strikingly than the famous Stanford Prison Experiment. Male college students were divided randomly into "guards" and "inmates" in a mock prison for a two-week role-play experiment. In less than a day, the guards began bullying and brutalizing the inmates, and the inmates started developing the depression, uncontrollable weeping, rage, and anxiety of real-life prisoners. By Day Two, the prisoners revolted and the guards put down the rebellion by blasting them with fire extinguishers. By Day Seven, the experimenters decided they had to terminate the experiment early before anyone was permanently damaged.[22]

The attitude changes in the subjects almost defy belief. One guard wrote in his diary before the experiment, "As I am a pacifist and non-aggressive individual, I cannot see a time when I might maltreat other living things."[23] By Day Five, here's what the same student wrote:

> This new prisoner, 416, refuses to eat. That is a violation of Rule Two: "Prisoners must eat at mealtimes," and we are not going to have any of that kind of shit. . . . Obviously we have a troublemaker on our hands. If that's the way he wants it, that's the way he gets it. We throw him into the Hole ordering him to hold greasy sausages in each hand. After an hour, he still refuses. . . . I decide to force feed him, but he won't eat. I let the food slide down his face. I don't believe it is me doing it. I just hate him more for not eating.[24]

The power of situations to wreak havoc on conscience is hard to believe—but, in experiment after experiment, the evidence is irrefutable. Consider the famous Milgram shock experiments.[25] Two people out of three will administer what they think are near-fatal electric shocks to an innocent volunteer if an experimenter orders them to. But not a single person who heard the experiment described believed that they would do it. Apparently, the situation takes over when we're actually in it. Give the shocker a teammate and the result is even more dramatic: if the teammate won't administer the next shock, only 10 percent of people obey the experimenter. But if the teammate goes along with the next shock, compliance shoots up to 90 percent. Conscience is affected by social pressure to an extent few of us would believe possible.

In a corporate culture, this incredible plasticity of conscience creates perhaps the biggest challenge to reformers. If you can't trust your own conscience to tell you the difference between right and wrong, how are you supposed to do what's right? Remember what we've learned so far: the stakes in business are high, the corporate culture puts out powerful cues, the wider culture reinforces them, and no settled guidelines about morality in competitive settings push hard in the opposite direction. It isn't surprising that the result is ethical self-deception on a grand scale.

It may sound as though I'm saying dishonesty is a social disease that's nobody's fault. That's not my intention at all. The goal is to understand, not to make excuses. In fact, I am not a great believer in the idea that to understand all is to forgive all. People make their choices under constraints, including psychological ones—but in the end every sane adult is still accountable for the choices she makes. We should never forget that not everyone gives in to social pressures. If my conscience lets me down, the fact remains that it's *my* conscience—not the company's conscience, and not society's conscience.

I believe it's customary to end on an optimistic note. My basic message has been that ethics, culture, economics, and psychology all pose tremendous challenges to efforts at corporate reform. Changing the rules of conduct for corporate lawyers won't necessarily change the conduct, because it has nothing to do with changing the ethos, the culture, the economics, or the psychology that make up the moral world of corporate America. People who think there are magic vaccines or magic bullets are fooling themselves.

But challenging isn't the same as impossible. Even if Wall Street does have new scandals to deal with, the insider trader scandals of the '80s haven't recurred. The savings and loan crisis is history. Messes can be cleaned up, even if we know that the crooks will always be with us, and sometimes they won't even realize that they're crooks.

What advice can I offer to lawyers? Is it really true that forces you are barely aware of can disconnect your conscience as thoroughly as the Stanford prison guards or the administrators of electric shocks? If the answer is yes, then how can anyone deal with forces they are barely aware of?

I have four suggestions. First, all the experimental studies suggest that cognitive dissonance disconnects the wires of conscience slowly and one step at a time. That's what C. S. Lewis suggests, and I am certain that he's right. We get cooked like the legendary frog who doesn't notice that he is being boiled as long as the water is heating up slowly. If that's right, then it's important to give ourselves some kind of warning. Set yourself some telltale sign—something that you *know* is wrong. Write down on a piece of paper: "I will never backdate a document." Or "I will never let a co-worker get blamed for something that was my fault." Or "I will never paper a deal that I don't understand." Or "I will never do anything that I couldn't describe to my dad while looking him in the eye." Pick your telltale sign carefully—and, the moment the alarm rings, evacuate the building.

Second, I'd like to take a cue from Stanley Milgram's electric-shock experiments. When Milgram debriefed his compliantly murderous subjects afterward, he asked them whose fault the shocks were: the scientist who ordered the shocks, the victim who provoked them by getting wrong answers on a test, or the subject who administered them. Not too surprisingly, the subjects usually blamed the other two. My advice, then, is to notice when you're blaming someone else. Right or wrong, the very fact that you're blaming it on the CFO or the accountant is a telltale sign that your own conscience is on the road to perdition.

Lastly, I want to suggest that a certain amount of self-doubt and self-skepticism is not such a bad thing. Moral meltdowns happen when the reactor overheats. There is a kind of euphoria that comes from working on big cases, big deals, for high-energy businesses and high-powered clients. I know from personal experience how intoxicating it is, but I think it's a bad idea to trust euphoria. My version of Socrates' "know yourself!" is "doubt yourself!" This is hard advice in a nation that admires self-confident, don't-look-back leaders. "Doubt yourself!" sounds like a recipe for neurosis. But without some healthy skepticism, the temptation to take your cues from the client-executive with the most hubris may be unavoidable. Icarus is a lousy role model.

I'd like to end with a better role model. That is Louis Brandeis, who was a successful corporate lawyer before he went to the Supreme Court. Among Brandeis's papers, a biographer discovered a memorandum he wrote to himself, entitled "The Practice of Law." Earlier, I quoted Elihu Root's famous dictum that the lawyer's job is not to tell the client what he can't do, but to figure out how he can do it. Brandeis's was rather different. He wrote: "Advise client what he should have—not what he wants." In the Enron case, only one person ever followed Brandeis's dictum—Sherron Watkins, the accountant who sent Kenneth Lay the famous anonymous letter telling him to beware the Ides of Fastow. It should have been a lawyer.

A New Role for Lawyers? The Corporate Counselor after Enron[1]

Robert W. Gordon[2]

Law and the Enemy: Libertarian Antinomianism

In recent years many lawyers have taken on the values of and completely identified with their business clients, some of whom see law as an enemy or a pesky nuisance. Such lawyers say things like, "Helping our clients is good because they create wealth, innovation, and jobs; while their adversaries, the people we help them fight, small-minded vindictive bureaucrats and greedy plaintiffs' lawyers, create nothing and destroy innovation and enterprise. We help our clients work around the constraints on their autonomy and wealth-maximizing activities."

I call this the viewpoint of the libertarian antinomian, because it rests on an express contempt for, and disapproval of, law and regulation. Tax law, products liability tort law, drug law, health and safety law, environmental law, employment discrimination law, toxic waste cleanup law, foreign corrupt payments law, SEC disclosure regulation, and the like are all shackles on risk-taking initiative. They interfere with maximizing profits, and anything that does that must be bad.

Law as Neutral Constraint: The Lawyer as Risk-Manager

This viewpoint is much like the first, but without the negative normative spin. Adverse legal consequences are not an evil, they are just a fact. In this view, law is simply a source of "risk" to the business firm; it is the lawyers' task to assess and, to the extent possible, reduce it. These lawyers do not feel a moral imperative, as libertarians do, to defy or undercut the law; but neither do they feel one to comply.

The outputs of law in the regulatory state are not norms that express views of right conduct or desirable states of the world, but simply tariffs on conduct. The lawyer objectively assesses the risks, then games the rules to work around the constraints and lower the tariffs as much as possible. If some constraints are unavoidable he "not only may but should" advise breaking the rules and paying the penalty if the client can still make a profit.

These two story lines were not available in the case of Enron, for the obvious reasons that managers were looting the companies for their own benefit while concealing debts and losses from workers and investors. When the lawyers and accountants outwitted the pesky regulators—who, had they known what was happening, might have put a stop to it—they were not helping heroic outlaws add value to the economy and society by defying timid convention, but enabling, if not abetting, frauds and thieves. Nor were the professionals objectively, if amorally, assessing risks and weighing benefits against costs of efficient breach. It seems not to have occurred to them that outsiders might find out that the many-sided trans-actions with special entities were not actually earning any real returns, but merely concealing debts and losses, and that when that happened, Enron's stock price would tumble, and with it, all the houses of cards secured by that stock. The company they advised is now facing at least seventy-seven lawsuits as a result of its conduct. At best, the lawyers were closing their eyes to the risk of disaster; at worst, they were helping to bring it on.

The lawyers have been relying instead on different stories, somewhat in conflict with one another.

"We Din' Know Nothin'": The Lawyer as Myopic or Limited-Function Bureaucrat

These are claims that the lawyers were not at fault because their role was limited: We didn't know, we weren't informed; the accountants said the numbers were okay; management made the decisions; our representation was restricted to problems on the face of the documents or to information submitted to us.

Many of these claims of innocent ignorance now look pretty dubious. Some of the outside law firms, such as Vinson and Elkins (V and E) and

Andrews and Kurth, in fact worked closely with Andersen accountants in structuring many of the transactions. Sometimes lawyers made notes that they needed further information or managers' or the board's approval to certify a deal, but signed opinions and proxy statements even if they never got it. Sometimes they expressed doubts about the deals. An in-house lawyer, Jordan Mintz, once even hired an outside law firm to look more closely into some of Fastow's deals. Ronald Astin of V and E repeatedly objected to some of Fastow's deals, saying they posed conflicts or weren't in Enron's best interests; but when Fastow persisted, Astin expressed unease to in-house attorneys or executives but not to the board. Moreover, in V and E's report on the whistleblower Watkins's allegations, Astin minimized suspected problems. In the end, the doubting lawyers never pressed the issues.[3]

Some of their claims of limited knowledge are plausible, however, because Enron never trusted any one set of lawyers with extensive information about its operations—it spread legal work out to more than a hundred law firms. If one firm balked at approving a deal, as V and E occasionally did, Enron managers would go across town to another, more compliant firm such as Andrews and Kurth. Even Enron's general counsel, James Derrick, had no means of controlling or supervising all of the legal advice the company was receiving, because the different divisions all had their own lawyers and outside firms. It is this layering of authority, fragmentation of responsibility, and decentralization that has made it possible for the chairman, CEO, and board of directors of Enron, as well as the lawyers, to claim that they did not know much about what was going on in their own company. One question for lawyers—as well as for senior managers and board members—is whether they can conscientiously and ethically do their jobs and exercise their functions as fiduciaries in organizations structured to diffuse responsibility and prevent their access to the big picture.

The Lawyer as Advocate

The classic defense of the corporate lawyer's role, both most often advanced and held in reserve if other defenses fail, is of course that we are advocates, whose duty is zealous representation of clients. We are not like auditors, who have duties to the public; our duties are only to our clients. Our job is to help them pursue their interests and put the best construction on their conduct that the law and facts will support without intolerable strain, so as to enable them to pursue any arguably legal ends by any arguably legal means. The paradigmatic exercise of the adversary-advocate's role is the criminal defense lawyer's; and the role is a noble role, both because it furthers the client's freedom of action and protects his rights against an overbearing state, and because it facilitates the proper determination of his claims and defenses.

For the advocate the law is a medium of action and discursive moves, an arsenal of procedures, and a field of argumentation and negotiation. Ultimate responsibility for determining the facts and interpreting the law rests with other actors and institutions—the authoritative decision-makers, especially the courts. The lawyer does not look for truth or justice, although of course to play his role he needs to know what courts are likely to say, and how far he can get them to see the facts and bend the rules his client's way. As one of Enron's tax advisors put it recently, speaking of the company's complex tax avoidance transactions, "The government is not going to like these deals. People can disagree on what works within the written rules. . . . If you know the rules you don't have to break the rules, you just use them. That's what lawyers and accountants do."[4] The lawyer is a specialist playing a differentiated role in an overall process (the adversary system) that will, if it functions property, approximate (we hope) truth and justice in the aggregate.

The advocate is subtly different from the other lawyer-types I have mentioned. Unlike the antinomian and the neutral risk-assessor, the advocate is not hostile or indifferent to law. Law, to the advocate, is binding if the rules and facts are clear and there is no plausible basis for spinning them. To put this another way, the advocate is loyal to the law seen as the outer boundaries of the arguably legal, the point beyond which facts and law can no longer be stretched. He will push up to the boundaries, and even to creative plausible extensions of the boundaries, but not beyond. And unlike the myopic bureaucrat, the advocate wants to know everything relevant to representing the client.

What is less clear and more debated about the corporate-lawyer-as-advocate is whether he has any obligation to try to induce his clients to comply with the law. It is clear that the lawyer may not actively help clients engage in what he knows to be a crime or a fraud. It is not at all clear what steps lawyers should take to prevent this from happening, to encourage the client to walk in the paths of legality, or to respond if the client strays off the paths. Most state ethics codes impose stricter requirements on lawyers than do the ABA's Model Rules—they say that lawyers who become aware of fraud, especially if it has been accomplished through lawyers' efforts, must try to get clients to correct the wrong, and that if the client does not comply, the lawyer may or must withdraw and disaffirm any documents he has helped to prepare; and if serious harm is likely to result, may or must disclose to relevant parties or authorities.[5]

In the post-Enron debates—as in the wake of past corporate scandals —the view of the lawyer-as-advocate has most often been invoked to resist rule changes that would give corporate lawyers positive obligations as monitors or gatekeepers of the legality of corporate conduct, especially by requiring them to report, if all else fails, managers' violations of law to authorities. Law firms and bar associations almost always take the position that such reporting requirements would turn lawyers into "cops," "snitches," or "informers," and thus pervert their function as confidential advisors and advocates. If clients do not trust their lawyers, they will not be candid and forthcoming with the information that the lawyers need to do their job.

But what is their job? One view is that the lawyer needs the information simply so that he can present the best case for his client as an effective adversary advocate, so as not to be sandbagged by prosecutors, regulators, or adversaries who know more than he does and have access to facts more exculpatory than the client may suspect. But another—which one hears just as often, or more so, from the corporate bar—is that the lawyer needs his client's trust so that he can learn about possibly illegal plans and take steps to stop them. The argument for confidentiality here recognizes that one of the lawyer's functions is to monitor compliance and head off wrongdoing—not just to put the best face on things if the client goes ahead and breaks the law. This function is (weakly) recognized in the Comments to the ABA's Model Rules of Professional Conduct:

> The lawyer is part of a judicial system charged with upholding the law. One of the lawyer's functions is to advise clients so that they avoid any violation of the law in the proper exercise of their rights. . . . Almost without exception, clients come to lawyers in order to determine what their rights are and what is, in the maze of laws and regulations, deemed to be legal and correct. . . . Based upon experience, lawyers know that almost all clients follow the advice given, and the law is upheld.[6]

This comment and the policy arguments against allowing lawyers to breach client confidences seem, however, to be among the few contexts in which the bar officially recognizes some sort of duty of lawyers to advise compliance with the law. The bar does not prescribe giving such advice as a duty, or suggest any sanction for failing to provide it. It fiercely resists attempts by legislatures or regulators to impose any such obligations.

And the bar does not help at all to clarify what would seem to be the crucial issue, which is what view of "the law," or "the bounds of the law," the zealous advocate should take when giving a client legal advice about a prospective course of action. Should "the law" in this context be the same as the "law" in adversary proceedings charging the client with misconduct, i.e., construction of the applicable legal regime as any arguably legal, even if strained, interpretation of facts and law that favors the client? The strong advocacy view of the lawyer's role says yes: in advising the client, the lawyer may look forward to the defenses of the client's conduct that an advocate might raise in future adversary proceedings (i.e., a regulatory action, criminal prosecution, or civil lawsuit) down the road. As long as those defenses of the conduct are colorable, the lawyer-advocate may properly advise the client to engage in the conduct. Of course, if the client is likely to lose despite the availability of a colorable defense, the lawyer as neutral risk-assessor must also inform the client of that risk.

Inadequacy of the Excuses

The Enron and similar scandals illustrate the limits of all these standard stories as adequate accounts of the corporate lawyer's proper role.

Despite their increasing popularity among practicing and some academic lawyers, the profession surely has to reject out of hand libertarian-antinomian and neutral-risk-assessment theories of its appropriate role and ethics. Both construe the client's interests and autonomously chosen goals as supreme goods, and law as a set of obstacles that the lawyer helps to clear out of the way. The antinomian ranges the lawyer alongside his client as an opponent of law, someone who sees law as merely an imposition and a nuisance. The lawyer as risk-assessor also views legal norms, rules, institutions, and procedures in a wholly alienated fashion from the outside, as a source of opportunity and risk to his client.

Some might dispute whether even ordinary citizens of a liberal-democratic republic may, consistent with their enjoyment of its privileges and protections, legitimately adopt such a hostile or alienated attitude toward its laws. People who participate in self-rule through the representatives they elect—constrained by the constitutional limits their ancestors have adopted in conventions or by amendments—and whose lives are mostly benefited from the restraints law puts on private predation and public oppression, should generally internalize the norms and purposes of their legal system and voluntarily respect and obey even the laws they do not particularly like.

Others might reply that so long as they outwardly conform to its commands citizens may adopt whatever attitude toward law they please. This response comes from our admirable liberal respect for individual dignity and autonomy, and the consequent reluctance to coerce the inner souls of the unwilling. Fair enough; but the pragmatic limits of this position derive from the sociological fact that unless people in fact internalize the norms and respect the general obligation to obey the law, they will tend to violate it when they can get away with it. That is a recipe for anarchy, because all law depends on voluntary compliance, on my willingness to keep my hands off of your property even when nobody can see me stealing it, and to report my taxable income honestly even though I know only one percent of returns are audited. Societies whose leaders and institutions have conditioned their members into contempt for law and its norms and purposes are plagued by theft, fraud, crime, unenforceable contracts, uncollectible taxes, valueless currencies, and general civil strife. Evidently, this does not mean that society will fall apart unless everyone feels that they must obey every law all the time. In all societies, people obey some laws instinctually, some willingly, and others grudgingly; and they ignore or routinely violate others that they think do not matter all that much. But a general disposition in most people to respect the laws and the purposes behind them really does seem to be a precondition to peaceful, prosperous, cooperative, and orderly social life, which is why good societies put a lot of effort into socializing their citizens into dispositions of general law-abidingness.

However one comes out on this broader argument does not, it seems to me, much affect the question at issue here: whether lawyers representing public corporations may confront the legal system as alienated outsiders, determined to work around it and minimize its effects to the extent it gets in the way of the client's projects. To this the right answer ought to be, unequivocally, no. I will discuss first the corporate clients, then their lawyers.

People who defend corporations' taking a "bad man's" approach to law sometimes seem to suggest that business entities should have special privileges—more leeway than individual persons—to game and evade regulations they do not like, because, as engines of growth, job creation, innovation, and shareholder wealth, they are heroic actors on the social scene, a breed of Nietzschean supermen, beyond good and evil. The taxes, regulations, and liabilities that government pygmies and plaintiffs' lawyers keep trying to impose on them, on the other hand, are often foolish and inefficient, the product of ignorant populism or envy or special-interest rent-seeking. This attitude plays well in boom periods, but it sounds a lot less convincing when defrauded and impoverished employees and investors are licking the wounds from their losses and looking to more, not less, regulation to protect them in the future. Anyway, it is basically an incoherent position. A strong state and effective legal system are preconditions, not obstructions, to successful capitalism, ones capable of legislating and enforcing an adequate infrastructure of ground rules creating stable currencies, defining and enforcing property rights, contracts, and rules for the transparent and fair operation of markets, and deterring frauds, thefts, torts, discrimination, abuses of labor, and harms to competition, health, safety, and the environment.

Of course, the laws in force are not always those businesses would prefer, nor are regulations anywhere near optimally efficient. But though businessmen running large public corporations love to grumble about the SEC, the EPA, and OSHA—and products-liability class-action suits—they are hardly in a position to claim that they are like Jim Crow southern blacks, or vagrants picked up and accused of crimes: powerless outcasts and victims. Big American business firms are not discrete and insular minorities. They have exceptional access to influence in legislatures, administrative agencies, and the courts through government advisory commissions, trade associations, lobbies, and lawyers.

Indeed, it is precisely because of their exceptional power to collectivize and command resources and employees, and to influence governments, that American legal tradition and popular opinion have usually concluded that corporations need to be more, and not less, constrained by law than ordinary citizens. If corporations cheat on or evade their taxes, the treasury loses billions; if corporations bribe politicians or officials, whole governments may be corrupted; and if corporations ignore environmental restraints, entire ecosystems may be wiped out. When it became clear that the financial statements of Enron, WorldCom, Tyco, Adelphia, and Global Crossing could no longer be trusted, investors fled the markets en masse.

It may be that a natural person cannot be compelled to internalize the values promoted by law, or to feel an obligation to obey the law, without violating his or her dignity or freedom of conscience. But a company has no soul to coerce, dignity to offend, or natural freedom to restrain. Nor can it be schooled by parents, educators, and peers into a general disposition toward sociability or law-abidingness. It can only have the character that its managers, contracts, and organizational incentives and the legal system build into it. It is a creature of law made to serve limited social purposes. Since we are free to construct the character of these artificial persons, we should construct them for legal purposes as good citizens, persons who have internalized the public values expressed in law and the obligation to obey even laws they do not like, for the sake of the privileges of the law that generally benefits them as well as the rest of us.

Nothing in this conception prevents the good corporate citizen from challenging taxes and laws he thinks are unfairly or improperly applied to him; or trying to change them through political action. But it does foreclose the amoralist's argument, that the corporation should be free to ignore, subvert, or nullify the laws because the value it contributes to society justifies its obeying the higher-law imperatives of profit-seeking and shareholder-wealth creation. If the artificial person is constructed as a good and law-abiding person, it follows that the manager who ignores or tries to nullify the valid objectives of law and regulation is not acting as a responsible or faithful agent of his principal, the good corporate citizen.

If the corporation should be constructed and presumed to have the interests of a good, law-respecting citizen, so should its lawyers (even more so). Lawyers are not simply agents of clients—they are also licensed fiduciaries of the legal system, "part of a judicial system charged with upholding the law," to use the ABA's words.[7] They do not have, as the dissenting citizen does, the option of taking up a position outside the legal order, rejecting the norms and public purposes of the legal system and limiting themselves to a grudging and alienated outward compliance with such of its rules as they think they cannot safely or profitably violate when their interest or inclination is to do so. The lawyer is, by vocation, committed to the law.

Toward an Alternative Conception of the Corporate Counselor's Role

The view I am pressing here of the corporate counselor's role is neither new nor unorthodox. It is in fact one of the traditional conceptions of the counselor's role in our legal culture, with a pedigree quite as venerable and considerably more respectable than the rival notion of the lawyer as zealous advocate or hired gun. It was regularly invoked by leading lawyers throughout the nineteenth century and surfaced as an express ethical standard in the ABA's first Canons of Ethics, promulgated in 1908:

> Canon 32: No client, corporate or individual, however powerful, nor any cause, civil or political, however important, is entitled to receive, nor should any lawyer render, any service or advice involving disloyalty to the law, whose ministers we are . . . or deception or betrayal of the public. . . . [T]he lawyer . . . advances the honor of his profession and the best interests of his client when he renders service or gives advice tending to impress upon the client and his undertaking exact compliance with the strictest principles of moral law. He must also observe and advise his client to observe the statute law, though until a statute shall have been construed and interpreted by competent adjudication, he is free and entitled to advise as to its validity and as to what he conscientiously believes to be its just meaning and extent.[8]

In the post–World War II era, a group of lawyers and legal academics—including Lon Fuller, Willard Hurst, Hart and Sacks, and Beryl Harold Levy—theorized, from hints dropped by such Progressive lawyers as Brandeis and Adolf Berle (who disagreed on everything else but concurred on this), the role of the new corporate legal counselor as a "statesman-advisor." The counselor represents his client's interest "with an eye to securing not only the client's immediate benefit but his long-range social benefit." In negotiating and drafting contracts, collective bargaining agreements, or reorganization plans, the lawyer is a lawmaker of "private legislation" and "private constitutions," a "prophylactic avoider of troubles, as well as pilot through anticipated difficulties."[9] The emphasis is on creative compliance with government regulators and labor unions, and on harmonious stable compromises with contract partners and the workforce. It is a vision founded on a very particular model of corporate leadership as the ideal business client, what we now call the "managerialist" model (Berle named the lawyer-executive Owen D. Young of General Electric as the exemplar of vanguard corporate leadership)—business leaders who had made their peace with the New Deal, accepted unions as the price of stability, and whose lawyers moved in and out of government and co-drafted regulations in semi-captured regulatory agencies. The vision also assumed the model of stable corporate law-firm relations that prevailed until the 1970s: a single firm composed of partners for life, who did virtually all of the legal work for companies that retained them indefinitely, rarely questioned their bills, and formed ties of trust and confidence with the senior partners. The "wise-counselor" vision of the lawyer's role found its way into the Joint Report prefacing the ABA's 1969 Model Code of Professional Responsibility and portions of the Code itself,[10] and according to Erwin Smigel's 1964 study of Wall Street law firms, had been completely internalized by the partners of those firms.[11]

Since the 1970s, this conception of the wise-counselor-lawyer-statesman has been in decay. It is no longer recognized by most corporate lawyers as a norm. It has almost no institutional support in the rules and disciplinary bodies that regulate the profession. Some academic lawyers still support some version of it; and so too do some judges and regulators. It resurfaces on occasion after business disasters such as the savings-and-loan and Enron scandals. The SEC, IRS, banking regulators, and the courts have sporadically revived it and brought enforcement actions in its spirit. Bar commissions on professionalism sometimes nostalgically evoke it. Yet even where it still has some residual influence there are no effective sanctions behind it.

My idea is this: that there be established a separate professional role for a distinct type of lawyer, the Independent Counselor, with a distinct ethical orientation, institutionalized in a distinct governance regime of ethical codes, liability and malpractice rules, special statutory duties and privileges, and judicial rules of practice. Clients could for most purposes decide whether they wished to be represented by counselors or ordinary attorneys, making clear by contract and representations to the outside world which role they wanted the lawyer to occupy. For some legal purposes, however, clients would be required to act through counselors. "Counselor" would be primarily an elective role that lawyers could move in and out of, could assume for particular representations or transactions or purposes, and then resume the role and function of regular lawyer. But it might also be a role regularly institutionalized in practice settings. Lawyers could organize law firms, branches, or offices within client organizations, consisting only of counselors. The counselor's role might eventually evolve into a distinct profession, one organized into separate law firms, or counselors' offices within firms or within client organizations.

This idea is only in an embryonic stage of its development. If it ever caught on as a practical possibility there would of course be many, many details to be worked out. Before that day comes, it hardly seems worth-while to try to fill out the fine points of what is at present only a hypothet-ical and possibly completely utopian scheme. So I will limit my job here to trying to spell out what I think would be the essential elements of the counselor's role.

The most basic is this: that the lawyer engaged as a counselor adopt an independent, objective view of the corporate agents' conduct and plans and their legal validity. This emphatically does not mean that the coun-selor must take up an adversary stance to the client, or an attitude of in-difference toward its welfare; indeed, as its lawyer, she ought to view the company's legitimate aims and objectives sympathetically and to give advice that will generally further those aims. Nor does it mean that her advice must be invariably conservative and obstructive, that she must be the unhelpful kind of lawyer who constantly tells managers that they can-not do what they want to do; counselors can and should be as creative as any other good lawyers in devising means to accomplish clients' objectives that will overcome and work around legal objections, and in devising innovative arguments that will alter and expand the boundaries of the existing law. But whatever advice the counselor gives, she should: (a) con-strue the facts and law of the client's situation as a sympathetic but objec-tive observer such as a judge, committed to serving the law's spirit and furthering its public purposes, would construe them; (b) impute to the corporate client the character of the good citizen, who has internalized legal norms and wishes to comply with the law's legitimate commands and purposes while pursuing its own interests and goals; and (c) be based on an interpretation and practical application of the law to the client's sit-uation that helps the client, so constructed, to satisfy rather than subvert the purposes of the law.

When the counselor asserts facts or makes a legal claim or argument to authorities or third parties—outside the context of fully adversary pro-ceedings where all interested parties have effective access to relevant facts and legal knowledge necessary to forming the opinion—they should gen-erally be facts and arguments that a fair-minded and fully informed ob-server could accept as plausible and correct. For example, if the counselor is giving a legal opinion on the validity of a client's proposed conduct or transaction, she cannot leave out important facts that might cast doubt on her conclusions, or slant the facts so as to obscure difficulties with the conclusions. If she is not sure that her client's agents have been giving her the important facts, or reporting them accurately, she has to ask questions until satisfied or refuse to give the opinion. In other words, she should give the kind of report that a lawyer hired to be an independent investigator and analyst of a client's situation would be expected to give. Unlike the Enron lawyers, she may not accept limits on the scope of her representation that would effectively prevent her from doing the counselor's job; nor may she permit her opinion or conclusions to be used to give cover or respectability to actions she has not really had a chance to look into.

The notion that the counselor's role has to be consistent with the law's public purposes, and should further rather than frustrate those purposes —and that she should give candid, truthful, and undistorted reports to authorities and third parties—does not mean that she must become an informer or enforcement officer. Nor does it mean that the lawyer has to accept regulators' or adversaries' construction, or an ultra-conservative and risk-averse construction, of the law's purposes: she is perfectly entitled to present an innovative view of the law and facts that favors what her client wants to do, so long as it is a view that she thinks a judge or other competent lawmaker would actually be likely to accept. But the conception of the role does pretty clearly imply that if a counselor wants to press on a client's behalf an adventurous, strained, or ingenious interpretation of existing law, or a construction of fact that an objective observer might reasonably think partial and one-sided and potentially misleading, she must do so in a way that flags the contentious nature of what she is proposing and thus permits its adequate testing and evaluation. If no effective adversary process and independent adjudicator is available to test it—not in the hypothetical distant future but here and now—the counselor has either to refrain from pushing the envelope or give intended audiences signals sufficient to inform them of the legal riskiness of getting involved with the plan. Technical, cosmetic, or literal disclosure or compliance that in practical effect is nondisclosure or noncompliance is ruled out under this conception. So is tax evasion parading as tax-minimization. So is trying to sneak a legally dubious transaction under the noses of regulators or third parties whom the lawyers know are too overburdened or unsophisticated or uninformed to discover the potential problems with it.

Is this idea for reviving the counselor's role an idle dream? Perhaps it is. But the status quo—a situation in which lawyers effectively facilitate or passively acquiesce in and enable corporate frauds, in the name of a noble idea of advocacy that has been ludicrously misapplied to the context of corporate advice-giving—is not tolerable. At least some corporate lawyers may wish to revive the ideal of independent counseling which has, until very recent times, been one of the most inspiring regulative ideals of their profession. And even if they do not, a society that wants its corporations to be good citizens, as well as efficient profit-maximizers, may insist on reviving it, or something like it, against their opposition.

Appendix
Suggestions for Further Reading

Introduction

Readers who wish to further explore the intellectual foundations of the critical turn in legal ethics scholarship should probably start with philosopher David Luban's *Lawyers and Justice: An Ethical Study* (1988)(which I was unable to include in this reader because of its publisher's copyright permissions policies). Similarly, William H. Simon's *The Practice of Justice: A Theory of Lawyers' Ethics* (1998) defines the field, as we further examine in considering one of his earlier articles in chapter 5. Robert W. Gordon is another "founding father" who is also highly regarded for his outstanding ethic of service in encouraging the efforts of newer scholars. Other founding mothers and fathers include Richard Abel, Derrick Bell, Gerald López, Carrie Menkel-Meadow, Russell Pearce, Deborah Rhode, Lucie White, and David Wilkins.

For additional literature documenting the shifts away from public interest law in many students' career objectives through law school, see Robert V. Stover, *Making and Breaking It: The Fate of Public Interest Commitment during Law School* (1989); Howard S. Erlanger and Douglas A. Klegon, "Socialization Effects of Professional School: The Law School Experience and Student Orientations to Public Interest Concerns," 13 *L. and Soc. Rev.* 11 (1979); and Robert Granfield, "Constructing Professional Boundaries in Law School: Reactions of Students and Implications for Teachers," 4 *S. Cal. Rev. L. and Women's Stud.* 53 (1994).

Leading work exploring interconnections between legal ethics and the process of law school education includes Eleanor W. Myers, "'Simple Truths' about Moral Education," 45 *Am. U. L. Rev.* 823 (1996); Deborah L. Rhode, "Missing Questions: Feminist Perspectives on Legal Education," 45 *Stan. L. Rev.* 1547 (1993); David Wilkins, "Two Paths to the Mountain Top:

The Role of Legal Education in Shaping the Values of Black Corporate Lawyers," 45 *Stan. L. Rev.* 1981 (1993). There is also a great deal of literature exploring the connections between teaching legal ethics and clinical legal education. One favorite is James E. Moliterno, "In House Live-Client Clinical Programs: Some Ethical Issues," 67 *Fordham L. Rev.* 2377 (1999).

A lively CLS critique every law student should read is Duncan Kennedy, "Legal Education and the Reproduction of Hierarchy," 32 *J. Legal Educ.* 591 (1982). Readers may also want to be on the lookout for a soon-to-be-published N.Y.U. collection of Duncan Kennedy's work.

An excellent scholar doing paradigm-shifting work on legal ethics and civil government lawyers is Kathleen Clark. See, e.g., Kathleen Clark, "Do We Have Enough Ethics in Government Yet: An Answer from Fiduciary Theory," 1996 *U. Ill. L. Rev.* 57 (1996). There is also a good symposium issue on the general topic, "Symposium, Government Lawyering," 61 *Law and Contemporary Problems* 1 (1998). Another leading scholar on the ethics of government lawyers is Bruce Green. See, e.g., "Must Government Lawyers 'Seek Justice' in Civil Litigation?" 9 *Widener J. Pub. L.* 235 (2000), and literature cited in Appendix for chapter 5.

The enormous questions involving lawyers' ethical responsibilities in the face of the USA Patriot Act and other government measures designed to curtail civil liberties in response to the current terrorist threat are only beginning to be explored by legal ethics scholars. David Cole has been an eloquent and outspoken commentator on the importance to lawyers and others of preserving these civil liberties. See, e.g., David Cole, "The New McCarthyism: Repeating History in the War on Terrorism," 38 *Harv. C.R.-C.L. L. Rev.* 1 (2003). See also Nadine Strossen, "Maintaining Human Rights in a Time of Terrorism: A Case Study in the Value of Legal Scholarship in Shaping Law and Public Policy," 46 *N.Y.L. Sch. L. Rev.* 373 (2003). Former government lawyer Jesselyn Radack was discharged from her position at the U.S. Department of Justice and threatened with criminal prosecution after she publicly disagreed with U.S. Attorney General John Ashcroft's position that U.S. citizen Taliban fighter John Walker Lindh was not constitutionally entitled to legal representation before being interrogated after his capture in Afghanistan. Radack has published a piece considering the ethics implications of government lawyer whistleblowing, "The Government Attorney-Whistleblower and the Rule of Confidentiality: Compatible at Last," 17 *Geo. Legal Ethics* 125 (2004). See also James Moliterno, "The New Politically Motivated Bar Discipline" (unpublished draft manuscript).

Chapter 1

Further readings on the sociology of the profession include the classics: Philip Elliott, *The Sociology of Professions* (1972), Elliott Friedson, *The Profession of Medicine* (1970), and Magali Sarfatti Larson, *The Rise of Professionalism* (1977). An excellent collection of writing exploring the ideology of the legal profession is *Professions and Professional Ideology in America* (Gerald L. Geison, ed., 1983). An article in which Abel demonstrates his commitment to an alternative legal ethics is Richard L. Abel, "Choosing, Nurturing, Training and Placing Public Interest Law Students," 70 *Fordham L. Rev.* 1563 (2002) (discussing the need to create alternative prestige hierarchies to encourage students to go into public interest law).

Another major article by Wilkins on professional regulation is David B. Wilkins, "Legal Realism for Lawyers," 104 *Harv. L. Rev.* 468 (1990). For pioneering critical work on the history, effects, and purposes of the bar's unauthorized practice restrictions, see Deborah L. Rhode, "Policing the Professional Monopoly: A Constitutional and Empirical Analysis of Unauthorized Practice Prohibitions," 34 *Stan. L. Rev.* 1 (1981).

A few examples of the work of newer scholars who are investigating the implications of professional ideology from varying perspectives include Tanina Rostain, "Ethics Lost: Limitations of Current Approaches to Lawyer Regulation," 71 *S. Cal. L. Rev.* 1273 (1998); Susan G. Kupfer, "Authentic Legal Practices," 10 *Geo. J. Legal Ethics* 33 (1996); Amy R. Mashburn, "Professionalism as Class Ideology: Civility Codes and Bar Hierarchy," 28 *Val. U. L. Rev.* 657 (1994); and Elizabeth Chambliss, "Professional Responsibility: Lawyers, a Case Study," 69 *Fordham L. Rev.* 817 (2000).

Chapter 2

(By Ben Holt, J.D., American University Washington College of Law, 2005). While not a focal point of the writings selected in this reader, there is a rich literature on the colonial and post-revolutionary periods of the American legal profession. For example, in Lawrence M. Friedman, *A History of American Law* (2d ed., 1985), the author provides a narrative history of the profession from its earliest origins to the modern period. For another account tracing the legal profession from the pre-revolutionary period, see Charles W. Wolfram, "Toward a History of the Legalization of Legal Ethics-I Origins," 8 *U. Chi. L. Sch. Roundtable* 469 (2001).

The debate over the republican origins of modern legal ethics norms has produced much scholarship. For a defense of the republican revival, see Rob Atkinson, "Reviving the Roman Republic: Remembering the Good Old Cause," 71 *Fordham L. Rev.* 1187 (2003). Atkinson maintains that civic republicanism, by disrupting the focus on liberal legality, reinforces one's ability to imagine alternative ways of organizing the legal profession. Critics have argued that those seeking to reinvigorate a republican past have glossed over values that were integral to earlier republican projects but would seem repugnant today. For a viewpoint that critiques the downplaying of past racial prejudice in the republican revival, see Derrick Bell and Preeta Bansal, "The Republican Revival and Racial Politics," 97 *Yale L. J.* 1609 (1988).

The place of turn-of-the-century legal ethics has also been hotly contested among those studying the legal profession. Some accounts have attempted to look backwards selectively in the hopes of valorizing particular actors or arrangements, while others have taken a more condemnatory view of the legal profession in the early twentieth century. For an argument in favor of retaining certain aspects of early twentieth-century elite legal culture, see William H. Simon, "Babbit v. Brandeis: The Decline of the Professional Ideal," 37 *Stan. L. Rev.* 565 (1985). A further question concerning turn-of-the-century legal ethics is to what extent members of the legal profession, and in particular those fashioning ethical rules, held dominant or coherent views. For an account stressing the conflict, and the ambiguity that resulted therefrom, among the drafters of the 1908 Canons of Professional Responsibility, see Susan D. Carle, "Lawyers' Duty to Do Justice: A New Look at the History of the 1908 Canons," 24 *Law and Soc. Inquiry* 1 (1999).

Virginia Drachman's larger project detailing the struggles of women to gain access to the legal profession is collected in *Sisters in Law: Women Lawyers in Modern American History* (1998). Another prominent work is D. Kelly Weisberg, "Barred from the Bar: Women and Legal Education in the United States 1870–1890," 28 *J. Legal Educ.* 485 (1977). J. Clay Smith Jr. has collected the voices of many African-American women lawyers from the 1890s to the present in *Rebels in Law: Voices in History of Black Women Lawyers* (1998). *African Americans and the Legal Profession in Historical Perspective* (Paul Finkelman, ed., 1992), collects many good journal and law review articles. Kermit L. Hall has edited an excellent volume with numerous perspectives on outsiders to the bar and other themes in *The Legal Profession: Major Historical Interpretations* (1987). For a short treatment of the methodological tools used by many contemporary historians, and exemplified in the selection excerpted here on Sadie Alexander by Kenneth Mack, see William E. Forbath, Hendrick Hartog, and Martha Minow, "Introduction: Legal Histories from Below," 1985 *Wis. L. Rev.* 759.

For more analyses of demographic and practice area transformations in the later twentieth century, see Robert L. Nelson, "The Future of American Lawyers: A Demographic Profile of a Changing Profession in a Changing Society," 44 *Case W. Res. L. Rev.* 345 (1994); and Barbara Curran, "The Legal Profession in the 1980s: A Profession in Transition," 20 *Law and Soc'y Rev.* 19 (1986). The disturbing trends toward increasing racial disparity in college and professional school enrollments are documented in The National Urban League, *The State of Black America* (1998).

Chapter 3

There is a rich and growing literature on the history of the NAACP. Accounts of *Brown v. Board of Ed.* include Loren Miller, *The Petitioners: The Story of the Supreme Court of the United States and the Negro* (1966); Richard Kluger, *Simple Justice: The History of Brown v. Board of Education and Black America's Struggle for Equality* (1975); and Juan Williams, *Eyes on the Prize* (1988). The best general account of the NAACP's earliest years, including documentation of some of its test case strategies, is Charles Flint Kellogg, *NAACP: A History of the National Association for the Advancement of Colored People, 1909–1920* (1972).

August Meier and Elliott Rudwick have written a series of classic articles on the NAACP's internal politics and other topics. These articles are collected in their book, *Along the Color Line: Explorations in the Black Experience* (1976). Mark Tushnet's two books on the NAACP from the 1920s to the 1960s, *Making Civil Rights Law* (1994) and *The NAACP's Legal Strategy against Segregated Education, 1925–1950* (1987), offer excellent, law-focused accounts of the organization's legal campaigns and the legal and political obstacles its leaders faced.

In addition to the article excerpted in this chapter, my work on legal ethics issues and the history of the NAACP includes "How Should We Theorize Class Interests in Thinking about Professional Regulation? The Early NAACP as a Case Example," 12 *Cornell J. L. and Pub. Policy* 571 (2003); "From Buchanan to Button: Legal Ethics and the NAACP (Part II)," 8 *U. Chi. Roundtable* 281 (2001); and "Elite Privilege and Public Interest

Lawyering," 20 *Law and Hist. Rev.* 153 (2002) (responding to comments by David Wilkins).

Law review articles summarizing the Supreme Court's race jurisprudence during the period of the NAACP's public impact litigation campaigns include, among many others, Randall Kennedy, "Race Relations Law and the Tradition of Celebration: The Case of Professor Schmidt," 86 *Colum. L. Rev.* 1622 (1986); Benno C. Schmidt Jr., "Principle and Prejudice: The Supreme Court and Race in the Progressive Era. Part 1: The Heyday of Jim Crow," 82 *Colum. L. Rev.* 444 (1982); and Michael J. Klarman, "The Racial Origins of Modern Criminal Procedure," 99 *Mich. L. Rev.* 48 (2000). For a critique of how insider scholarship on civil rights has excluded outsider voices, see Richard Delgado, "The Imperial Scholar: Reflections on a Review of Civil Rights Literature," 132 *U. Pa. L. Rev.* 561 (1984). See also Richard Delgado, "The Imperial Scholar Revisited: How to Marginalize Outsider Writing, Ten Years Later," 140 *U. Pa. L. Rev.* 1349 (1992).

The fiftieth anniversary of *Brown v. Board of Education* in 2004 has led to the publication of many symposia that examine the legacy of this landmark decision, sometimes through eulogistic lenses and sometimes through more critical ones. See, e.g., "Symposium: *Brown* at Fifty," 117 *Harv. L. Rev.* 1334 (2004); "*Brown*@50 Symposium," 47 *How. L. J.* 299 (2004); "*Brown v. Board of Education*: A Moot Court Argument," 52 *Am. L. Rev.* 1343 (2003); "Symposium: *Brown v. Board of Education* after Forty Years: Confronting the Promise," 36 *Wm. and Mary L. Rev.* 547 (1995). See also Charles J. Ogletree Jr., *Reflections on the First Half Century of* Brown v. Board of Education (2004); Derrick Bell, Brown v. Board of Education *and the Unfulfilled Hopes for Racial Reform* (2004); James T. Patterson, Brown v. Board of Education: *A Civil Rights Milestone and Its Troubled Legacy* (2001); *What* Brown v. Board of Education *Should Have Said* (Jack M. Balkin, ed., 2001); *Race, Law, and Culture: Reflections on* Brown v. Board of Education (Austin Sarat, ed., 1997). An enormous outpouring of commentary also took place in the popular press, which could easily be researched in LEXIS.

With respect to the 1960s and 1970s poverty law movement, historian Martha F. Davis has written an award-winning book, *Brutal Need: Lawyers and the Welfare Rights Movement, 1960–1973* (1993). (Martha Davis later left full-time academia to become Legal Director of the National Organization for Women.) Classic law review literature by movement lawyers who were examining legal ethics issues in relation to their work includes Stephen Wexler, "Practicing Law for Poor People," 79 *Yale L. J.* 1049 (1970);

Edgar S. and Jean Camper Cahn, "Power to the People or the Profession? The Public Interest in Public Interest Law," 79 *Yale L. J.* 1005 (1970); and Gary Bellow, "Turning Solutions into Problems: The Legal Aid Experience," 24 *NLADA Briefcase* 106 (August 1977).

Literature championing the ADR movement and exploring the special ethics issues raised by ADR includes Carrie Menkel-Meadow's "Ethics in Alternative Dispute Resolution: New Issues, No Answers from the Adversary Conception of Lawyers' Responsibilities," 38 *S. Tex. L. Rev.* 407 (1997); and "When Litigation Is Not the Only Way: Consensus Building and Mediation as Public Interest Lawyering," 10 *Wash. U. J. L. and Pol'y* 37 (2002), as well as many other of her articles. A critique of the hopes placed in ADR from a feminist perspective is Trina Grillo, "The Mediation Alternative: Process Dangers for Women," 100 *Yale L. J.* 1545 (1991). One of the first articles to raise such questions about ADR was Richard Delgado et al., "Fairness and Formality: Minimizing the Risk of Prejudice in Alternative Dispute Resultion," 1985 *Wis. L. Rev.* 1359.

A short sampling of other interesting work exploring ADR and legal ethics issues includes Jennifer Gerarda Brown, "Ethics in Environmental ADR: An Overview of Issues and Some Overarching Questions," 34 *Val. U. L. Rev.* 403 (2000); Phyllis E. Bernard, "Community and Conscience: The Dynamic Challenge of Lawyers' Ethics in Tribal Peacemaking," 27 *U. Tol. L. Rev.* 821 (1996); and Kimberlee K. Kovach, "New Wine Requires New Wineskins: Transforming Lawyer Ethics for Effective Representation in a Non-Adversarial Approach to Problem Solving: Mediation," 28 *Fordham U. L. J.* 935 (2001).

Classics on public interest lawyering include Gary Bellow, "Steady Work: A Practitioner's Reflections on Political Lawyering," 31 *Harv. C.R.-C.L. L. Rev.* 297 (1996) (reflections on his practice two decades after the article excerpted here); Susan D. Bennett, "On Long-Haul Lawyering," 25 *Fordham Urb. L. J.* 771 (1998) (exploring long-term commitments needed to pioneer new forms of transactional lawyering for community development organizations in poor communities); John O. Calmore, "A Call to Context: The Professional Challenges of Cause Lawyering at the Intersection of Race, Space, and Poverty," 67 *Fordham L. Rev.* 1927 (1999) (exploring the intersection of race and class inequality and how these affect lawyering); Stephen Ellmann, "Client-Centeredness Multiplied: Individual Autonomy and Collective Mobilization in Public Interest Lawyers' Representation of Groups," 78 *Va. L. Rev.* 1103 (1992); Nancy Polikoff, "Am I My Client? The Role Confusion of a Lawyer Activist," 31 *Harv. C.R.-C.L. L.*

Rev. 443 (1996) (gay rights activist reflecting on line between activism and client representation); Deborah Rhode, "Class Conflicts in Class Actions," 34 *Stan. L. Rev.* 1183 (1982) (groundbreaking article on conflicts issues in group representation); William B. Rubenstein, "Divided We Litigate: Addressing Disputes among Group Members and Lawyers in Civil Rights Campaigns," 106 *Yale L. J.* 1623 (1997) (exploring conflicts issues in civil rights litigation); William H. Simon, "The Dark Secret of Progressive Lawyering: A Comment on Poverty Law Scholarship in the Post-Modern, Post-Reagan Era," 48 *U. Miami L. Rev.* 1099 (1994) (critiquing client-centered lawyering literature); and Paul R. Tremblay, "Acting 'a Very Moral Type of God': Triage among Poor Clients," 67 *Fordham L. Rev.* 2475 (1999) (proposing ethics standards for legal services lawyers' triage decisions in deciding how to allocate limited resources among needy clients). See also Martha Matthews, "Ten Thousand Tiny Clients: The Ethical Duty of Representation in Children's Class-Action Cases," 64 *Ford. L. Rev.* 1435 (1996); Stanley S. Herr, "Representation of Clients with Disabilities: Issues of Ethics and Control," 17 *N.Y.U. Rev. L. and Soc. Change* 609 (1989); Ann Southworth, "Collective Representation for the Disadvantaged," 67 *Ford. L. Rev.* 2449 (1999). An excellent bibliography collecting and organizing citations to this vast literature is "Bibliography to the Conference on the Delivery of Legal Services to Low-Income Persons: Professional and Ethical Issues," 67 *Ford. L. Rev.* 2731 (1999). One of many important symposia was "Symposium: Theoretics of Practice: The Integration of Progressive Thought and Action," 43 *Hastings L. J.* 771 (1992).

A new textbook on public interest law practice is Martha R. Mahoney, John O. Calmore, and Stephanie M. Wildman, *Social Justice: Professionals, Communities, and Law: Cases and Materials* (2003).

Chapter 4

Recent reflective pieces on client-centered or collaborative lawyering include Ascanio Piomelli, "Appreciating Collaborative Lawyering," 6 *Clinical L. Rev.* 427 (2000) (examining critiques and defenses of this model); Alex J. Hurder, "Negotiating the Lawyer-Client Relationship: A Search for Equality and Collaboration," 44 *Buff. L. Rev.* 71 (1996). Miller reflects on the ethics issues raised by telling client stories in "Telling Stories about Cases and Clients: The Ethics of Narrative," 14 *Geo. J. Legal Ethics* 1 (2000).

Additional work by Gerald López exploring various facets of the rebellious/community lawyering model includes "Reconceiving Civil Rights Practice: Seven Weeks in the Life of a Rebellious Collaboration," 77 *Geo. L. J.* 1603 (1989); "Lay Lawyering," 32 *UCLA L. Rev.* 1 (1989); and "The Work We Know So Little About," 42 *Stan. L. Rev.* 1 (1989). For an assessment of the use of community-based stories in lawyering in the domestic violence context, see Jane Murphy, "Lawyering for Social Change: The Power of the Narrative in Domestic Violence Law Reform," 21 *Hofstra L. Rev.* 1243 (1993). Writing on community organizing and law reform includes William Quigley, "Reflections of Community Organizers: Lawyering for Empowerment of Community Organizations," 21 *Ohio N.U.L. Rev.* 455 (1994); and Scott L. Cummings and Ingrid V. Eagly, "A Critical Reflection on Law and Organizing," 48 *UCLA L. Rev.* 443 (2001).

Articles exploring legal ethics issues in the community lawyering movement include Michael Diamond, "Community Lawyering: Revisiting the Old Neighborhood," 32 *Colum. Hum. Rts. L. Rev.* 67 (2000); and Shauna I. Marshall, "Mission Impossible? Ethical Community Lawyering," 7 *Clinical L. Rev.* 147 (2000). A symposium on the intersections among collaborative lawyering, legal ethics, and alternative dispute resolution can be found in 17 *Ohio St. J. On Disp. Resol.* 431 (2002).

For an essay bridging the collaborative and community lawyering movements, see Lucie E. White, "Collaborative Lawyering in the Field: On Mapping Paths from Rhetoric to Practice," 1 *Clinical L. Rev.* 157 (1994). Another outstanding article for readers who enjoy Lucie White is "To Learn and Teach: Lessons from Driefontein on Lawyering and Power," 1988 *Wisc. L. Rev.* 699.

Chapter 5

"Critical Legal Studies Symposium," 36 *Stan. L. Rev.* 1 (1984), captures the basic history of the critical legal studies movement from the perspectives of its founders. *Critical Legal Studies* (James Boyle, ed., 1994), provides a good general reader. Another classic reader, edited by a prominent CLS practitioner with a strong activist bent, is *The Politics of Law: A Progressive Critique* (David Kairys, ed., 1982). This is also available in a later edition collecting somewhat different works. An early William Simon article that explicitly invokes Brandeis in support of his ethical discretion model is

"Babbitt vs. Brandeis: The Decline of the Professional Ideal," 37 *Stan. L. Rev.* 565 (1985).

Literature exploring other aspects of the ethical dimensions of the exercise of prosecutorial discretion includes Fred C. Zacharias, "The Professional Discipline of Prosecutors," 792 *N. C. L. Rev.* 721 (2001); Bruce A. Green and Fred C. Zacharias, "Regulating Federal Prosecutors' Ethics," 55 *Vand. L. Rev.* 381 (2002); Stanley Z. Fisher, "The Prosecutor's Ethical Duty to Seek Exculpatory Evidence in Police Hands: Lessons from England," 68 *Ford. L. Rev.* 1379 (2000); and Erwin Chemerinsky, "The Role of Prosecutors in Dealing with Police Abuse in Los Angeles," 8 *Va. J. Soc. Pol'y and L.* 305 (2001). A fascinating literature is also beginning to explore prosecutors' ethical obligations with regard to post-conviction DNA testing and innocence claims. See, e.g., Peter Neufeld, "Legal and Ethical Implications of Post-Conviction DNA Exonerations," 35 *New Eng. L. Rev.* 639 (2001).

A general discussion of the intersection of critical race theory and legal practice can be found in Eric K. Yamamoto, "Critical Race Praxis: Race Theory and Political Lawyering Practice in Post–Civil Rights America," 95 *Mich. L. Rev.* 821 (1997). An applied ethics discussion using critical race theory to distinguish between the appropriate and inappropriate use of criminal defense strategies based on claims of culture is Leti Volpp, "(Mis)identifying Culture: Asian Women and the 'Cultural Defense,'" 17 *Harv. Women's L. J.* 57 (1994).

Tony Alfieri's numerous writings on critical race theory and legal ethics include "Lynching Ethics: Toward a Theory of Racialized Defenses," 95 *Mich. L. Rev.* 1063 (1997); "Defending Racial Violence," 95 *Colum. L. Rev.* 1301 (1995); "Race-ing Legal Ethics," 96 *Colum. L. Rev.* 800 (1996); and "Impoverished Practices," 81 *Geo. L. J.* 2567 (1993). For a critique of Alfieri's positions by a criminal defense lawyer turned clinical law professor, see Abbe Smith, "Burdening the Least of Us: 'Race Conscious' Ethics in Criminal Defense," 77 *Tex. L. Rev.* 1585 (1999).

David Wilkins explicates and defends his racial obligation thesis—i.e., his claim that black lawyers and, presumably, other lawyers of color as well, owe special ethical obligations to their communities of origin—in "Identities and Roles: Race, Recognition, and Professional Responsibility," 57 *Md. L. Rev.* 1502 (1998); see also David Wilkins, "Race, Ethics and the First Amendment: Should a Black Lawyer Represent the Ku Klux Klan," 63 *Geo. Wash. L. Rev.* 103 (1995). For a somewhat different perspective on the intersection between racial identity and lawyering, see Margaret M. Russell, "Beyond 'Sellouts' and 'Race Cards': Black Attorneys and the Strait-jacket of Legal Practice," 95 *Mich. L. Rev.* 766 (1997).

Emerging scholarship from the LatCrit movement that sometimes touches on legal practice issues includes Elizabeth M. Iglesias and Francisco Valdes, "LatCrit at Five: Institutionalizing a Postsubordination Future," 78 *Den. L. Rev.* 1249 (2001); Maureen Ebben and Norma Guerra Gaier, "Telling Stories, Telling Self: Using Narrative to Uncover Latinas' Voices and Agency in the Legal Profession," 19 *Chicano-Latino L. Rev.* 243 (1998); and Leslie Espinoza and Angela P. Harris, "Afterword: Embracing the Tar-Baby–LatCrit Theory and the Sticky Mess of Race," 85 *Cal. L. Rev.* 1585 (1997).

Readers interested in *intersectionality*—i.e., the intersection between various forms of identity-based critical theory—and legal ethics and prac-tice issues might want to start with Kimberlé Williams Crenshaw, "Mapping the Margins: Intersectionality, Identity Politics, and Violence against Women of Color," 43 *Stan. L. Rev.* 1241 (1991). See also Darren Hutchinson, "Identity Crisis: 'Intersectionality,' 'Multidimensionality,' and the Development of an Adequate Theory of Subordination," 6 *Mich. J. Race and L.* 285 (2001).

There are many excellent readers that collect representative works in the fields of critical race theory and feminist legal theory. A few of these include *Global Critical Race Feminism: An International Reader* (Adrien Katherine Wing, ed., 2000); *Critical Race Feminism* (Adrien Katherine Wing, ed., 1997); *Critical Race Theory: The Cutting Edge* (Richard Delgado and Jean Stefancic, eds., 2d ed., 2000); *Critical White Studies: Looking be-hind the Mirror* (Richard Delgado and Jean Stefancic, 1997); and *Feminist Legal Theory: Foundations* (D. Kelly Weisberg, ed., 1993). An excellent short primer introducing critical race theory is Richard Delgado and Jean Ste-fancic, *Critical Race Theory: An Introduction* (2001).

Empirical studies of women's lawyering include Kathleen E. Hull and Robert L. Nelson, "Gender Inequality in Law: Problems of Structure and Agency in Recent Studies of Gender in Anglo-American Legal Profes-sions," 23 *L. and Soc. Inquiry* 681 (1998); and Dana Crowley Jack and Rand Jack, "Women Lawyers: Archetype and Alternatives," 57 *Fordham L. Rev.* 933 (1989). For a sociologist's account refuting claims that women and men practice law differently, see Cynthia Fuchs Epstein, "Faulty Frame-work: Consequences of the Difference Model for Women in the Law," 35 *N. Y. L. Sch. L. Rev.* 309 (1990).

Readings addressing the sameness/difference debate about women's lawyering include Margaret Jane Radin, "Reply: Please Be Careful with

Cultural Feminism," 45 *Stan. L. Rev.* 1567 (1993); Naomi R. Cahn, "Styles of Lawyering," 43 *Hastings L. J.* 1039 (1992); Ann Shalleck, "The Feminist Transformation of Lawyering," 43 *Hastings L. J.* 1071 (1992); Joan Williams, "Deconstructing Gender," 87 *Mich. L. Rev.* 797 (1989); and Suzanna Sherry, "Civic Virtue and the Feminine Voice in Constitutional Adjudication," 72 *Va. L. Rev.* 543 (1986).

Literature on the ethics of care movement includes Theresa Glennon, "Lawyering and Caring: Building an Ethic of Care into Professional Responsibility," 43 *Hastings L. J.* 1175 (1992); and Stephen Ellmann, "The Ethic of Care as an Ethic for Lawyers," 81 *Geo. L. J.* 2665 (1993). See also Carrie Menkel-Meadow, "What's Gender Got to Do With It? The Politics and Morality of an Ethic of Care," 22 *N.Y.U. Rev. L. and Soc. Change* 265 (1996) (book review of philosopher Joan Tronto's work on the ethics of care).

An article exploring what a law school inspired by a feminist ethics might look like is Jennifer Gerarda Brown, "'To Give Them Countenance': the Case for a Women's Law School," 22 *Harv. Women's L. J.* 1 (1999). Readers who enjoyed Phyllis Goldfarb's excerpt comparing feminist and clinical legal ethics will also enjoy Phyllis Goldfarb, "Creating a New Tango: Re-Imagining Gender," 9 *Cardozo Women's L. J.* 443 (2003).

Chapter 6

There is a large and growing literature defining the *law and literature* movement; in this chapter I sought to include some examples most relevant to themes within the field of legal ethics. Other articles of particular note in relation to legal ethics questions include work by Bergman's colleague, Michael Asimov, looking at *bad* lawyers, "Embodiment of Evil: Law Firms in the Movies," 48 *UCLA L. Rev.* 1339 (2001); and "Bad Lawyers in the Movies," 24 *Nova L. Rev.* 533 (2000). Anthony Chase has combined the history of the critical legal studies movement with cultural studies in "Toward a Legal Theory of Popular Culture," 1986 *Wis. L. Rev.* 527. Carole Shapiro has examined images of women lawyers from a feminist perspective in "Women Lawyers in Celluloid: Why Hollywood Skirts the Truth," 25 *U. Toledo L. Rev.* 955 (1995). Carrie Menkel-Meadow has pursued topics in legal ethics and literature; see, e.g., "Can They Do That? Legal Ethics in Popular Culture: Of Characters and Acts," 48 *UCLA L. Rev.* 1305 (2001). Marc Galanter has analyzed jokes for their insights into popular conceptions of lawyer roles; some of his articles include "Changing Legal Consciousness in America: The View from the Joke Corpus," 23 *Cardozo L. Rev.* 2223 (2002); and "The Faces of Mistrust: The Image of Lawyers in Public Opinion, Jokes, and Political Discourse," 66 *U. Cin. L. Rev.* 805 (1998).

Two books investigating law and culture from different critical perspectives are Paul Bergman and Michael Asimov, *Reel Justice: The Courtroom Goes to the Movies* (1996); and Richard H. Weisberg, *Poethics and Other Struggles of Law and Literature* (1992).

Chapter 7

There have been many recent symposia that collect writing from various perspectives about the connections between legal ethics and religious commitment. These include: "Symposium, Law, Religion and Identity," 26 *Law and Soc. Inquiry* 95 (2001); "Symposium, Rediscovering the Role of Religion in the Lives of Lawyers and Those They Represent," 26 *Fordham Ur. L. J.* 821 (1999); "Symposium, The Relevance of Religion to a Lawyer's Work: An Interfaith Conference," 66 *Fordham L. Rev.* 1075 (1998); and "Symposium, Faith and the Law," 27 *Tex. Tech. L. Rev.* 911 (1996).

Anthony Cook's work combines an inquiry into spirituality in African-American churches and critical approaches to lawyering for social change. See, e.g., Anthony E. Cook, "Foreword: Towards a Postmodern Ethics of Service," 81 *Geo. L. J.* 2457 (1993); "Beyond Critical Legal Studies: The Reconstructive Theology of Dr. Martin Luther King, Jr.," 103 *Harv. L. Rev.* 985 (1990); and "The Spiritual Movement Towards Justice," 1992 *U. Ill. L. Rev.* 1007.

Some of the "deans" of such lines of inquiry into the connections between religion and legal ethics include Thomas Shaffer, whose book *On Being a Christian and a Lawyer: Law for the Innocent* (1981) sparked renewed interest in this area, and Robert M. Cover, "Forward: Nomos and Narrative," 97 *Harv. L. Rev.* 4 (1983). See also Robert F. Drinan, S.J., "A Challenge to Lawyers," 38 *Cath. Law.* 274 (1998).

Chapter 8

Literature taking critical perspectives on corporate lawyers' ethical responsibilities in counseling corporate clients seems to come in waves that correspond to cycles of corporate scandals. In the era of failed savings and loans, important articles included David B. Wilkins, "Making Context Count: Regulating Lawyers after Kaye, Scholer," 66 *S. Cal. L. Rev.* 1145 (1993); and William Simon, "The Kaye Scholer Affair: The Lawyer's Duty of Candor and the Bar's Temptations of Evasion and Apology," 23 *Law and Soc. Inquiry* 243 (1998).

Post-Enron, Susan Koniak, among others, stands out as a passionate and lively commentator. See, e.g., Susan P. Koniak, "When the Hurlyburly's Done: The Bar's Struggle with the SEC," 103 *Colum. L. Rev.* 1236 (2003); Susan P. Koniak, "Corporate Fraud: See, Lawyers," 26 *Harv. J. L. and Pub. Pol'y* 195 (2003).

Empirical studies include sociologist Robert L. Nelson's work in *Partners with Power: The Social Transformation of the Large Law Firm* (1988), and "Ideology, Practice, and Professional Autonomy: Social Values and Client Relationship in the Large Law Firm," 37 *Stan. L. Rev.* 503 (1985). See also David B. Wilkins and G. Mitu Gulati, "What Law Students Think They Know about Elite Law Firms: Preliminary Results of a Survey of Third Year Law Students," 69 *U. Cin. L. Rev.* 1213 (2001).

A complex article critiquing corporate ideologies concerning "efficient" levels of compliance with regulatory law is Cynthia A. Williams, "Corporate Compliance with the Law in the Era of Efficiency," 76 *N. C. L. Rev.* 1265 (1998).

Other interesting recent work exploring legal ethics issues in corporate law practice includes Susanna M. Kim, "Dual Identities and Dueling Obligations: Preserving Independence in Corporate Representation," 68 *Tenn. L. Rev.* 179 (2001); Milton C. Regan Jr., "Corporate Norms and Contemporary Law Firm Practice," 70 *Geo. Wash. L. Rev.* 931 (2002); and Milton C. Regan Jr., "Professional Responsibility and the Corporate Lawyer," 13 *Geo. J. Legal Ethics* 197 (2000).

It is fitting in a legal ethics reader that started with a reference to David Luban's earlier legal ethics reader, *The Good Lawyer,* to end with references to his work as well. On corporate lawyers' ethics, see, e.g., David Luban, "The Noblesse Oblige Tradition in the Practice of Law," 41 *Vanderbilt L. Rev.* 717 (1988), and "The Social Responsibilities of Lawyers: A Green Perspective," 63 *Geo. Wash. L. Rev.* 955 (1995).

Notes

Notes to the Introduction

1. Susan Wolf, "Ethics, Legal Ethics, and the Ethics of Law," in *The Good Lawyer: Lawyers' Roles and Lawyers' Ethics* (David Luban, ed., 1983).

2. See David Held, *Introduction to Critical Theory: Horkheimer to Habermas* (1980) (discussing history of critical theory).

3. See *Cause Lawyering: Political Commitments and Professional Responsibilities* (A. Sarat and S. Scheingold, eds., 1998); *Cause Lawyering and the State in a Global Era* (A. Sarat and S. Scheingold, eds., 2001).

4. *Lawyers in Society* (Richard L. Abel and Philip S.C. Lewis, eds., 1988–89).

5. *Lawyers in Society: An Overview* (Richard L. Abel and Philip S.C. Lewis, eds., 1995).

Notes to Chapter 1

ABEL

1. Reprinted by permission from 59 *Texas Law Review* 639 (1981).

2. Connell Professor of Law, University of California at Los Angeles School of Law.

3. *ABA Code of Professional Responsibility* (1971).

4. *ABA Model Rules of Professional Conduct* (1982).

5. *Model Rules Discussion Draft* Preface, at ii.

6. *Model Rules Final Draft* Rule 1.3.

7. *Id.* Rule 1.4.

8. *Id.* Rule 1.7. See also *American Lawyer's Code* Rules 2.1, 2.4.

9. *Model Rules Final Draft* Rule 1.15.

10. *Model Rules Discussion Draft* Rule 3.12, Comment.

11. Compare *Model Rules final Draft* Rule 8.1 and *id.* Rule 7.1 with *id.* Rule 3.3 and *id.* Rule 4.1.

HALLIDAY

1. Reprinted by permission from *Beyond Monopoly: Lawyers, State Crises, and Professional Empowerment* (University of Chicago Press, 1987).

2. Research Fellow, American Bar Foundation.

WILKINS

1. Reprinted by permission from 105 *Harv. L. Rev.* 799 (1992).

2. Kirkland & Ellis Professor of Law & Director, Program on Legal Profession, Harvard University Law School.

3. President's Council on Competitiveness, *Agenda for Civil Justice Reform in America* I, 1–3 (1991).

4. See John T. Curtin, Remarks to the House of Delegates 4 (August 13, 1991) (unpublished manuscript, on file at the Harvard Law School Library).

5. Commission on Evaluation of Disciplinary Enforcement, American Bar Association, Report to the House of Delegates iii (1991).

WHITE

1. Reprinted by permission from 77 *Cornell L. Rev.* 1499 (1992).

2. Louis A. Horvitz Professor of Law, Harvard University Law School.

3. Clifford Geertz, *Person, Time and Conduct in Bali* (Yale Southeast Asia Program, Cultural Report Series No. 14, 1966), in *The Interpretation of Cultures* 360 (1973).

4. *Id.* at 3.

5. See Clifford Geertz, *Works and Lives: The Anthropologist as Author* (1988).

6. See, e.g., Catharine A. MacKinnon, *Feminism Unmodified: Discourses on Life and Law* (1987); Catharine A. MacKinnon, *Toward a Feminist Theory of the State* (1989).

7. See Ellen C. DuBois et al., "Feminist Discourse, Moral Values, and the Law —a Conversation," 34 *Buff. L. Rev.* 11 (1985).

8. *Id.* at 73–76.

9. Angela P. Harris, "Race and Essentialism in Feminist Legal Theory," 42 *Stan. L. Rev.* 581, 590–601 (1989). [Note: Excerpt of this is in chapter 5—Ed.]

10. Richard Delgado & Jean Stefancic, "Images of the Outsider in American Law and Culture: Can Free Expression Remedy Systemic Social Ills?" 77 *Cornell L. Rev.* 1258 (1992).

11. See Nancy Fraser, *Unruly Practices: Power, Discourse, and Gender in Contemporary Social Theory* 17–34 (1989); Robin West, "Feminism, Critical Social Theory and Law," 1989 *U. Chi. Legal F.* 59; Nancy Fraser, *The Uses and Abuses of French Discourse Theories for Feminist Politics* (1989) (unpublished manuscript, on file with the author).

Notes to Chapter 2

INTRODUCTION

1. See Clyde Spillenger, "Elusive Advocate: Reconsidering Brandeis as a People's Lawyer," 105 *Yale L.J.* 1445, 1473 (1996).

2. Indeed, the ABA did not remove a question asking about race from its membership application until 1956. John A. Matzko, untitled, unpublished manuscript, on file with the editor. The best source of information about the ABA's early history is John A. Matzko's richly detailed "The Early Years of the American Bar Association, 1878–1928" (1984) (unpublished Ph.D. dissertation, University of Virginia), a portion of which was originally to appear here but had to be cut for space reasons from the final draft. It is a great loss to critical scholarship on the legal profession that this work is not in print.

3. Robert Stevens, *Law School: Legal Education in America from the 1850s to the 1980s* 24 (1983). This book is an excellent source generally for understanding the history described here.

4. Richard L. Abel, *American Lawyers* 90, 100 (1989).

5. Ted Gest, "Law Schools' New Female Face," *U.S. News and World Report*, April 9, 2001, at 76.

P E A R C E

1. Reprinted by permission from 6 *Geo. J. Legal Ethics* 242 (1992).

2. Professor of Law, Fordham University School of Law.

3. George Sharswood, "An Essay on Professional Ethics," 32 *A.B.A. Rep.* 1 (5th ed. 1907).

4. "Canons of Ethics," 33 *A.B.A. Rep.* 575 (1908).

5. *Model Code of Professional Responsibility* (1983).

6. *Model Rules of Professional Conduct* (1983).

7. Hazard, *supra*, at 1244.

8. *See* Bernard Bailyn, *The Ideological Origins of the American Revolution* 24–93 (1967); and Gordon Wood, *The Creation of the American Republic, 1776–1787* 46–90 (1969).

9. J.G.A. Pocock, "The Machiavellian Moment Revisited: A Study in History and Ideology," 53 *J. Mod. Hist.* 49 (1981).

10. Bailyn, *supra*, at 35.

11. William Michael Treanor, Note, "The Origins and Original Significance of the Just Compensation Clause of the Fifth Amendment," 94 *Yale L.J.* 694, 699 (1985). *See* Wood, *Creation, supra*, at 53; Gordon Wood, *The Radicalism of the American Revolution* 104–5 (1991).

12. Wood, *Creation, supra*, at 61–63.

13. *Id.* at 134.

14. Wood, *Radicalism, supra*, at 106.

15. Treanor, "Origins," *supra*, at 699.

16. Wood, *Radicalism, supra*, at 252–53.

17. Drew R. McCoy, *The Last of the Fathers: James Madison and the Republican Legacy* 193–194 (1989).

18. Wood, *Radicalism, supra*, at 253.

19. *Id.* at 254 (discussing *The Federalist No. 35* [Alexander Hamilton]).

20. *Id.* at 324.

21. Robert W. Gordon, "The Independence of Lawyers," 68 *B.U. L. Rev.* 1, 14 (1988).

22. *Id.*

23. Alexis de Tocqueville, *Democracy in America* 270 (J. P. Mayer, ed. and George Lawrence, trans., 1969).

24. *Id.* at 268.

25. *Id.* at 35.

26. *Id.* at 53–54.

27. *Id.* at 54, 30.

28. *Id.* at 81–82.

29. *Id.* at 81.

30. *Id.* at 84.

31. *Id.* at 87.

32. *Id.* at 96–97 (quoting *Rush v. Cavenaugh*, 2 Pa. 187, 189 (1845)).

SPAULDING

1. Reprinted by permission from 71 *Fordham L. Rev.* 1397 (2003).

2. Acting Professor of Law, University of California, Berkeley School of Law.

3. *See* Norman W. Spaulding, "Reinterpreting Professional Identity," 74 *U. Colo. L. Rev.* 1 (2003).

4. Erich Auerbach, *Mimesis: The Representation of Reality in Western Literature* 20 (Willard R. Trask, trans., Princeton University Press 1953) (1946).

5. David Hoffman, *A Course of Legal Study, Addressed to Students and the Profession Generally* (2d ed. 1836) (1817) [hereinafter *Course*].

6. *Id.* at 103.

7. *Id.* at 26–27.

8. G. Edward White, *The Marshall Court and Cultural Change, 1815–1835*, at 79 (1988).

9. Maxwell Bloomfield, "David Hoffman and the Shaping of a Republican Legal Culture," 38 *Md. L. Rev.* 673, 684 (1979).

10. Bloomfield, *supra*, at 687.

11. *Id.* at 684.

12. Susan D. Carle, "Lawyers' Duty to Do Justice: A New Look at the History of the 1908 Canons," 24 *Law and Soc. Inquiry* 1, 11 (1999).

13. Hoffman, *supra*, at 746.

14. *Id.* at 747.

15. Carle, *supra*, at 9.

16. Memorial, in Hon. George Sharswood, *An Essay on Professional Ethics*, 76 & 81 (5th ed. 1884).

17. *Id.* at 97 (quoting Chief Justice Gibson).

18. *Id.* at 96, 98; see also *id.* at 92.

19. Russell G. Pearce, "Rediscovering the Republican Origins of the Legal Ethics Codes," 6 *Geo. J. Legal Ethics* 241, 261–67 (1992).

20. Gerald J. Postema, *Moral Responsibility in Professional Ethics*, at 169 in *Ethics and the Legal Profession* (Michael Davis & Frederick A. Elliston, eds., 1986).

GORDON

1. Reprinted by permission from 68 *B.U.L. Rev.* 1 (1988).

2. Chancellor Kent Professor of Law and Legal History, Yale Law School.

3. "Study and specialized knowledge of the law give a man a rank apart in society and make of lawyers a somewhat privileged intellectual class. The exercise of their profession daily reminds them of this superiority; they are the masters of a necessary and not widely understood science; they serve as arbiters between the citizens; and the habit of directing the blind passions of the litigants toward the objective gives them a certain scorn for the judgement of the crowd." A. De Tocqueville, *Democracy in America* 243 (J. Mayer and M. Lerner, eds., G. Lawrence, trans. 1966).

4. See J. Matthews, *Rufus Choate: The Law and Civic Virtue* 147–91 (1980).

5. R. Ferguson, *Law and Letters in American Culture* 16–20 (1984).

6. See B. Bledstein, *The Culture of Professionalism* 1–45, 80–128, 171–96 (1976).

7. A. Chroust, *The Rise of the Legal Profession in America: The Revolution and the Post-revolutionary Era* 49 n. 176 (1965).

8. In the English institutional context in which the advocacy ideal of loyalty to the client was classically articulated, the equilibrating mechanism is the "cab-rank" principle, requiring the barrister to take the brief text offered and to argue that client's position, whatever it may be. Not only will the opposing position be heard in court, but the same barrister may be arguing the other side in the following week. The cab-rank principle was one of several that English lawyers adopted to achieve independence from powerful client-patrons. See generally W. Boulton, *A Guide to Conduct and Etiquette at the Bar of England and Wales* 6, 32–41 (6th ed. 1975); D. Duman, *The English and Colonial Bars in the Nineteenth Century* 40–50 (1983). For a concise description of the cab-rank principle and its role in preserving the independence of barristers, *see* Alexander, *The History of the Law as an Independent Profession and the Present English System*, in *The Lawyer's Professional Independence: Present Threats/Future Challenges* 14–18 (1984).

Under the English system, theoretically, the resources of advocacy cannot be concentrated in the hands of those clients best able to pay for them. I say "theoretically" because in fact the English and American systems converge much more than a superficial description implies. The cab-rank principle applies only to barristers; solicitors may and do continuously represent the same clients and positions. Solicitors in turn establish continuing relations with barristers' chambers. *See* J. Flood, *Barristers' Clerks* 69–81 (1983). And the cab-rank rule is widely circumvented through having barristers' clerks tell solicitors that the boss is "too busy" at the moment to take the brief of an undesirable client. See *id.* at 80. For a fascinating account of these doorkeepers, see generally *id.*

9. See P. Strum, *Louis D. Brandeis: Justice for the People* 38–41 (1984).

10. See *id.*

11. See J. Hurst, *The Growth of American Law: The Law Makers* 306 (1950).

12. See N. Schachner, *Alexander Hamilton* 173–83, 432 (1946).

13. See G. Gawalt, *The Promise of Power: The Emergence of the Legal Profession in Massachusetts, 1760–1840* 39, 74 (1979).

14. Gordon, *"The Ideal and the Actual in the Law": Fantasies and Practices of New York City Lawyers, 1870–1910,* in *The New High Priests: Lawyers in Post–Civil War America* 67 n.6 (G. Gawalt, ed., 1984).

SPILLENGER

1. Reprinted by permission from 105 *Yale L.J.* 1445 (1996).

2. Professor of Law, University of California at Los Angeles School of Law.

3. *See* Alpheus Thomas Mason, *Brandeis: A Free Man's Life* 77–95 (1946).

4. See, e.g., David Luban, *Lawyers and Justice: An Ethical Study* at xxiii, 169–74, 237–38 (1988) [hereinafter Luban, *Lawyers and Justice*].

5. *See* Charles W. Wolfram, *Modern Legal Ethics* 946 (1986).

6. Louis D. Brandeis, "The Opportunity in the Law," 39 *Am. L. Rev.* 555, 559 (1905), reprinted in Brandeis, *Business—A Profession* 329, 337 (1914).

7. See Robert A. Burt, *Two Jewish Justices: Outcasts in the Promised Land* 13–14 (1988).

8. Brandeis, *Opportunity in the Law, supra.*

9. Lucie E. White, "Subordination, Rhetorical Survival Skills, and Sunday Shoes: Notes on the Hearing of Mrs. G.," 38 *Buff. L. Rev.* 1 (1990) [Ed. Note: excerpted in chapter 4 below].

10. Gordon, *Independence of Lawyers, supra,* 33.

11. Luban, *Lawyers and Justice, supra* at 238.

12. William H. Simon, "Ethical Discretion in Lawyering," 101 *Harv. L. Rev.* 1083, 1128 (1988) [Ed. Note: excerpted in chapter 5].

13. Thomas L. Shaffer, "The Legal Ethics of Radical Individualism," 65 *Tex. L. Rev.* 963, 972–84 (1987).

14. Luban, *Lawyers and Justice, supra* at 238.

AUERBACH

1. Reprinted by permission from *Unequal Justice: Lawyers and Social Change in Modern America* 40 (Oxford University Press, 1976).

2. Professor of History, Wellesley College.

3. "Lawyers's Code of Ethics," 13 *Bench and Bar* 44 (May 1908).

4. New York State Bar Association, 3 *Proc.* 67 (1879).

5. Lawrence M. Friedman, "Law Reform in Historical Perspective," 13 *St. Louis Uni. L. J.* 356, 358, 370–371 (1969).

DRACHMAN

1. Reprinted by permission from 28 *Ind. L. Rev.* 227 (1995).

2. Arthur Jr. and Lenore Stern Professor of American History, Tufts University.

3. "Bar Group Assails Rivals of Lawyers," *N.Y. Times,* August 19, 1930, at 16.

4. "Sane Suggestions," 14 *Women Law. J.* 9, 9 (1926).

5. *Women Law. J.* 6, 6 (1919).

6. "'Girl Lawyer has Small Chance for Success,' Says Mrs. Lesser," *Boston Saturday Evening Traveller,* June 8, 1912, at 2.

7. BVI questionnaire no. 18 (March 2, 1920) (on file in the BVI Collection at the Schlesinger Library) [hereinafter referred to as "BVI questionnaire" without cross-reference].

8. BVI questionnaire no. 131 (March 27, 1920).

9. Letter from Gertrude Smith to Inez Milholland (no date available) (on file in the Inez Milholland Papers at the Schlesinger Library, reel 2, folder 21).

10. BVI questionnaire no. 200.

11. BVI questionnaire no. 146 (March 7, 1920).

12. BVI questionnaire no. 199 (April 6, 1920).

13. Rose Young, "Your Daughter's Career," 61 *Good Housekeeping* 470 (1915).

14. Letter from Betty Reynolds Cobb to Emma P. Hirth (April 9, 1920) (BVI Collection, box 9, folder 142).

15. *Id.*

16. *Id.*

17. BVI questionnaire no. 251 (March 1, 1920).

18. "Lady Lawyers," *Ebony* 19 (August 1947).

MACK

1. Reprinted by permission from 87 *Cornell L. Rev.* 1405 (2002).

2. Assistant Professor of Law, Harvard University Law School.

3. President's Comm. on Civil Rights, *To Secure These Rights: The Report of the President's Committee on Civil Rights* (1947).

4. See Sadie Tanner Mossell Alexander, "Women as Practitioners of Law in the United States," 1 *Nat'l B.J.* 56, 61 (1941).

5. Jerold S. Auerbach, *Unequal Justice: Lawyers and Social Change in Modern America* (1976).

6. See, e.g., Virginia G. Drachman, *Sisters in Law: Women Lawyers in Modern American History* 215–25 (1998).

7. See Nancy F. Cott, *The Grounding of Modern Feminism* 215–39 (1987); Drachman, *supra,* at 191–249; Barbara Allen Babcock, "Feminist Lawyers," 50 *Stan. L. Rev.* 1689, 1702 (1998) (reviewing Drachman, *supra*).

8. *See* J. Clay Smith Jr., *Introduction: Law Is No Mystery to Black Women,* in *Rebels in Law: Voices in History of Black Women Lawyers* 1, 5 (J. Clay Smith Jr., ed., 1998) (attributing this term to Barbara Omolade).

9. This is a paraphrase of the question that Audre Lorde answers in "The Master's Tools Will Never Dismantle the Master's House," in *Sister Outsider: Essays and Speeches by Audre Lorde* 110, 110–11 (1984) ("What does it mean when the tools of a racist patriarchy are used to examine the fruits of that same patriarchy?").

MENKEL-MEADOW

1. Reprinted by permission from 44 *Case W. Res. L. Rev.* 621 (1994).

2. Professor of Law, Georgetown University Law Center.

3. Richard L. Abel, *American Lawyers* 108 (1989).

4. *Id.* at 110.

5. Steven Keeva, "Unequal Partners: It's Tough at the Top for Minority Lawyers," *A.B.A.J.,* February 1993, at 50, 50.

6. 433 U.S. 350, 383 (1977) (holding that advertising by attorneys may not be subjected to blanket suppression).

7. See, e.g., Brotherhood of R. R. Trainmen v. State Bar of Va. ex rel. Va. State Bar, 377 U.S. 1 (1964); NAACP v. Button, 371 U.S. 415 (1963).

Notes to Chapter 3

INTRODUCTION

1. 163 U.S. 537 (1896).

2. 347 U.S. 483 (1954).

3. 371 U.S. 415 (1963).

SMITH

1. Reprinted by permission from *Emancipation: The Making of the Black Lawyer 1844–1944* (University of Pennsylvania Press, 1993).

2. Professor of Law, Howard University School of Law.

CARLE

1. Reprinted by permission from 20 *Law and History Rev.* 97 (2002).

2. Professor of Law, American University Washington College of Law.

3. 347 U.S. 483 (1954).

4. See "Third Annual Meeting of the Niagara Movement, August 26–29, 1907," Joel Spingarn, Manuscript Division, Moorland-Spingarn Research Center, Howard University, Box 95-14, Folder 554; "List of Legal Committee Members," *ibid.,* Folder 557.

5. See *Constitution and By-Laws of the Niagara Movement,* in *Pamphlets and Leaflets by W.E.B. DuBois,* 59, 61 (H. Aptheker, ed., 1986) .

6. See *In re Neuman,* 255 N.Y.S. 438, 169 A.D. 638 (1915).

7. New York County Lawyers' Association Opinion [hereinafter NYCLA Op.] No. 50 (1914), in *Opinions of the Committees on Professional Ethics of the Association of the Bar of the City of New York and the New York County Lawyers' Association* 540 (1956).

8. NYCLA Op. No. 89 (1916), in *Opinions of the Committees on Professional Ethics,* 563.

9. 371 U.S. 415 (1963).

MCNEIL

1. Reprinted by permission from *Groundwork: Charles Hamilton Houston and the Struggle for Civil Rights* (University of Pennsylvania Press, 1990).

2. Professor of History, University of North Carolina at Chapel Hill.

BELL

1. Reprinted by permission from 85 *Yale L.J.* 470 (1976).

2. Visiting Professor of Law, New York University School of Law.

3. U.S. 449 (1958).

BELLOW AND KETTLESON

1. Reprinted by permission from 58 *B.U.L. Rev.* 337 (1978).

2. Gary Bellow was a Professor of Law at Harvard Law School; he passed away in 2000. For more about him and his career as a public interest advocate, see a memorial website posted on his behalf at www.garybellow.org (last visited on May 5, 2004). Jeanne Charn (then Kettleson) is a Lecturer, Director of the Hale & Dorr Legal Services Center, Bellow-Sacks Access to Civil Legal Services Project, Harvard Law School.

3. Address by Sargent Shriver to the National Advisory Committee on Legal Services, Office of Economic Opportunity, in Washington, D.C. (February 1966). Sargent Shriver played a major role in establishing the national legal services program, now funded through the Legal Services Corporation.

Notes to Chapter 4

INTRODUCTION

1. For a general discussion of the legal ethics issues raised by this genre of scholarship, see Binny Miller, "Telling Stories about Cases and Clients: The Ethics of Narrative," 14 *Geo. J. Legal Ethics* 1 (2000).

DINERSTEIN

1. Reprinted by permission from 32 *Ariz. L. Rev.* 501 (1990).

2. Professor of Law and Director, Disability Rights Clinic, American University Washington College of Law.

3. *Model Code of Prof'l Responsibility* EC 7-7 (1980).

4. Simon, "Ethical Discretion in Lawyering," 101 *Harv. L. Rev.* 1083, 1084 n.1 (1988). [Ed. note: Excerpted in chapter 5.]

WHITE

1. Reprinted by permission from 38 *Buff. L. Rev.* 1 (1990).

2. Louis A. Horvitz Professor of Law, Harvard University Law School.

MILLER

1. Reprinted by permission from 93 *Mich. L. Rev.* 485 (1994). This excerpt has been edited by the author, who made minor changes from the originally published version.

2. Professor of Law and Director, Criminal Justice Clinic, American University Washington College of Law.

JACOBS

1. Reprinted by permission from 27 *Golden Gate U.L. Rev.* 345 (1997).

2. Professor of Law, DePaul University College of Law.

3. Carl O. Ward et al., "The Nonverbal Mediation of Self-Fulfilling Prophecies in Interracial Interaction," 10 *J. Experimental Soc. Psychol.* 109 (1974).

4. J. Schwartzbaum et al., "Physician Breach of Patient Confidentiality among Individuals with Human Immunodeficiency Virus (HIV) Infection: Patterns of Decision," 80 *Amer. J. of Pub. Health* 829 (1990).

5. Francis Terrell and Sandra Terrell, "An Inventory to Measure Cultural Mistrust among Blacks," 5(3) *The W.J. of Black Stud.* (1981).

6. Francis Terrell and Sandra Terrell, "Race of Counselor, Client Sex, Cultural Mistrust Level and Premature Termination from Counseling Among Blacks," 31 *J. of Counseling Psychol.* 371 (1984).

LÓPEZ

1. Reprinted by permission from *Rebellious Lawyering: One Chicano's Vision of Progressive Law Practice* (Westview Press, 1992).

2. Clinical Professor of Law, New York University School of Law.

CRUZ

1. Reprinted by permission from 5 *Clinical L. Rev.* 1999.

2. Professor of Law, University of New Mexico Law School.

3. *Model Code of Professional Responsibility,* Canon 7 (1983).

4. Rosemary J. Coombe, "The Properties of Culture and the Politics of Possessing Identity: Native Claims in the Cultural Appropriation Controversy," 6 *Can. J.L. and Jurisprudence* 249, 279 (1993) (citation omitted).

5. Oren Lyons, "When You Talk about Representing Tribal Clients, You Are Talking about the Future of Indian Nations," in *Rethinking Indian Law* at v (Nat'l Law. Guild, Comm. on Native Am. Struggles, ed., 1982).

HWANG

1. Reprinted by permission from 9 *Asian L.J.* 83 (2002).

2. Managing Attorney, Asian Pacific Islander Legal Outreach, San Francisco, California.

3. Dale Minami, quoted in *Rafu Shimpo,* April 19, 1997, at 3.

4. Eric Yamamoto, "Critical Race Praxis: Race Theory and Political Lawyering Practice in Post–Civil Rights America," 95 *Mich. L. Rev.* 821, 828–29 (1997).

5. Yamamoto, *supra,* at 830.

6. Gerald Lopez, *Rebellious Lawyering* 38 (1992).

7. *See* Richard Delgado and Jean Stefancic, "Symposium: *Brown v. Board of Education* after Forty Years: Confronting the Promise: The Social Construction of *Brown v. Board of Education*: Law Reform and the Reconstructive Paradox," 36 *Wm. and Mary L. Rev.* 547, 568–69 (1995).

8. [Ed. Note: Derrick Bell's interest convergence thesis proposes that minorities only achieve gains when it is in the interest of the majority to grant them. *See* Derrick A. Bell Jr., "*Brown v. Board of Education* and the Interest-Convergence Dilemma," 93 *Harv. L. Rev.* 518, 523 (1980).]

9. Dale Minami, "Asian Law Caucus: An Experiment in the Alternative," 3 *Amerasia J.* 28, 29 (1975).

10. Welfare Reform Act of 1996, Pub. L. No. 104–193, § 400 (1996).

11. See Welfare Reform Act of 1996 § 402, 8 U.S.C. § 1612 (2002).

12. Agricultural Research, Extension, and Education Reform Act of 1998, Pub. L. No. 105–85, § 508, 112 Stat. 523, 579 (1998).

Notes to Chapter 5

INTRODUCTION

1. See John Henry Schlegel, "Notes Toward an Intimate, Opinionated, and Affectionate History of the Conference on Critical Legal Studies," 36 *Stan. L. Rev.* 391, 406 (1984) (noting the social context from which CLS emerged, including "disillusion and hostility arising from the Vietnam War, Watergate, and the nation's political shift to the right").

GABEL AND HARRIS

1. Reprinted by permission from 11 *N.Y.U. Rev. L. and Soc. Change* 369 (1982–83).

2. Peter Gabel is Professor of Law and Director of the Institute for Spirituality and Politics at New College of California. Paul Harris is retired.

3. See Karl Klare, "Judicial Deradicalization of the Wagner Act and the Origins of Modern Legal Consciousness, 1937–1941," 62 *Minn. L. Rev.* 265 (1978); Freeman, "Legitimizing Racial Discrimination through Antidiscrimination Law: A Critical Review of Supreme Court Doctrine," 62 *Minn. L. Rev.* 1049 (1978).

SIMON

1. Reprinted by permission from 101 *Harv. L. Rev.* 1083 (1988).

2. Professor of Law, Columbia University School of Law.

3. See G. Bellow and B. Moulton, *The Lawyering Process* 586–91 (1978).

DAVIS

1. Reprinted by permission from 67 *Fordham L. Rev.* 13 (1998).

2. Professor of Law, American University Washington College of Law.

3. *Luke* 12:48 (King James version).

4. Louis D. Brandeis, *Other People's Money, and How the Bankers Use It* 62 (1914).

5. See Kenneth J. Melilli, "Prosecutorial Discretion in an Adversary System," 1992 *B.Y.U.L. Rev.* 669, 671.

6. *See* Noryal Morris, "Race and Crime: What Evidence Is There that Race Influences Results in the Criminal Justice System?" 72 *Judicature* 111, 112 (1988); Joseph F. Sheley, "Structural Influences on the Problem of Race, Crime, and Criminal Justice Discrimination," 67 *Tul. L. Rev.* 2273, 2275–76 (1993); Alan J. Tomkins et al., "Subtle Discrimination in Juvenile Justice Decisionmaking: Social Scientific Perspectives and Explanations," 29 *Creighton L. Rev.* 1619, 1632 (1996).

7. See United States v. Weaver, 966 F.2d 391, 392 (8th Cir. 1992) (explaining that factors that created reasonable suspicion included fact that defendant was a "'roughly dressed' young black male"); see also United States v. Brignoni-Ponce, 422 U.S. 873, 886–87 (1975) (stating that a person's "Mexican appearance" in an area near the U.S.–Mexico border is a relevant factor in creating reasonable suspicion that the person is an illegal alien, but "standing alone it does not justify stopping all Mexican-Americans to ask if they are aliens"); United States v. Harvey, 16 F.3d 109, 113 (6th Cir. 1994) (Keith, J., dissenting) (noting that the majority upheld a pretextual traffic stop despite the police officer's admission that he was motivated to make stop based on fact that "there were three young black male occupants in an old vehicle").

8. See United States v. Robinson, 414 U.S. 218, 242 (1973) (Marshall, J., dissenting) ("The majority's fear of overruling the 'quick ad hoc judgment' of the police officer is thus inconsistent with the very function of the [Fourth] Amendment—

to ensure that the quick ad hoc judgments of police officers are subject to review and control by the judiciary").

9. See Courtland Milloy, "Unequal Justice in P.G.?" *Wash. Post,* February 25, 1996, at B1 (describing an event in Prince George's County, Maryland, where white officers observed three white adults smoking crack cocaine in a car with a baby and neither made arrests nor filed charges).

10. The criteria that generally guide "plain view" searches are set forth in Coolidge v. New Hampshire, 403 U.S. 443 (1971).

11. See Batson v. Kentucky, 476 U.S. 79 (1986) (holding that a prosecutor must establish a race-neutral reason for using a peremptory strike against African American member of jury pool).

12. Charles H. Lawrence III, "The Id, the Ego, and Equal Protection: Reckoning with Unconscious Racism," 39 *Stan. L. Rev.* 317, 322 (1987).

13. The *Model Code of Professional Responsibility* states: "The responsibility of a public prosecutor differs from that of the usual advocate; his duty is to seek justice, not merely to convict. This special duty exists because: (1) the prosecutor represents the sovereign and therefore should use restraint in the discretionary exercise of governmental powers, such as in the selection of cases to prosecute." *Model Code of Professional Responsibility* EC 7-13 (1981).

14. See Berger v. United States, 295 U.S. 78, 88 (1935); *Model Code of Professional Responsibility* EC 7-13 ("The responsibility of a public prosecutor differs from that of the usual advocate; his duty is to seek justice, not merely to convict"); *Model Rules of Professional Conduct* Rule 3.8 cmt. (1983) (describing a prosecutor's responsibilities "to see that [a] defendant is accorded procedural justice and that guilt is decided upon the basis of sufficient evidence"); Standards Relating to the Admin. of Criminal Justice Standard 3-1.2(c) (1992) ("The duty of the prosecutor is to seek justice, not merely to convict").

HING

1. Reprinted by permission from 47 *Stan. L. Rev.* 901 (1995).

2. Professor of Law and Asian American Studies, University of California, Davis.

3. E.g., Ashley Dunn, "King Case Aftermath: A City in Crisis," *L.A. Times,* May 2, 1992, at A1 (reporting that lacking confidence in the police, merchants in Koreatown armed themselves for protection against looters); David Freed, "Under Fire: Guns in Los Angeles County," *L.A. Times,* May 17, 1992, at A27 (reporting that merchants and residents in Koreatown armed themselves for protection during the uprising); Al Kamen and Ruben Castaneda, "Koreans Bear Arms to Protect Businesses," *Wash. Post,* May 2, 1992, at A1 (reporting that Korean business owners armed themselves with rifles, shotguns, and semiautomatic weapons to protect their stores from looters and arsonists).

4. "Listening to America with Bill Moyers: In Search of a Common Destiny" (Public Affairs television broadcast, May 5, 1992).

5. See Martin Luther King Jr., "I Have a Dream," Keynote Address for the March on Washington (August 28, 1963), in *A Testament of Hope: The Essential Writings and Speeches of Martin Luther King Jr.* 217, 219 (James Melvin Washington, ed., 1986).

6. William H. Simon, "Ethical Discretion in Lawyering," 101 *Harv. L. Rev.* 1083, 1120 (1988).

7. *Id.* at 739 (citing Talcott Parsons, "A Sociologist Looks at the Legal Profession," in *Essays in Sociological Theory* 370, 384 [rev. ed. 1958]).

ALFIERI

1. Reprinted by permission from 51 *Stan. L. Rev.* 935 (1999).

2. Professor of Law and Director, Center for Ethics and Public Service, University of Miami School of Law.

3. William H. Simon, *The Practice of Justice: A Theory of Lawyers' Ethics* 7–11 (1998).

4. *Id.* at 7.

5. *Id.* at 4.

6. *Id.* at 9.

7. *Id.*

8. *Id.*

9. *Id.* at 8.

10. *Id.* (emphasis added).

11. *Id.* at 10.

12. *Id.* at 225 n.32; see also *id.* at 211.

13. *See Model Rules of Professional Conduct* Rule 1.2(a) (1998) (requiring lawyer to abide by client's decisions on certain topics).

MENKEL-MEADOW

1. Reprinted by permission from 2 *Va. J. Soc. Pol'y and Law* 75 (1994).

2. Professor of Law, Georgetown University Law Center.

3. Carrie Menkel-Meadow, "Portia in a Different Voice: Speculations on a Women's Lawyering Process," 1 *Berkeley Women's L. J.* 39 (1985).

4. Cynthia F. Epstein, *Deceptive Distinctions,* 72–98 (1988) (asserting that gender differences in moral development may be "all in the mind" of the perceiver).

HARRIS

1. Reprinted by permission from 42 *Stan. L. Rev.* 581 (1990).

2. Professor of Law, University of California, Berkeley School of Law.

3. Jorge Luis Borges, *Labyrinths: Selected Stories and Other Writings* 64 (D. Yates and J. Irby, eds. 1964).

4. *Id.* at 65.

5. *Id.* at 66.

6. Audre Lorde, "Age, Race, Class, and Sex: Women Defining Difference," in *Sister Outsider* 122 (1984).

7. Patricia Williams, "On Being the Object of Property," 14 *Signs* 5 (1988).

8. *Id.* at 6–7.

9. *Id.* at 6.

10. *Id.*

11. *Id.* at 11.

12. *Id.* at 10.

13. *Id.* at 24.

14. *Id.* at 22.

15. Minow, *Justice Engendered, supra,* at 34–38.

16. Zora Neale Hurston, *How It Feels to Be Colored Me,* in *I Love Myself When I Am Laughing . . . and then Again When I Am Looking Mean and Impressive,* 152 (A. Walker, ed., 1979).

17. *Id.* at 153.

18. *Id.* at 154.

19. Hurston, "What White Publishers Won't Print," in *I Love Myself When I Am Laughing, supra,* at 169.

20. Barbara Johnson, "Thresholds of Difference: Structures of Address in Zora Neale Hurston," in *"Race," Writing, and Difference,* 322–23 (H. L. Gates Jr., ed., 1986).

GUINIER

1. Reprinted by permission from 24 *N.Y.U. Rev. L. and Soc. Change* 1 (1998).

2. Bennett Boskey Professor of Law, Harvard University Law School.

3. Lani Guinier, Michelle Fine, and Jane Balin with Ann Bartow and Deborah Lee Stachel, "Becoming Gentlemen: Women's Experiences at One Ivy League Law School," 143 *U. Pa. L. Rev.* 1, 2 (1994).

4. Elizabeth Mertz, Wamucii Njogu, and Susan Gooding, "What Difference Does Difference Make? The Challenge for Legal Education," at 5 (1996) (unpublished manuscript, on file with author).

5. Catherine Krupnick, "Women and Men in the Classroom: Inequality and Its Remedies," 1 *On Teaching and Learning: J of the Harv-Danforth Center* 18 (1985).

6. Susan Sturm, "From Gladiators to Problem-Solvers: Connecting Conversations about Women, the Academy, and the Legal Profession," 4 *Duke J. Gender L. & Pol'y.* 119, 121 (1997) (labeling the dominant model of legal education and lawyering which "celebrates analytical rigor, toughness, and quick thinking").

7. See Uri Treisman, "Studying Students Studying Calculus: A Look at the Lives of Minority Mathematics Students in College," 23 *C. Mathematics J.* 362, 366–369 (1992) (encouraging peer group study sessions which dramatically improved the performance of African-American and Latino students in calculus; this program was designed to simulate the studying styles of successful Asian students).

GOLDFARB

1. Reprinted by permission from 75 *Minn. L. Rev.* 1599 (1991).

2. Professor of Law, Boston College Law School.

3. Sophocles, *Antigone,* in *The Theban Plays* 125 (E. F. Watling, trans., 1962).

4. See Carol Gilligan, *In A Different Voice: Psychological Development and Moral Theory* (1982).

5. Catharine MacKinnon, "Feminist Discourse, Moral Values and the Law: A Conversation," 34 *Buff. L. Rev.* 11, 159 (1985).

6. *Id.* at 159; see also *id.* at 114 ("If the sexes are unequal, and perspective participates in situation, there is no ungendered reality or ungendered perspective").

7. See, e.g., Martha Nussbaum, *The Fragility of Goodness: Luck and Ethics in Greek Tragedy and Philosophy* 60 (1986).

8. See *id.* at 51.

9. *Id.* at 52.

Notes to Chapter 6

BERGMAN

1. Reprinted by permission from 48 *U.C.L.A. L. Rev.* 1393 (2001).

2. Professor of Law, University of California at Los Angeles School of Law.

3. Richard M. Nixon, "The Quotations Pages: Quotations by Author–Richard M. Nixon," at http://www.quotationspage.com/quotes.php3?author=Richard+M.+Nixon (last visited April 13, 2001).

4. See Fed. R. Evid. 804(b)(2).

5. *Counselor at Law* (Universal Pictures, 1933).

6. *Lawyer Man* (Warner Bros., 1933).

7. *The Verdict* (20th Century Fox, 1982).

8. *Philadelphia* (Clinica Estetico and TriStar Pictures, 1992).

9. *The Accused* (Paramount Pictures, 1988).

10. *An Act of Murder* (Universal International Pictures, 1948).

11. *Class Action* (20th Century Fox and Interscope Communications, 1991).

ATKINSON

1. Reprinted by permission from 105 *Yale L.J.* 177 (1995).

2. Ruden, McClosky, Smith, Schuster, and Russell Professor of Law, Florida State University College of Law.

3. Kazuo Ishiguro, *The Remains of the Day* (1989). The book is already well on its way to canonical status. It won the 1989 Booker Prize and was the basis for the movie *The Remains of the Day* (Columbia Pictures, 1993), which received eight Academy Award nominations including Best Picture, Best Director, Best Actor, and Best Actress. Susannah Herbert, "Gloom Is All that Remains of the Day," *Daily*

Telegraph (London), March 23, 1994, at 9. In this essay, I follow the book, though the differences are not material for my purposes except, perhaps, in the final scene.

4. Ishiguro, *supra,* at 6.

5. *Id.* at 9.

6. *Id.* at 147.

7. *Id.* at 149.

8. Stephen L. Pepper, "The Lawyer's Amoral Ethical Role: A Defense, A Problem, and Some Possibilities," 1986 *Am. B. Found. Res. J.* 623.

9. Ishiguro, *supra,* at 199.

10. *Id.* at 149.

11. Ishiguro, *supra,* at 149.

12. *Id.* at 116–117.

13. *Id.* at 114.

14. Ishiguro, *supra,* at 200.

15. *Id.* at 199–200.

16. *Id.* at 199.

17. *Id.* at 149.

18. William H. Simon, "The Ideology of Advocacy: Procedural Justice and Professional Ethics," 1978 *Wis. L. Rev.* 40.

19. Ishiguro, *supra,* at 148.

20. *Id.* at 149.

21. *Id.*

22. David Luban, *Lawyers and Justice: An Ethical Study* 160 (1988).

Notes to Chapter 7

CARTER

1. Reprinted by permission from 26 *Fordham Urb. L.J.* 985 (1999).

2. William Nelson Cromwell Professor of Law, Yale Law School.

3. David Tracy, *Plurality and Ambiguity* (1989).

4. Kenneth Starr, "Christian Life in the Law," 27 *Tex. Tech. L. Rev.* 1360 (1996).

5. *Id.*

PEARCE

1. Reprinted by permission from 27 *Tex. Tech. L. Rev.* 1259 (1996).

2. Professor of Law, Fordham University School of Law.

3. Martin Buber, *On Judaism* (Nahum N. Glatzer, ed., 1967).

4. *Id.* at 112.

5. Martin Buber, *I and Thou* 163 (Walter Kaufman, trans., 1970).

6. Martin Buber, *On Judaism, supra,* at 111.

7. *Leviticus* 19:2.

8. *Leviticus* 19:9–10.

9. *Leviticus* 19:18.

10. *Leviticus* 19:34.

11. *Isaiah* 1:15–17.

12. Rabbi Alexander Schindler, "Sermon on the Installation of Rabbi Sharon Kleinbaum at Congregation Beth Simchat Torah" 9 (September 11, 1992) (quoting Rabbi Leo Baeck).

13. Rabbi Joseph B. Soloveitchik, *Halakhic Man* 94 (1983).

14. Eugene B. Borowitz, *Reform Judaism Today: What We Believe* 13–14 (1977).

15. Heschel, *supra* at 165–166.

16. Martin Buber, *Tales of the Hasidim: The Early Masters* 169 (Olga Marx, trans., 1947).

17. Alfred S. Cohen, "On Maintaining a Professional Confidence," 7 *Halacha and Contemp. Soc'y* 84 (1984).

18. Gordon Tucker, "The Confidentiality Rule: A Philosophical Perspective with Reference to Jewish Law and Ethics," 13 *Fordham Urb. L.J.* 99 (1985).

19. *Deuteronomy* 16:20.

20. *Leviticus* 19:15.

21. *Leviticus* 19:34.

22. *Proverbs* 31:8.

23. *Proverbs* 31:9.

24. Russell G. Pearce, "Jewish Lawyering in a Multicultural Society: A Midrash on Levinson," 14 *Cardozo L. Rev.* 1613 (1993).

25. Buber, *On Judaism, supra* at 111.

SHAFFER

1. Reprinted by permission from 23 *Ga. L. Rev.* 1201 (1989).

2. Robert E. and Marion D. Short Professor Emeritus, Notre Dame Law School.

3. Thomas L. Shaffer, *American Legal Ethics* 698–703 (1985).

4. *John* 8:7.

5. Raymond Chandler, *The Long Goodbye* 193 (1954) (Ballantine ed. 1971).

Notes to Chapter 8

INTRODUCTION

1. David Luban, *Lawyers and Justice* 206 (1988).

2. *Id.* at 234.

LUBAN

1. Frederick Haas Professor of Law and Philosophy, Georgetown University Law Center.

2. Geoffrey C. Hazard Jr., "Lawyers and Client Fraud: They Still Don't Get It," 6 *Geo. J. Legal Ethics* 701, 720 (1993).

3. C. S. Lewis, "The Inner Ring," *in They Asked for a Paper: Papers and Addresses* 146 (1962).

4. *Id.* at 147.

5. Here I'm adopting the analysis of my colleague Don Langevoort. *See* Donald C. Langevoort, "Managing the 'Expectations Gap' in Investor Protection: The SEC and the Post-Enron Reform Agenda," 48 *Vill. L. Rev.* 1139 (2003).

6. 421 F.2d 1174 (2d Cir. 1970).

7. Bill Bratton, "Enron and the Dark Side of Shareholder Value," 76 *Tul L. Rev.* 1275, 1293 (2002).

8. Melvin J. Lerner, *The Belief in a Just World: A Fundamental Delusion* (1980).

9. *Id.* at 20–21.

10. Robert Swaine, *The Cravath Firm and Its Predecessors, 1819–1947,* 667 (1946).

11. Ronald H. Coase, "The Nature of the Firm," 4 *Economica* 386 (1937).

12. Robert Jackall, *Moral Mazes: The World of Corporate Managers* 17–25 (1987).

13. Bratton, *supra,* at 1293.

14. Jackall, *supra,* at 91–100.

15. Michael Lewis, *Liar's Poker* 164–70 (1989).

16. Donald C. Langevoort, "The Organizational Psychology of Hyper-Competition: Corporate Irresponsibility and the Lessons of Enron," 70 *Geo. Wash. L. Rev.* 968 (2002).

17. Former dot-commer Michael Wolff portrayed this world vividly in his 1998 bestseller *Burn Rate.*

18. Leon L. Festinger and J. M. Carlsmith, "Cognitive Consequences of Forced Compliance," 58 *J. Abnormal and Soc. Psychol.* 203 (1959); see also the discussion in Lee Ross and Richard E. Nisbett, *The Person and the Situation: Perspectives of Social Psychology* 66 (1991), and additional sources cited there.

19. I discuss this paradox at greater length—including extensive references to the social psychology literature—in David Luban, "Integrity: Its Causes and Cures," 72 *Fordham L. Rev.* 279 (2003).

20. See, e.g., Solomon E. Asch, "Effects of Group Pressures upon the Modification and Distortion of Judgment," in *Groups, Leadership, and Men* (H. Guetzkow, ed., 1951). See Nisbett and Ross, *supra,* at 30–35.

21. John Darley and Bibb Latané, "Bystander Intervention in Emergencies: Diffusion of Responsibility," 8 *J. Personality and Soc. Psychol.* 377 (1968); Bibb Latané and John Darley, *The Unresponsive Bystander: Why Doesn't He Help?* (1968); for a literature review, see Bibb Latané and Steve Nida, "Ten Years of Research on Group Size and Helping," 89 *Psychol. Bull.* 308 (1981).

22. Craig Haney et al., "Interpersonal Dynamics of a Simulated Prison," 1 *Int'l. J. Criminology and Penology* 69, 81 (1973); Philip Zimbardo et al., "The Mind Is a Formidable Jailer: A Pirandellian Prison," *N.Y. Times Mag.,* April 8, 1973. There is a

terrifically interesting slide show and analysis of the Stanford Prison Experiment, put together by lead experimenter Philip Zimbardo, available on the Internet. Philip B. Zimbardo, "Stanford Prison Experiment: A Simulation Study of the Psychology of Imprisonment Conducted at Stanford University," at http://www.prisonexp.org.

23. Craig Haney and Philip Zimbardo, "The Socialization into Criminality: On Becoming a Prisoner and a Guard," in *Law, Justice, and the Individual in Society: Psychological and Legal Issues* 207 (Tapp and Levine, eds., 1977).

24. *Id.* at 207–9.

25. These famous experiments are described in Stanley Milgram, *Obedience to Authority: An Experimental Approach* (1974).

GORDON

1. Reprinted by permission from 35 *Conn. L. Rev.* 1185 (2003).

2. Chancellor Kent Professor of Law and Legal History, Yale Law School.

3. The transactions were detailed in two fine journalistic analyses of the Enron lawyers' role. See Mike France, "What About the Lawyers?" *Bus. Wk.,* December 23, 2002, at 58; Ellen Joan Pollock, "Limited Partners: Lawyers for Enron Faulted Its Deals, Didn't Force Issue," *Wall St. J.,* May 22, 2002, at A1.

4. Peter Behr and Carrie Johnson, "Enron Probe Now Focuses on Tax Deals," *Wash. Post,* January 21, 2003, at E1 (quoting Robert J. Hermann).

5. See, e.g., *Model Rules of Professional Conduct* Rule 1.6(b) (2003) (stating that "a lawyer may reveal [confidential] information . . . to the extent the lawyer reasonably believes necessary"); *Conn. Rules of Professional Conduct* Rule 1.6(b) (2003) (stating that "a lawyer shall reveal such information to the extent the lawyer reasonably believes necessary").

6. *Model Rules of Professional Conduct* Rule 1.6 cmt. 1, 3 (1983) (requiring the confidentiality of information).

7. *Model Rules of Professional Conduct* Rule 1.6 cmt. 1 (1983).

8. American Bar Association, *Code of Professional Ethics* Canon 32 (1908). Notice that the lawyer's advice on the statute is not to be the construction that most favors the client, but the lawyer's independent view. *See* Susan D. Carle, "Lawyers' Duty to Do Justice: A New Look at the History of the 1908 Canons," 24 *Law and Soc. Inquiry* 1, 2, 18–26 (1999), on the debate among elite lawyers over the appropriate relative scope of client and public-regarding norms in the drafting of the Canons.

9. Beryl Harold Levy, *Corporation Lawyer: Saint or Sinner?* 151, 153 (1961).

10. See, e.g., *Model Code of Professional Responsibility* EC 7–3, EC 7–4 (1969) (clearly distinguishing the lawyer's roles of advocate and counselor and suggesting that in the counselor's role the lawyer has far less latitude to exploit uncertainties and ambiguities in the law for his client's benefit than in adversary proceedings).

11. Erwin O. Smigel, *The Wall Street Lawyer: Professional Organization Man?* 341–54 (1969).

Index

About the Editor

Susan D. Carle is Professor of Law at American University Washington College of Law.